SPART
CNN
LIVE FROM NEW YORK,
IT'S SATURDAY NIGHT!

S
N
L

Saturday Night Live

THE BOOK

BY ALISON CASTLE

Interview with Lorne Michaels

Principal Photography by
Edie Baskin
Mary Ellen Matthews

Design by Pentagram

TASCHEN

The show's very first home base, designed by Eugene Lee in 1975.

TRY STORE

Studio 8H in the early 1990s.

UPDATE

DO NOT
EAT PROPS

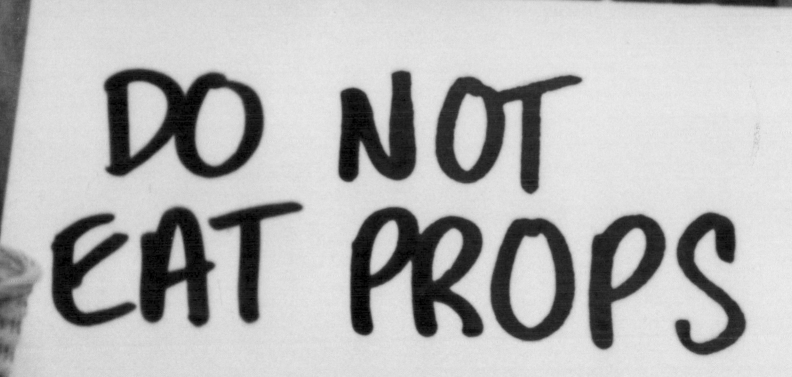

Table of Contents

_ M–T W

Foreword

T–F S _

I've been told enough times to lose count that guests invited to *Saturday Night Live* often inquire as to when the show is "taped." The answer, of course, is 11:30 p.m. on Saturday. It's a *live* show. To not know this is to miss the true magic of the whole enterprise. The fact that *SNL* is live informs its *entire character.* Anything could happen. As Lorne Michaels is wont to say, "We don't go on because we're ready. We go on because it's 11:30." It's a huge, beautiful, mind-blowing risk to take week after week, and they've been doing it for going on 40 years.

Each episode of *SNL* is created in just six days. Monday afternoon, the host arrives to meet the cast and writers for the first time. Sketches are written in a sleepless frenzy and submitted by Wednesday for the read-through. Rehearsals begin Thursday. Short films and commercial parodies are shot and edited in the 48 hours before the show airs. Rewrites, cuts, and changes to the lineup happen during the 90 minutes between dress rehearsal and air. Costumes are still being sewn in the final minutes before the cold open. What starts leisurely at the pitch meeting on Monday afternoon rapidly gathers pace as the days go by, building up to a feverish gallop toward the finish line by Saturday evening. Then, suddenly, everything clicks into place when the clock strikes 11:30. Every time you see a performer break character, look right at you, and say, "Live from New York, it's Saturday Night," you're witnessing a minor miracle in the making.

Yet there is so much more that makes *SNL* truly unique. It puts theater on television. It's a continuous forum for new talent and an ongoing study in the evolution of humor. It counts among its alumni many of the greatest comic talents of multiple generations and its catchphrases are indelibly marked in our collective memory. If you've ever bonded with a stranger over an obscure *SNL* reference, you know exactly what I mean. It's that crazy, reliable, seemingly immortal institution that we have each connected with at some point in our lives, or can never disconnect from.

This book is made for anyone who has ever loved the show, and especially for those who have *always* loved it. The fact that the structure of the six-day cycle has remained consistent since the show's beginnings affords the possibility of a cross-section through time in the guise of a day-by-day breakdown. Many of the faceless names that scroll in the end credits are shown working behind the scenes as the week progresses, leading up to the moment the pages go black and the show begins. Lorne Michaels imparts some insight into his experience as executive producer in the Q&A. The final part of the book is an illustrated reference guide covering all seasons from 1975 to 2014 and showcasing the transformation of the bumper artwork and graphics through the years. To distill material from the *SNL* archives—covering close to 800 episodes—into 500 intelligible pages was something of an impossible task. But then again, the impossible is what *SNL* does every week.

We've got a great show for you. Stick around.

SNL's Formative Years: A Brief History

The Little Engine that Could—and Did

Since televisions became ubiquitous in American households, the midnight hour—once a time for dreaming—has become a time for watching. Sleepless viewers tuned to NBC on October 11, 1975, at 11:30 p.m., many of whom may have expected to see a *Tonight Show* repeat, probably thought that they *were* dreaming: with no introduction, two unknown young men appeared live on screen and began performing something the likes of which nobody had seen before. The first, Michael O'Donoghue, read nonsensical phrases from a book, beginning with, "I would like...to feed your fingertips...to the wolverines," and pausing while the second, John Belushi, dutifully repeated each phrase in a thick foreign accent. Then O'Donoghue abruptly clutched his heart and collapsed onto the floor. Belushi paused, raised his eyebrow, and did the same. Posing as the stage manager, a third man, Chevy Chase, entered the set and feigned confusion before breaking character and announcing to the camera: "Live from New York, it's Saturday Night!" In that instant, television, which had become a thing deemed so uncool by almost anyone who knew what "cool" meant, experienced the first seismic tremors of a major paradigm shift. *Saturday Night Live* was, and still is, a show that dared to take significant risks, challenge the censors (network and moral), and promote the work of offbeat writer-performers. The brainchild of a group of nonconformist kids seemingly given free reign by the network, *SNL* took the road less traveled aboard a runaway freight train. The rest, of course, is history: that road less traveled is now a bustling four-lane highway.

SNL, poised to begin its 40th season at the time of this writing, is a storied institution, indelibly woven into the fabric of America's cultural heritage. Generations of Americans have grown up watching it with religious zeal. The ranks of esteemed alumni read like a "Who's Who" of the past four decades in comedy (the list is too preposterously long to enumerate). But of all the people that have worked to make *SNL* the success that it is, one name stands out above all others. That name is Lorne Michaels.

Rocking the Boat at 30 Rock

Let's rewind a bit. In early 1975, NBC was looking to produce a new late-night comedy variety show to air Saturdays at 11:30 p.m., a slot previously filled by reruns of *The Tonight Show.* Johnny Carson had let it be known that he wanted the network to find a replacement for the poorly rated repeats of his hit show, so NBC chief executive Herb Schlosser hired Dick Ebersol, director of late-night weekend programming, to come up with an idea for a new show to fill the slot. His brief, detailed in a three-page memo addressed to NBC network president Robert T. Howard, dated February 11, 1975, proposed an "effort to create a new and exciting program," originating "from the RCA Building in New York City, if possible live…It would be a variety show, but it would have certain characteristics. It should be young and bright. It should have a distinctive look, a distinctive set, and a distinctive sound…The show should not only seek to develop new young talent, but it should get a reputation as a tryout place for talent…With proper production and promotion, 'Saturday Night' can become a major show in television that people will talk about."

Ebersol's choice to produce this new endeavor was comedy writer Lorne Michaels, a Los Angeles–based Canadian who had won an Emmy the previous year for his work on a Lily Tomlin special. Relatively unknown to the affiliates, and usually dressed in jeans and sneakers, 30-year-old Michaels didn't stand out as the sort of producer NBC brass liked to gamble on. Yet Ebersol was adamant that Michaels had what it took to chart new territory in the dusty terrain of late-night comedy. Michaels's vision for the show was that it should provide topical satire with bite, and give viewers the impression "that the network had gone home and a bunch of kids had slipped into the studio to put on a show."

There was no reliable precedent for the type of show this was going to be. Times had changed since Sid Caesar's *Your Show of Shows* went off the air 20 years prior, and despite apparent similarities, the more recent *Laugh-In* (for which Michaels had worked as a writer) was so tailored to the conservative mainstream that it was in fact the antithesis of the kind of show Michaels dreamed of doing. In 1975, to a generation that was eager to move past the uptight, conservative mentality of the Nixon years, TV sketch comedy seemed stale and played out. Inspired by the absurdist type of humor pioneered in the UK by Monty Python, Michaels wanted to revive the tradition for a new generation of young Americans, with subversive humor and hip musical acts to boot. In fact, he had a lot of ideas that Ebersol liked enough to insist to the network, over a series of meetings, that Michaels be the executive producer. NBC accepted, and on April 1, 1975 (ha ha), Michaels signed the contract and prepared to move to New York City.

Ebersol and Michaels set up camp at 30 Rockefeller Plaza in midtown Manhattan, nine stories above the former soundstage assigned to the show: Studio 8H (previously home to Arturo Toscanini and the NBC Symphony Orchestra). Long, narrow, and not particularly spacious, the studio wasn't ideally suited to a live sketch comedy show. To solve this problem, Michaels hired the first of many people that would grudgingly come from outside of the television field to work on the show: theater set designer Eugene Lee. The self-avowed hippie's looks may have unsettled the network execs, but Lee got to business right away repurposing Studio 8H. He tore out the seating that was situated at the north end of the studio and installed elevated bleachers along the east and north sides, preserving access to the studio from both hallways while providing backstage areas underneath the seating and allowing the audience to have a wider, better vantage point for sketches that would be performed in various spots around the studio. He designed the home base and the music stage to have the feel of a comfortably shabby basement jazz club—very New York, very theatrical, and very un-TV. (Lee still designs sets for the show today.)

Before leaving Los Angeles, Michaels had recruited budding young comedians Chevy Chase (initially as a writer) and Laraine Newman. The first writers Michaels approached in New York were *National Lampoon*'s Michael O'Donoghue and Anne Beatts, both of whom declared themselves allergic to television, a thing they referred to as "a lava lamp with sound." Paradoxically, this meant they were a perfect fit for Michaels's outsider mentality; his persuasive pitch won them over. Several of Michaels's other early hires were fellow Canadians: his first wife, writer Rosie Shuster; his friend from Toronto, comedian Gilda Radner; musical director Howard Shore; and pianist/bandleader Paul Shaffer. Actor/playwright Garrett Morris, like Chase, was also promoted to cast member after being hired as a writer. Apprentice positions were filled by writer Alan Zweibel and comedy duo Al Franken and Tom Davis. The 17th floor of 30 Rock was filling up with what NBC vice president Dave Tebet called "a motley crew," as well as the distinctive odor of marijuana (yes, the rumors are true, drugs were ubiquitous in those days). Former Johnny Carson writer Herb Sargent, the only writer of the bunch with bona fide television experience, was brought on as script supervisor (eliciting, perhaps, a tiny sigh of relief from network execs).

Though the budget was fiercely negotiated by Michaels and Ebersol, it was lean—only seven cast members could be hired, and Michaels would have to run a tight ship. He had his eye on Gilda Radner's friend Dan Aykroyd,

MGMNYAT HSB
2-049102E171002 06/20/75
ICS IPMMTZZ CSP
1 2122478300 MGM TDMT NEW YORK NY 06-20 0806P EST
ZIP 10020

THIS MAILGRAM WAS TRANSMITTED ELECTRONICALLY BY WESTERN UNION TO A POST OFFICE NEAR YOU FOR DELIVERY

NBC ATTN LORNE MICHAELS ROOM 408
30 ROCKEFELLER PLAZA
NEW YORK NY 10020

THIS MAILGRAM IS A CONFIRMATION COPY OF THE FOLLOWING MESSAGE:

2122478300 TDMT NEW YORK NY 861 06-20 0806P EST
PMS DICK EBERSOL CARE BEVERLY HILLS HOTEL, DLR
9641 SUNSET BLVD
BEVERLY HILLS CA 90213
DICK:

"SATURDAY NIGHT", AS IT IS NOW CONCEIVED BREAKDOWN INTO THE FOLLOWING AREAS OF CONTENT. EACH FEATURE IS COMPETITIVE FOR TIME WITHIN THE SHOW BUT THE DOMINANCE OF ONE DOES NOT MEAN THE EXCLUSION OF THE OTHERS FLEXIBILITY AND ADAPTABILITY IS THE KEYNOTE.

ROTATING GUEST HOST:
THERE WILL BE A GUEST HOST FOR EACH PROGRAM, THE REQUISITE QUALITY I AM LOOKING FOR IS SPONTANEITY. FAME AND TALENT WOULD NOT HURT. NO MORE THAN FIVE HOSTS WILL BE CONTRACTED BEFORE OUR FIRST SHOW ON OCTOBER 11. I WOULD LIKE TO BE AS RESPONSIVE AS POSSIBLE TO VIEWER REACTION. HOSTS WHO ARE COMFORTABLE AND SUCCESSFUL WITHIN THE SATURDAY NIGHT FORMAT WILL, OF COURSE, DO MORE THAN ONE SHOW. HOWEVER, THERE WILL BE PROVISION FOR AN AMPLE SPRINKLING OF ONE TIME ONLY GUEST HOST.

ARTIST WITH WHOM WE HAVE DISCUSSED THE POSSIBILITY OF HOSTING ARE BETTE MIDLER, LILY TOMLIN, GEORGE CARLIN, RICHARD PRYOR, PAUL SIMON, AND ROBERT KLEIN. WE SHOULD HAVE SOME INDICATION OF WHOM THE HOST FOR SHOWS ONE THROUGH SIX WILL BE SOMETIME IN LATE JULY.

MUSICAL GUESTS:
THERE WILL BE TWO MAJOR MUSICAL GUESTS PER SHOW, THE EMPHASIS HERE IS MORE THEATRICAL OR POP RATHER THAN HARD ROCK. WE ARE LOOKING FOR PERFORMERS-WITH A STRONG SENSE OF LIVE-TELEVISION SHOWMANSHIP, ENERGY AND VISUAL PRESENTATION. JOHN HEAD WILL COORDINATE THIS.

REGULAR FEATURES:
A: A FILM BY ALBERT BROOKS: ALBERT WILL BE WRITING, DIRECTING, PRODUCING AND, MORE OFTEN THAN NOT, APPEARING IN A FIVE MINUTE FILM EACH WEEK FOR AT LEAST THE FIRST SEVEN SHOWS. ALBERT HAS ALREADY TALKED TO SUCH DIVERSE TALENT AS PETER BOYLE AND JOHN LENNON ABOUT THE POSSIBILITY OF CAMEO APPEARANCES. I HAVE EXTENDED A GREAT DEAL OF CREATIVE FREEDOM TO HIM ON THESE FILMS AND ALL INDICATIONS POINT

5241 (R2-74)

REPLY BY MAILGRAM – SEE REVERSE SIDE FOR WESTERN UNION'S TOLL – FREE PHONE NUMBERS

Dated June 20, 1975, this letter from Lorne Michaels to producer Dick Ebersol describes his plans for the show.

PAGE 2

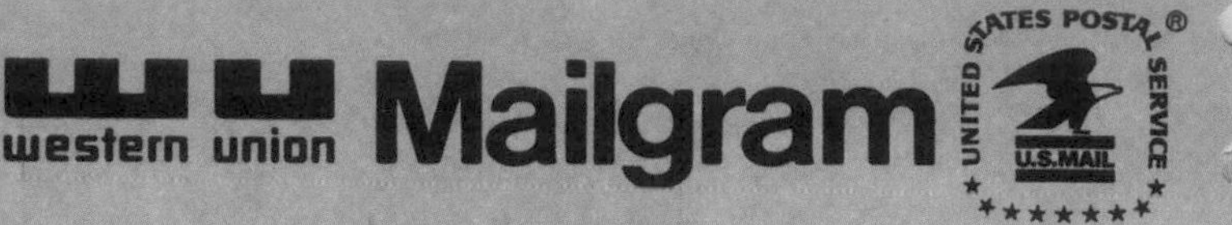

THIS MAILGRAM WAS TRANSMITTED ELECTRONICALLY BY WESTERN UNION TO A POST OFFICE NEAR YOU FOR DELIVERY

TO HIGH HUMAN EXPECTATIONS.
B: JIM HANSON AND MUPPETS: JIM HANSON HAS AGREED TO CREATE A TOTALLY NEW GROUP OF MUPPETS FOR SATURDAY NIGHT. THESE WILL BE ADULT PUPPETS SO THERE WILL BE NO PROBLEMS ABOUT THEIR STAYING UP LATE. AS TO WHAT THESE MUPPETS WILL DO OR SAY, I REALLY HAVE NOT MUCH OF AN IDEA. HOWEVER, JIM SEEMS TO FEEL THEY CAN BE RELIED UPON. THIS SEGMENT WILL BE DONE LIVE AND MAY INVOLVE NUMBERS OF REPERTORY CAST.
C: REPERTORY CAST: WILL BE COMPOSED OF THREE MEN AND THREE WOMEN. THAT MAKES SIX ALTOGETHER. EACH SHOW THEY WILL APPEAR IN SKETCHES, BLACKOUTS, VIGNETTES, AND CHARACTER MONOLOGUE; MOST OF WHICH WILL DEAL WITH MATTERS OF TOPICAL INTEREST. ALSO, I WILL BE WORKING WITH THE REPERTORY CAST IMPROVISATIONALLY THROUGHOUT THE PRE-PRODUCTION PERIOD SO THAT, HOPEFULLY, A FAMILY FEELING WILL EXIST BY THE TIME OF THE FIRST SHOW. AGAIN, AS CHARACTERS OR SKETCHES ARE MET WITH FAVORABLE RESPONSE, THEY WILL BE INTEGRATED INTO THE SHOW ON A CONTINUING BASIS. NOTE- WHEN THE GUEST HOST HAS APPROVEN ABILITY IN SKETCH/COMEDY, HE OR SHE WILL WORK WITH THE REPERTORY COMPANY.

DOCUMENTARY:
THERE WILL BE A FILM UNIT ATTACHED TO THE SHOW UNDER THE DIRECTIONS OF AWARD-LOSING FILM MAKER GARY WEIS WHICH WILL, MOST WEEKS, PROVIDE US WITH A FOUR OR FIVE MINUTE MINI-DOCUMENTARY. THE SUBJECT MATTER OF THESE FILMS WILL BE GENERALLY LIGHT IN TONE AND SHOULD REFLECT THE OFF-BEAT TASTE AND STYLE OF MISTER WEIS. EXAMPLE. "THE MIDGETS OF MASSACHUSETTS"

LIVE REMOTES:
THE POSSIBILITY EXISTS THAT ON OCCASION WE WILL DO LIVE REMOTES IN AND AROUND MANHATTAN. A GOOD EXAMPLE OF THIS FEATURE IS A MOVIE REVIEW IDEA WE HAVE DISCUSSED.

COMMERCIAL PARODIES:
IT IS CURRENTLY INTENT THAT PRE-TAPED COMMERCIAL PARODIES (FOR EXAMPLE "POLAND THIS WINTER") BE STUDDED THROUGHOUT THE SHOW. MINGLING ON OCCASION WITH COMMERCIALS WHICH ARE NOT PARODIES, THESE THREE-RECORDED MOMENTS ARE ENORMOUSLY HELPFUL IN PACING A LIVE SHOW.

INSTRUCTIONAL FILM:
ALSO AS A PACING DEVICE, WE HAVE INSTITUTED A SEARCH FOR PERIOD TRAINING FILMS. ALREADY AT THE LOS ANGELES PUBLIC LIBRARY A RESOURCEFUL TOM SCHILLER HAS UNCOVERED A SHORT TRAINING FILM ON PROPER CONDUCT DURING THE COFFEE BREAK.

NEW TALENT:
THERE WILL BE THREE NEW TALENT ACTS ON EACH SATURDAY NIGHT. TWO OF THESE WILL BE STAND-UP COMICS. THE THIRD WILL MORE THAN LIKELY BE A VARIETY OR MUSICAL ACT. EACH PERFORMER WILL BE OPTIONED FOR THREE OR MORE APPEARANCES SHOULD THE AUDIENCE RESPOND FAVORABLY.

MOCK DOCUMENTARY:
ON OCCASION SATURDAY NIGHT WILL PRESENT A FIVE OR SIX MINUTE

5241 (R2-74)

REPLY BY MAILGRAM – SEE REVERSE SIDE FOR WESTERN UNION'S TOLL – FREE PHONE NUMBERS

PAGE 3

western union **Mailgram**

UNITED STATES POSTAL SERVICE U.S. MAIL

THIS MAILGRAM WAS TRANSMITTED ELECTRONICALLY BY WESTERN UNION TO A POST OFFICE NEAR YOU FOR DELIVERY

MOCK-DOCUMENTARY SIMILAR IN STYLE TO THE "REPORTS ON DUTCH TUCK DISEASE" (C.B.C.) AND THE BEVERLY HILLS ORDINANCE MAKING IT ILLEGAL TO BE FAT. (TOMLIN SPECIAL) SUBJECT UNDER CONSIDERATION INCLUDES THE BERMUDA TRIANGLE (INTERSECTION IN BERMUDA OHIO) AND APHRODESIACS. NOTE- THE "MOCK-DOCS" WILL BE USED MOSTLY TO SUPPORT SHOWS HOSTED BY SINGERS.

ADDENDA:
I HAVE MADE NO ATTEMPT HERE, OBVIOUSLY, TO PRESENT A LOCKED-IN SHOW FORMAT. AS THE WRITERS AND PRODUCTION STAFF ASSEMBLE IN NEW YORK ON JULY 7, AND ARE EXPOSED TO THESE CONCEPTS, THE ABOVE IDEAS WILL BEGIN TO GROW, NEW FEATURES WILL BE ADDED AND A SHOW WILL EVOLVE- A SHOW WITH VITALITY AND HUMOR: A SHOW WITH STYLE.

IF NOT, REMEMBER THEY ARE ALL ON SIX WEEK OPTIONS. REGARDS,
LORNE

20:06 EST

MGMNYAT HSB

REPLY BY MAILGRAM – SEE REVERSE SIDE FOR WESTERN UNION'S TOLL – FREE PHONE NUMBERS

5241 (R2-74)

as well as *National Lampoon's* Bill Murray, but decided to hold auditions before filling any of the remaining three spots. Over two days in August of 1975, more than 200 hopefuls turned out, including yet another young, talented TV hater: John Belushi. *Everyone* had been telling Michaels that Belushi was perfect for the show, but their first meeting earlier that summer hadn't gone particularly well (Belushi had shouted "TV sucks!" repeatedly). However, by this time the buzz around the show made it seem like the holy grail for young comedians, so Belushi swallowed his pride and came to audition. By the time it was his turn, he'd been waiting for hours and his screams of frustration had been audible all the way upstairs in the audition room; but any unease Belushi's antics may have provoked was assuaged when he began to perform. He proved himself uncannily capable of harnessing his wild side and channeling his energy into his characterizations.

Aykroyd also dutifully came to audition, despite having already met Michaels (at the insistence of Gilda Radner). And he, too, was made to wait for hours, before bursting into the audition room to declare that he was leaving to catch a plane to Los Angeles; whether this was a tactical or honest move is hard to say, but he got the job. Among the other standouts from the auditions was Jane Curtin, whose deadpan delivery and dry humor earned her the seventh spot. (Bill Murray lost out to Aykroyd and Belushi, though he would join the cast in the second season.)

Winging It

Saturday Night Live was the early, favorite title for the show. But there was a problem: it was already taken—by Howard Cosell, who was slated to launch a primetime comedy variety show that fall on ABC. So Michaels settled for *NBC's Saturday Night.* When Cosell's show premiered, and tanked, the cast and writers at NBC (correctly) predicted its rapid demise. Though the show had taken the name they wanted, they did claim something in return. Cosell's show featured a repertory group called the Prime Time Players (one of whom turned out to be Bill Murray); Michaels's cheeky cast decided to call themselves the Not Ready for Prime Time Players. (The name *Saturday Night Live* came up for grabs and was adopted during season 2.)

The cast and crew spent the month of September hoping for the best and preparing for the worst. There had been talk about whether there should be a revolving cast of recurring hosts or even a permanent host (early on, Albert Brooks's name was tossed around), but Michaels wanted to test the waters before settling on a formula. Stand-up comedian George Carlin was selected to be the host of the first episode, along with a bunch of special guests, including Andy Kaufman. By all accounts, they were making it up as they went along, and nobody really dared to think the show would last through the first season. The premiere was rough around the edges, but its vibe was electrifying. Andy Kaufman performed his now-iconic Mighty Mouse routine; the Killer Bees and Jim Henson's "Land of Gorch" Muppets made their first appearances; Chevy Chase delivered the fake news with sardonic aplomb; and if there were any doubts about the show's antiestablishment slant, the subversive mockumentary short *Show Us Your Guns* laid them to rest.

Ratings were shaky at first, but the fan base was out there, and they were watching. Michaels knew it would take some time for things to fall into place, and he reckons that happened around the fourth show, after which (despite Michaels's threatening to quit unless NBC agreed to his choice of lighting director) the rest of the season sailed by relatively smoothly. The ratings inched up throughout the season as the show generated more and more buzz, but it wasn't until the show won a staggering five Emmy Awards in May of 1976 (including Best Comedy-Variety Series) that NBC knew it had a hit show on its hands.

Anyone who watched the show in those early years remembers what an impact it had. But watching those shows now, younger generations might wonder what all the fuss was about. Today's media is flooded with content for every imaginable taste. Many of us don't really even watch "TV" anymore—we watch clips on the Internet and we stream shows on our iPads. We can hardly fathom how truly *original* the show was because the context has been forgotten. Anyone under the age of 30 could be forgiven for being unable to grasp how Kubrick's *2001: A Space Odyssey* blew people's minds; they've seen so many exquisitely produced, futuristic CGI films that Kubrick's masterpiece looks painfully dated to them. But they're missing the point: Kubrick's film shifted the paradigm. In the history of sci-fi cinema, it delineated a point on either side of which are the films that came before it, and those that came after. For comedy, *SNL* did the same.

Lorne Michaels on set in 1975.

Up, Up, and Away

But it wasn't always smooth sailing. By its fifth season, *SNL*—still strong in the ratings—was starting to grow a bit worse for wear; Chase had left in the second season (replaced by Murray), and Aykroyd and Belushi left after the fourth. The Killer Bees, the Coneheads, the Nerds, the Blues Brothers, the Widettes, Roseanne Roseannadanna, Emily Litella, Nick the Lounge Singer, and Samurai Futaba had become the stuff of legend, but the more the audience wanted to see these bits, the more the cast and writers tired of them. Something had to happen or the show's mojo would evaporate completely.

The cast seemed ready to move on, and it became clear to Michaels that the show needed to reinvent itself in the form of new blood. As the fifth season neared its end, he told the network he needed six months or so to regroup, recruit a new cast, and prepare a relaunch. But NBC, bolstered by the show's success, had already renewed the show for its sixth season, which would begin in September 1980. A lot of soul-searching ensued, and Michaels eventually concluded that he was not prepared to risk failure by rushing things. He was too burned out to start from scratch with so little time, so he chose to quit while he was ahead. The last episode of season 5 closed with a shot of the ON AIR sign going off. Neither he nor any of the cast and writers believed the show would survive. Diehards may see this as a mercy killing, but Michaels just needed to step away from the success he was afraid to compromise. If *SNL* was going to fly too close to the sun, it had to be without him.

NBC's choice for Michaels's successor came as somewhat of a surprise: Jean Doumanian, an associate producer whose primary role had been in the talent department. She and Michaels were close, but nobody had elicited Michaels's opinion in the matter, which made the whole affair slightly awkward. Doumanian had the task of recruiting not only an entirely new cast, but new writers and crew members as well, since most had defected after Michaels's departure. The sixth season was plagued with conflict and problems, and the last straw came in March of 1981, when Doumanian chose to defend cast member Charles Rocket after he unexpectedly dropped an f-bomb on air. She had been responsible for hiring 18-year-old newcomer Eddie Murphy, but by the time he emerged the next season as the star of the show, Doumanian was long gone.

Unbeknownst to Doumanian, the network had already approached *SNL* co-founder Dick Ebersol about taking over. After her departure and a month-long hiatus, the show resumed under Ebersol. He vowed to recreate the spirit of *SNL*'s early years by asking for Michaels's blessing (which was granted) and by bringing back as many key original players as possible. Michaels suggested

'SNL' producer: 'It'll be better next week'

By JOSEF ADALIAN

LORNE Michaels says he's "still standing"

still tuned in to see whether the veteran sketch comedy series would be

NBC Unveils Live Latenight Show Oct. 11.

Live comedy-variety will return to network television Oct. 11 on NBC.

Reportedly the brainchild of NBC president Herb Schlosser, the show will air 11:30 p.m.-1 a.m. on every

Saturday, Novembe

Only time will tell if new 'SNL' is improved

A brief history lesson: It was 11 years ago, as an NBC veep

Steve

who presided over its *Mee-ow.*

Ebersol likes to make

POST TV Plus

Lorne Michaels' 'Saturday Night' promise:

'I won't give up!'

By JOSEF ADALIAN

LORNE Michaels says

Saturday Night boss: I'm quitting

POST DEC 3 1977

By JEFF WEINGRAD

LORNE MICHAELS, pro-

He reaffirms now that the demanding schedule was th

C18

THE NE

Lorne Michaels Vows To Stay With His Show

By BILL CARTER

Angry at persistent critics of "Saturday Night Live" and at NBC executives for failing to come to his support, Lorne Michaels, the comedy

"I was surprised and angered again at Warren's comments," Mr. Michaels said. He said he had held discussions earlier this year with Don Ohlmeyer, the president of NBC's West Coast division. "I got a clear set of marching orders about

The press has always kept close tabs on SNL's ups and downs, particularly during the tumultuous period in the 1980s surrounding Lorne Michaels's five-year hiatus.

O'Donoghue, who accepted the offer while, in characteristic fashion, declaring that he planned to give the show a "decent Viking funeral." True to form, O'Donoghue berated the cast on his first day back on the 17th floor of 30 Rock, accusing them of being too risk-averse and making a show of spray-painting "DANGER" in huge letters on the pristine office wall. Undeterred by O'Donoghue's antics and trusting Michaels's advice, Ebersol gave him almost complete creative control over the writing. Ebersol was so committed to bringing the show back to its roots that he convinced Chevy Chase to host the first show. In the cold open of April 11, 1981, Chase waxes nostalgic in a storeroom full of old Land Shark, Killer Bee, and Conehead costumes; he rescues Mr. Bill from a trash can, who tells him, "Hey, Chevy, we can make a comeback."

Initially, the chemistry between Eddie Murphy and Joe Piscopo was the glue that held the show together and helped it recover from the ratings slump suffered in season 6. Then Ebersol further bolstered the cast by bringing in Julia Louis-Dreyfus the following season, and in season 10, as cast member Jim Belushi put it, he "basically pulled a Steinbrenner, he went out and bought the best comic talent out there." Though it was a departure from the founding principle of the show (to cultivate young, new talent), hiring Martin Short, Christopher Guest, and Billy Crystal proved to be a remarkably shrewd move on Ebersol's part. Season 10, which also featured considerably more pretaped material than ever before, was an immensely successful year for the show, both commercially and critically; but it would be Ebersol's *SNL* swan song. As season 11 loomed, Ebersol, tired of missing weekends with his family (and unable to convince the network to move the show to Friday night or prerecord it in its entirety), decided it was time to move on.

Director Dave Wilson (left) and executive producer Dick Ebersol in 1985, shortly before Lorne Michaels returned to the show.

Jean Doumanian (center) looks over a script with Ellen Burstyn. Doumanian's tenure as executive producer was cut short in March of 1981 after less than a full season.

Bringing It All Back Home

The previous year, Lorne Michaels had produced a pretaped primetime sketch comedy show, *The New Show*, for NBC. Despite appearances by *SNL* cast and host alums such as Buck Henry, Franken and Davis, Laraine Newman, Gilda Radner, Candice Bergen, and Steve Martin, the show failed to gain foothold in the primetime lineup and was cancelled after nine episodes. Programming head Brandon Tartikoff beseeched Michaels, who had left *SNL* at a high point in the ratings, to return to the show at a time when the ratings were finally soaring again. Paradoxically, it was a tough act to follow.

A change of producer means a changing of the guards, thus Ebersol's all-star cast was disbanded. Many crew members who had defected after

Michaels's departure returned, while Michaels set about casting a whole new set of players, including Joan Cusack, Robert Downey Jr., Anthony Michael Hall, Jon Lovitz, Dennis Miller, and Randy Quaid. But it wasn't going to be easy. By all accounts, season 11 was a train wreck—the change of style and substance was so abrupt that audiences floundered. Michaels, undeterred, persevered to rebuild what he cared about more than anything else. This would be the first of many times he would patiently ride out the inevitable awkward phase following a cast turnover. By the following season, with Dana Carvey, Phil Hartman, Jan Hooks, and Kevin Nealon newly on board, Michaels's comeback finally began to crystallize. Rather than pretending that season 11 wasn't a flop, Michaels chose to stick his neck out by having Madonna, who had hosted the first episode of season 11, make a cameo appearance for the *Dallas*-inspired cold open of the season 12 premiere to announce, "Concerning last year's entire season...it was all a dream, a horrible, horrible dream." Like many calculated risks Michaels has made in his career, it paid off. He has been with the show ever since, and today he is the most influential figure in late-night television.

The Legend Endures

The early years of *SNL* were magical. You had to stay up to watch the show back then. You stayed up Saturday nights and you watched the Not Ready for Prime Time Players at 11:30. Then the 1980s brought us VCRs, the 1990s brought us TiVo, and the 2000s brought us streaming. Though a little bit of the magic is lost when you don't watch the show live (or, for those in Central and Pacific time zones, almost live), in recent years the Internet has played an important role in keeping *SNL* relevant to younger generations. On Sundays, links to the previous night's sketches are posted around the web, and many of these have famously gone viral. With its video archives now available almost in their entirety on the web, *SNL* is never more than a click away.

A lot has happened since *SNL* changed TV forever, and a lot has stayed the same. When Michaels returned in 1985, so, too, did the old habits. His office was set back up as if he had never left, with his desk and fish tank in the same spots, and looks pretty much the same today. The weekly schedule remains virtually identical to that of the early seasons. Eugene Lee and Akira Yoshimura are still designing sets. At 91, Phil Hymes is still designing the lighting. During the writing of this introduction, Don Pardo, the show's legendary announcer since day one, passed away at the age of 96—the same week that *SNL* picked up another five Emmy Awards (no other show in history has won more). Pardo's voice will be sorely missed when season 40 premieres, but the show must go on. And it will.

Long live *SNL*.

SATURDAY NIGHT LIVE
SHOW 90
4-22-78

Show 90, which featured Steve Martin's King Tut, the Blues Brothers, and the Festrunk Brothers ("Two wild and crazy guys"), not only was a high point of season 3 but is considered by many as one of the show's greatest.

Monday–Tuesday

Tabula rasa. On Monday the six-day timer is reset to zero. Everything begins again when the host arrives to meet the team and share sketch ideas. Tuesday is when the writing happens. Tuesday is when all the good ideas have to become good sketches to survive.

MONDAY-TUESDAY / MEETINGS

After a Sunday off, usually spent sleeping, people filter in throughout the day on Monday. Informal meetings and brainstorming sessions punctuate the day, but the late-afternoon writers' meeting (also referred to as the pitch meeting), when the host meets with the writers and cast members, is when things really get back into full swing and the week officially begins. In the early years, this group membered around a dozen people. Now, over 30 people cram into Lorne Michaels's 17th-floor corner office, most sitting on the floor, while latecomers are left to hover at the open doorway. Michaels sits at his desk, which still occupies the same spot it did in 1975, and the host sits on a chair in front of the desk. For the next hour or so, each writer and cast member takes a turn at pitching sketch ideas, to which the host responds with comments or suggestions.

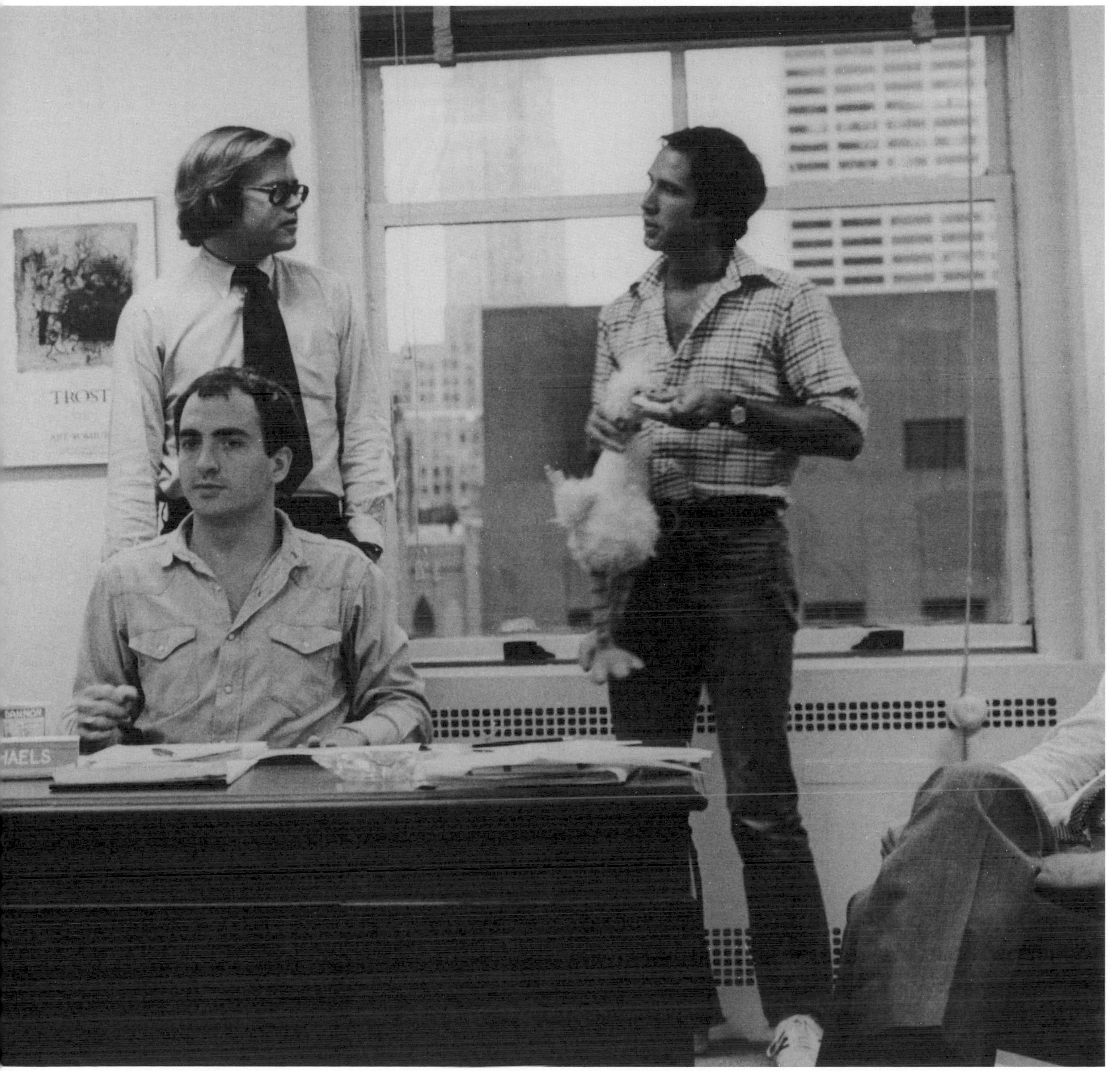

Lorne Michaels (seated), Dick Ebersol, and Chevy Chase in Michaels's office on the 17th floor of 30 Rockefeller Plaza in 1975.

Seen from the doorway of Michaels's office: cast and writers (led by Fred Armisen) filing in for the Monday writers' meeting. (2011)

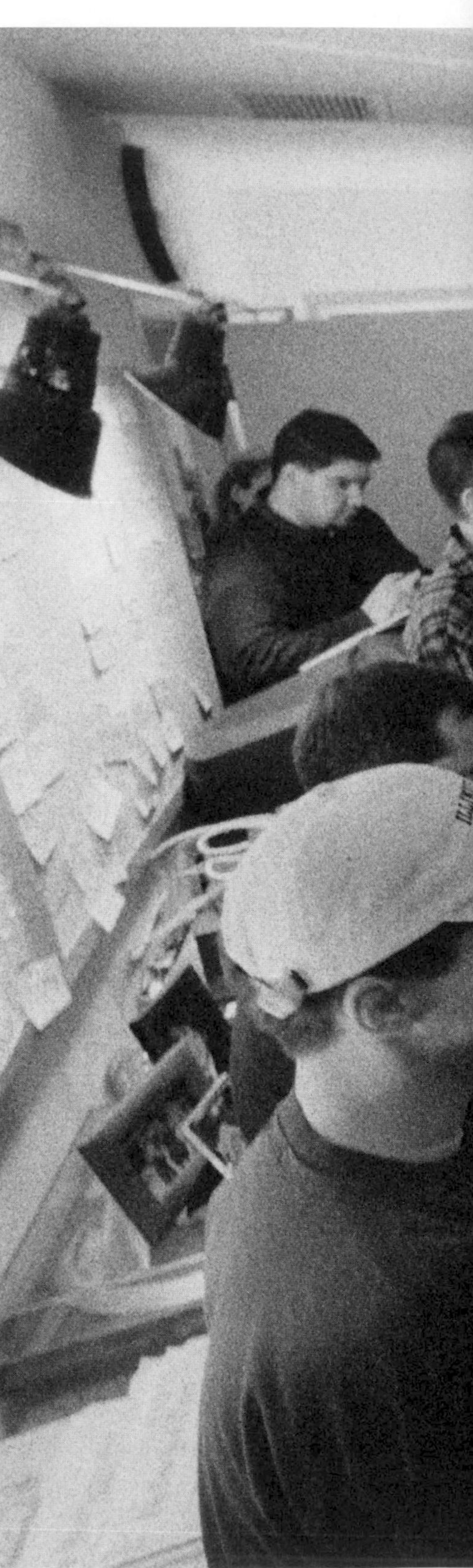

Season 26 writers and cast members pitching sketch ideas for the week's show.

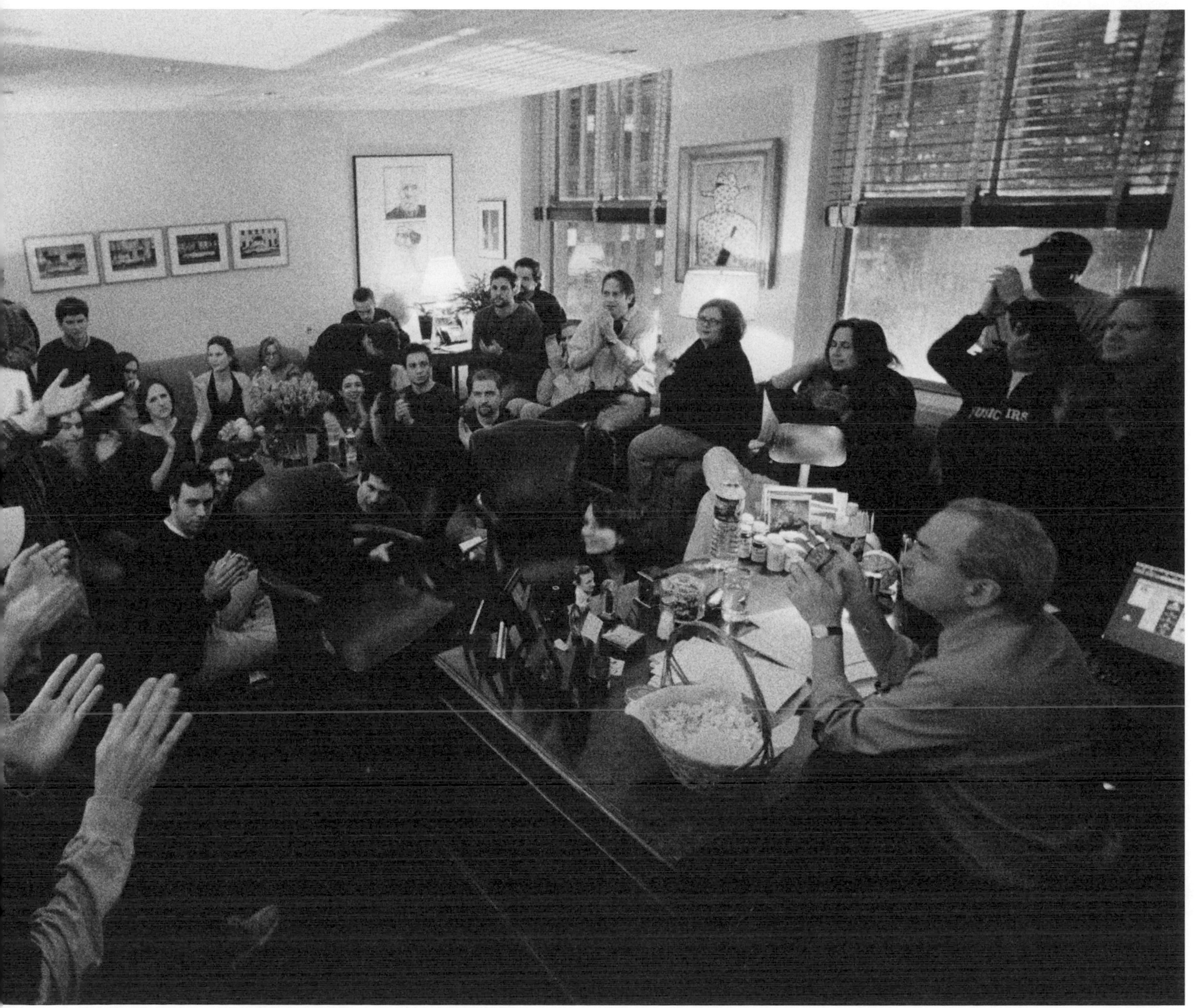

Dan Aykroyd, Michael O'Donoghue, and John Belushi. (1975)

At your convenience, we have things to discuss.

1976

Note to Lorne Michaels from head writer O'Donoghue.

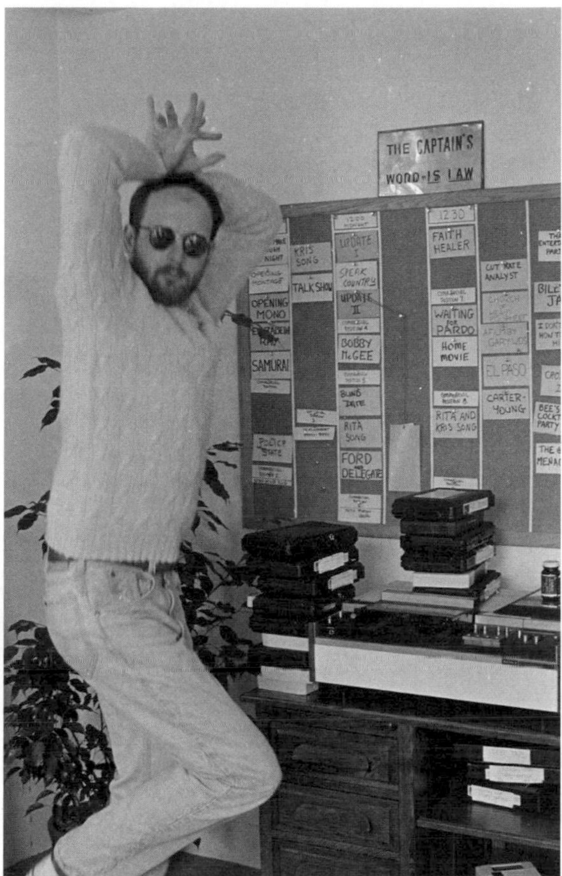

O'Donoghue doing the Antler Dance in Michaels's office. The "Captain's Word Is Law" sign, a gift given to Michaels in 1975, still hangs in the same spot above the bulletin board.

MONDAY-TUESDAY / WRITING

After Monday's writers' meeting, while the writers disperse to begin working on their sketches, Michaels makes notes of the host's feedback to relay to them. Some work in groups, or pair up with cast members to work on character pieces. Each writer and cast member has a shared office down the hall from Michaels's, and this is where they typically hole up through the night on Tuesday to finish their sketches by Wednesday morning. Though there is no time clock or official office hours, leaving early on Tuesday is generally considered poor sportsmanship. Staying late into the night, or at least sticking around to offer moral or creative support, has become something of a venerable tradition that most still subscribe to.

Chevy Chase in 1975.

Most writing happens in the 17th-floor offices down the hall from the writers' room.
THIS PAGE: Michael O'Donoghue and John Belushi. (1975) **OPPOSITE:** Fred Armisen, John Mulaney, and Bobby Moynihan. (2011)

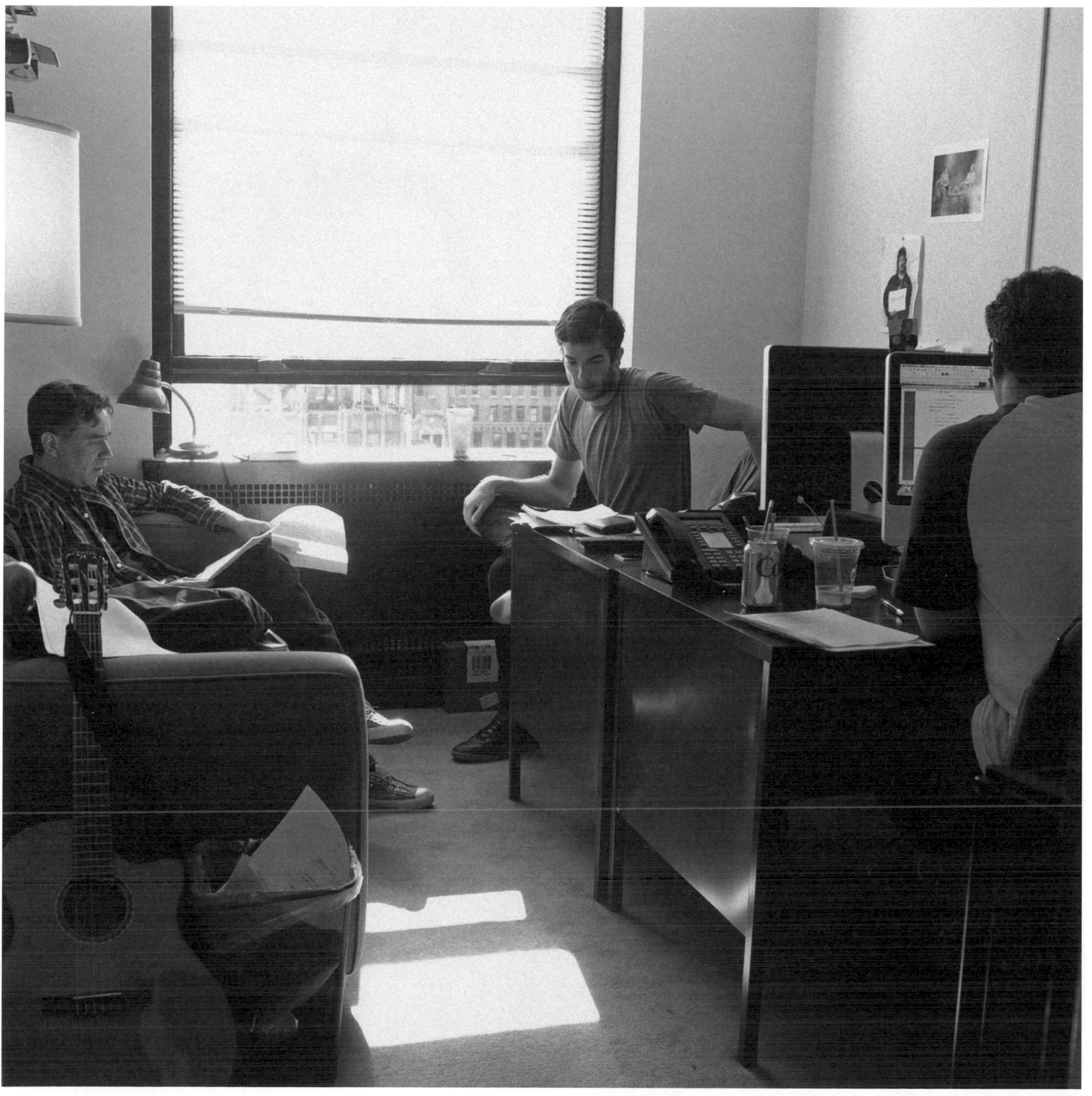

Laraine Newman and Gilda Radner. (1975)

Writer Marilyn
Suzanne Miller. (1975)

Chris Parnell and Will
Ferrell with Katreese
Barnes. (ca. 2002)

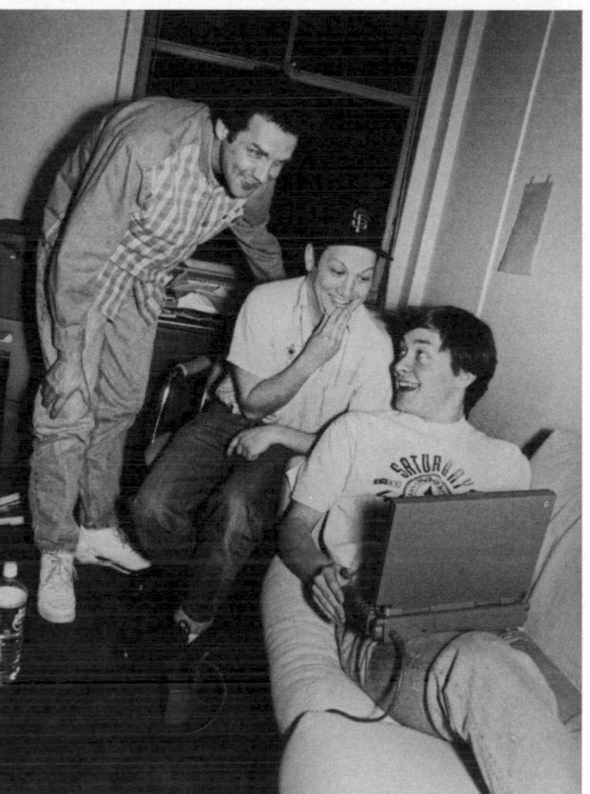

Norm Macdonald, Rob Schneider,
and Lewis Morton. (ca. 1993)

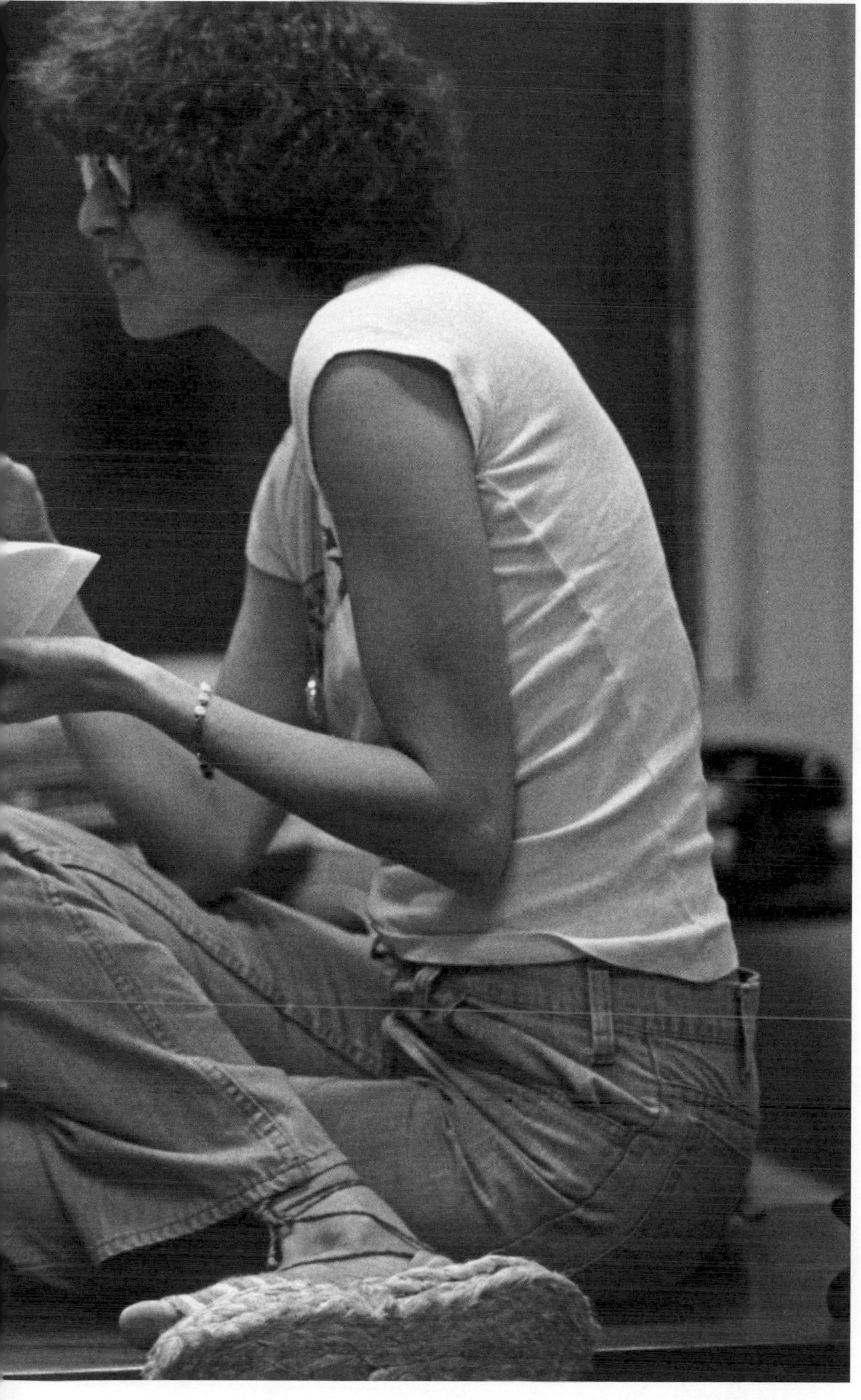

Writers Michael O'Donoghue and Anne Beatts. (1975)

MONDAY-TUESDAY / WRITING

→7 →7A →8 →8A →9 →9A →10

KODAK TRI X PAN FILM KODAK SAFETY FIL

→19 →19A →20 →20A G K H →21A →22

KODAK SAFETY FILM KODAK TRI X PAN

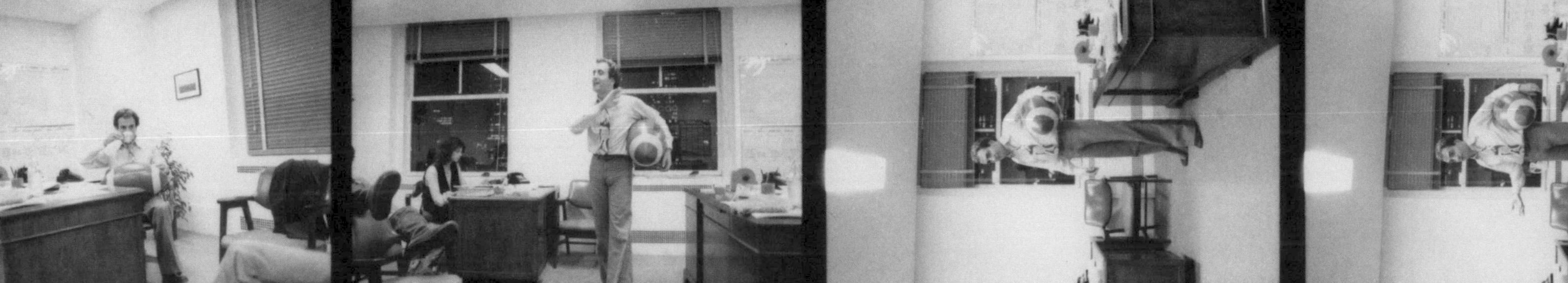

THIS PAGE: Writer Rob Klein working with Andy Samberg. (2011)
OPPOSITE: Scenes from Lorne Michaels's office. (1975)

Wednesday

Sketches are finalized, submitted, and performed at the read-through. Decisions are made. Picks are announced. Writers meet with set and costume designers, makeup and hair artists, and the director to begin the process of bringing the sketches to life.

WEDNESDAY / READ-THROUGH

The read-through is the second in a series of hurdles that a sketch must clear to make it to the live broadcast (the first being the head writers' selection of the 40 scripts to be read). At around 4 p.m. on Wednesday, the host, the head writers, the director, and the cast members take their seats around a large conference table in the writers' room. Staff from the various departments sit in tightly packed chairs around the room, a handful spilling out into the hall. With no fanfare or introduction, Michaels takes his seat at the head of the table and begins reading the stage directions of the first script—the signal that the read-through is under way. Except for a short break at the halfway point, roughly the next three to four hours are spent reading through the scripts.

Afterwards, Michaels adjourns to his office to consult with the head writers, producers, and host to determine the lineup for Saturday's dress rehearsal. The complexity of the selection process really can't be overstated; sketches that got a lot of laughs at the read-through are usually good candidates, but there are many factors at play. Michaels has to consider the show as a whole—the rhythm, tone, balance, and the like. The supervising producer and director weigh in about possible complications with fitting the sketches in the studio, whether there will be enough time to rehearse the show, and the logistics of potential pretapes. In addition to all of these factors, the host's personal preferences and the distribution of roles among cast members are taken into account. (Sometimes, when Michaels likes a sketch that won't work for that week's show, he will suggest that the writer resubmit it later, and some iconic pieces, including "VH1: Behind the Music [Cowbell]," were resubmits.)

While this meeting is taking place behind the closed door of Michaels's office, everyone else waits on pins and needles for the announcement that the "picks" are in, which typically takes two hours or more after the end of the read-through. Then they file into Michaels's office to look at the bulletin board on which are pinned index cards indicating the sketches selected for the lineup. Predictably, reactions range from elation to disappointment.

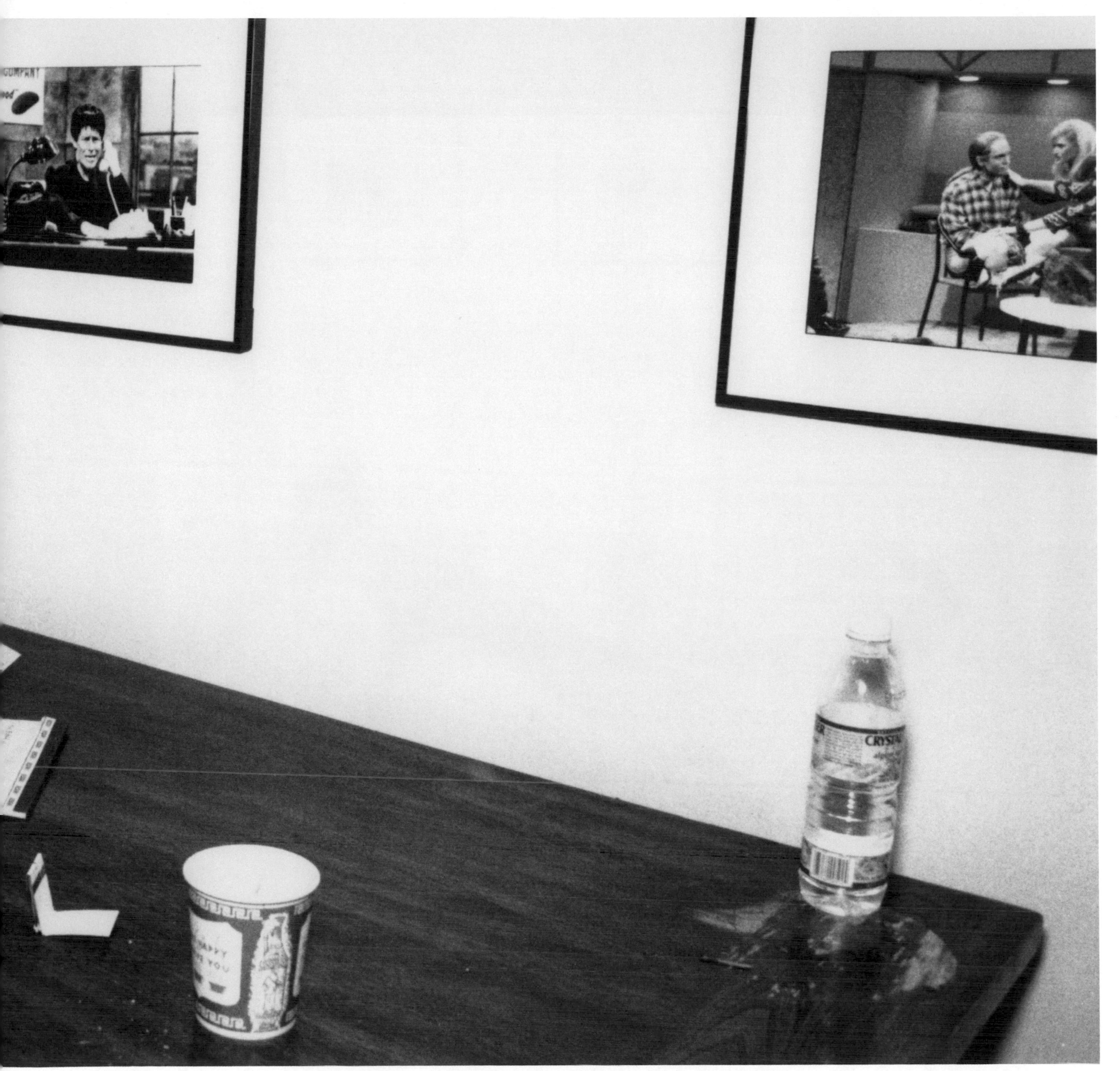

Most writers stay up until the wee hours of Wednesday morning to finish their sketches in time for the read-through. Sarah Silverman, seen here, was a writer and featured player for the 1993-94 season.

This unidentified writer has either given up or rewarded himself with a nap.

BELOW AND RIGHT: Script bundles being stacked and distributed. A complete set of 40 scripts is given to each cast and crew member attending the read-through.

Amy Poehler, Kristen Wiig, and Casey Wilson performing a dance number at read-through. (2008)

Jay Pharoah, Bill Hader, and Paul Brittain. (2011)

Each person seated at the table for the read-through has his/her own designated seat. Lorne Michaels sits at the head of the table (left, between the windows), the host sits to his right, and the head writer to his left. (1994)

The passage from one sketch to the next at read-through is punctuated by the sounds of scripts being tossed to the floor. The aftermath (seen here in the 1980s) is a familiar sight to anyone who has ever worked on the show.

WEDNESDAY / DESIGN

Just up the hall from the writers' room is the design room, and this is where the design meeting happens Wednesday night after the picks are announced. First, the director and designers gather around a plan of Studio 8H to map out the location of each sketch. Then, sketch by sketch, the writers consult with the director and designated set designer about the set, after which they proceed to the table around which are seated the costume designers and the heads of hair and makeup to give their notes. By around midnight, everyone has dispersed but the set designers, who work late into the night to complete the designs so that construction can begin early the next morning.

Set designers Eugene Lee (left) and Akira Yoshimura, seen here in the fall of 1975, still design for the show today.

Set designer Keith Ian Raywood at his drafting table during a Wednesday-night session. (2014)

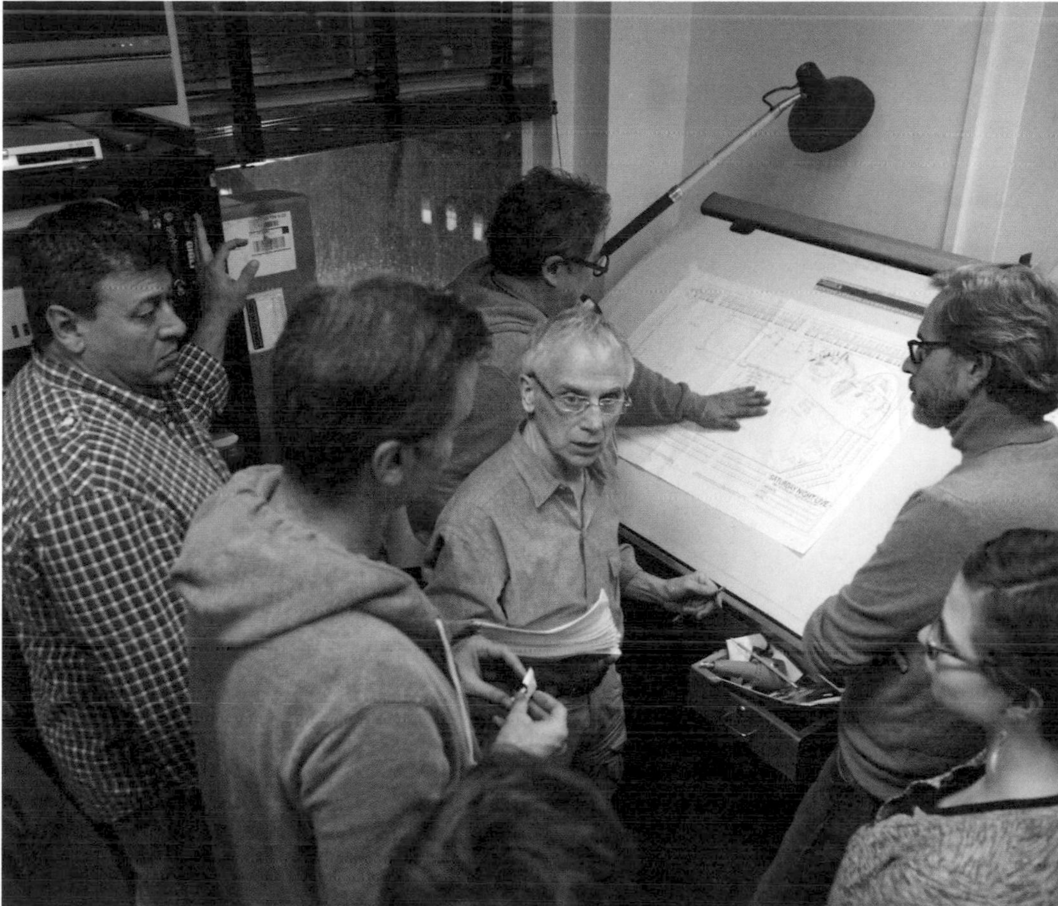

LEFT: Once the picks are in, the director (Don Roy King, center) confers with writers, designers, and assistants to discuss the designs for each of the week's sketches. **BELOW:** During the design meeting, costume and wardrobe brainstorming happens at a nearby table (seen here, from left to right: Dale Richards, Tom Broecker, and Eric Justian).

Once all the others have gone home, the four set designers stay late to finish their designs. Left to right: Eugene Lee, Akira Yoshimura, N. Joseph DeTullio, and Keith Ian Raywood. (All photos this spread, 2014)

Thursday–Friday

After a few days of relative peacefulness, Studio 8H comes roaring to life again as the action moves from the 17th to the 8th floor of 30 Rock. Cue cards are written by the hundreds. Rehearsals begin. Writers rewrite. Extras are cast. Network censors are placated. Musical arrangements and graphics are created. Pretapes and bumper photos are produced and shot. Sets are built; props are selected. Costumes and wigs are researched, sourced, and designed. Finally, the running order for Saturday's dress rehearsal is established.

THURSDAY-FRIDAY / REHEARSALS

Music rehearsals begin at 2 p.m. on Thursday and sketch rehearsals run from 3:30 until 8 p.m. Thursday's rehearsal schedule, which includes roughly a third of the week's sketches, is established Wednesday night after the announcement of the picks, and indicates when and where each cast member and writer is due for rehearsal. When they arrive in Studio 8H to rehearse, cue cards are ready and basic props and furniture have already been placed on the sets—the bare minimum needed for blocking. At least three passes at each sketch are required—first a dry block, during which the writer(s) and director guide the cast members through the sketch, and then two or more on-camera rehearsals that the director monitors from the control room to fine-tune the camera blocking. Meanwhile, the writers, who convene Thursdays at noon, work on rewrites; the head writers lead these meetings, giving their suggestions and passing on notes from other departments as to how the sketches should be reworked and tweaked. They begin with the pretapes, then move on to sketches to be rehearsed Thursday, and lastly they tackle sketches slated for Friday rehearsal. By the end of Thursday, all rewrites are complete (unless a new sketch is added to the lineup). On-camera rehearsals continue Friday in the same manner for the remaining sketches.

Lorne Michaels with the season 1 writing team in Studio 8H.

Martin Short in character as Ed Grimley. (ca. 1984)

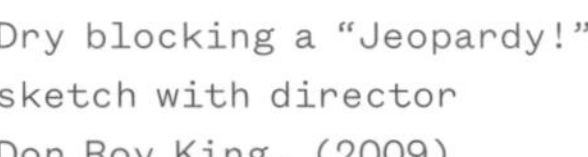

Dry blocking a “Jeopardy!” sketch with director Don Roy King. (2009)

Recognizable from the many monologues throughout the years that have featured shots of the audience, the wooden swivel chairs on the studio floor have been in use since the show began. Seen here in the early 1990s, left to right: Phil Hartman, writer Christine Zander, set designer Keith Ian Raywood, and producer Marci Klein.

Chevy Chase splayed on the floor of Studio 8H. (1975)

3:52:19PM
SNL

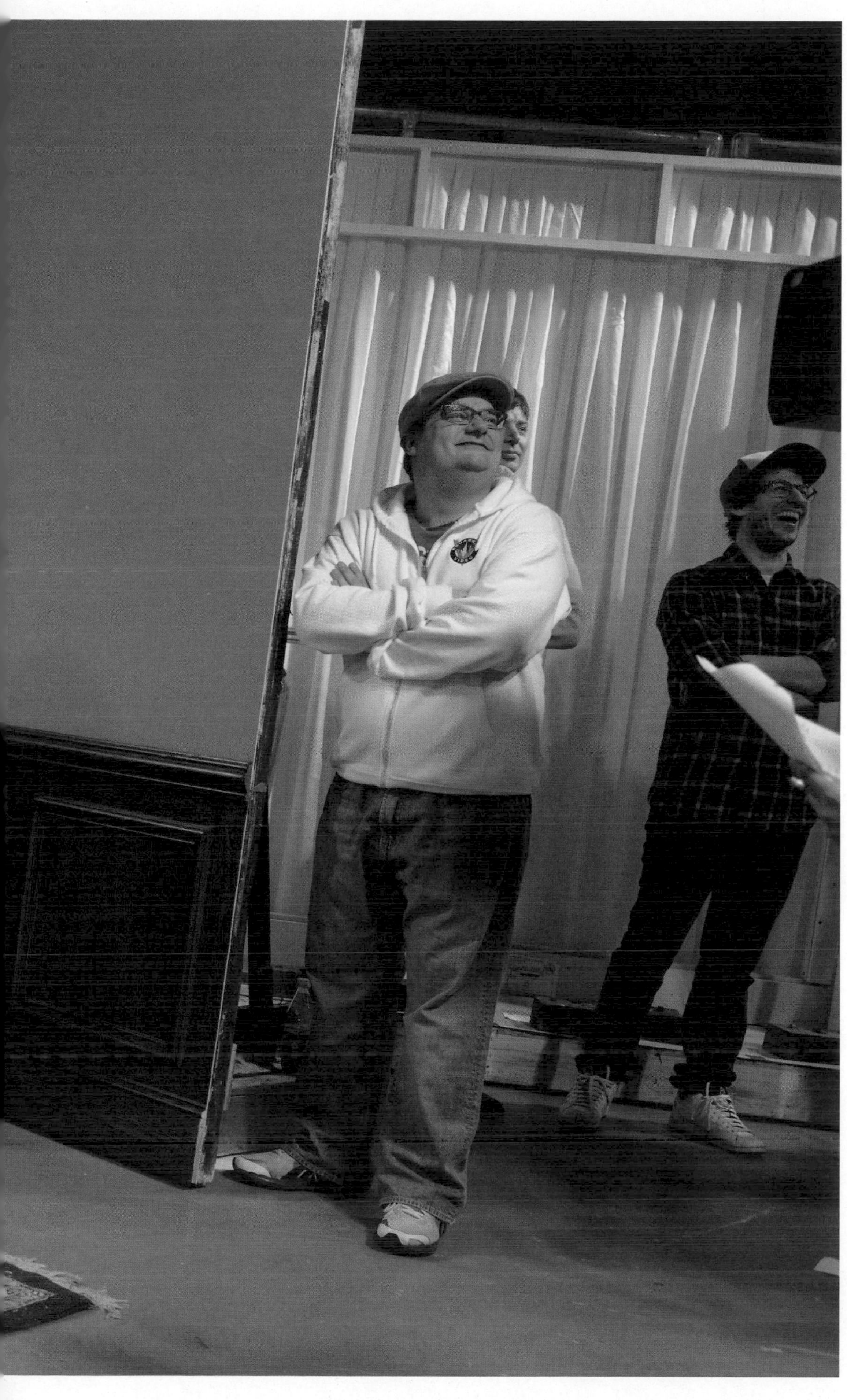

Offstage, Bobby Moynihan, Mike O'Brien, and Andy Samberg watch the monitor as "Five-Timers' Club" inductee Justin Timberlake (far left) rehearses with fellow members Steve Martin, Chevy Chase, and Martin Short. (2013)

Arcade Fire band members Régine Chassagne and Win Butler racing down the hallway toward Studio 8H.

Host Bryan Cranston rehearses “What Up with That?” with Kenan Thompson, Jay Pharoah, and Fred Armisen. (2010)

Musical directors Paul Shaffer and Howard Shore. (1975)

A private concert for stage manager Chris Kelly as Bruce Springsteen rehearses. (2002)

Choreographer Danielle Flora (right) works with cast members for a “Gangnam Style” routine with special guest Psy. (2012)

THURSDAY-FRIDAY / SETS

At the crack of dawn on Thursday morning, set construction begins at a massive former shipbuilding site in Brooklyn's Navy Yard. Sets are built to be broken down into pieces that can fit into the elevators at 30 Rock, and they are driven in by truck as they are completed. Meanwhile, the production designer responsible for set dressing visits prop houses to select furniture and accoutrements that will be delivered in time for set dressing on Saturday morning.

Sets are constructed at Stiegelbauer Associates, located in Brooklyn's Navy Yard.

S.N.L
1 Twins
Principal Frye (Rush)
M Hearings c/o (Rush)
8 Big Cats
9 French Dance
10 Universal Studios
11 Little Mermaid
12 Big Joe
STEIGELBAUER ASSOCIATES

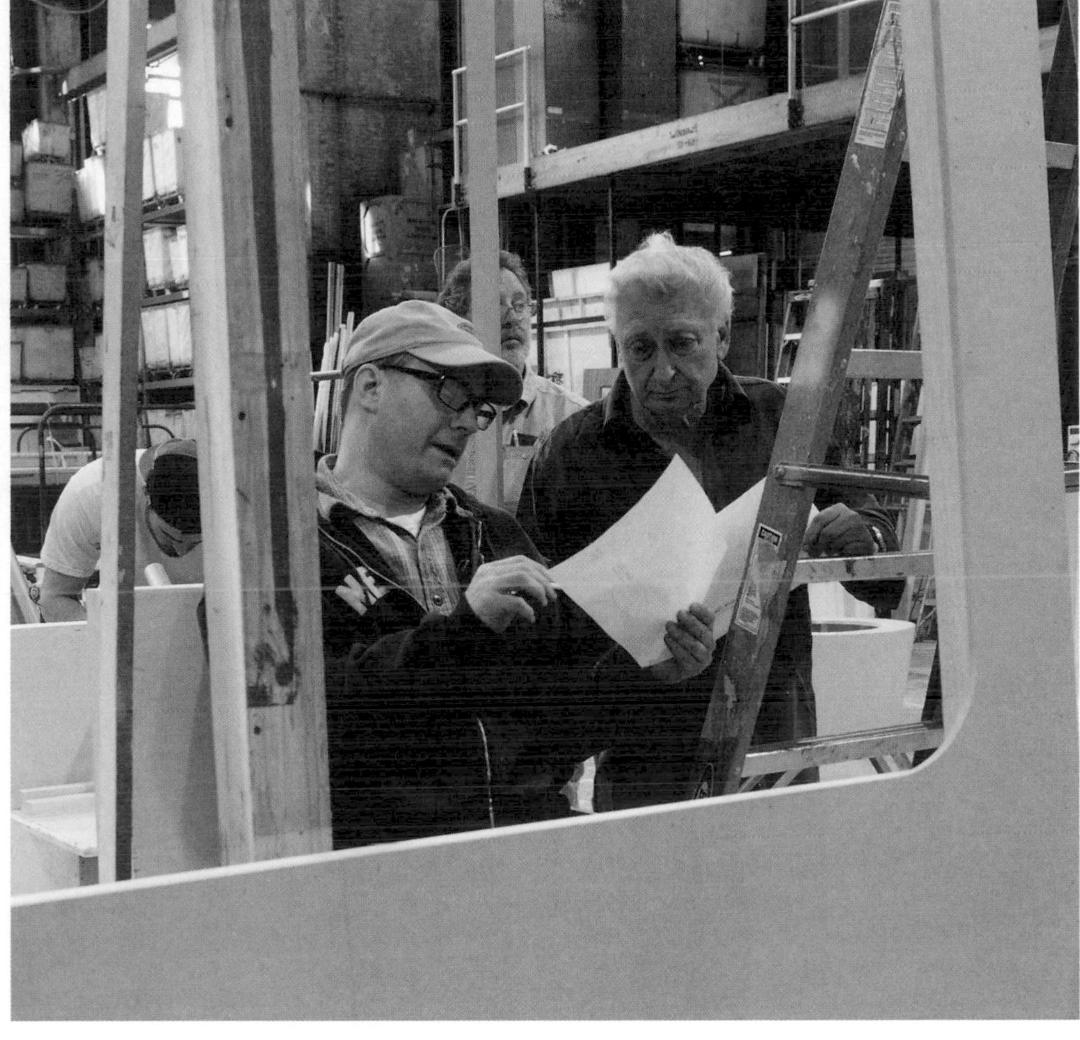

Scenes at the Navy Yard set-building shop: Designer N. Joseph DeTullio (**OPPOSITE**) studies sketches and reference images; some set elements, such as this "Jeopardy!" game board (**TOP**), are saved for reference or future use; DeTullio confers with shop foreman Steve DeMaria (**BOTTOM RIGHT**). (All photos this spread, 2014)

THURSDAY-FRIDAY / COSTUMES, HAIR, AND MAKEUP

Performers never appear on air without makeup, rarely without wigs (often what looks like a person's real hair is actually an "own wig" that facilitates quick changes), and always dressed by the costume and wardrobe department. These departments spend Thursday and Friday researching, shopping, designing, and creating. The wardrobe and wig archives are scoured for usable pieces—whenever possible, existing clothing is modified or resized and wigs are restyled or "refronted"—and rush orders are placed for anything not on hand. Costume designers make sketches and work with pattern makers to create original costumes on site. Meanwhile, in the special effects and makeup labs, crew members take on whatever challenges the scripts offer up, be it a monster's head, an exploding whale carcass, or a body flying through the air. The more demanding the task, the more fun they have making it happen.

Since script changes continue to filter in until the show goes live, the designers must not only prepare in advance, they must be ready to modify anything at a moment's notice. It is not uncommon, for example, for a costume hot off the sewing machine to be run down the hall to the quick-change booths and appear on air in a period of minutes.

The storage room in the makeup lab is home to a vast collection of of plaster casts and molds, including head casts of each current cast member as well as frequent hosts and special guests. (2009)

The wardrobe department uses a whiteboard to cross-reference cast members and sketches in which they appear. (2011)

Costume designer Eric Justian (left) fitting a fat suit on Darrell Hammond, to Jimmy Fallon's great amusement. (1998)

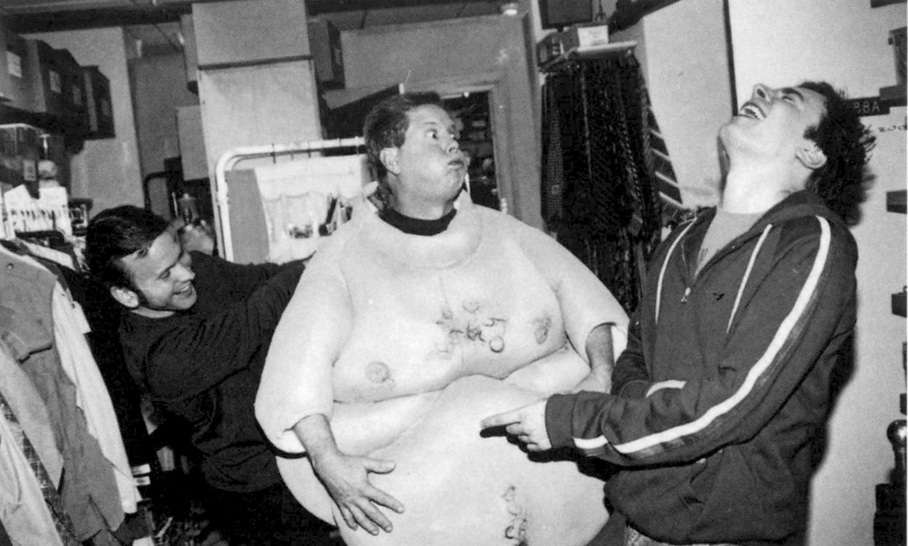

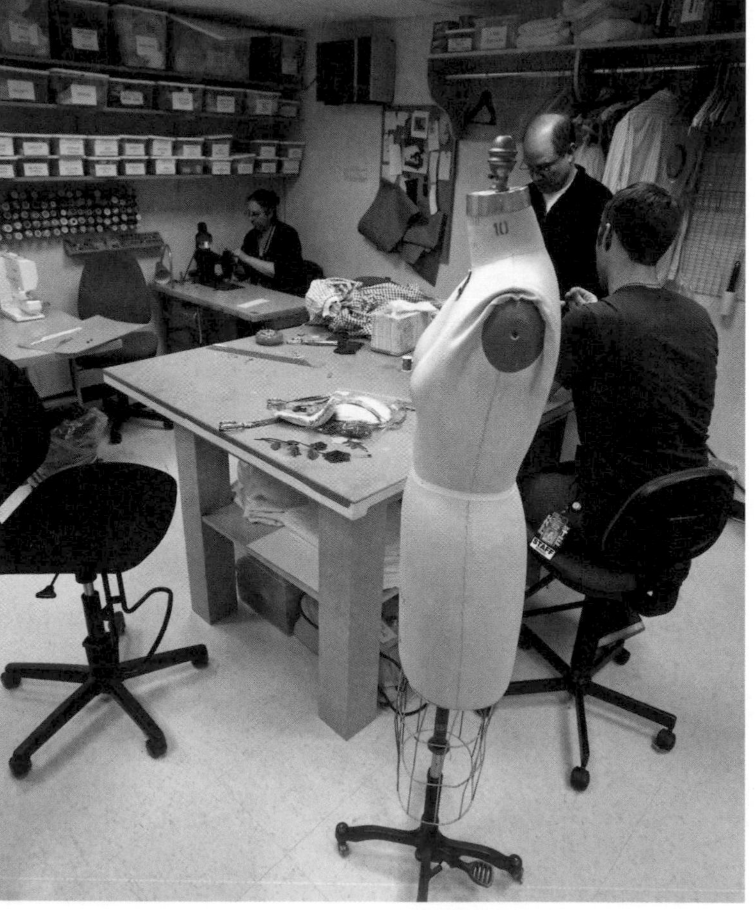

Down the hall from Studio 8H is where most costumes are sewn. Dale Richards (standing) is a member of a team of highly skilled men and women who make or alter nearly every costume worn on the show. (2009)

Costume designer
Tom Broecker in the
wardrobe archives.
(mid-1990s)

The hair department is led by Bettie O. Rogers, seen here in 2013 working on a wig for Justin Timberlake while hair stylist Inga Thrasher looks on.

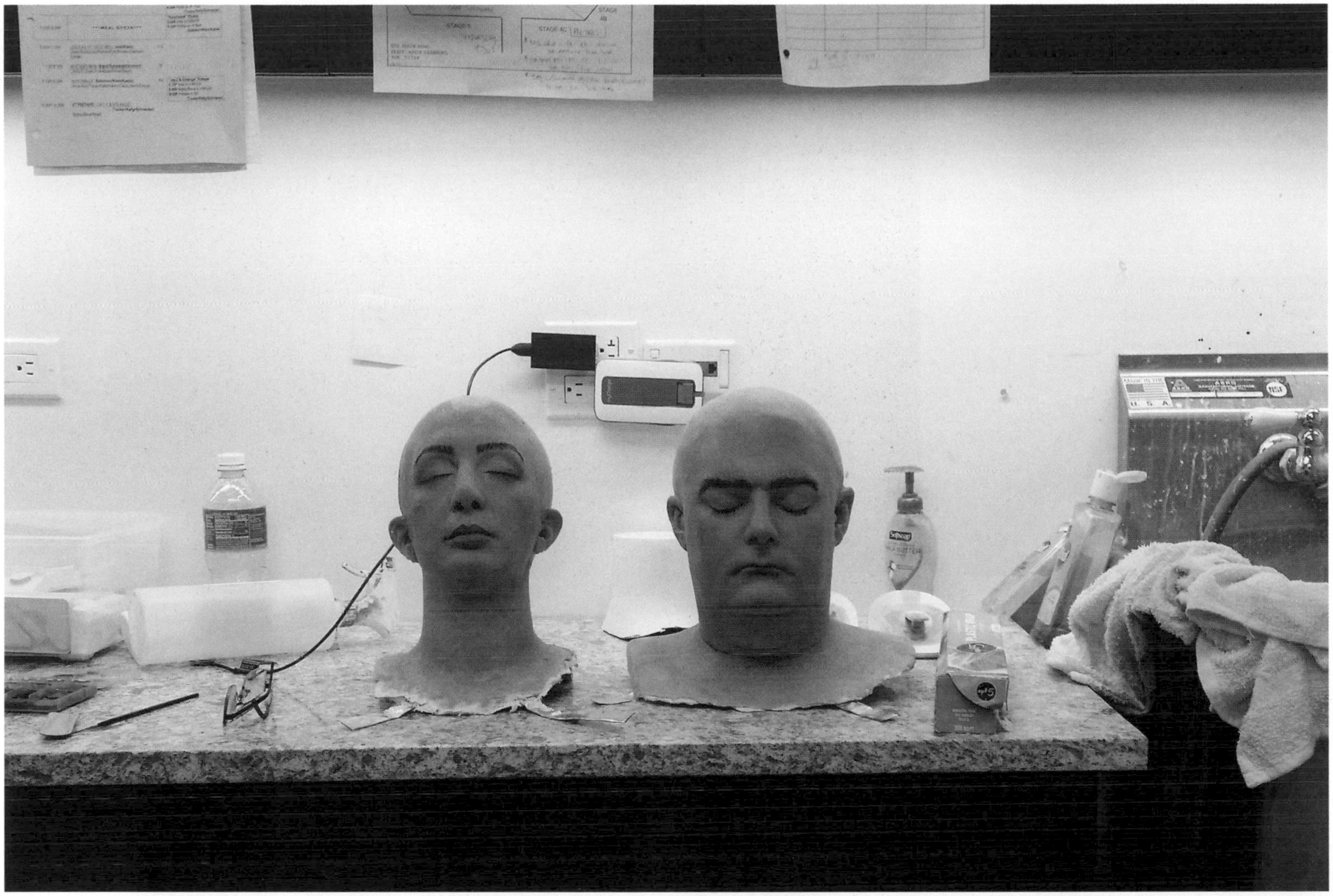

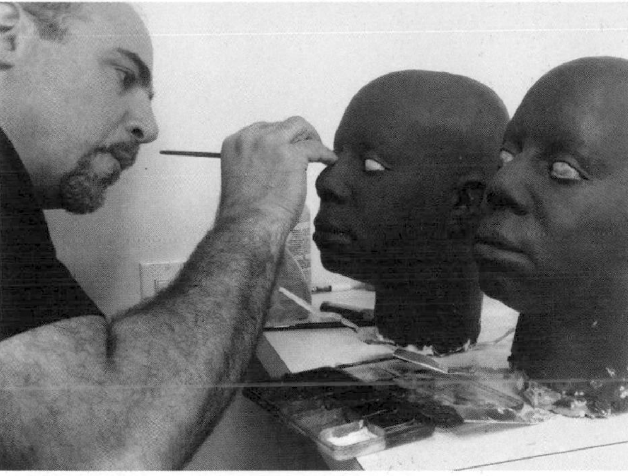

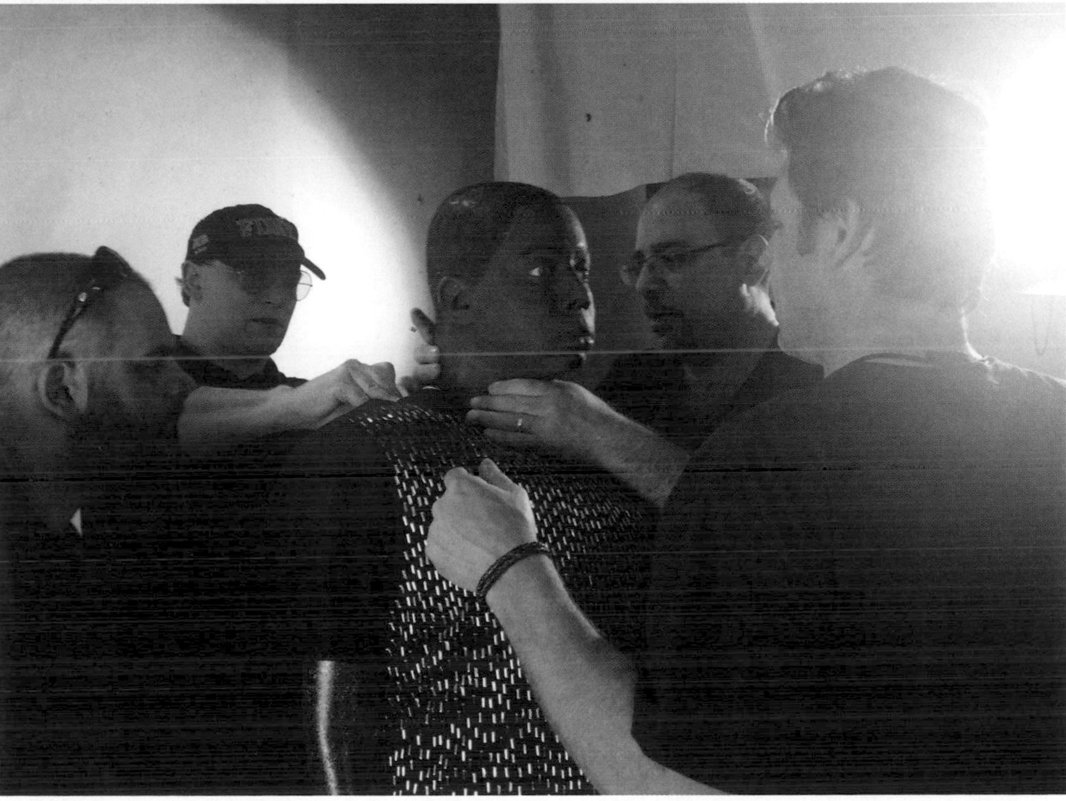

For the 2014 short "When Will the Bass Drop?", which called for three characters' heads to explode, chief SNL makeup artist Louie Zakarian created lifelike heads to be mounted on the stunt dummies. **ABOVE:** Zakarian puts finishing touches on two Kenan Thompson heads (one to be used to test the explosion on set). **RIGHT:** special effects experts help mount the stunt dummy on the shoot. **TOP:** Nasim Pedrad and Bobby Moynihan's likenesses are ready to be rigged with explosives.

THURSDAY-FRIDAY / PHOTO AND PROMO SHOOTS

The portraits of the host and musical guest that air during the show's commercial breaks are called "bumpers," and the shoots for these take place Thursday afternoons in Studio 8H. After a few days of brainstorming and pre-production, the photographer usually has no more than an hour or two to complete the shoot.

The main promos that air on TV to promote the upcoming episode are recorded on Thursday afternoons in Studio 8H. Writers pitch a number of ideas, several of which are shot with a view to choosing a few variations for airing. Though cue cards are provided, ad libs sometimes trump the scripted dialogue after a few takes are in the can.

Photographer Mary Ellen Matthews shooting bumpers for Will Ferrell's second time hosting. (2009)

Michael O'Donoghue lends a hand (and a leg) as Edie Baskin shoots a bumper for Candice Bergen's Christmas 1976 show.

Jane Curtin, Laraine Newman, and Gilda Radner. (ca. 1976)

Mary Ellen Matthews shooting bumper photos of Jon Hamm (**LEFT**, 2010) and U2 (**BELOW**, 2009).

RIGHT: Edie Baskin, whose hand-tinted photographs defined SNL's visual identity in the 1970s, seen here at work. **OPPOSITE:** Baskin's daughter, Bella Bronson, assists during Louis C.K.'s bumper shoot. (2014)

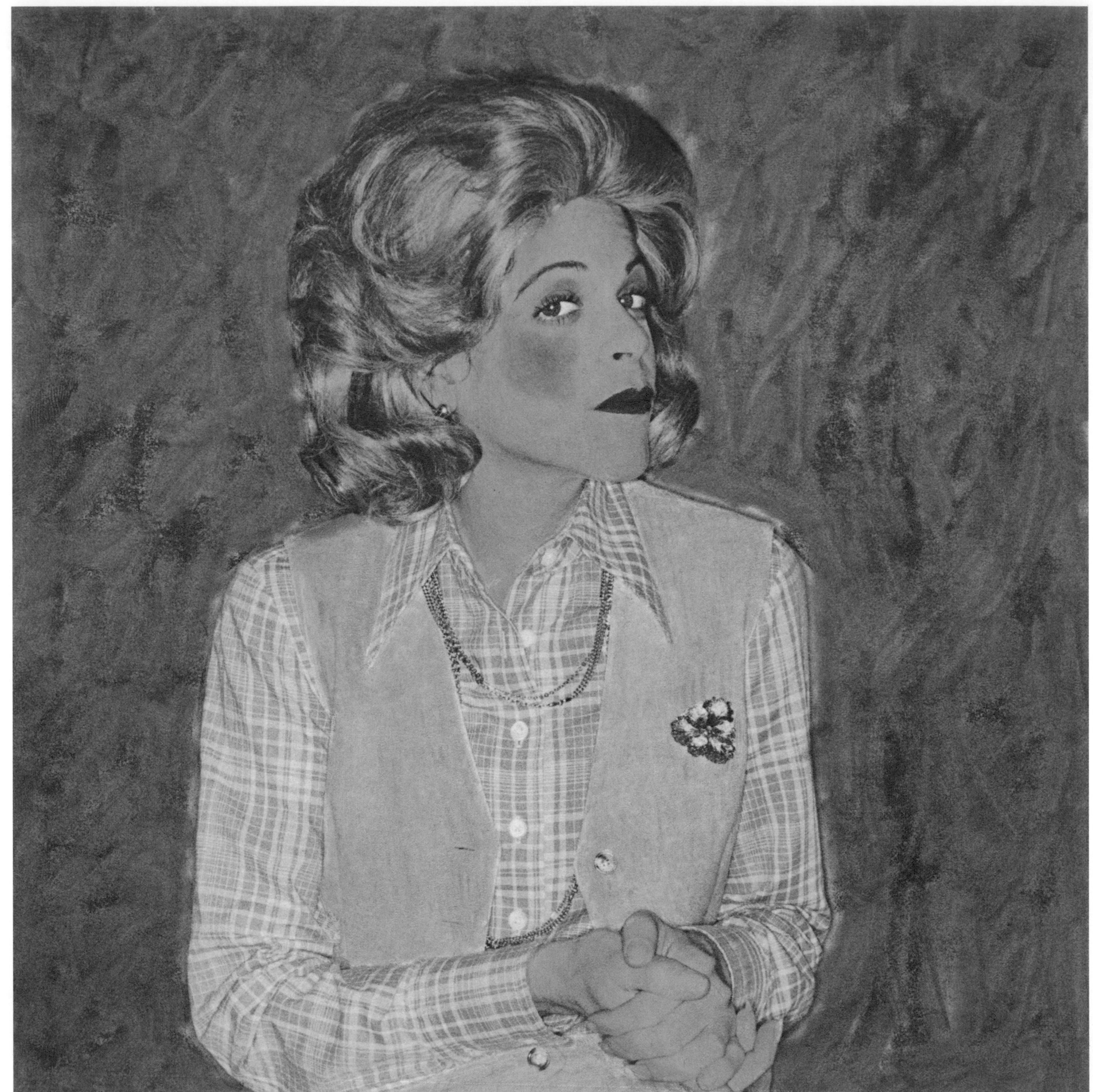

Edie Baskin's hand-tinted portraits of Gilda Radner as Baba Wawa and John Belushi as Samurai Futaba. (1977)

Lorne Michaels overseeing promo shoots with Madeline Kahn and Spartan cheerleaders Craig and Arianna, played by Will Ferrell and Cheri Oteri (**RIGHT**, 1995), and Steve Martin (**ABOVE**, 1989).

Kenan Thompson joined Jimmy Fallon on the roof of 30 Rock to shoot the promo for Fallon's December 2013 show.

Producer Marci Klein supervises the two Donalds (Donald Trump and Darrell Hammond as his doppelganger) for Trump's April 2004 promo.

Betty White and Jay-Z. (2010)

Bill Hader in character as Stefon mugs for lighting designer Phil Hymes in preparation for a promo shoot. Behind him are hair stylist Inga Thrasher, writer John Mulaney, and stage manager Gena Rositano. (2011)

THURSDAY-FRIDAY / PRETAPES

Pretapes are pieces shot in advance of the live show, including short films, commercial parodies, and title sequences for sketches. With very limited time for pre-production, shooting of pretapes begins Thursday or Friday, in the studio or on location, and usually runs into early Saturday morning. Juggling the schedule so that the host and cast members can attend their studio rehearsals and be on set for pretapes is just one of the many complex responsibilities of the supervising producer.

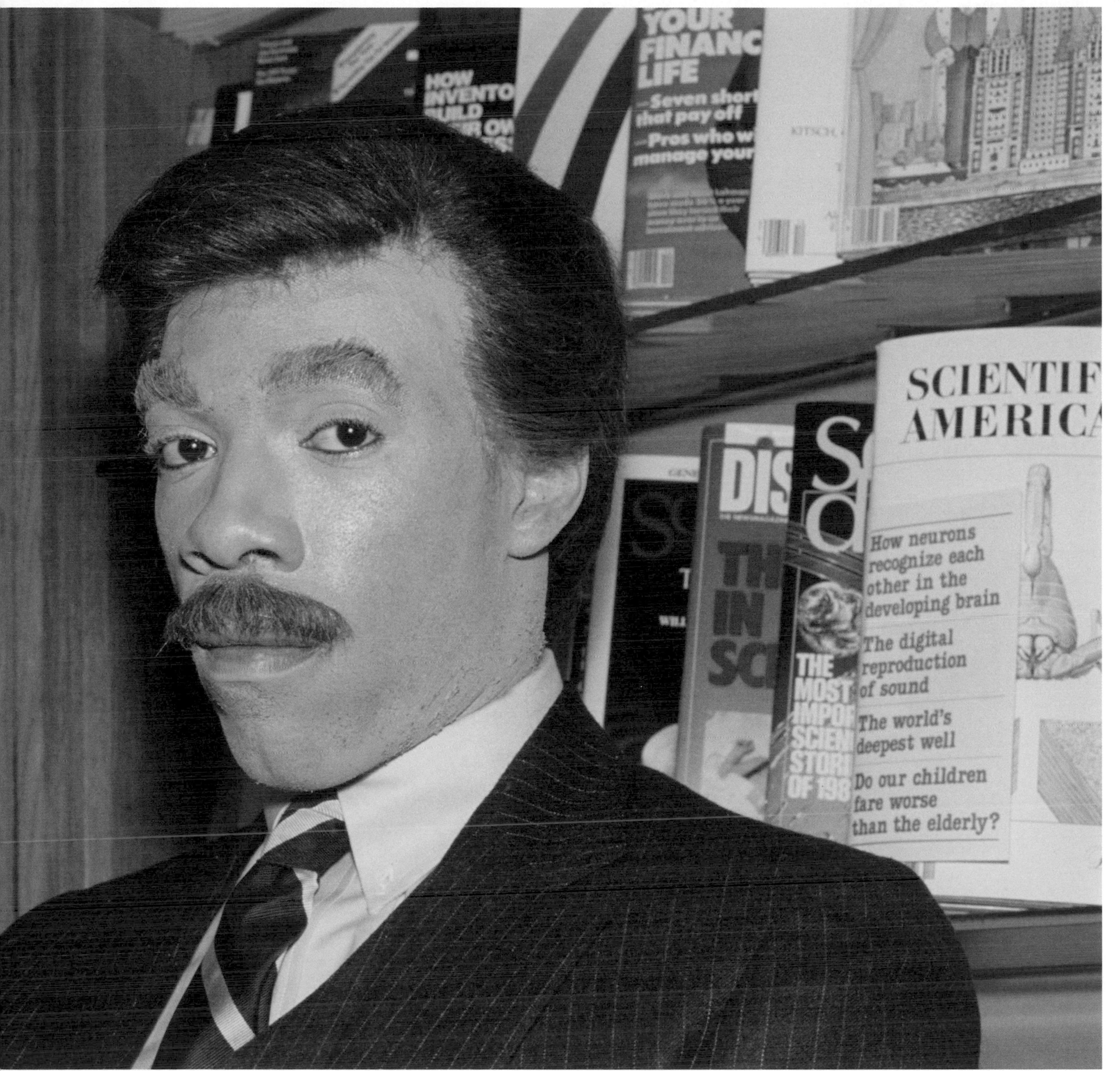

Eddie Murphy in whiteface for the short film “White Like Me” (1984), in which he goes undercover to experience a day in the life of a white man.

Fred Armisen and Maya Rudolph as Barack and Michelle Obama shooting the "Cosby Show"-inspired title sequence of "The Obama Show." (2012)

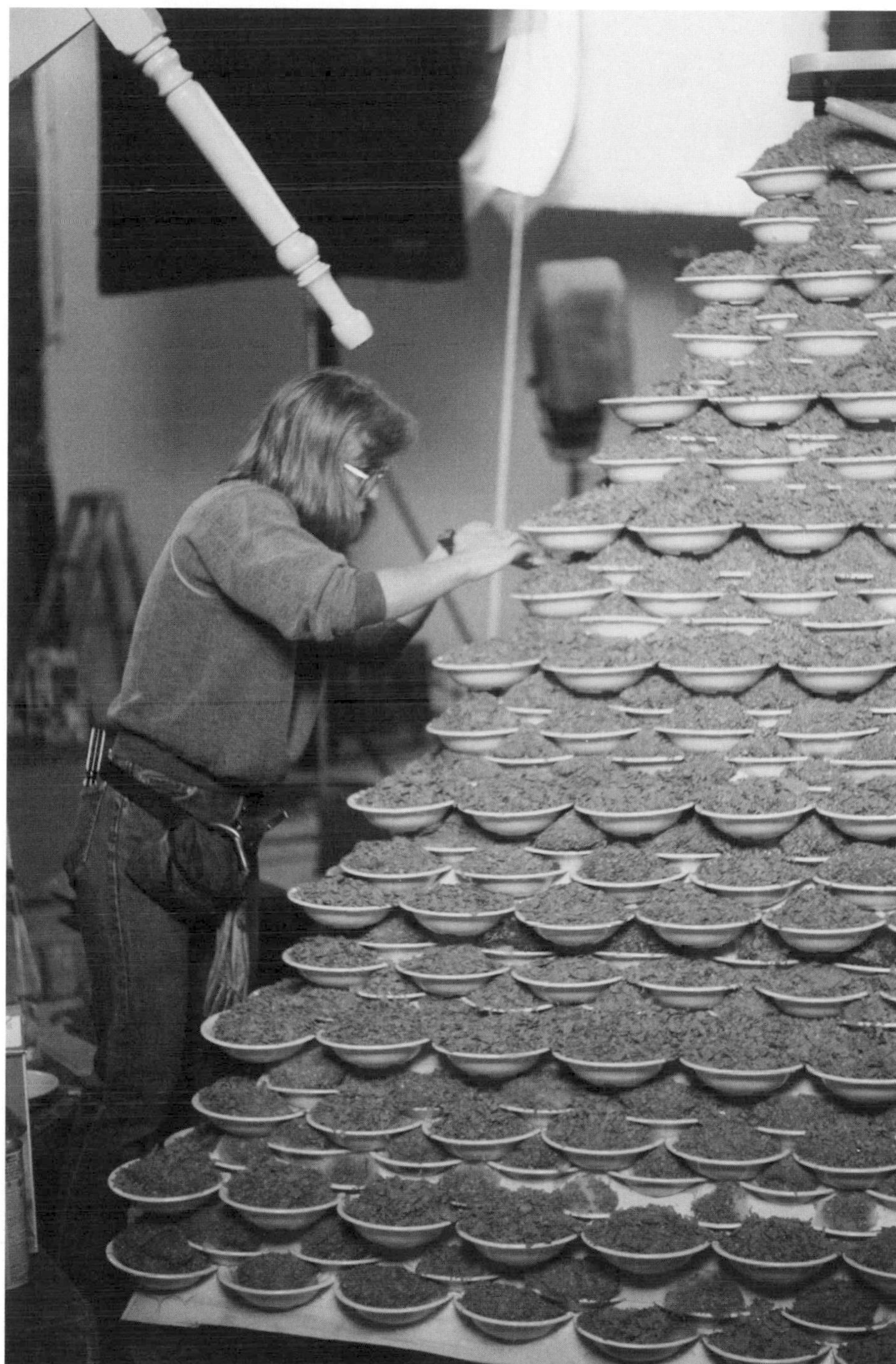

Prepping a pyramid of cereal bowls for the 1989 commercial parody "Colon Blow."

Producer/director James Signorelli (left) on set with Peyton Manning (rear) for the "Meatloaf Lovers" commercial-parody shoot. (2007)

Directors Matt & Oz shooting "Blockbuster" with Bobby Moynihan, Lady Gaga, and Mike O'Brien. (2013)

Short-film director Rhys Thomas (left) talks with writer Zach Kanin on the set of "More Hobbit." (2013)

Claymation sensation Mr. Bill began his career in a 1976 Super 8 home movie submitted by amateur filmmaker Walter Williams. Williams was subsequently hired as a writer on the show and produced more than 20 Mr. Bill shorts.

Michael Cera made a special appearance alongside host Jonah Hill in the parody trailer "Me," a takeoff of Spike Jonze's "Her" in which the protagonist falls in love not with a virtual woman but with his own doppelganger. (2014)

Lonely Island's Andy Samberg, Jorma Taccone, and Akiva Schaffer (**RIGHT,** in "The Creep," 2011) created over 100 SNL Digital Shorts between 2007 and 2012, including the iconic "Lazy Sunday" and "Dick in a Box." **ABOVE RIGHT:** Andy Samberg in "The Roommate." (2011) **ABOVE LEFT:** Jon Hamm and Justin Bieber in "The 100th Digital Short." (2012)

Steven Spielberg, Bill Hader, and Andy Samberg shooting "Laser Cats 7" in Lorne Michaels's office. (2012)

A

In this episode of "MacGruber," Will Forte's character learns that his father is MacGyver (in a cameo by Richard Dean Anderson), which means his real name is "MacGruber MacGyver." With Kristen Wiig and camera operator John Rosenblatt. (2009)

George Harrison and Paul Simon shooting the cold open for the Thanksgiving 1976 episode.

Akiva Schaffer on the set of SNL Digital Short "Three-Way (The Golden Rule)" with Lady Gaga, Andy Samberg, and Justin Timberlake. (2011)

Storyboard and original artwork from "The Ambiguously Gay Duo," written by Robert Smigel and designed by J.J. Sedelmaier. A regular feature on SNL's "TV Funhouse" animated series beginning in 1996, it featured the voices of Stephen Colbert and Steve Carrell as Ace and Gary.

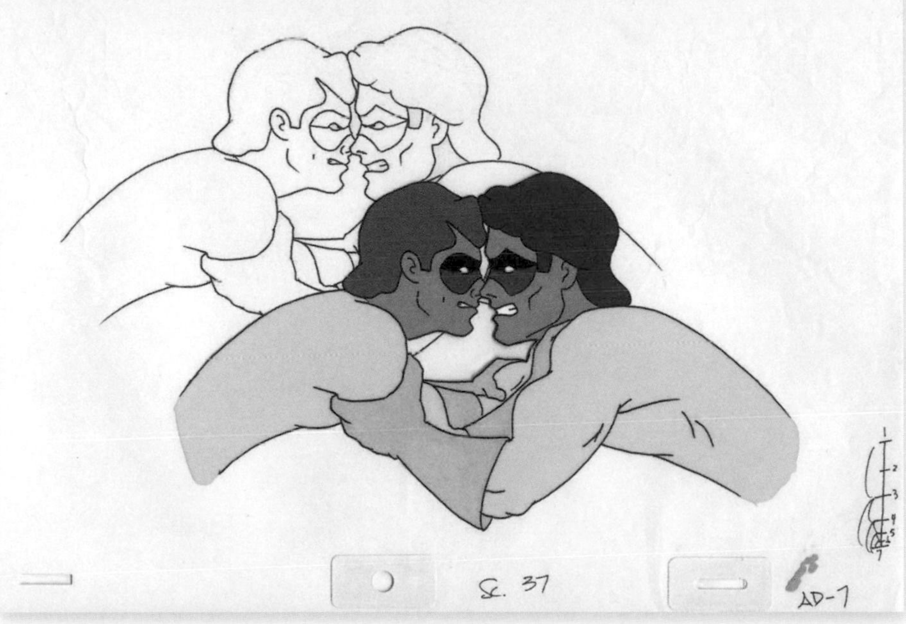

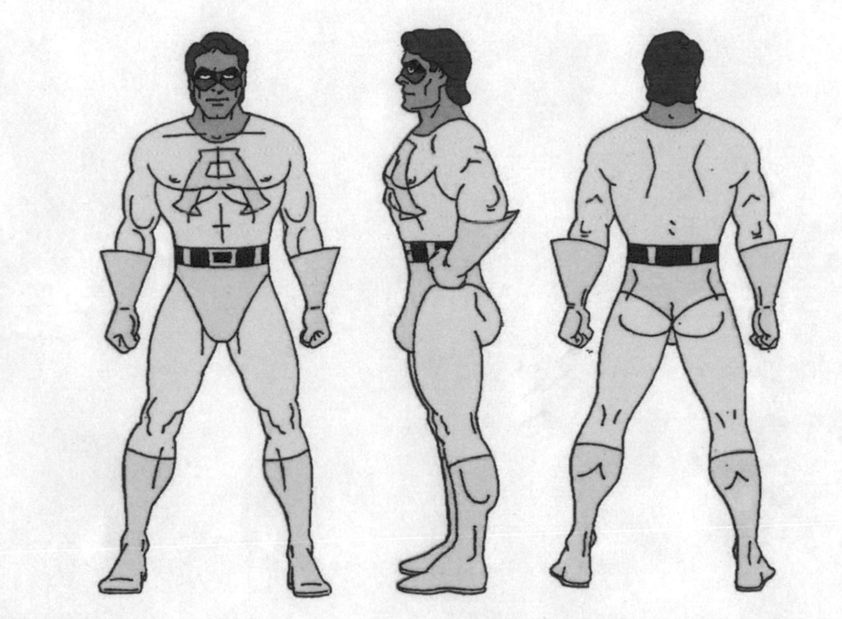

A
ROBERT SMIGEL
FILMED PROGRAM

Saturday

Sets are completed and dressed. Rehearsals in costume. Last-minute script changes. Cue-card writers in overdrive. Backstage meal break. Dress rehearsal in front of a live audience. Last-minute cuts and rewrites as the final countdown to the live show begins.

SATURDAY / RUN-THROUGHS

By the time Saturday run-throughs begin at 1 p.m., the sets have been constructed and dressed, costumes and wigs are (for the most part) ready, and cue cards have been updated to reflect script changes. In the hallway leading to Studio 8H, the quick-change booths and hair/makeup stations—one for each cast member—are set up. Most crew members walk around with a photocopy of the rundown pinned to their clothing, which lists the order in which each sketch will be rehearsed as well as the running order for the dress rehearsal. (The order of sketches for the run-through is determined by the studio layout and bears no resemblance to the actual running order for the dress rehearsal.) Any time there is a change to the dress-rehearsal lineup, new photocopies on paper of a different color are distributed.

The performers rehearse, for the first time in costume and wigs. Producers and other concerned parties keep an eye on the many monitors in the halls and offices to identify possible issues with wigs, costumes, sets, lighting, and the like. If the cold open is still being written on Saturday, it is usually rehearsed last.

Director Beth McCarthy-Miller watches as host dresser Donna Richards and Dean Nichols of wardrobe remove Robert De Niro's pants. (2002)

Left to right: writers Kent Sublette, James Anderson, and Steve Higgins with Kristen Wiig as Gilly. (2009)

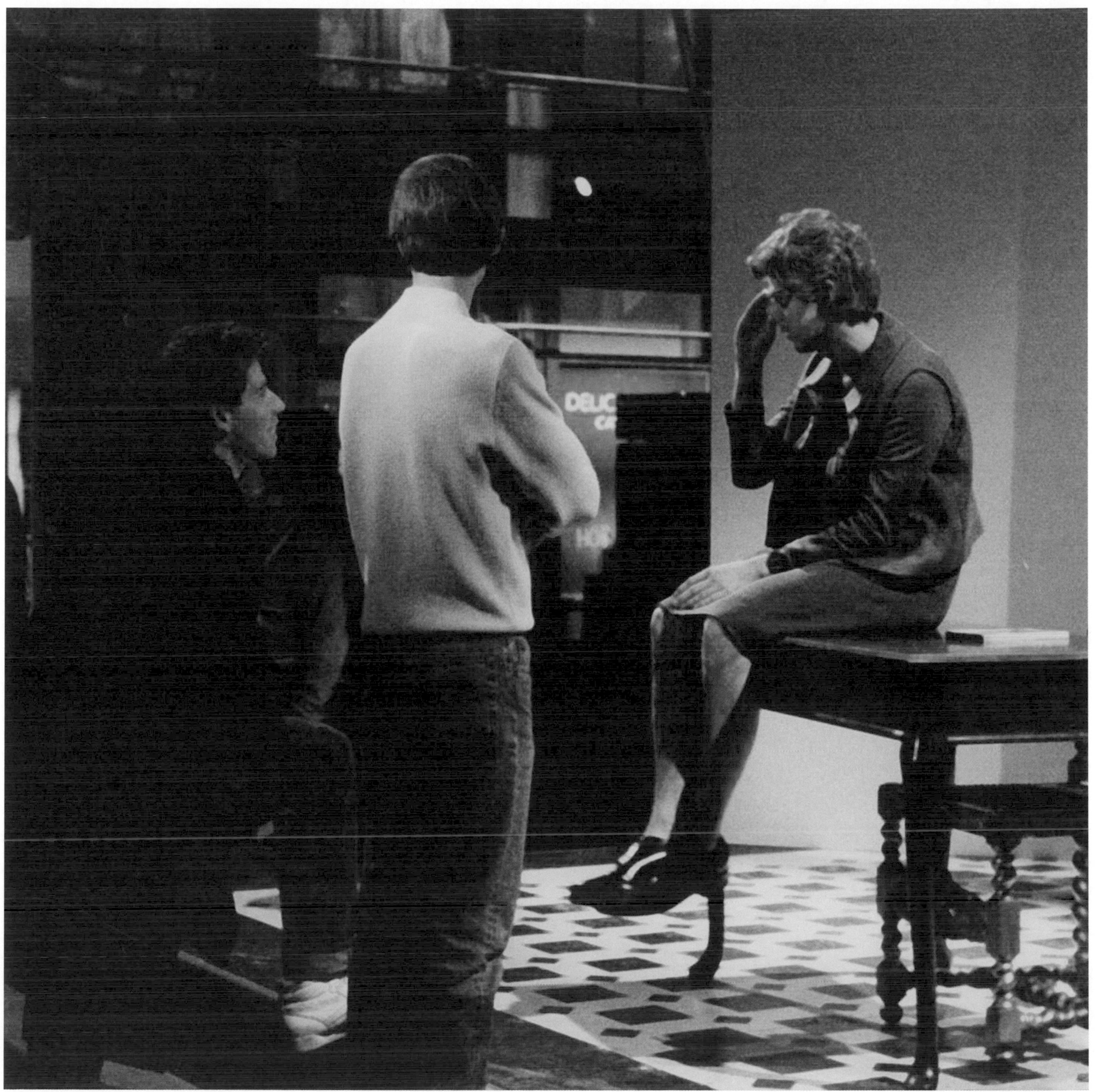

Dana Carvey, as Church Lady, taking a break during rehearsal. (1980s)

Will Ferrell (as Harry Hugs for the sketch “Happy Smile Patrol”) in the hallway outside Studio 8H. (1999)

Chevy Chase is almost unrecognizable with this prosthetic nose. (1977)

Mary Gross and Julia Louis-Dreyfus in the “Simulated Cat Fight” cold open of May 5, 1984. Spinal Tap members Christopher Guest, Michael McKean, and Harry Shearer (seen here during the dress rehearsal) didn't appear in the live version of the sketch.

Host Seth Rogen rehearsing "Rivista Della Televisione" with Bill Hader as Vinnie Vedecci. Since the director relies on dialogue or visual cues for switching camera angles, a sketch featuring a character speaking in gibberish posed an unusual challenge. The solution: Hader used hand gestures to provide cues to the director in the control room. (2009)

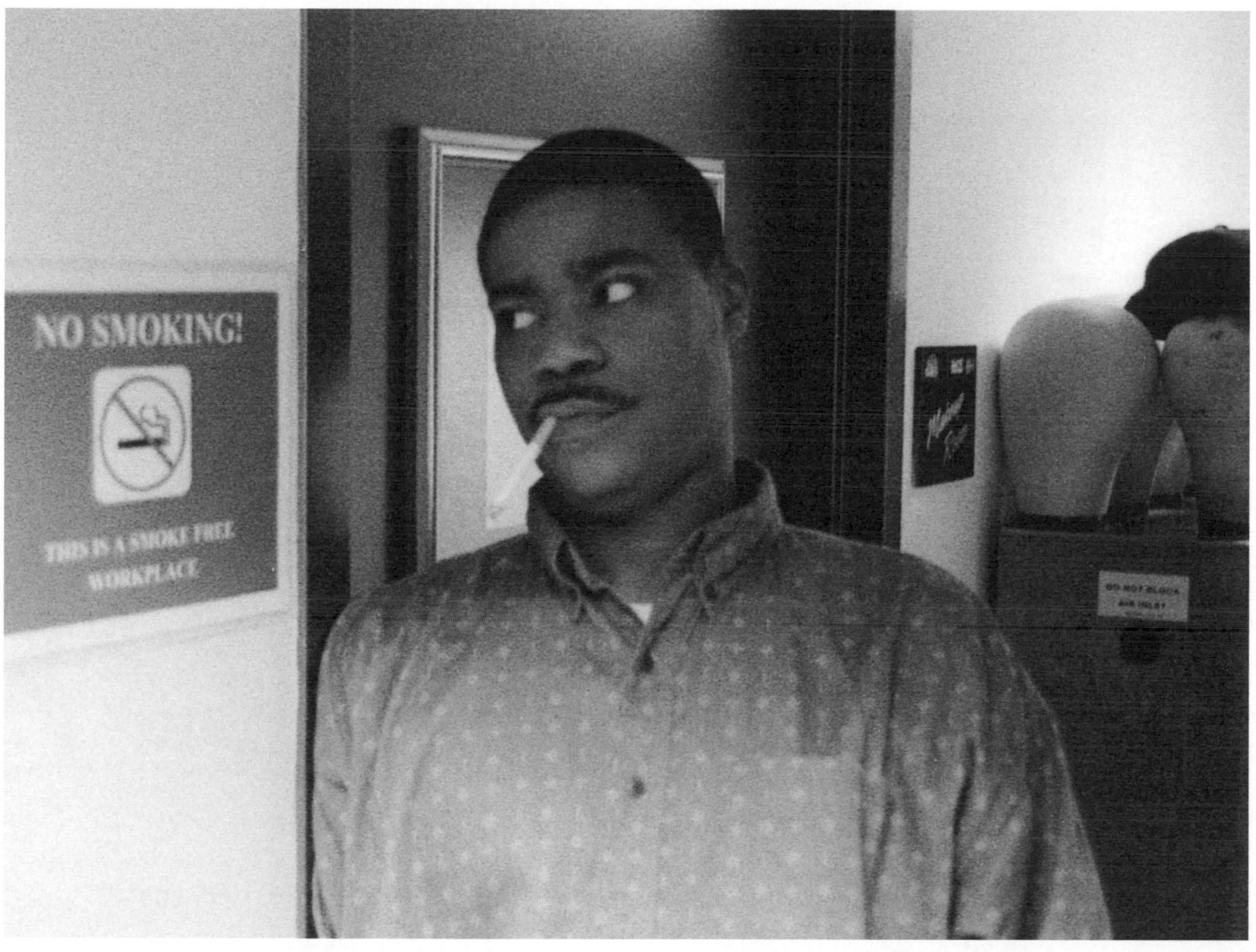

Tracy Morgan backstage, “observing” workplace smoking regulations. (ca. 2001)

Jan Hooks as Nancy Reagan. (Late 1980s)

Jon Lovitz and Phil Hartman. (Late 1980s)

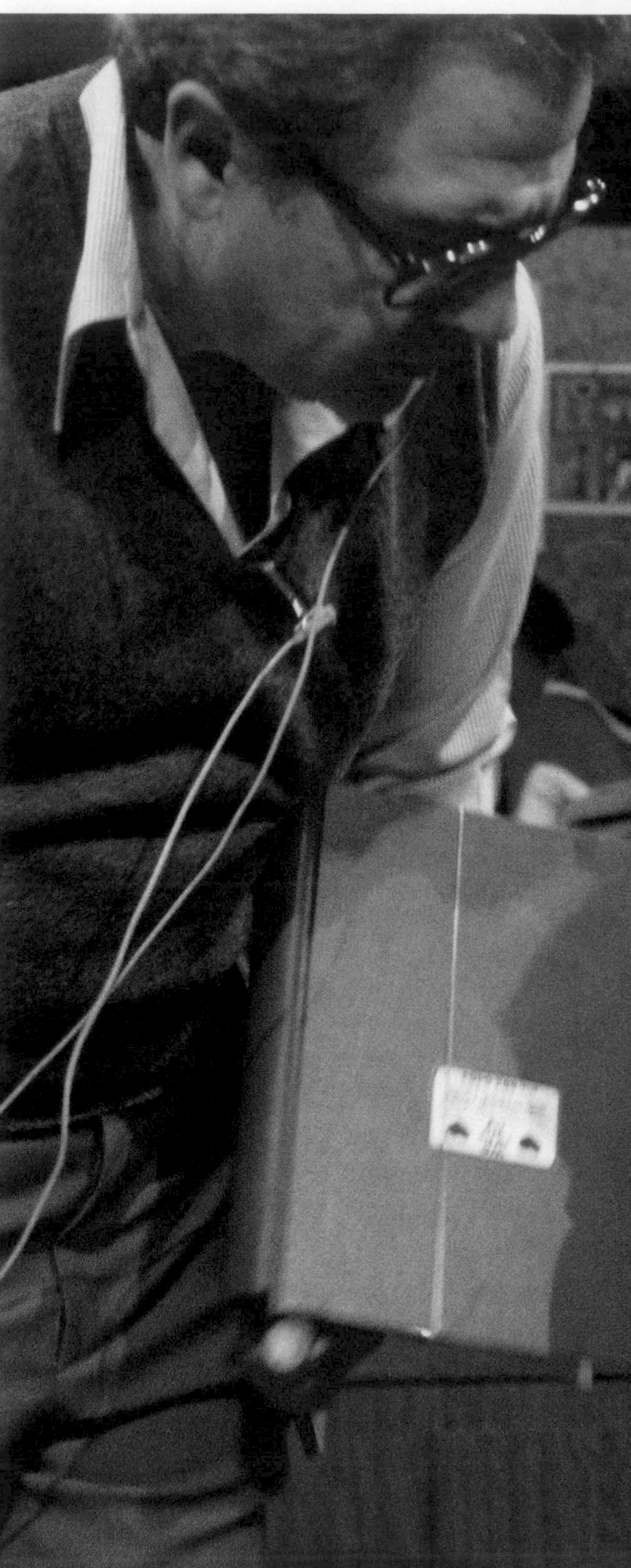

Tina Fey and writer Paula Pell as lesbian audience members for the Lucy Lawless monologue. (1998)

Stage manager Joe Disco
with Drew Barrymore and
Tim Kazurinsky. (1982)

Christopher Walken in “Angel of Death.” (2000)

Phil Hartman with Victoria Jackson, Jan Hooks, and Nora Dunn in a rehearsal of “Planet of the Enormous Hooters.” (1989)

Will Ferrell and Colin Quinn. (1998)

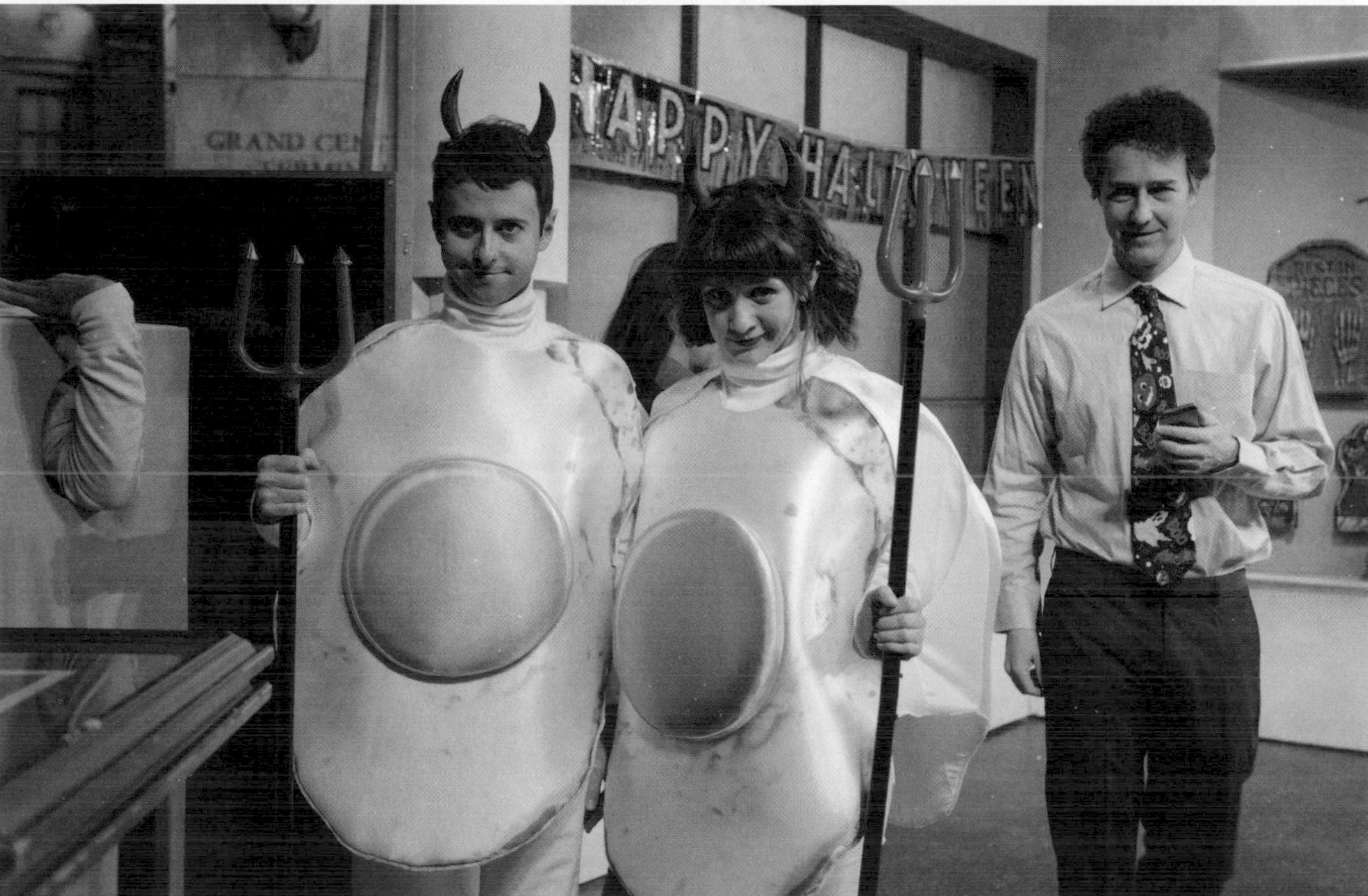

Deviled Eggs John Milhiser and Noël Wells with Edward Norton on set for “The Steve Harvey Show.” (2013)

ABOVE: Writer Tom Schiller with Dan Aykroyd as Gregnovich on the set of "Love, Russian Style." (1976)
OPPOSITE: Lorne Michaels, Elliott Gould, and cast rehearing a Killer Bees sketch. (1976)

→17
→17A
→18
→18A
→19
→19A
SAFETY FILM 5063
KODAK SAFETY FILM 5063
KODAK SAFETY FILM 5063

→23
→23A
→24
→24A
→25
→25A
KODAK SAFETY FILM 5063
KODAK SAFETY FILM 5063

→29
→29A
→30
→30A
→31
→31A
AK SAFETY FILM 5063
KODAK SAFETY FILM 5063

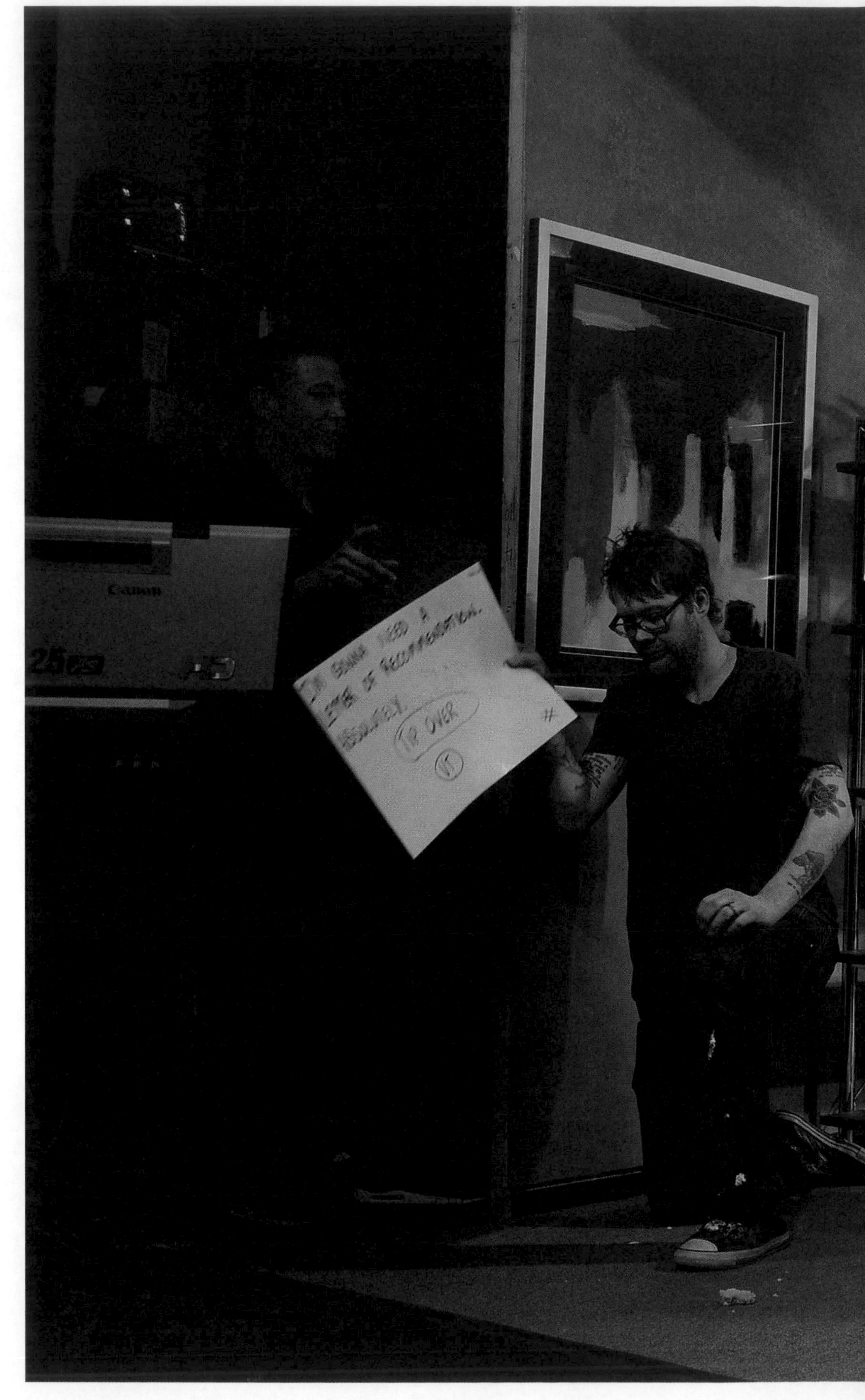

Louis C.K. and Beck Bennett in "Office Boss." (2014)

The ebullient Sweeney Sisters, played by Jan Hooks and Nora Dunn, made regular appearances on the show between 1986 and 1989.

Kristen Wiig and Miley Cyrus in the “Rock-a-Billy Lady Party Moisturizing Facial Cream” sketch. (2011)

Laraine Newman and Dan Aykroyd, as Christy Christina and E. Buzz Miller, rehearse the "E. Buzz Miller's Exercise World" sketch. Aykroyd's character was inspired by a man who ran a stand in Tahiti that sold postcards of topless native women, and Christy was inspired by… well, according to Newman, she was "pretty much an eyelash distance from a porn sidekick." OPPOSITE: Newman poses with her character's greatest assets. (1978)

Parody “CSI: Sarasota” promo starring Betty White and Rachel Dratch as elderly crime fighters. “They’ve got a license to kill… and a license to drive before sundown.” (2010)

Garrett Morris and Dan Aykroyd in "The Pepsi Syndrome." (1979)

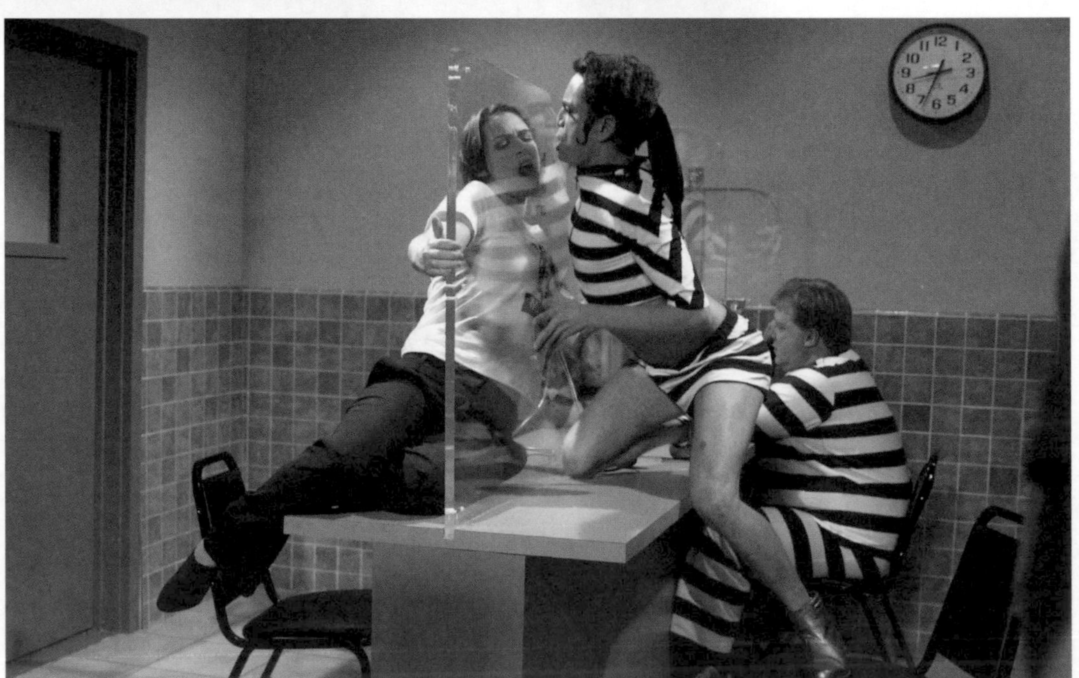

Mango, in prison for shoplifting, shares a steamy moment with visitor Winona Ryder in this sketch that made light of Ryder's recent shoplifting arrest. (2002)

Christopher Walken's recurrent sketch "The Continental" was shot from the point of view of the woman he was attempting to seduce. The hand he kisses here is that of camera operator Joe De Bonis. (1992)

Guest Art Garfunkel rehearsing a sketch that required him to poke his head through a hole in the wall; Bill Murray takes advantage of the situation to sneak up on him for a tickle. (1978)

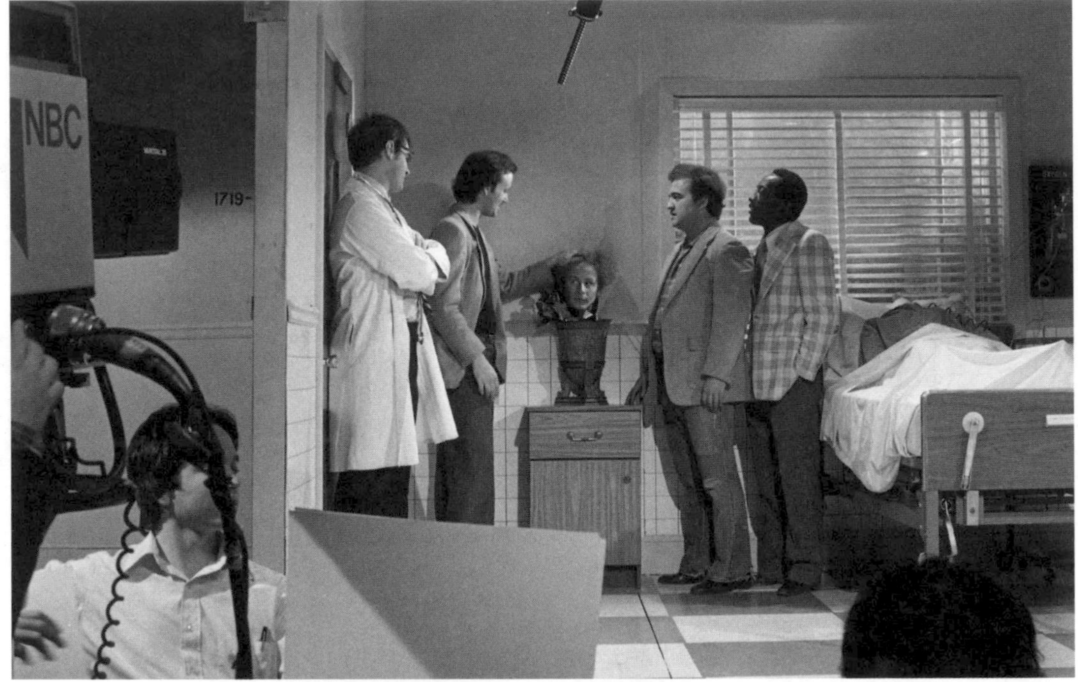

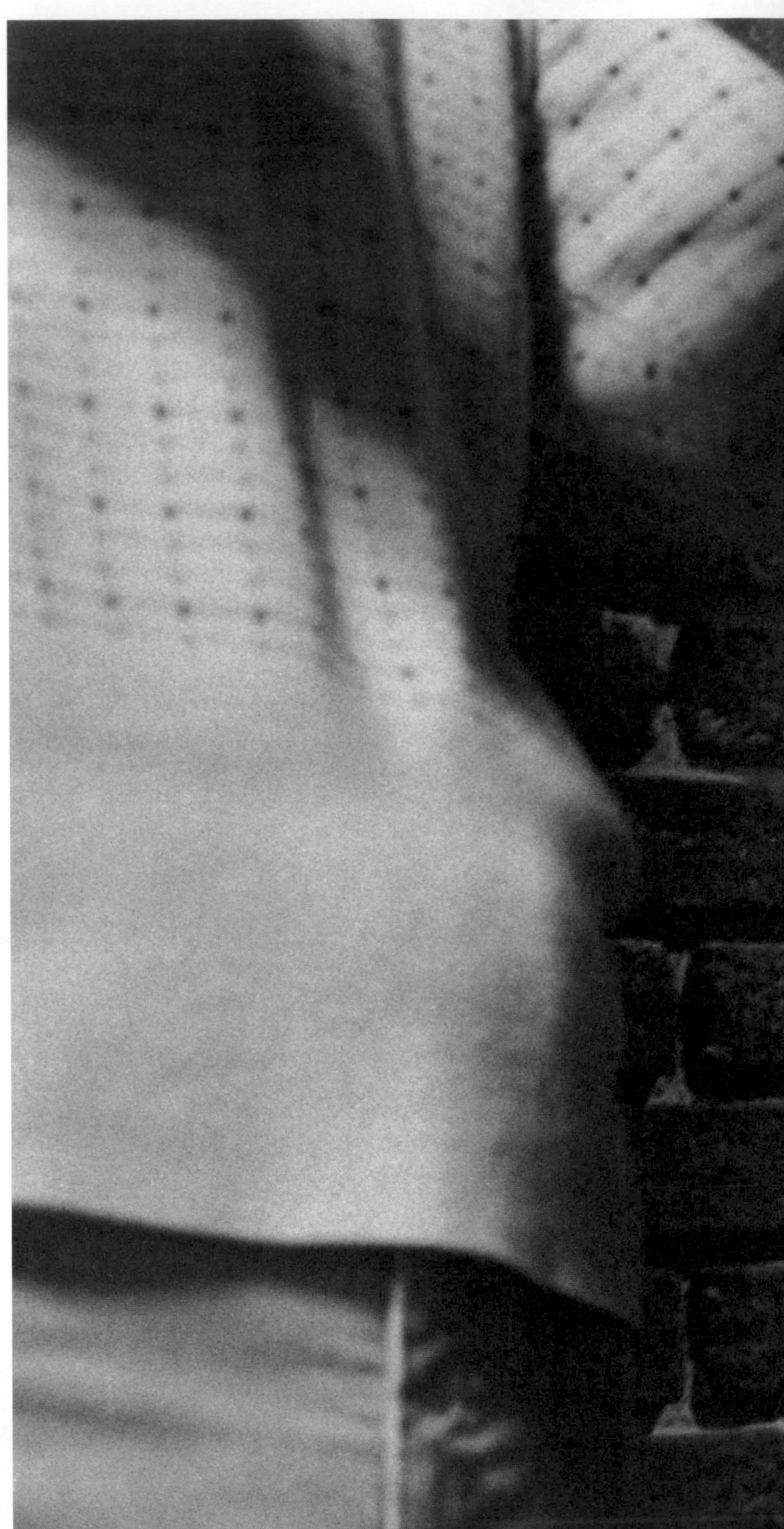

John Belushi and
Dan Aykroyd in "The
Untouchables." (1976)

Jon Lovitz and William Shatner rehearsing the sketch “Star Trek V: The Restaurant Enterprise.” (1986)

For the goodnights of Kristen Wiig's final show as a cast member, she danced with host Mick Jagger, Lorne Michaels, and the cast to "She's a Rainbow," performed by Arcade Fire. Here, Wiig and Jagger rehearse. (2012)

Bob Dole impressionist Norm Macdonald with the senator shortly after he lost the 1996 election to Bill Clinton.

Vice-presidential hopeful Sarah Palin backstage with Alec Baldwin and Lorne Michaels, while Tina Fey can be seen playing Palin on the monitor. (2008)

Senator Hillary Clinton on set with Amy Poehler. (2008)

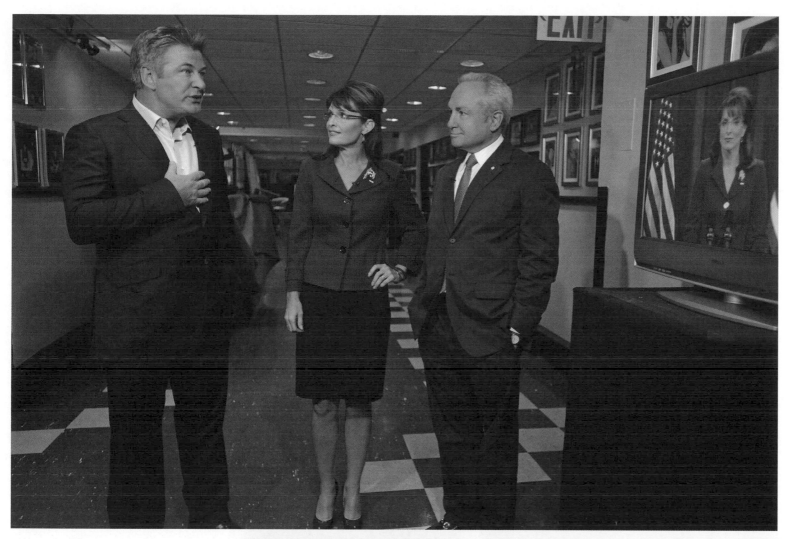

Al Gore on set with writer James Downey. (2000)

SATURDAY / "WEEKEND UPDATE" AND MONOLOGUE REHEARSAL

The late-afternoon meal break is followed by the monologue and "Weekend Update" rehearsals. "Weekend Update" is rehearsed just once. The "Update" writing department keeps their eyes on breaking news as they work on the jokes continually throughout the day; meanwhile guests rehearse their appearances off set and the graphics department scurries to prepare the visuals. "Update" rehearsals end at around 7:30 p.m., just as the audience is about to enter the studio for the dress rehearsal.

Seth Meyers and Amy Poehler at the “Weekend Update” desk during rehearsal. (ca. 2004)

As Sally O'Malley, Molly Shannon rehearses a guest appearance on "Weekend Update." (2010)

"Weekend Update" head writer Herb Sargent with Chevy Chase. (1976)

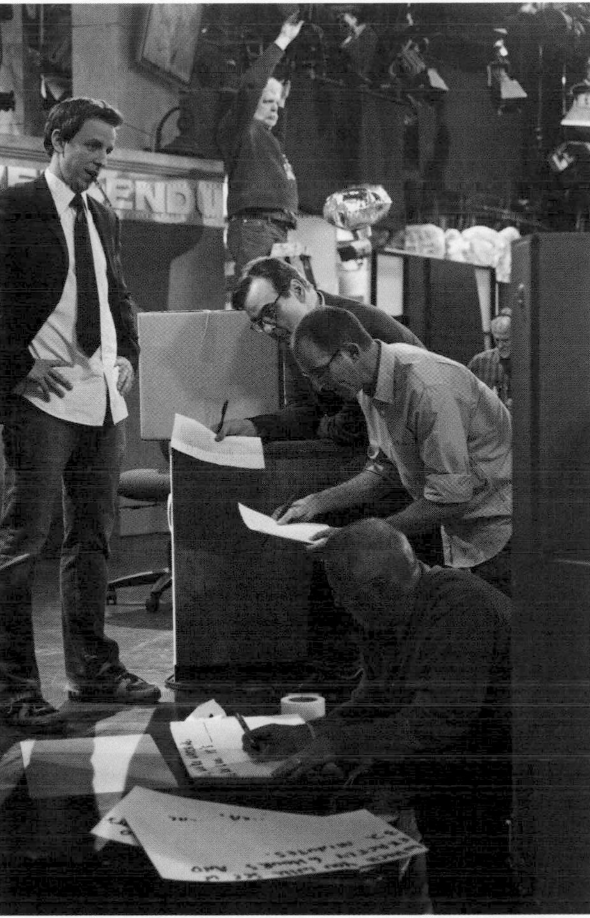

Seth Meyers, Steve Higgins, and Doug Abeles give script changes directly to cue card scribe Wally Feresten. (2009)

Writer Alan Zweibel with Jane Curtin. (1979)

Bill Hader waiting for his cue to slide over to the "Update" desk as Stefon. (2012)

KODAK 5054 TMZ

Cue cards for "Weekend Update" are a work in progress right up until the last moments before the segment goes on air.

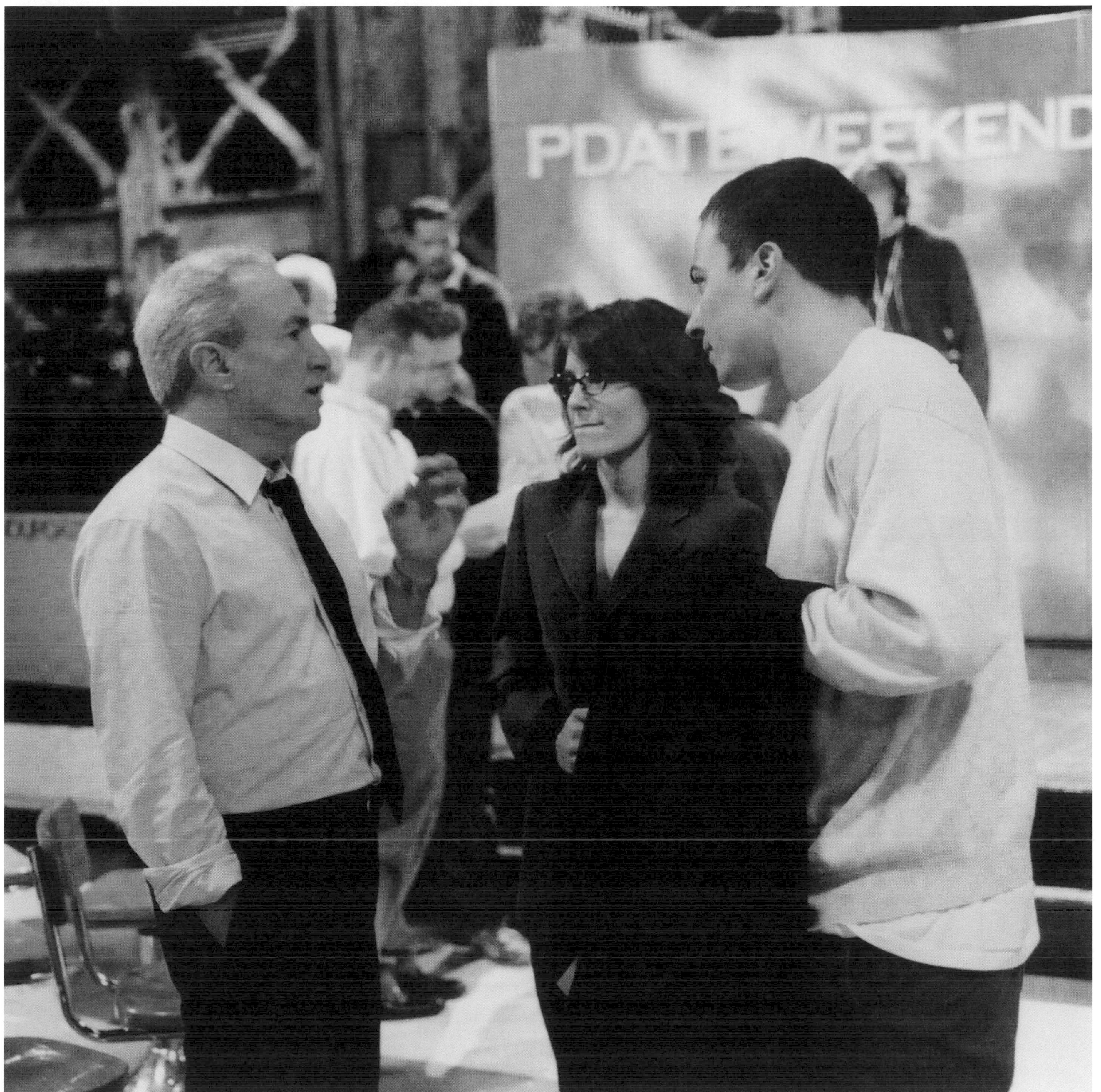

Tina Fey and Jimmy Fallon, seen here with Lorne Michaels, anchored "Update" together from 2000 to 2004.

Monologue rehearsals, **CLOCKWISE FROM TOP:** Bryan Cranston (2010), Zooey Deschanel (with Steve Higgins, 2012), Steve Guttenberg (1986), and Cameron Diaz (with Will Ferrell and Steve Higgins, 2002).

Will Ferrell, being made up as George W. Bush for the cold open, reviews dialogue for his monologue with Wally Feresten. (Passing behind Ferrell is writer Colin Jost) (2012)

SATURDAY / BACKSTAGE

In the hours before the live show, the atmosphere backstage is electric. Despite the mounting pressure, the ambiance is as jovial as it is businesslike. Cast members wander around in costume as if they weren't. A we're-all-in-it-together camaraderie unites the team.

After the dress rehearsal, which runs from 8 to about 10 p.m., the show must be cut down to 90 minutes. In Lorne Michaels's 9th-floor office, whose windows overlook Studio 8H, the producers meet with the host and head writers to determine the final running order and to decide which sketches to cut and which should be shortened or rewritten. Around 10:30, the cast and writers file into the office to discuss the changes. While this is going on, the script department works in the adjoining office to integrate changes as they are submitted.

When the final script is compiled, around 30 minutes before air, it is delivered to the director in the control room, who studies the blocking changes and then holds a meeting with the five camera operators to give last-minute instructions. While this is going on, the stagehands meet to go over the final running order as it pertains to the moving of scenery and props; the cue cards are rewritten yet again; the host and cast members' dressers, makeup artists, and hairstylists plan where quick-changes will take place for performers appearing in back-to-back sketches; and the players prepare to take their places on set for the cold open. Meanwhile, the audience is already seated in the studio, watching the *SNL* warm-up act and house band.

Lorne Michaels surrounded by "Video Vixens" Shelley Duvall, Gilda Radner, Laraine Newman, and Jane Curtin. (1977)

Gilda Radner unfazed
as the Land Shark
gobbles John Belushi's
arm backstage. (1976)

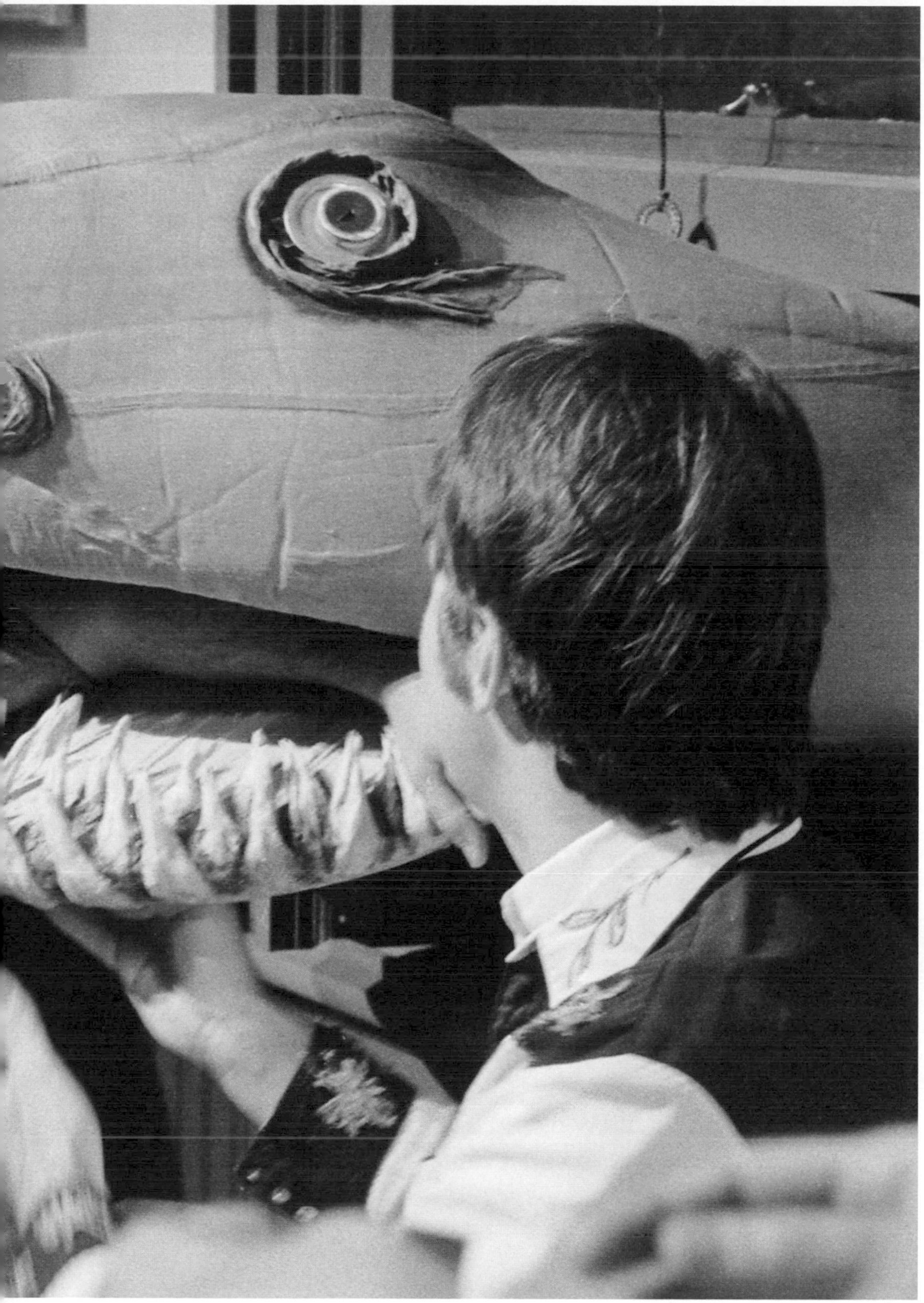

Dan Aykroyd backstage wearing his Beldar Conehead prosthetic.

Jimmy Fallon (as Jarret) and Seth Meyers (as Jonathan Feinstein) in costume for “Jarret’s Room.” (2001)

Season 3 cast and crew in the greenroom during meal break. (1977)

Tarzan (Kevin Nealon) grabs a snack. (ca. 1989-90)

Amy Poehler at the page desk outside Studio 8H. (ca. 2003-2004)

Hair stylist John Quaglia tends to Phil Hartman in the hair and makeup room. Seated behind him are Kevin Nealon and Jan Hooks.

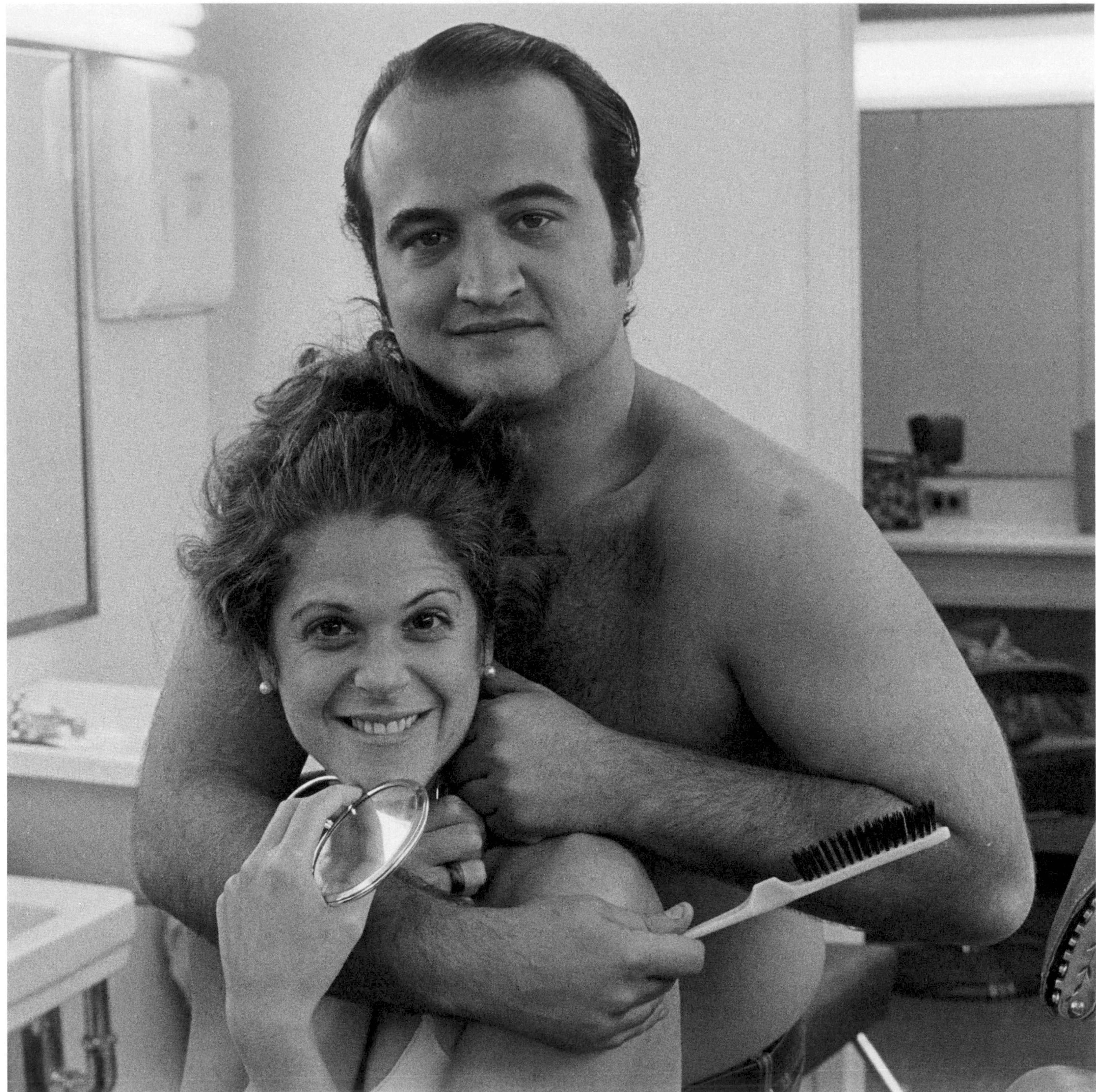

Gilda Radner and John Belushi share a tender moment in the hair and makeup room. (1976)

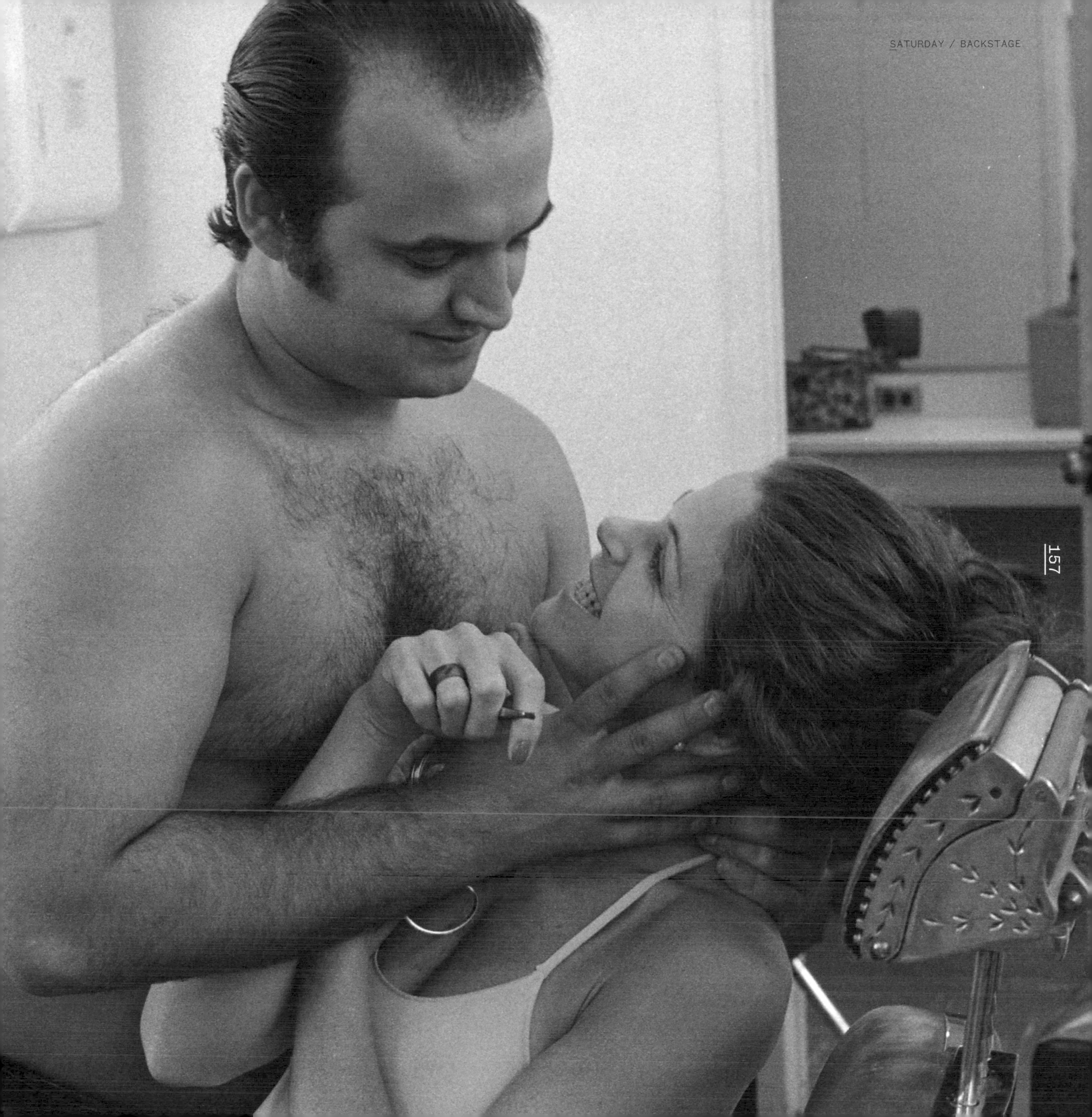

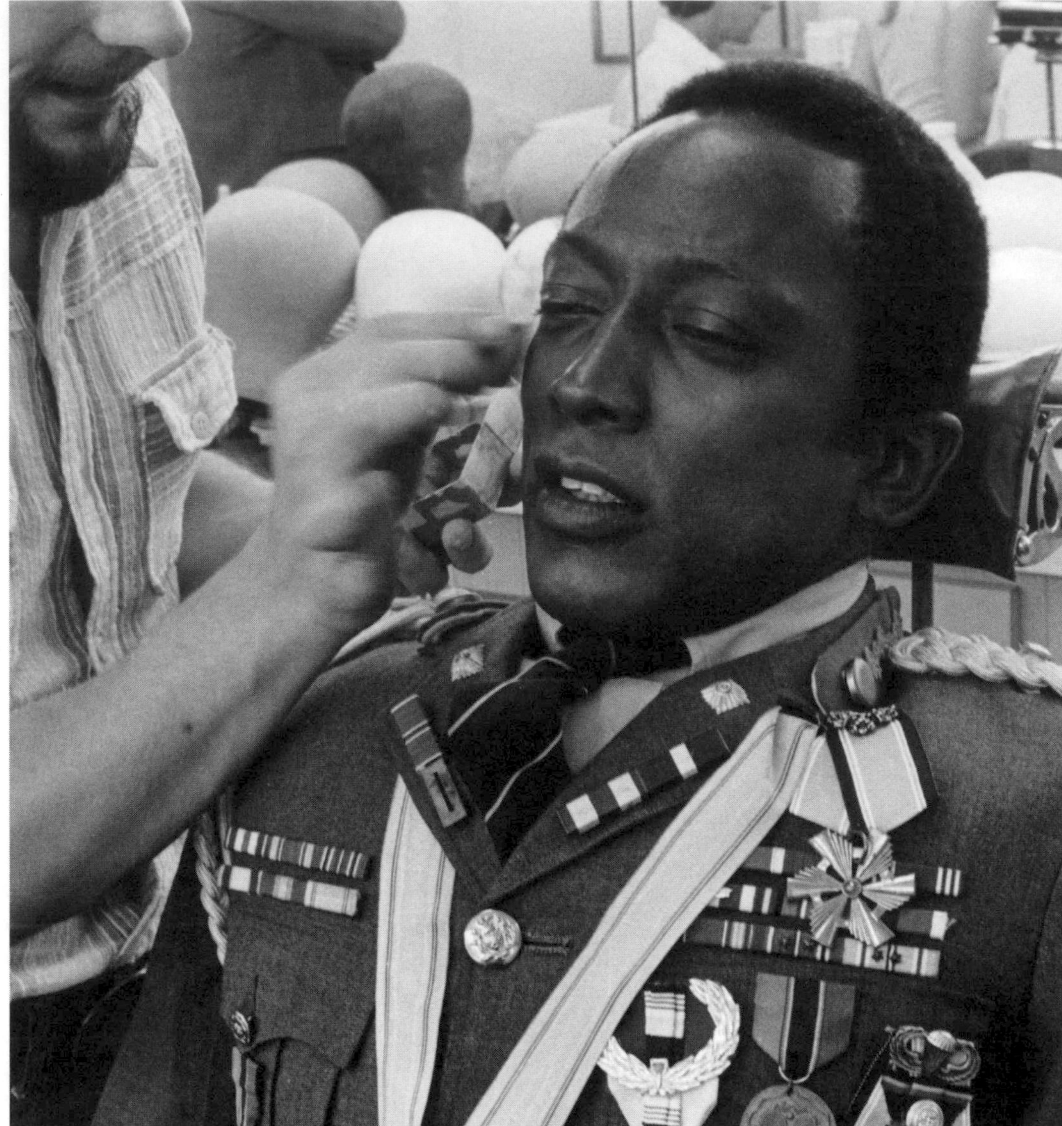

Makeup transformations, **CLOCKWISE FROM LEFT:** Garrett Morris as Idi Amin (1976), Fred Armisen as Prince (2012), and Dana Carvey as George Michael (1989).

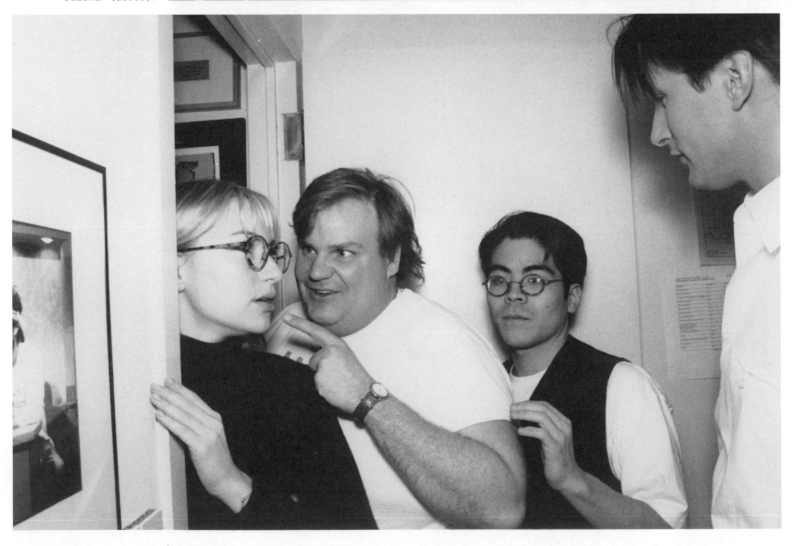

Filing into Lorne Michaels's 9th-floor office for the meeting between dress and air: **RIGHT,** Erik Kenward, Scott Wainio, Maya Rudolph, Tracy Morgan, Meredith Walker, and Geno Rositano. (ca. 2001-2002) **BELOW,** Erin Maroney, Chris Farley, Ryan Shiraki, and Billy Baldwin (1990s).

Lorne Michaels at his desk during the meeting between dress and air, surrounded by cast and crew members including director Beth McCarthy-Miller (seated, foreground) and Stacey Foster (seated to Michaels's left). (ca. 2003)

162

15 KODAK 5053 TMY
163

Seagram's
CLUB SODA

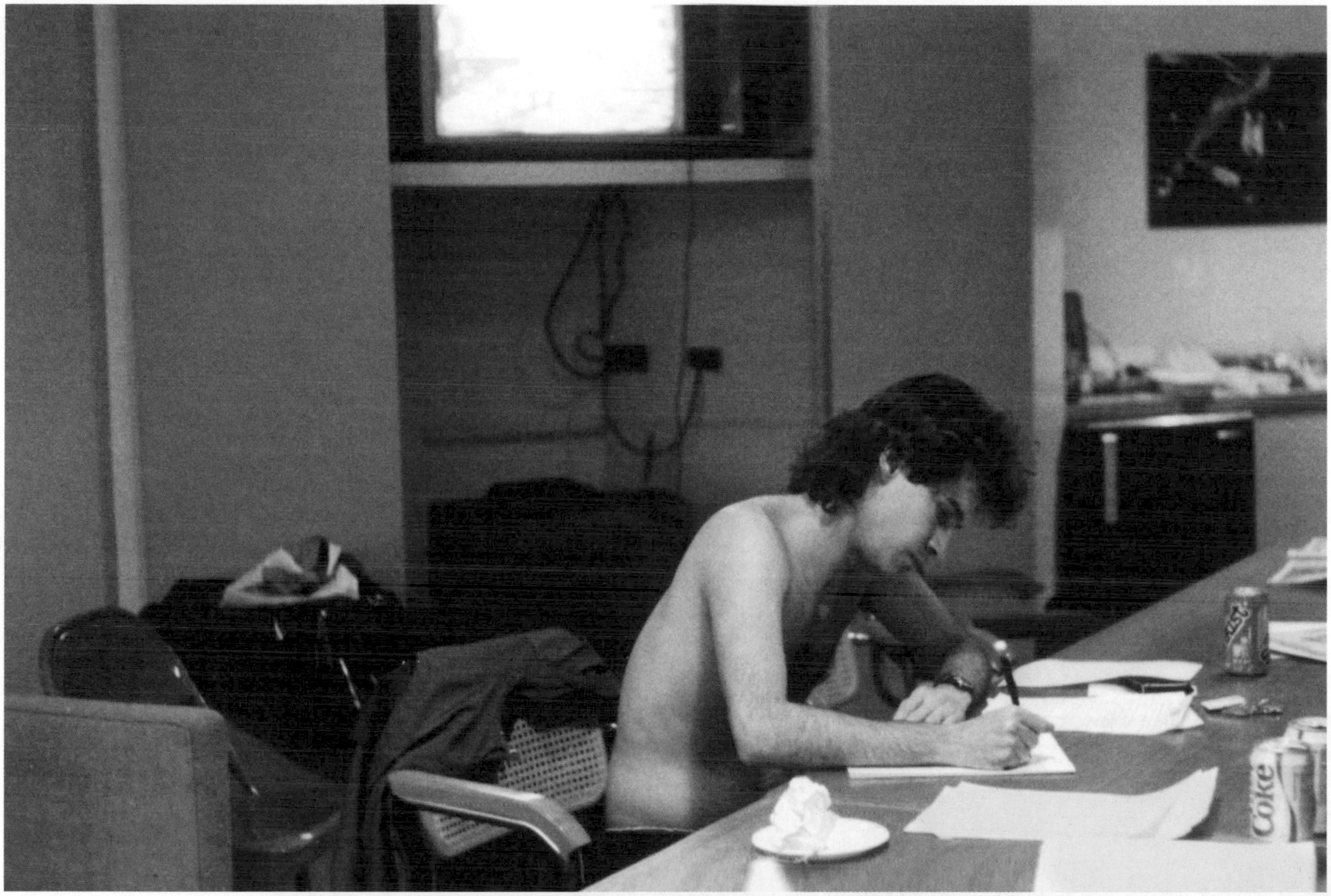

Scenes from the meeting room adjoining Lorne Michaels's 9th-floor office during the 90 minutes between dress and air: **OPPOSITE,** A. Whitney Brown (1986); **ABOVE,** Dennis Miller (1987); Steve Higgins (**RIGHT**) and Michael Che (**FAR RIGHT**) go over script changes with Abbey Lieber (2014).

Script assistants compile the show's final script (**BELOW**) before it is delivered to the director in the control room at 11 p.m. (**RIGHT**). (2014)

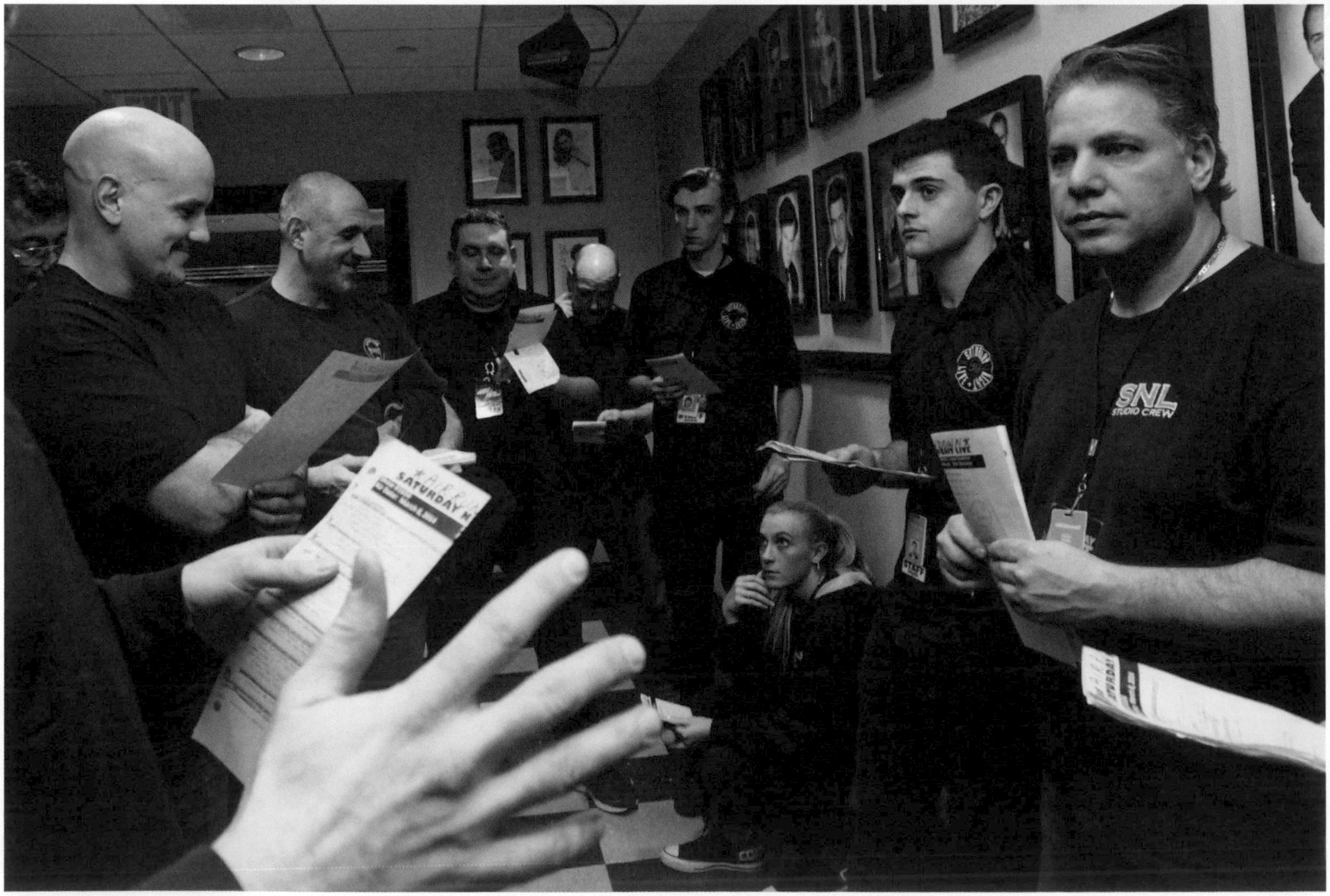

Stagehands meet shortly before the live broadcast to discuss the running order as it pertains to the movement of scenery and props. (2014)

At 11:10 p.m., director Don Roy King (standing, left) goes through blocking changes with the show's five camera operators. (2014)

CUE CARD DE
HAT DO YOU
ANT FROM ME?

Cue-card scribes make last-minute changes. **OPPOSITE:** Jentle Phoenix and Shannon Hellman (1994); **ABOVE,** Peter Levin and William Smeal (2009).

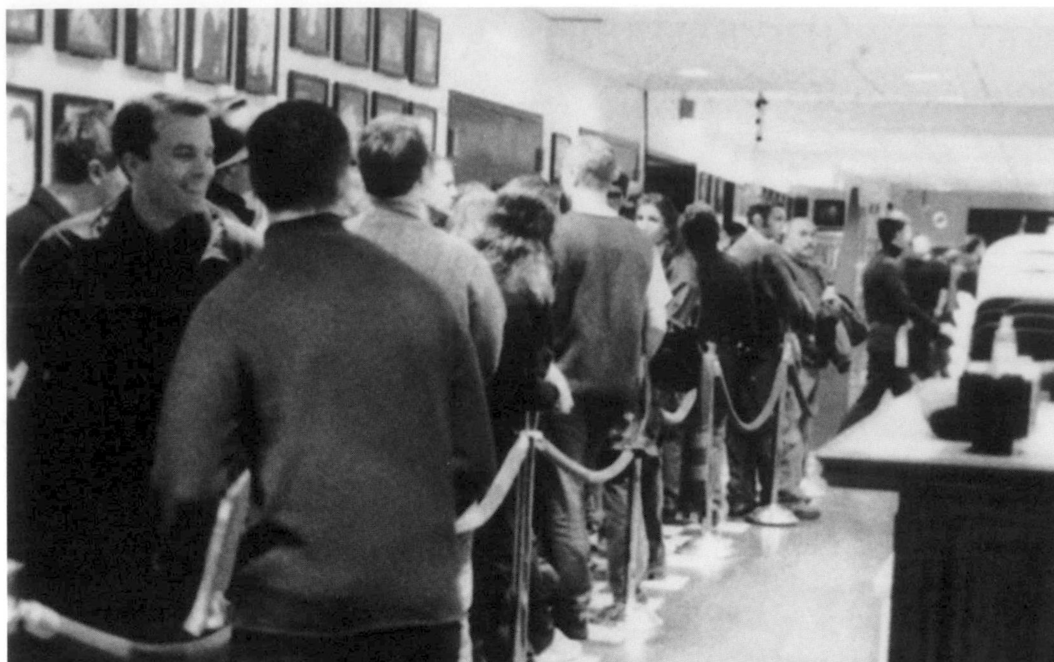

Audience members line up in the hallway leading to Studio 8H.

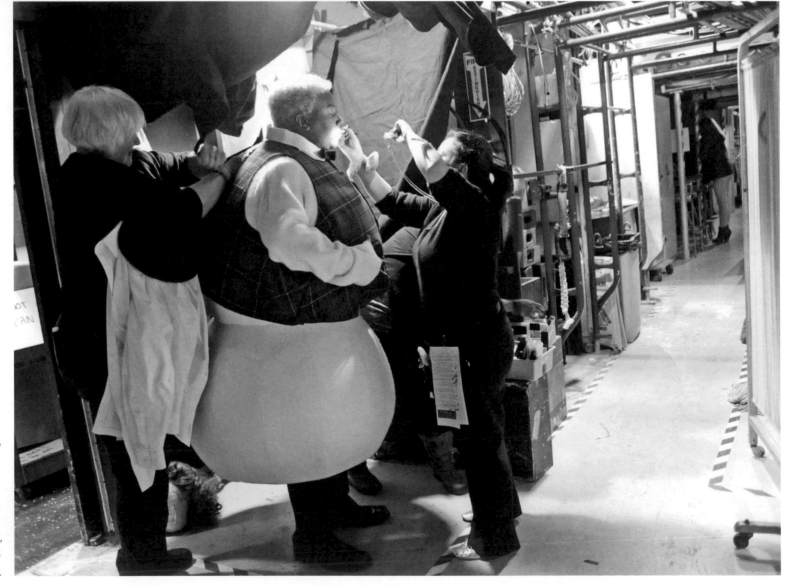

In the quick-change area beneath the bleachers at the entrance to Studio 8H, Kenan Thompson (with Vicki Jo DeRocker and Kathy O'Donnell) becomes Frosty the Snowman for the "Christmas Eve in Washington, D.C." cold open of December 18, 2010.

Former and current Barack Obama impressionists Fred Armisen and Jay Pharoah await their cues for the "Democratic Rally" cold open of September 15, 2012.

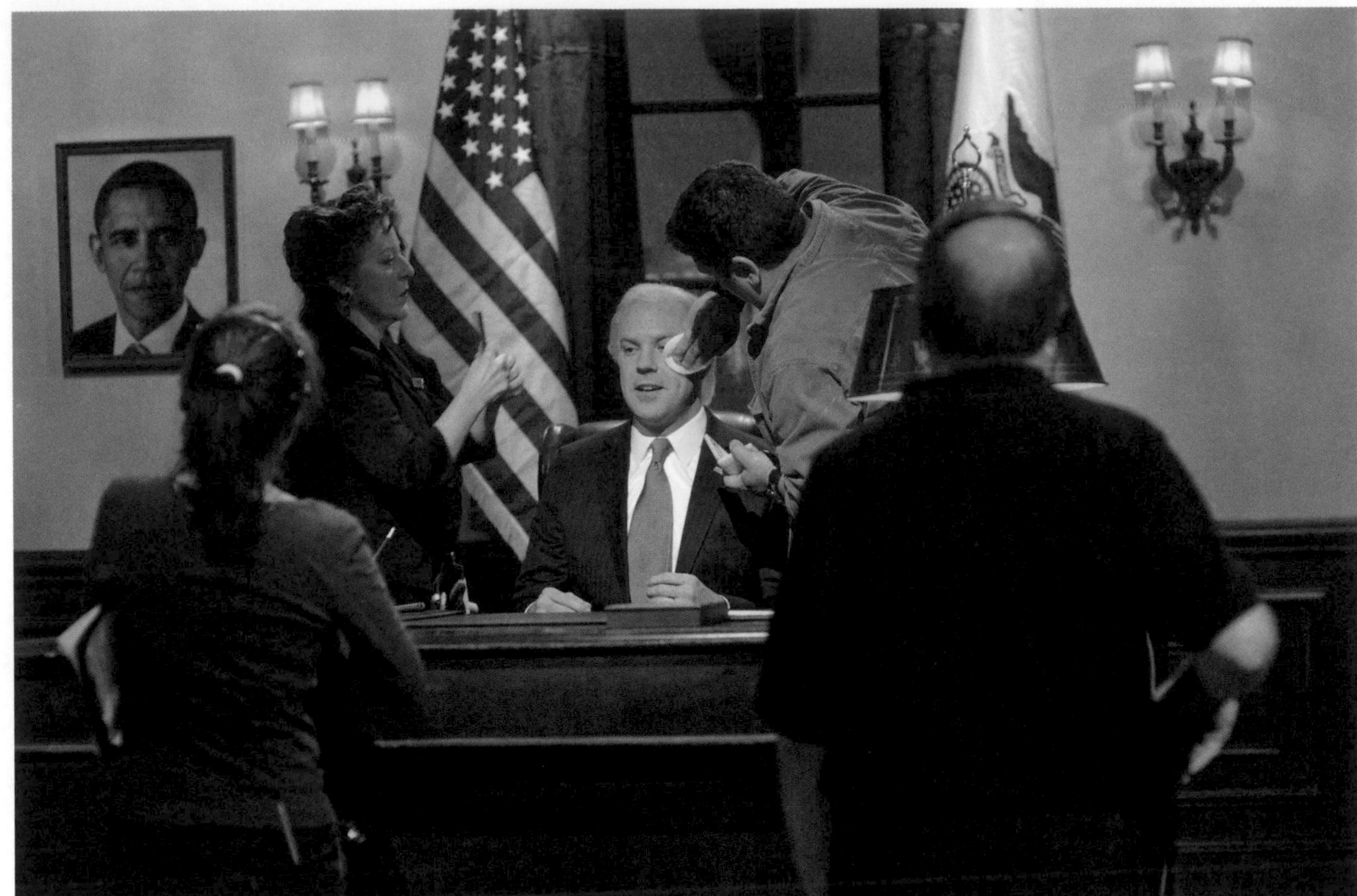

In the moments before the cold open: **ABOVE:** hair stylist Inga Thrasher and makeup artist Josh Turi touch up Jason Sudeikis (as Joe Biden, 2010); **RIGHT:** Darrell Hammond (as George W. Bush, 2001) reviews cue cards while Robin Day and Doug James put finishing touches on his hair and costume; **OPPOSITE:** Lorne Michaels leans in to confer with Chris Parnell (as George W. Bush, 2003).

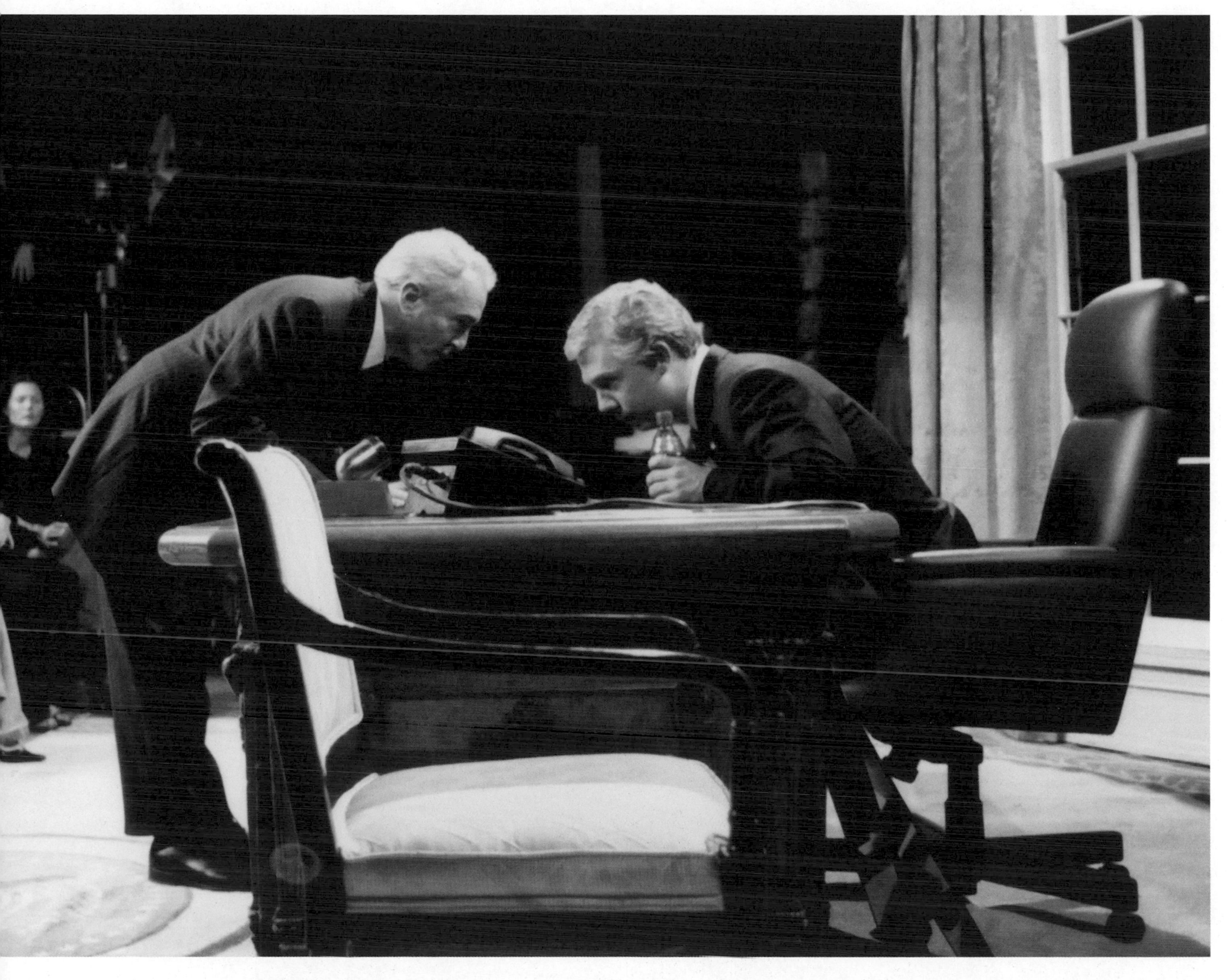

Saturday Night Live

N.B. With few exceptions, episodic photos are not taken during the live show but rather during the dress rehearsal. Any differences readers may notice between the photos herein and the actual broadcast (or, in some cases, photos of sketches that never aired) are due to changes or cuts that were made between the dress rehearsal and the live show.

Two minutes before air, the warm-up lighting dips to black and the cold-open lights come up. The performers enter the stage and take their places. Lorne Michaels checks his watch and gives last-minute notes. The house band stops playing at precisely 11:28:30. A hush of anticipation washes over the studio. The stage manager begins the countdown. There is a brief moment of total silence. The ON AIR sign lights up and the show begins.

Director Dave Wilson conducting the live show from the control room. (ca. 1988)

“Wolverines,” featuring John Belushi and Michael O’Donoghue, was the cold open of SNL’s debut episode.

SHOW #1-SHORT RUNDOWN

Air: 10/11/75

HOST: GEORGE CARLIN

AIR:

WOLVERINES
OPENING MONTAGE
GEORGE MONOLOGUE —
NEW DAD
BUMPER
Commercial #1

DON INTRO
BILLY PRESTON
TRIAL
DON INTRO
MIGHTY MOUSE
DON V.O.
MINI PADS
Commercial #2
DELTA PROMO

MISC MONOLOGUE —?
INTRO
JANIS IAN
SHARK BITE
JAMITOL GAY
BUMPER
Commercial #3 STAT. OF LIBERTY
STATION BREAK
Paul Simon Promo

WEEKEND UPDATE I
TRIOPENIN
BLAINE HOTEL
UPDATE II
VTR OPENING
MUPPETS
Commercial #4 PINBALL
Bumper

GEORGE MONOLOGUE — 3
ALBERT BROOKS FILM
~~ACADEMY OF BETTER CAREERS~~
Commercial #5 NEWSTAND

BEES & TAG ACADEMY OF BETTER CAREERS
DON INTRO
VALRI BROMFIELD
SHOW US YOUR GUN
Bumper
Commercial #6
STATION BREAK
LONDON TOWN CAR

GEORGE MONOLOGUE —
DON INTRO
BILLY PRESTON
Commercial #7
Bumper

HOME SECURITIES
TRIPLE TRACK
Bumper
Commercial #8 MICHAEL & ANN AT TABLE

INTRO
JANIS IAN
Bumper
Commercial #9
Bumper

CLOSING MONOLOGUE —
GOODNIGHTS
PROMO SLIDES
CREDITS

The original rundown of episode 1.

ABOVE: The September 29, 2001, season-premiere cold open featured Mayor Rudy Giuliani, surrounded by New York City police officers and firemen, announcing, "On our city's darkest day, our heroes met the worst of humanity with the best of humanity… Our hearts are broken, but they are beating— and they are beating stronger than ever." The emotional performance of "The Boxer" by Paul Simon that followed left not a dry eye in the house; then Lorne Michaels joined Giuliani on stage to ask, "Can we be funny?", to which the mayor replied, "Why start now?"

ABOVE: Phil Hartman, seen here in 1993, was the first cast member to portray Bill Clinton.
LEFT: As Gerald Ford in "Christmas Eve at the White House," Chevy Chase delivers one of his famous cold-open stumbles. (1975)

RIGHT: While giving a speech affirming Americans' rights to sexual freedom, speaker-elect Nancy Pelosi (Kristen Wiig) is interrupted by her assistant (Will Forte) and his slave, Filth, the "human ashtray." (Fred Armisen). (2006)
ABOVE RIGHT: Darrell Hammond as Bill Clinton with Molly Shannon as Monica Lewinsky. (1998)
TOP RIGHT: In season 1, Chevy Chase (here, as Gerald Ford in 1975) delivered 22 of the 24 "Live from New York, it's Saturday Night" intros (The other two were delivered by Garrett Morris and the actual President Ford.)

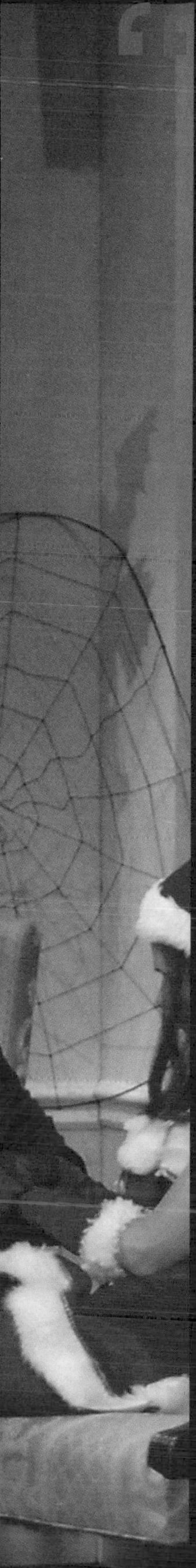

"Live from New York, it's Saturday Night!"

—**BARACK OBAMA**
(as himself) with Darrell Hammond and Amy Poehler as Bill Clinton and Hillary Rodham Clinton in "Halloween Party." (2007)

The legendary Don Pardo was SNL's announcer for the entire history of the show (with the exception of season 7) until his death, at the age of 96, in August 2014.

After “surprising” host Jimmy Fallon during an impression of him, Paul McCartney joins Fallon for a Christmas duet. (2013)

Host George Carlin delivering the show’s very first monologue on October 11, 1975.

Steve Martin donning a fake arrow-through-the-head during his monologue banjo routine: "I like to keep the laughs rolling even while I'm playing." (1976)

ABOVE: After passing out during his monologue from a minor leg injury, Tom Hanks goes backstage and, finding Abraham Lincoln, asks him, "What's happening? […] I'm dead?" Lincoln responds, "No, Tom, you're just an incredible pussy." (Incidentally, if you look carefully whenever the cameras go backstage, you'll often spot Abraham Lincoln and/or two showgirls and a llama. It's a thing.) **RIGHT:** Bryan Cranston pokes fun at the unusual spelling of his name in this song-and-dance

LEFT: Zach Galifianakis delivers his monologue to "Tomorrow" from the musical "Annie." (2011) **ABOVE:** Leonardo DiCaprio makes a cameo appearance during Jonah Hill's monologue. (2014)

Sid Caesar, an early pioneer of live TV sketch comedy, hosted SNL in 1983.

Kate Hudson, daughter of "Laugh-In" star Goldie Hawn, "reunites" with children of other "Laugh-In" stars.

Chris Parnell presents host Heather Graham with a "special" gift. (1999)

ABOVE: Lindsay Lohan's future self (Amy Poehler) warns her to "cool it with the partying, 'cause I'm totally beat." (2005)
TOP: After expressing regret about missing senior prom to host the show, Ashley and Mary-Kate Olsen are treated to SNL's version, complete with frilly dresses, limo, and date Jimmy Fallon. (2004)

"New Shimmer, for the greatest shine you ever tasted!"

—CHEVY CHASE (with Dan Aykroyd and Gilda Radner, 1976), touting the merits of Shimmer Non-Dairy Floor Wax. (This photo was taken during dress rehearsal—for the live show, Shimmer had its "real" label affixed.)

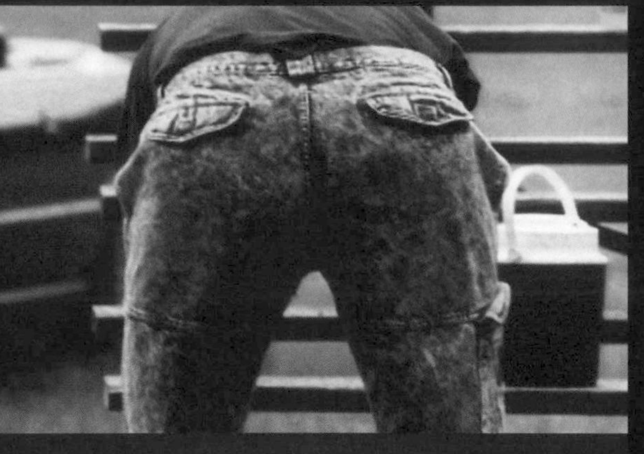

BAD
IDEA
JEANS

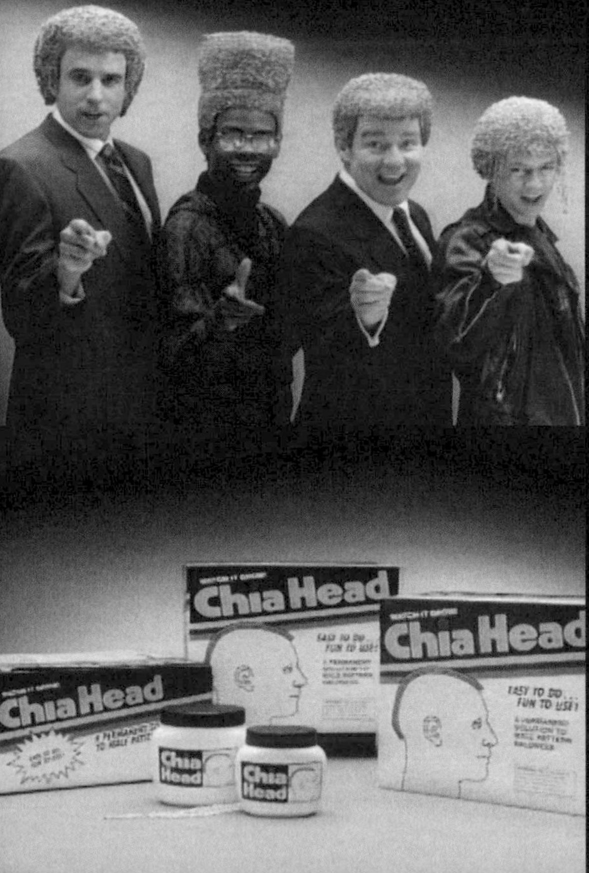

ABOVE: “How many bowls of your oat-bran cereal would it take to equal the fiber content of one bowl of Colon Blow? [...] It would take over 30,000 bowls.” Colon Blow (with Phil Hartman, 1989) **LEFT:** “Ain't enough turkey to feed this crowd! But yo mamma says pump it! Pump it up now! Pump it!” Nikey Turkey (with Chris Rock, 1990) **ABOVE RIGHT:** “I thought about it, and even though it's over, I'm going to tell my wife about the affair.” Bad Idea Jeans (1990)

ABOVE: “If you've got a big thirst, and you're gay, reach for a cold, tall bottle of Schmitts Gay.” Schmitts Gay (with Adam Sandler, 1991) **LEFT:** “You've tried all the hair-replacement products, but nothing seems to work. Well, now there's a solution. It's Chia Head.” Chia Head (with Kevin Nealon, Chris Rock, Phil Hartman, and David Spade, 1990) **TOP:** “Hear that sizzle? That's me! 550 degrees! Good thing I'm dead, or yow-wee!” The Cluckin' Chicken (with Phil

ABOVE: "Malibu Mystery Bishop is ready for a day at the beach, or a night of dancing!" Chess for Girls (1997) **LEFT:** "Finally, you can see your meat." Crystal Gravy (with Kevin Nealon, 1993) **LEFT:** "The Gas Right strip spreads the cheeks apart for a wider, more direct passageway. You hear that? Silence...." Gas Right Posterior Strips (with Fred Armisen, 2008)

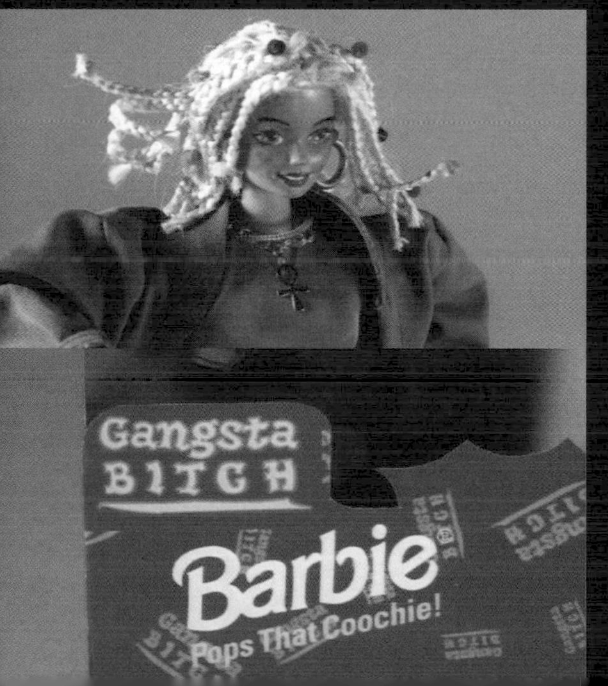

ABOVE: "This Mother's Day, don't give Mom that bottle of perfume. Give her something that says, 'I'm not a woman anymore. I'm a mom.'" Mom Jeans (with Maya Rudolph, Rachel Dratch, Tina Fey, and Amy Poehler, 2003) **RIGHT:** "Barbie comes direct with Jolly Ranchers, a pack of Newports, and a restraining order against her boyfriend, Tupac Ken." Gangsta Bitch Barbie (1995) **TOP:** "There's one drawback to the conventional air bag—it may save your life, but what do you eat while waiting for help to arrive?" Jiffy Pop Airbag (with Melanie Hutsell, 1992)

ABOVE: "Cologne for Dogs, from Calvin Klein. Now available at Macy's." Canis (1992)
TOP: "You know it's good, 'cause it's blue, BITCH!" E-Meth (with Aaron Paul, 2013)
TOP RIGHT: "It's like a big friendly lumberjack between your knees!" Big Brawn Feminine Napkins (with Will Ferrell, 1996)

"Because when you're in love, even five minutes apart can seem like an eternity." The Love

ABOVE: "If you're as busy as I am, every day you have to make a decision. Am I going to eat lunch? Or am I going to go to the bathroom? Now you never have to make that choice again." Jon Hamm's John Ham (with Jon Hamm, 2008)
RIGHT: "They taste good, and they've got the sugar I need to get me going in the morning." Little Chocolate Donuts (with John Belushi, 1977)

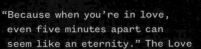

HAPPY FUN BALL
Warning: Pregnant women, the elderly and children under 10 should avoid prolonged exposure to Happy Fun Ball.

We just make change.
Paul McElroy
Service Representative

ABOVE: "If Happy Fun Ball begins to smoke, get away immediately. Seek shelter and cover head. Happy Fun Ball may stick to certain types of skin." Happy Fun Ball (1991)
LEFT: "With our experience, we're going to have ideas for change combinations that probably haven't occurred to you. If you have a fifty-dollar bill, we can give you fifty singles. We can give you forty-nine singles and ten dimes. We can give you twenty-five twos. Come talk to us." First Citiwide Change Bank (with James Downey, 1988)
TOP RIGHT: "Because you can't wait 'til afternoon." A.M. Ale (with David Koechner, 1995)

"Somewhere between cleanliness and godliness lies Compulsion, the world's most indulgent disinfectant." Compulsion by Calvin Kleen (with Jan Hooks, 1987)

ABOVE: "The only razor gutsy enough to give you 14 blades." Platinum Mach 14 (with Will Ferrell, 2000)
TOP: "Cookie dough right when you need it most. Be the dough." Cookie Dough Sport (with Chris Kattan, 1997)
TOP LEFT: "You gave him life. Now give him confidence." Nelson's Baby Toupees (with Bill Hader, 2006)

ABOVE: "It's the only hairball remover that cats ask for by name." Eych (1994) **LEFT:** "He's your best friend. Why not be his, and let him keep his balls?" Franklin's Dog Condoms (with Taran Killam as Brad Pitt, 2012) **BELOW:** "It's pizzazz that slides right up into my choch." NuvaBling (with Kate McKinnon, Cecily Strong, and Vanessa Bayer, 2013)

ABOVE: "Don't call this pizza. It's Almost Pizza. Pizza that's practically pizza in every way, except for a few key ones.... Dig in!" Almost Pizza (with Kristen Wiig, Nasim Pedrad, and Bill Hader, 2012) **TOP:** "The sassy new Mexican import that's made out of clay.... You can buy a cheaper car. But I wouldn't recommend it!" Adobe (with Phil Hartman, 1986) **RIGHT:** "Using Bosley's breakthrough technique, hair is harvested from the 'mezzanine' and brought to the head. Bosley (with Jason Sudeikis, Bobby Moynihan, Kristen Wiig, and Fred Armisen, 2010)

ust spray Shirt in a Can on those parts of
our body where a shirt would normally be...."

TOP LEFT: "It's not a Taco Town taco until we roll it up in a blueberry pancake, dip it in batter, and deep-fry it until it's golden brown." Taco Town (with Bill Hader, Jason Sudeikis, and

ABOVE: "With today's low-cut fashions, your coin slot is exposed to sun and wind that can leave your slot dry and flaky." Neutrogena Coin Slot Cream (with Lindsay Lohan and Kristen Wiig, 2006)

LEFT: "We've come to Temple Beth Shalom in Little Neck, New York, and asked Rabbi Mayer Taklas to circumcise eight-day-old Benjamin Kanter while riding in the back seat....To show you that our ride is possibly the finest, smoothest in the world, we've deliberately picked this road because of its rough, uneven surface." Royal Deluxe II (with Gilda Radner, 1977)

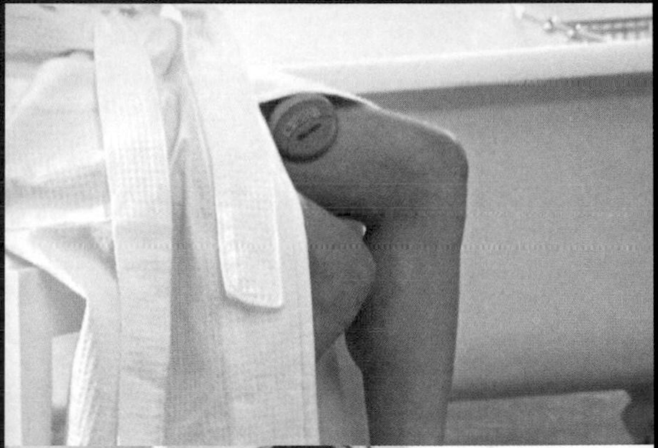

ABOVE: "It puts my mind at rest, and I sleep soundly. So soundly, I sleep through my first dump in the morning." Tylenol BM (with Alec Baldwin, 2005)

TOP: "It's a robot and it cleans my business—my lady business. And I like that." Woomba (with Tina Fey, 2004)

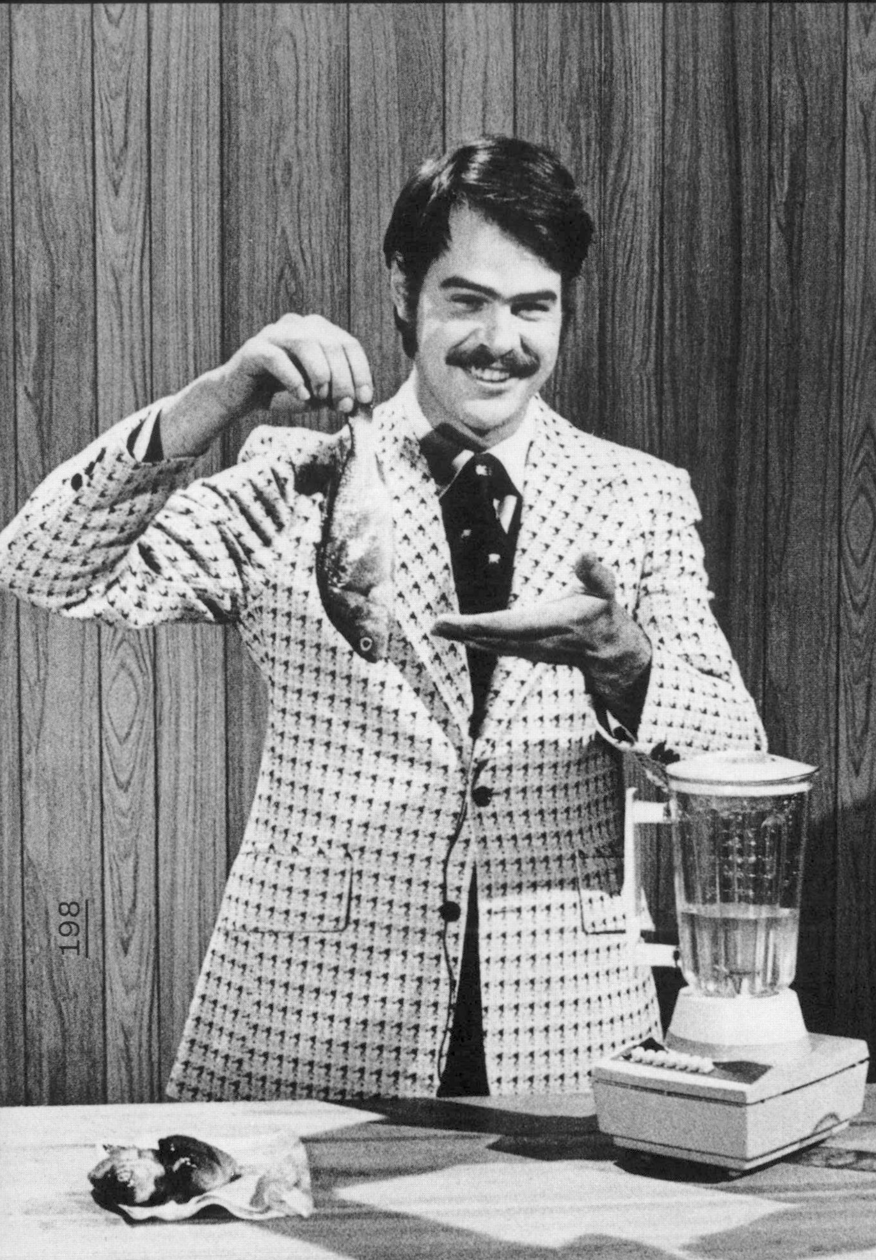

ABOVE: "Yes, fish-eaters, the days of troublesome scaling, cutting, and gutting are over." Super Bass-o-Matic '76 (with Dan Aykroyd, 1976)
LEFT: As Catherine Deneuve, Candice Bergen laments about the difficulty of being Catherine Deneuve. When she lifts her head, the perfume bottle is actually stuck to her face. Chanel no. 5 (1975)

SNL has made a meta art form out of bringing celebrities on to appear with their imitators. Here, Robin Gibb (Justin Timberlake) and Barry Gibb (Jimmy Fallon) of "The Barry Gibb Talk Show" perform with the real Barry Gibb. (By the way, that's Madonna in the background taking a picture.) (2013)

Season 6 cast members Gilbert Gottfried, Denny Dillon, Charles Rocket, and Matthew Laurance with host Charlene Tilton (center, 1981).

In this "Mary Tyler Moore" takeoff starring John Belushi as Lou Grant, Mary is dead from accidental poisoning by the idiotic Ted Baxter (Steve Martin). (1976)

The set of "Friends" was replicated for this spoof starring Matthew Perry (who played Chandler on the original show), Colin Quinn, Molly Shannon, Ana Gasteyer, Cheri Oteri, and Chris Kattan. As Joey, Perry breaks character to complain about Quinn's blatantly effeminate portrayal of Chandler. (1997)

Supervising producer Ken Aymong and Jimmy Fallon at the entrance to Studio 8H. (2004)

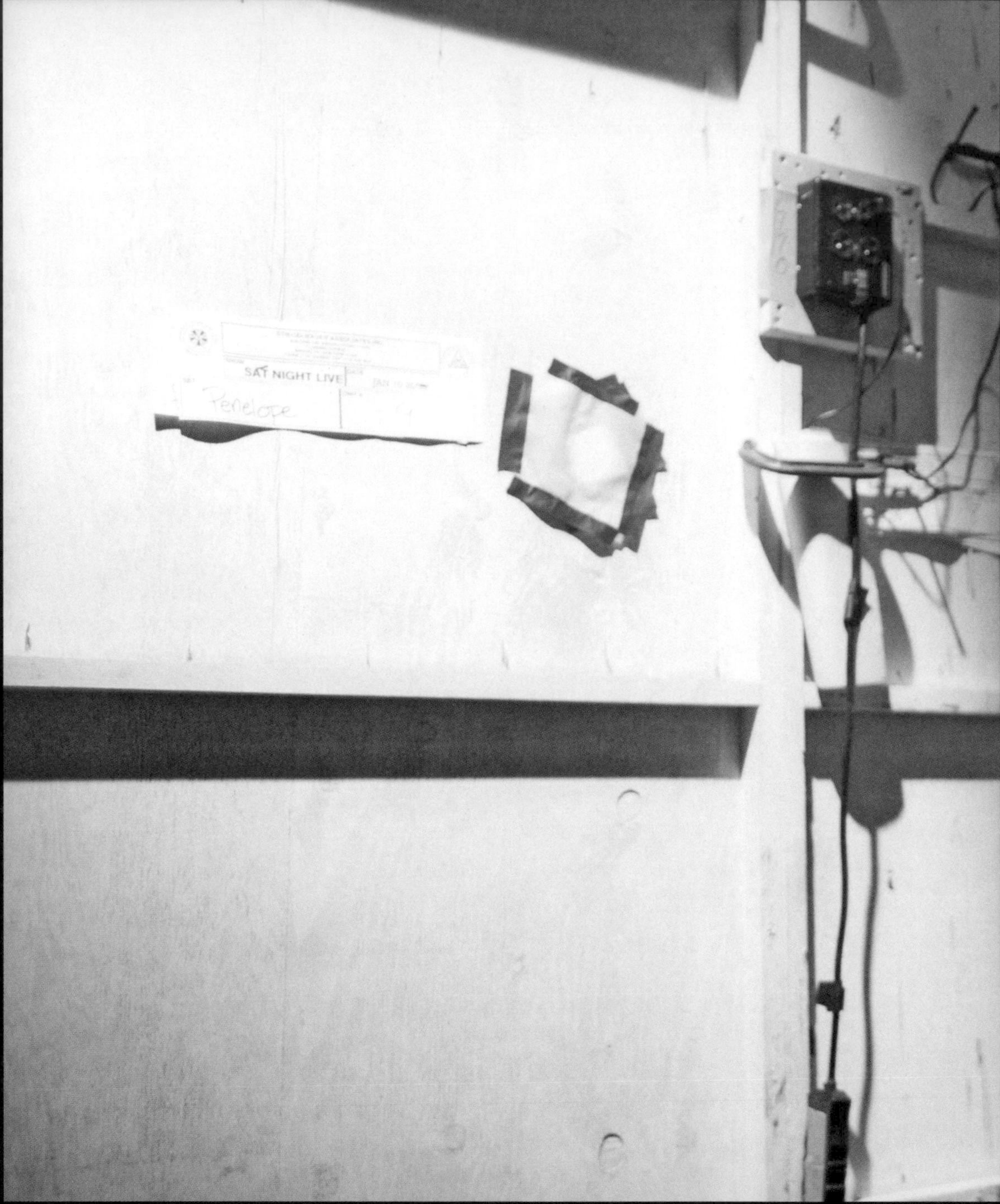

Liza Minnelli awaiting her cue to enter the stage. (2009)

With no time to lose between the cold open (in which she played Greta Van Susteren) and an appearance in Katy Perry's monologue, Kristen Wiig applies her makeup in the quick-change area. (2011)

Tracy Morgan as Rev. Al Sharpton. (ca. 2001-2002)

Supervising producer Ken Aymong at his station in the control room. (2011)

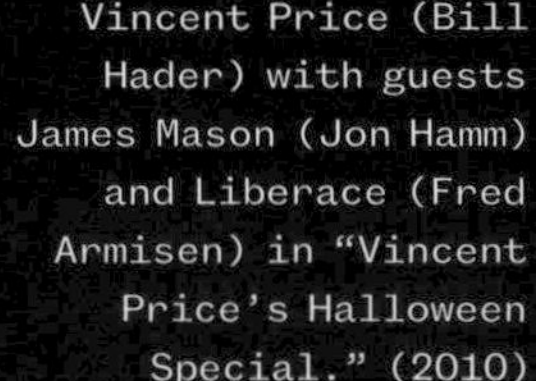

Vincent Price (Bill Hader) with guests James Mason (Jon Hamm) and Liberace (Fred Armisen) in “Vincent Price’s Halloween Special.” (2010)

ABOVE: "This Johnny Space Commander mask here is a pure fantasy toy. I mean, you know, kids can have a lot of fun with a toy like this, you know? Let me show you..." (Dan Aykroyd as Irwin Mainway on "Consumer Probe," 1977)
LEFT: Bryan Cranston (rear left) as Doo Doo Man in "What Up with That?" with compulsively interrupting host Diondre Cole (Kenan Thompson, center) and special guests Ernest Borgnine and Morgan Freeman. (2010)

ABOVE: Phil Hartman playing sidekick Ed McMahon to Dana Carvey's Johnny Carson, with Jon Lovitz as Andrew Dice Clay. (1990)

ABOVE: This sketch, "Salon Talk with Gene" (with Zach Galifianakis, Taran Killam, and Kristen Wiig) was cut after dress rehearsal. (2011)
LEFT: Jesse Jackson (Darrell Hammond) pays a visit to Nat X (Chris Rock) on "The Dark Side with Nat X." (1996)

ABOVE: “Safari Planet” host Brian Fellow (Tracy Morgan) with guest Karen Nathanton (Sarah Michelle Gellar). (1999)
TOP: David Frost (Eric Idle) struggles to stay awake while interviewing Richard Nixon (Dan Aykroyd) for 18-plus hours. (1977)

"No one can resist my Schweddy Balls."

—ALEC BALDWIN
as "Delicious Dish" guest Pete Schweddy, with Ana Gasteyer and Molly Shannon as hosts Margaret Jo McCullin and Terry Rialto. (1998)

ABOVE: Ben Stiller as Eddie Munster on "Sprockets." (1989)
TOP: "I'm Chillin'" with Onski (Chris Rock) and B Fats (Chris Farley). (1991)

ABOVE: "My credo is 'It is better to look good than to feel good.' You know what I am saying, and you know who you are." Billy Crystal on "Fernando's Hideaway." (1984)
RIGHT: "The Prince Show" with Fred Armisen, Maya Rudolph (as Beyoncé), and Steve Martin. (2006)
TOP: "That was awesome!" Chris Farley gets overly excited about having Martin Scorsese on his eponymous interview show. (1991)

BUTT, BUNS, REAR END, HINEY, CAN, TALENT, VULNERABILITY, AND BUTT. AND NOW, LET'S GO UP TO THE BOOTH WITH OUR COLOR LADY, PAT STEVENS.

ABOVE: During this "Succinctly Speaking" sketch, starring host Kathleen Fulmer (Nora Dunn) and guests Frankenstein (Phil Hartman), Tarzan (Kevin Nealon), and Tonto (Jon Lovitz), Hartman succumbed to a rare moment of uncontrollable laughter on air. According to Lovitz, Hartman began to laugh and quickly stopped himself; then "he was sitting there thinking how funny it must have looked to see Frankenstein laugh like that. And then that just made him like lose it." (1987) **TOP:** Dialogue for Peter Graves (Phil Hartman) from the "Sexiest Man Alive" sketch. (1987)

The elephant in the room: like Bob and Betty Widette (Dan Aykroyd and Jane Curtin), their friends Wilma and Earl Bass (Garrett Morris and host Cicely Tyson) are blissfully unaware of their abnormally large butts. (1979)

Dan Aykroyd as a Norge refrigerator repairman, with Bill Murray and Gilda Radner as "Nerds" Todd DiLaMuca and Lisa Loopner. (1978)

Pee-wee Herman as played by Mary Gross (with Joe Piscopo, **ABOVE,** 1984) and in a cameo (**RIGHT,** with Andy Samberg in the SNL Digital Short "Andy and Pee-wee's Night Out," 2011).

"Parents Home Video" was one of seven short films that Albert Brooks contributed during the first season. (1975)

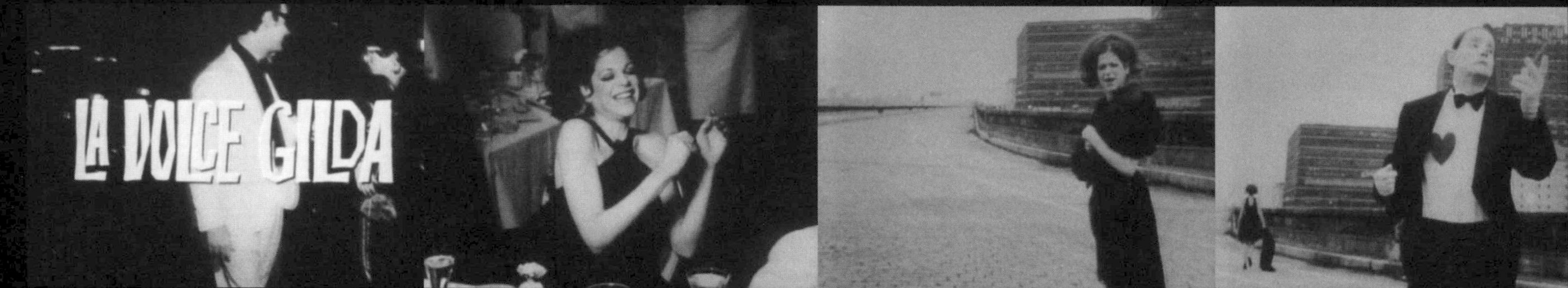

In Tom Schiller's Fellini-esque "La Dolce Gilda," Gilda Radner plays a starlet trying to escape the spotlight: "You know I love you, my little monkeys. But leave me my dreams. Dreams are like paper, they tear so easily." (1978)

When Eddie Murphy tired of playing Buckwheat, he suggested killing him off. The result was this fake "Nightline" piece of 1983 in which Buckwheat's assassination is played back in slow motion Zapruder-style and Murphy plays the role of the killer in a segment resembling actual footage of Lee Harvey Oswald. Ironically, the success of Buckwheat's assassination was such that he made four more appearances on the show.

In the mockumentary short "Synchronized Swimming," Martin Short and Harry Shearer play an ambitious yet utterly incompetent pair of synchronized swimmers. (1984)

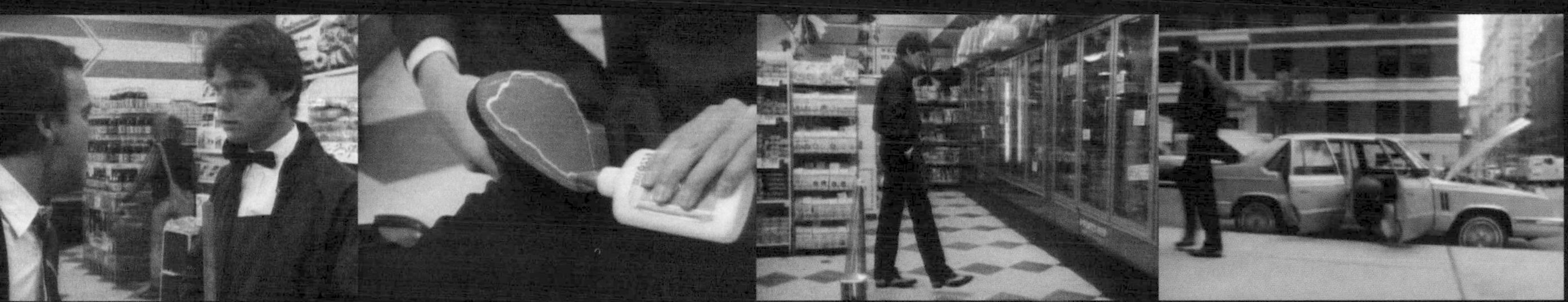

In "Walking After Midnight," grocery-store employee Rich Hall discovers the magical power of an automatic doormat and, using it to sole his shoes, finds a way to exact revenge on his malicious boss. (1984)

"Star Wars" screen-test fails: Han Solo (Kevin Spacey as Christopher Walken), Princess Leia (Ana Gasteyer as Barbara Streisand), and Darth Vader (Norm Macdonald as Burt Reynolds). (1997)

holidays

Ana Gasteyer stars in “Martha Stewart’s Home for the Holidays: Topless Christmas Special.” (1996)

A SERIES FINALE REGARDED BY MOST TV CRITICS AS “SATISFACTORY AT BEST” JERRY SEINFELD WAS TRANSFERRED TO A MAXIMUM SECURITY PRISON.

THAT FACILITY IS KNOWN AS...

“Seinfeld” ended its final episode with the main characters being sent to prison. In this short, “due to a series of sarcastic quips Jerry made to prison guards,” Seinfeld is transferred to “Oz.” (1999)

The first digital short by Lonely Island trio Andy Samberg, Akiva Schaffer, and Jorma Taccone to go viral was “Lazy Sunday,” starring Samberg and Chris Parnell. (2005)

Though the D-word was bleeped out for the live broadcast, the uncensored version of “Dick in a Box” (starring Justin

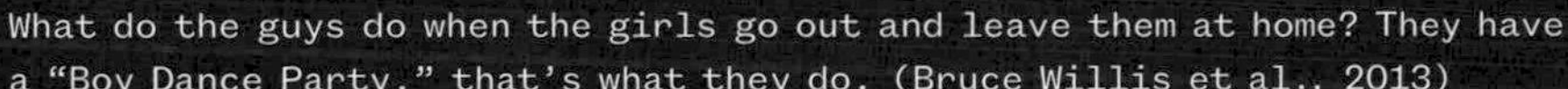

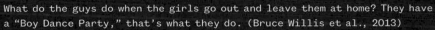

What do the guys do when the girls go out and leave them at home? They have a “Boy Dance Party,” that’s what they do. (Bruce Willis et al., 2013)

Caught busting a move at his ironing board, Kyle Mooney is “discovered” by promoter Beck Bennett in this short about the instantaneous rise and fall of a roommate turned club dancer. (2013)

In the short film “Me,” a spoof of the trailer for Spike Jonze’s film “Her,” the protagonist (Jonah Hill) falls in love with his operating system, a doppelganger of himself (played by Michael Cera). (2014)

The wildly popular short “(Do It On My) Twin Bed” celebrated the awkward experience of hooking up in your childhood bedroom. (2013)

As Blizzard Man, Andy Samberg baffles record execs with his cheesy, scatty rap style. (2014)

"Guess what. I got a fever. And the only prescription. Is more cowbell."

—CHRISTOPHER WALKEN

as "legendary" record producer Bruce Dickinson in "VH1: Behind the Music" (a.k.a. "More Cowbell.") This sketch, featuring Will Ferrell as an overzealous cowbell player and Walken as a huge cowbell enthusiast (with Chris Kattan, Jimmy Fallon, Chris Parnell, and Horatio Sanz as band members), is one of the top cult favorites in the history of SNL. You may notice that Ferrell's belly isn't protruding from his shirt in this photo, taken during the dress rehearsal. According to costume designer Eric Justian, "Will decided between the dress and air show to go back to a shirt that was too small. This shirt made us laugh so hard during his costume fitting, but we were uncertain if it was really appropriate. Will was right, too small is funny." In the live show, Fallon's struggle to keep a straight face was a losing battle. (2000)

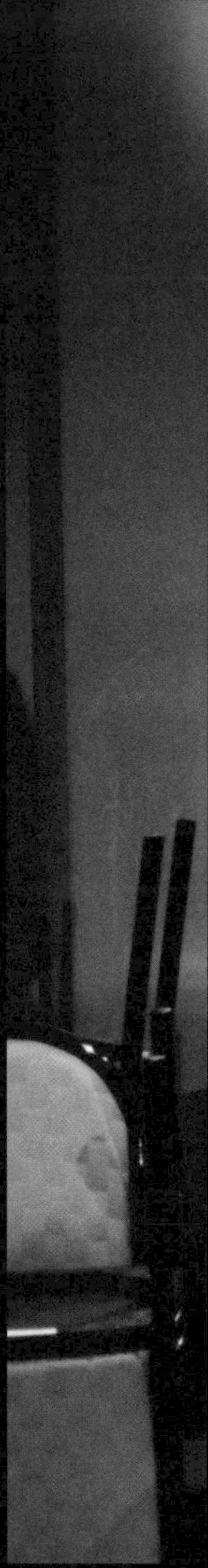

ABOVE: "Haaaiiii! Too hot in the hot tub! Burn myself!" Eddie Murphy in "James Brown's Celebrity Hot Tub Party." (1983)
RIGHT: Oversharers Virginia and Roger Klarvin ("Lovers" stars Rachel Dratch and Will Ferrell) make an awkward moment of a hot tub gathering with another couple (Winona Ryder and Jimmy Fallon) by overtly discussing their sexual passion for one another. (2002)

RIGHT: "It's time for androgyny…here comes Pat!" The genderless Pat (Julia Sweeney) proves frustratingly good at strip poker. (1992)

"Barney, we all agreed that your dancing was great… your presentation was very sexy. I guess, in the end, we all thought that Adrian's body was much, much better than yours." This Chippendales audition sketch, featuring Patrick Swayze and new featured player Chris Farley, was Farley's first true standout moment in the show. (1990)

WELCOME HOME
COLONEL ANGUS

LEFT: "Colonel Angus might be rough. Colonel Angus might not smell like a bed of roses. But, deep down, Colonel Angus is very sweet.... And if I overstay my welcome, just tap me on the head." Christopher Walken plays a colonel on a journey to the "Deep South" in this sketch rife with double entendres. (With Rachel Dratch, Chris Parnell, and Amy Poehler, 2003)
ABOVE: Kate: "Ali, now that you and I have both experienced each other's mutual joy, and the very essence of our being, can we still continue our friendship as if nothing has happened at all?" Ali: "Kate, I loves your hair and I like your smile, but you an ugly old white woman, so I won't be back for a while." Martin Short (as Katharine Hepburn) and Billy Crystal (as Muhammad Ali) in "The Kate

Gilda Radner and Garrett Morris as prostitute and pimp in “Little Old Ladies of the Night.” (1977)

ABOVE: Women won't give "Girl Watchers" Tom Hanks, Kevin Nealon, and Jon Lovitz the time of day. (1988)
LEFT: Martin Short as nervous defense attorney Nathan Thurm. (1985)

Jan Hooks as Bette Davis in "Video Will." (1989)

Beldar Conehead (Dan Aykroyd) vs. Joe Mel (Steve Martin) on "Family Feud." (With Bill Murray, 1978)

"Dick in a Box" singers (Andy Samberg and Justin Timberlake) compete

ABOVE: A professor of African American studies (Louis C.K.) struggles with clues like "It's been a minute since he got a job" on "Black Jeopardy!" (With Kenan Thompson, Jay Pharoah, and Sasheer Zamata, 2014) **TOP:** "Don't walk away from your telescreen, because it's time for the new 'Jeopardy 1999!' Now, here's your host: Art F-114." (With Dan Aykroyd, Laraine Newman, Chevy Chase, and Steve Martin, 1976.)

"Oh, rough. Just the way your mother likes it, Trebek?"

—DARRELL HAMMOND
as "Celebrity Jeopardy!" contestant Sean Connery, with Will Ferrell as Alex Trebek. (2000)

Andy Kaufman doing his now-iconic "Mighty Mouse" routine on episode 1. (1975)

Kristen Wiig as the Target Lady, with Justin Timberlake as her friend, Peg. (2009)

RIGHT: Will Ferrell and Ana Gasteyer as husband and wife music duo Marty Culp and Bobbi Mohan-Culp. (1999) **TOP RIGHT:** “Acting!” Jon Lovitz as Master Thespian.

"Oh, my God! It's Barbra! It's Barbra! You're beautiful! It's Barbra! Oh! I can die now!" "Coffee Talk" host Linda Richman (Mike Myers) and guests Liz Rosenberg (Madonna) and her mother (Roseanne Barr) freak out when their idol, Barbra

Wayne Campbell (Mike Myers) and Garth Algar (Dana Carvey) doing their extreme-closeup faces on "Wayne's World." (1991)

"Please welcome the greatest performer ever to have graced this earth, Charles Nelson Reilly." Will Ferrell as James Lipton, with Alec Baldwin, on "Inside the Actor's Studio." (2001)

DEAD honkey."

—**RICHARD PRYOR** trades racial epithets with Chevy Chase during a psychological evaluation in "Word Association." (1975)

"Michael, I know there must be a lot of pressure for you to play very well, and I can imagine that a night before a game, you must lie awake thinking, 'I'm not good enough. Everybody's better than me. I'm not going to score any points. I have no business playing this game.'" Stuart Smalley (Al Franken) offers confidence-boosting advice to Michael Jordan on "Daily Affirmation." (1991)

RIGHT: "Makin' copies… Randy the Rand Man!" Richard Laymer (Rob Schneider) provides annoying commentary while his colleague (Kevin Nealon) uses the copy machine. (1991)

RIGHT: During the live performance of this "Samurai Stockbroker" sketch, John Belushi (as Samurai Futaba) accidentally cut Buck Henry's forehead with his sword. Henry finished the sketch despite bleeding from the cut, and appeared for the remainder of the show with a bandage on his head. One by one, other cast members also appeared with bandages on their heads throughout the rest of the broadcast. (1976)

Gary (Jimmy Fallon): “Think we can take them, Ace?” Ace (Jon Hamm): “I think we Can-Can!” The Ambiguously Gay Duo comes to life in the “Dark, Clenched Hole of Evil” episode. (2011)

"Now watch and listen 'cause I'm ready to rule." The real Judy Sheindlin interrupts Cheri Oteri's impression of her to demonstrate her judicial skills. (1998)

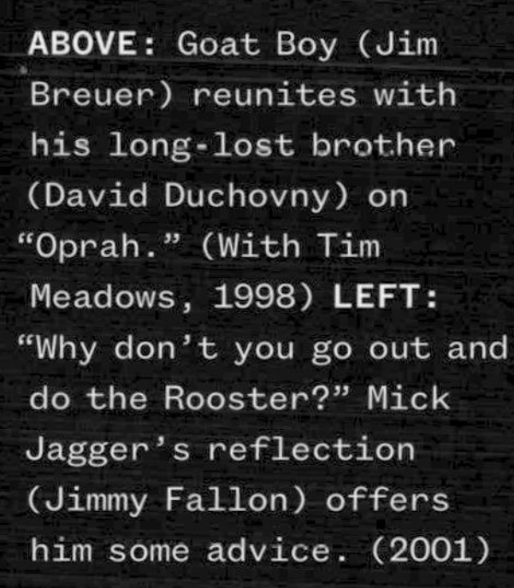

ABOVE: Goat Boy (Jim Breuer) reunites with his long-lost brother (David Duchovny) on "Oprah." (With Tim Meadows, 1998) **LEFT:** "Why don't you go out and do the Rooster?" Mick Jagger's reflection (Jimmy Fallon) offers him some advice. (2001)

Stage manager Chris Kelly hands Andy Samberg the prop falcon as past and future Falconers multiply between live takes of "The Falconer." (With host Kevin Spacey, right, 2006)

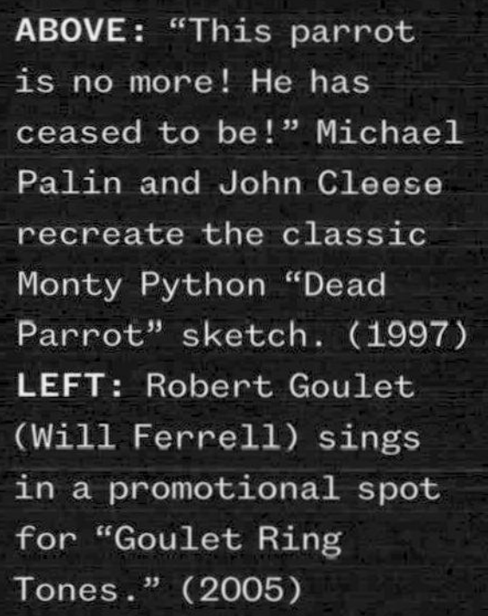

ABOVE: "This parrot is no more! He has ceased to be!" Michael Palin and John Cleese recreate the classic Monty Python "Dead Parrot" sketch. (1997)
LEFT: Robert Goulet (Will Ferrell) sings in a promotional spot for "Goulet Ring Tones." (2005)

RIGHT: "Toonces, look out!" "Dateline" anchors Stone Phillips and Jane Pauley (Mike Myers and Julia Sweeney) scream in terror as Toonces the driving cat loses control of the car. (1993)

"Say hi to your mother for me." Andy Samberg in "Mark Wahlberg Talks to Animals." (2008)

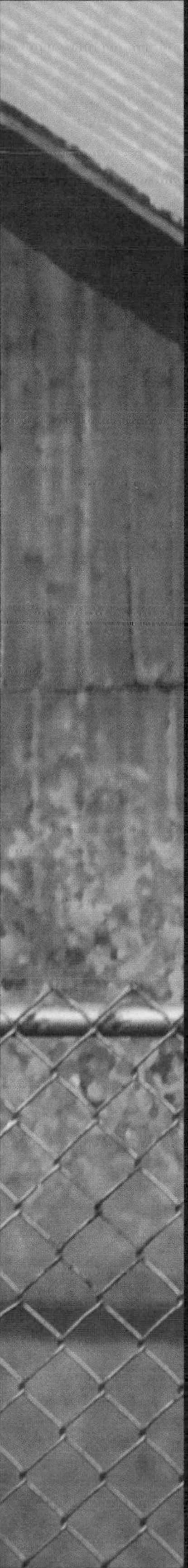

Eddie Murphy teaches important lessons to inner-city children in "Mr. Robinson's Neighborhood." (1982)

"I gotta be honest with you, buddy—I've been thinking about breaking that big, beautiful nose of yours." Mark Wahlberg confronts Andy Samberg backstage about his impression of him. (2008)

Phil Hartman as "Unfrozen Caveman Lawyer." (1992)

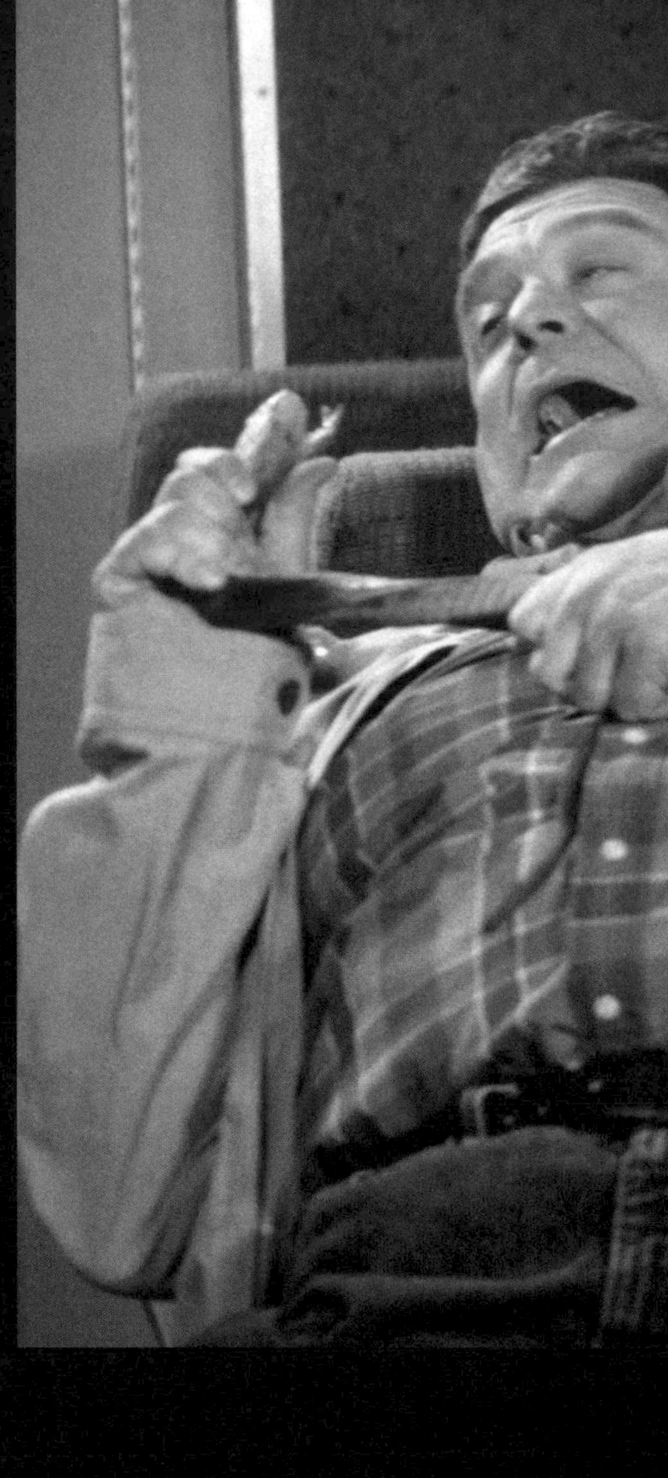

Conditions are less than ideal on "Deregulated Airline." (With Kevin Nealon, 1988)

Passengers John Goodman, Ana Gasteyer, and Tim Meadows face

As sketches finish, host dresser Donna Richards grabs hosts by the hand to lead them where they need to go as quickly as possible. **CLOCKWISE FROM ABOVE:** Russell Brand (2011), Emma Stone (2009), and Jon Hamm (2010).

ABOVE: Kristen Wiig performs on “Deep House Dish.” (2009)
LEFT: “Hey, my flute amp!” Aidy Bryant as a rap flautist on “What’s Poppin.’” (2014)
TOP: The first appearance of Bill Murray as small-time lounge singer Nick Summers. (1977)

Host Tom Hanks introduces Bruce Springsteen.

James Brown
(1980)

During the dress rehearsal of Frank Zappa's musical performance, Connie Conehead (Laraine Newman) makes an appearance on stage. (1978)

Aretha Franklin performing "United Together." (1980)

John Belushi does an impression of Joe Cocker during Cocker's

Kanye West, seen here performing "Power," was the first musical guest to completely transform the musical stage. (2010)

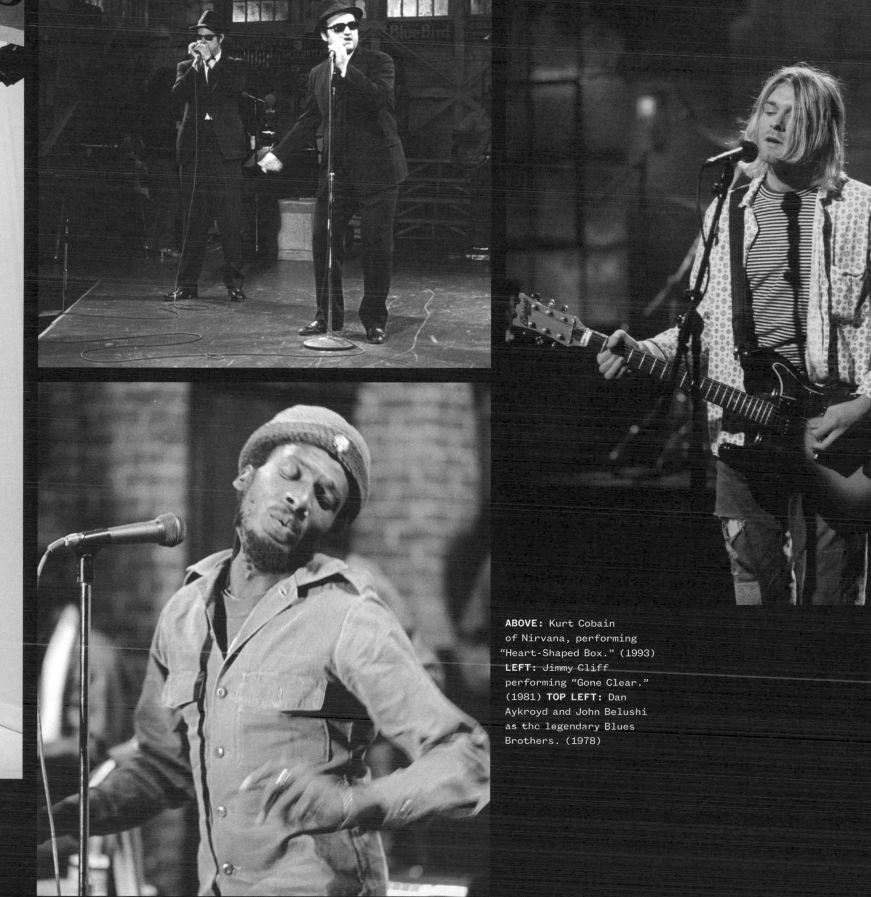

ABOVE: Kurt Cobain of Nirvana, performing "Heart-Shaped Box." (1993) **LEFT:** Jimmy Cliff performing "Gone Clear." (1981) **TOP LEFT:** Dan Aykroyd and John Belushi as the legendary Blues Brothers. (1978)

Lady Gaga performs a medley of “LoveGame,” “Bad Romance,” and “Poker Face.” (2009)

MC Hammer performing “Addams Groove.” (1991)

David Bowie performing “The Man Who Sold the World.” (1979)

ABOVE: Outkast performing their hit “Hey Ya.” (2003)
TOP: Devo performing “Jocko Homo.” (1978)

Elvis Costello singing
"Veronica." (1989)

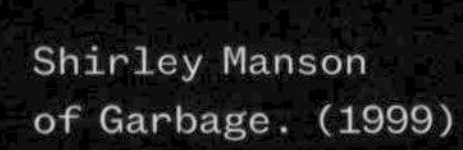

Shirley Manson
of Garbage. (1999)

Will Ferrell accompanies Green Day on cowbell during “East Jesus Nowhere.” (2009)

Prince performing “Party Up.” (1981)

Coldplay performing “Viva la Vida.” (2008)

Arcade Fire gives an encore performance for the audience, cast, and crew. (2007)

Seth Meyers having his blazer adjusted moments before "Weekend Update," (2011)

Seeing double: **ABOVE:** Fred Armisen as/with Governor David Paterson (2010) **RIGHT:** Gwyneth Paltrow joins Garth and Kat (Fred Armisen and Kristen Wiig, 2011) **OPPOSITE, FROM TOP:** Andy Samberg as/with Nicolas Cage (2012); Jimmy Fallon as/with Jerry Seinfeld (1999); Drunk Uncle (Bobby Moynihan, right) with Drunker Uncle (John Goodman, 2013); and Dana Carvey as/with Dennis Miller (1987).

WEEKENDUPDATEWE

264

ABOVE: "Oh…well, nevermind!" Chevy Chase tries to keep it together while Gilda Radner does Emily Litella. (1975)
TOP: During the commercial break before "Update," Seth Meyers and Amy Poehler review cue cards under the bleachers with Wally Feresten. (2007)

RIGHT: Colin Quinn and Bill Clinton (Darrell Hammond, 1999).
ABOVE RIGHT: "SNL Newsbreak" science editor Dr. Jack Badofsky (Tim Kazurinsky) with anchor Brad Hall. (1982)

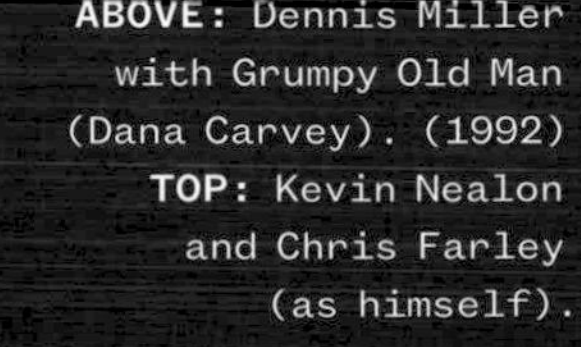

ABOVE: Dennis Miller with Grumpy Old Man (Dana Carvey). (1992) **TOP:** Kevin Nealon and Chris Farley (as himself).

Season 6 anchors Charles Rocket **(LEFT)** and Gail Matthius **(RIGHT)**. (1980)

Fred Armisen as American Apparel CEO Dov Charney, with Amy Poehler and Seth Meyers. (2008)

ABOVE; Joe Piscopo on "SNL Newsbreak." (1982)
TOP: Roseanne Roseannadanna (Gilda Radner) with Jane Curtin. (1979)

RIGHT: On Bill Hader's farewell show, Stefon ditches Anderson Cooper at the altar and runs off with his true love, Seth Meyers. (2013)

LEFT: Jane Curtin sneaks a giggle behind stargazer Bill Murray's Oscar-winner predictions board. (1978) **ABOVE:** Season 7 co-anchors Robin Duke and Brian Doyle-Murray. (1982) **ABOVE LEFT:** Cecily Strong with Seth Meyers's successor, Colin Jost. (2014) **TOP:** Drew Barrymore makes a surprise cameo to protest a joke Tina Fey made about her breasts. (With Amy Poehler, 2006)

"NEXT!"

—**TARAN KILLAM** as sardonic 1860s newspaper critic Jebidiah Atkinson, dismissing one abhorrent topic for the next. (2014)

"Love: the final frontier. These are the voyages of the Pacific Princess. Its mission: to explore passion and to boldly go to romantic ports of call." Captain Picard himself, Patrick Stewart, in "Love Boat: The Next Generation," with original "Love Boat" actor Bernie Kopell (as Doc). (Also featuring Phil Hartman as Worf, Tim Meadows as Geordi, and Al Franken as the alien Tog.) (1994)

TIC P

PLEASE DON'T
TELL HIM!

ABOVE: John Belushi as Beethoven, with Gilda Radner as Mrs. Beethoven and Laraine Newman as their maid. (1975) **LEFT:** Stevie Wonder (Eddie Murphy): "I am dark, and you are liiiiiight." Frank Sinatra (Joe Piscopo): "You are blind as a bat, and I have siiiiiight." Recording "Ebony and Ivory" for "Frank Sings Tunes the Young People Will Enjoy." (1982) **OPPOSITE:** "You know, we've kidded Ray a lot tonight, but blindness is nothing to kid about. So, we at 'Saturday Night,' with the network, set up sort of a matching fund and we were able to purchase this lovely painting in appreciation of Ray Charles and the courageous example he sets for all of us—besides being one heck of a good sport. And, so, in Ray's name, we're donating this painting to the Lighthouse of the Blind, in the hope that someday all will be able to see it." Mr. Mike (Michael O'Donoghue) presenting Charles with what he describes as a painting by Monet. (1977)

Kate McKinnon as Janis Joplin in “Vincent Price’s 1967 Halloween Special.” The sketch, cut after dress rehearsal, never aired. (2012)

“Normally, plants don’t have eyes, so it’s hard for me to trust them. Hence, googly eyes.”

—**CHRISTOPHER WALKEN**
in “Indoor Gardening Tips from a Man Who’s Very Scared of Plants.” (2008)

Chris Farley's iconic motivational speaker Matt Foley famously lives "in a van down by the river." (1994)

"Les Jeunes de Paris," guest starring Jean Dujardin. (With Taran Killam, 2014)

"Hey, you wanna dance? Me? Him? Me? Him? Him? Me? Me? Me? Him? Him? Me? Him?" Roxbury Guys Chris Kattan, Jim Carrey, and Will Ferrell. (1996)

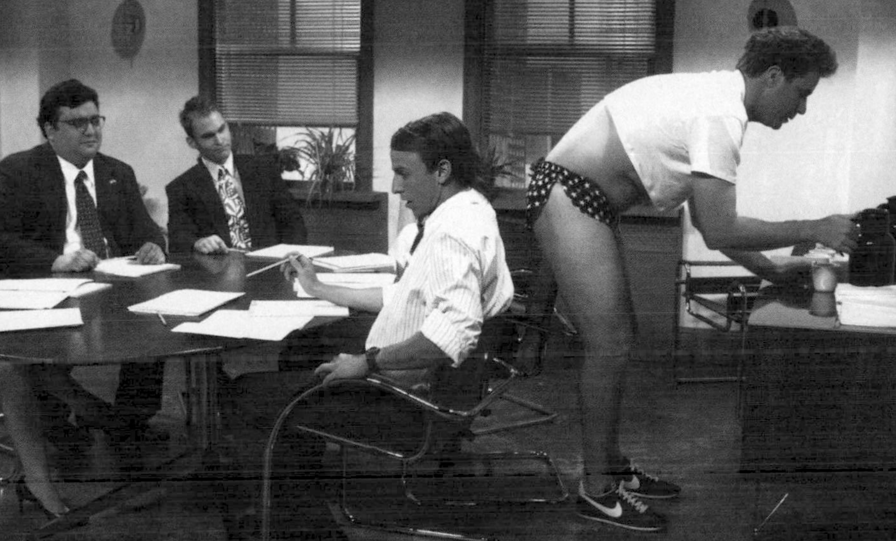

ABOVE: “The Franken and Davis Show” with Tom Davis and Al Franken. (1977) **LEFT:** “You do know that I love this country more than absolutely anything? Well, I’m sorry you had to see my ass cheeks, and my nugget pouch, and my bulge.” Will Ferrell as Dale McGrew in “Show Your Patriotism.” (2001)

LEFT: “Don’t worry about the other dancers, B-Town, I handpicked them myself. These guys are pros.” Paul Rudd as the director of Beyoncé’s “Single Ladies” video. With Justin Timberlake, Bobby Moynihan, Andy Samberg, and Beyoncé. (2008)

Mary Katherine Gallagher (Molly Shannon) makes a friend (Chris Farley) at St. Monica's Autumn Dance. (1997)

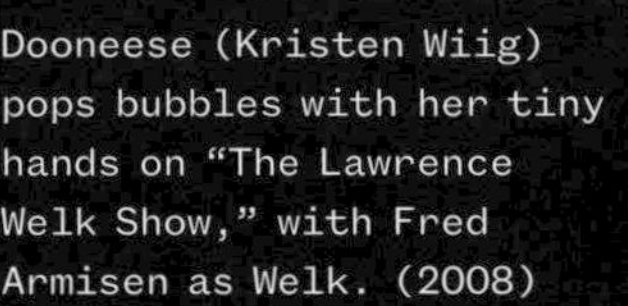

Dooneese (Kristen Wiig) pops bubbles with her tiny hands on "The Lawrence Welk Show," with Fred Armisen as Welk. (2008)

OPPOSITE: Backstage in costume for "Pageant Preview": Nasim Pedrad, Abby Elliott, Andy Samberg, Kristen Wiig, and Vanessa Bayer. (2011)

ON AIR.

"Unce …
tice …
fee tines
a mady."

—**EDDIE MURPHY**
as Buckwheat, performing "Three Times a Lady" from his album "Buh-Weet Sings." (1982)

Steve Martin and the Toot Uncommons perform the very memorable "King Tut." (1978)

"There we go! All ready for the trash. Now that's some garbage you can live with!" Phil Hartman in "Cooking with the Anal Retentive Chef." (1989)

"Oh, now I've done it, I've cut the dickens out of my finger.... I recommend natural coagulants, such as chicken liver. Another reason not to throw away the liver!" Dan Aykroyd as Julia Child, bleeding to death on "The French Chef." (1978)

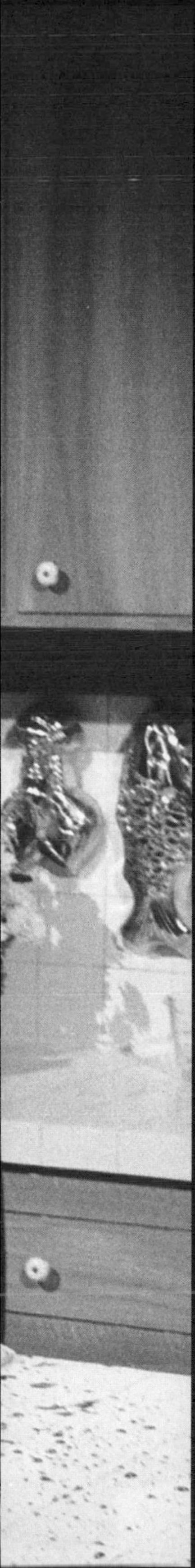

"Cheeseburger, cheeseburger, cheeseburger!" Dan Aykroyd as George in "Olympia Cafe." (With Ron Wood, Charlie Watts, and Rosie Shuster, 1978)

Gumby (Eddie Murphy) joins fellow comedians (Christopher Guest, Martin Short, and Billy Crystal) in Lishman's Deli to kvetch. (1984)

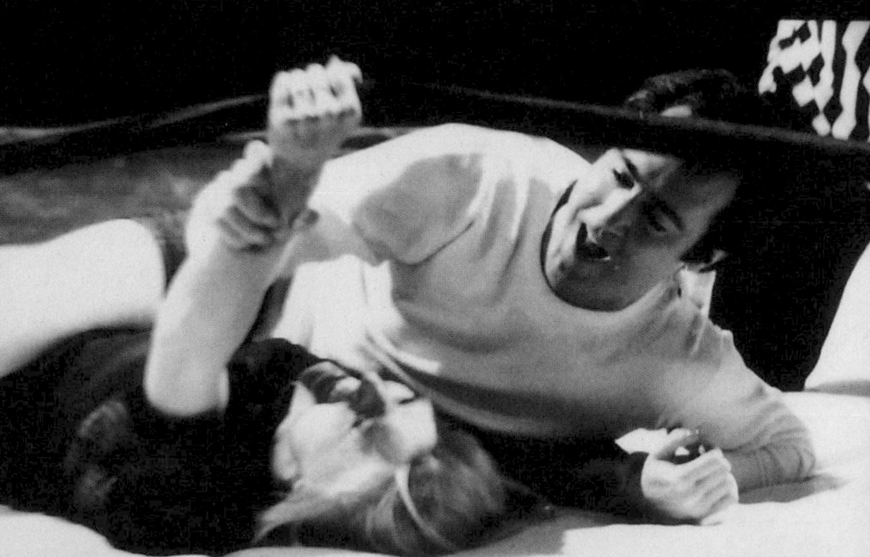

ABOVE: Andy Kaufman angered a lot of viewers with his faux-misogynist rants about women being inferior to men and his insistence on proving his superiority by wrestling women. (1979)
TOP: Kristen Wiig and Blake Lively in "Vagisil Superstars of Bowling Tournament 1989." (2009)

LEFT: Coach A. Whitney Brown consoles Phil Hartman for the loss of his arms during the "All-Drug Olympics." (1988) **OPPOSITE BOTTOM RIGHT:** "We have taken the world's most pathetic girly-man, and turned him into the embodiment of perfect pumptitude!" Dana Carvey as Hans, with Steve Martin and Kevin Nealon, on "Pumping Up with Hans and Franz." (1989)

"Oh! You box dirty!" Mayor Rudy Giuliani in "Janet Reno's Dance Party" with Will Ferrell. (1997)

Jim Henson (lower right) puppeteering King Ploobis with host Anthony Perkins (center) and cast members. His "Land of Gorch" Muppet sketches made 18 appearances on the show during the first two seasons. (1976)

Gilda Radner and Jane Curtin in "Mommie Dearest." (1978)

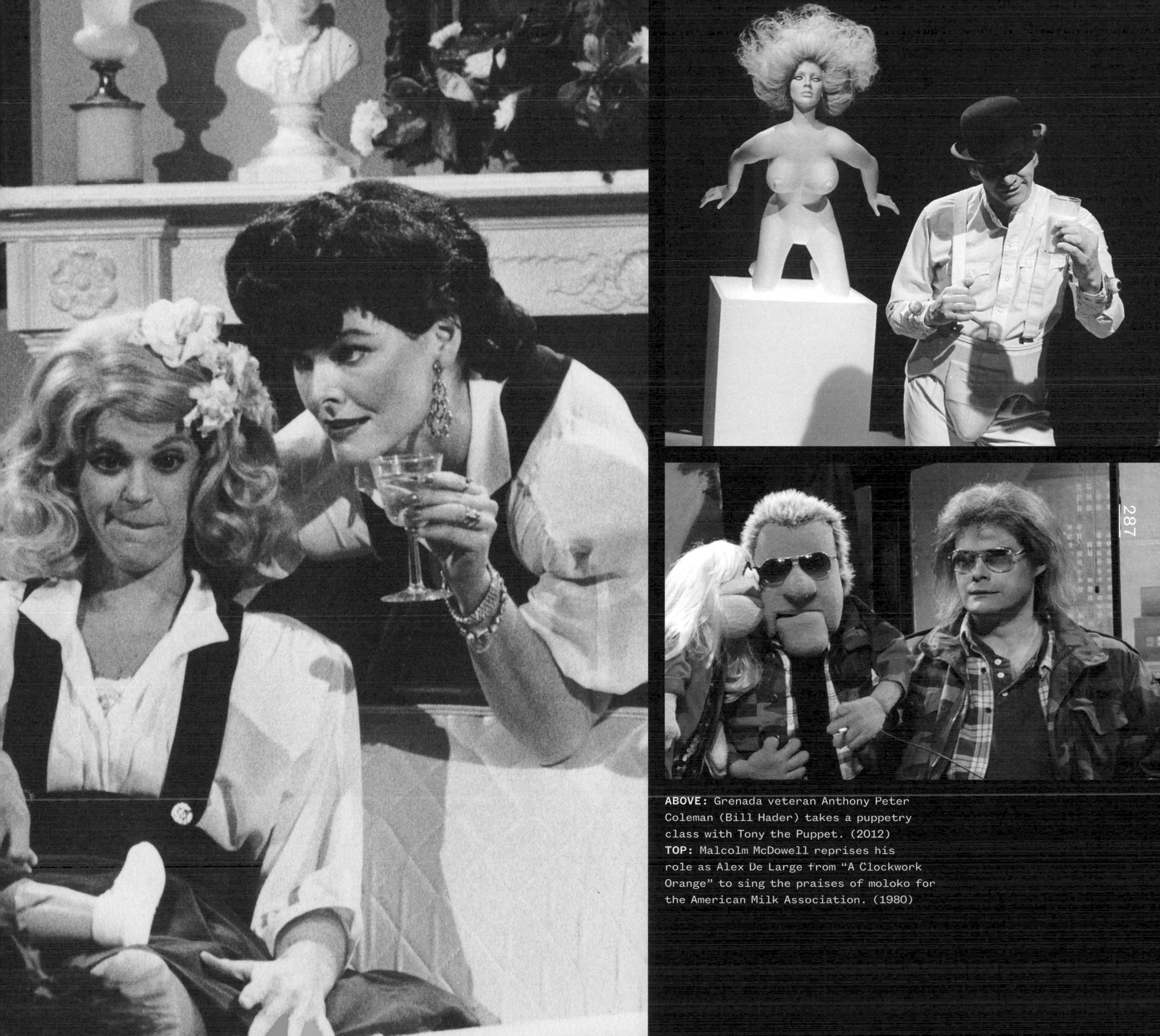

ABOVE: Grenada veteran Anthony Peter Coleman (Bill Hader) takes a puppetry class with Tony the Puppet. (2012)
TOP: Malcolm McDowell reprises his role as Alex De Large from "A Clockwork Orange" to sing the praises of moloko for the American Milk Association. (1980)

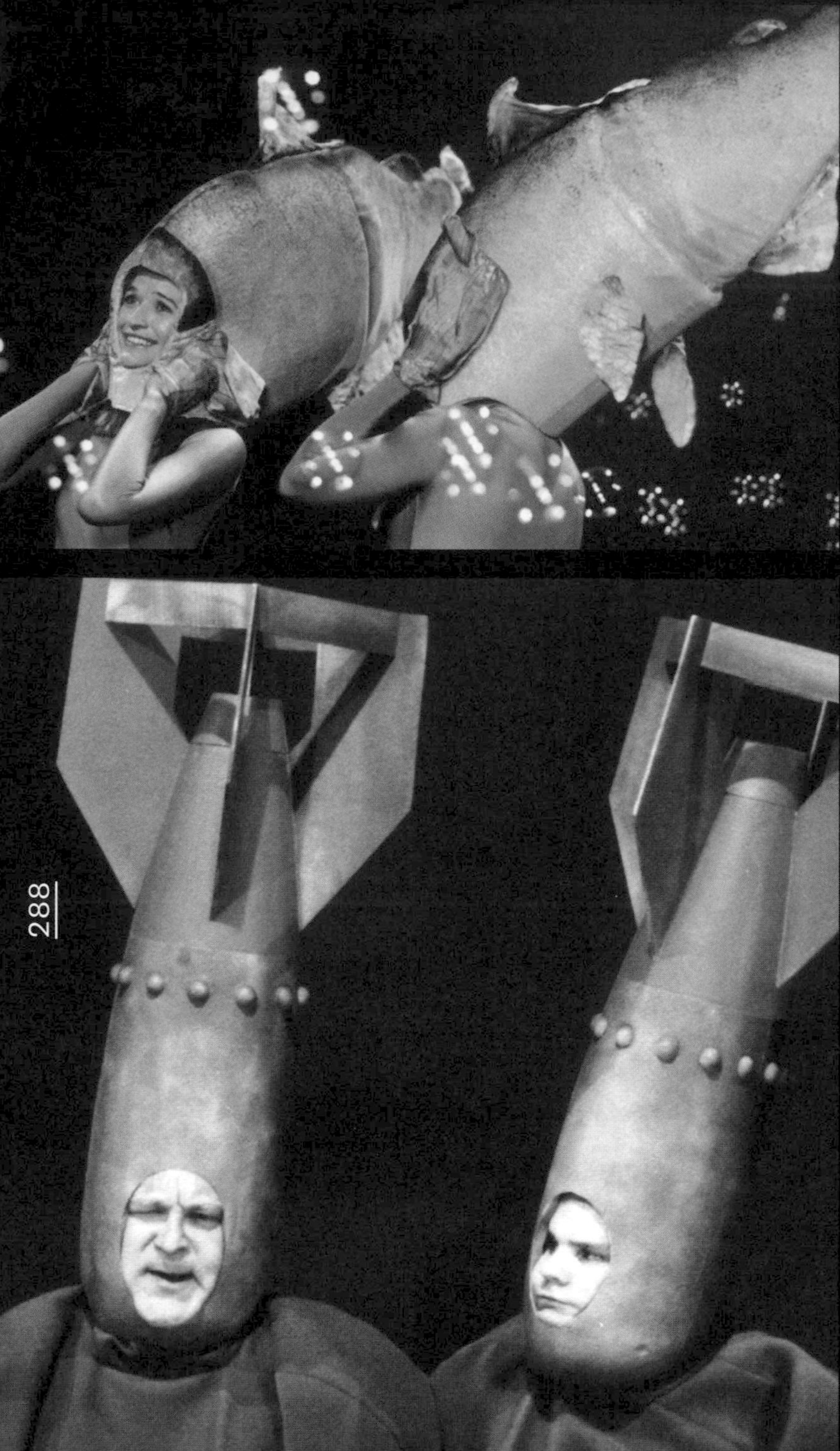

“Consume mass quantities!” Connie, Beldar, and Prymaat Conehead of Planet Remulak (played by Laraine Newman, Dan Aykroyd, and Jane Curtin). According to Aykroyd, the sketch was inspired by the film “This Island Earth,” in which the humans don’t seem to notice the very tall foreheads of the aliens. (1977)

ABOVE: John Goodman and Chris Farley in “Bombs,” a sketch that was cut after dress rehearsal. (1990)
TOP: Jan Hooks in “Salmon Spawning.” (1987)

RIGHT: "If it's not okay to have tooth decay, who you gonna call? Toothbrushers! I ain't afraid of no sweets!" Dr. Don McMullin, DDS, and his wife, Colleen, put up a saccharine front for trick-or-treaters between vicious arguments. (Norm Macdonald and Cheri Oteri, 1999)
TOP RIGHT: Shopkeepers Michaela Watkins and Fred Armisen are taken hostage by lamps Andy Samberg, Hugh Laurie, and Kristen Wiig. (2008)

In his bear costume for the VMA/Miley Cyrus sketch, Bobby Moynihan discusses the script with writer Tim Robinson. (2013)

Tim Kazurinsky chats with Eddie Murphy (as Gumby) between sketches. (1983)

291

"Bring it on down to
Wrappin'ville!" Justin

“My wife’s never gonna wanna see my penis again. Especially not since it’s been bunched up in this tight-ass unitard.” Kenan Thompson in “Dance of the Snowflakes,” in which performers put on happy faces while their inner thoughts, heard in voiceover, express regret and humiliation. (With John Goodman, Vanessa Bayer, and Aidy Bryant, 2013)

"I don't care what your momma says, Christmas time is nee-ear!" Horatio Sanz, Jimmy Fallon, Chris Kattan, and Tracy Morgan singing "I Wish It Was Christmas Today." (2000)

Filling in for an ailing Santa Claus, Hanukkah Harry (Jon Lovitz) disappoints children (Victoria Jackson and Mike Myers) with gifts of socks and slacks in "The Night Hanukkah Harry Saved Christmas." (1989)

Jon Lovitz bids goodnight with Jane's Addiction and special guest Flea. (1997)

Nasim Pedrad and Abby Elliott kiss Kristen Wiig as Arcade Fire plays during the goodnights of her farewell show. (2012)

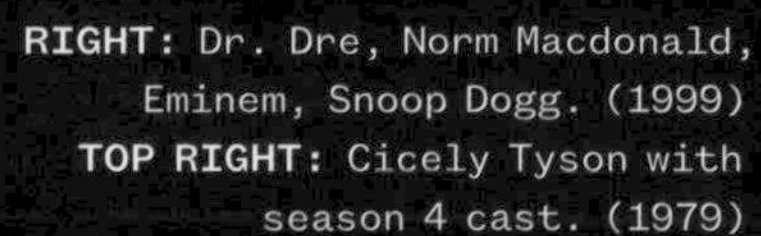

RIGHT: Dr. Dre, Norm Macdonald, Eminem, Snoop Dogg. (1999)
TOP RIGHT: Cicely Tyson with season 4 cast. (1979)

RuPaul, Muggsy Bogues, Charles Barkley, Kurt Cobain, and Dave Grohl. (1993)

Jimmy Fallon and the cast nod to the Killer Bees bumpers from Christmas 1975 (see following spread). (2011)

Fred Armisen and Bill Hader at the goodnights of their last show as cast members. (2013)

Season 1 cast and writers take to the ice at Rockefeller Plaza as the Killer Bees for the Christmas 1975 show.

Dear Lorne,

FROM THE DESK OF JASON PRIESTLEY

LORNE—
THANKS TO YOU AND
EVERYONE FOR
GIVING ME ONE OF
THE MOST REWARDING
AND ~~GREATEST~~
EXPERIENCES OF MY
LIFE—
I CAN'T WAIT TO DO
IT AGAIN—
JASON

Gilda July 3

Dear Lorne,
Thanks for the beautiful
birthday flowers — they
brightened the pit of despair
I'm just now pulling myself
out of — am still battling
fuckin cancer — looking
for the laughs — would
prefer to get back into
show business. I love you
Gilda

PAUL SIMON

Lorne —
Good show. Cast works.
Update funny. Commercial parodies
Excellent. No complaints. Good to
have you back. Details when next
we speak. Congrats etc.

Tom Brokaw

NBC

Lorne,
As I read all of
the SNL anniversary
pieces I have a
recurring thought:
you're the real star.
Without you Saturday
night would still be
just that.
Just think, you
customized a whole night.
Kind of like turning a
'55 Chevy into a 911.
Okay before. Better now.
Congratulations. Tom

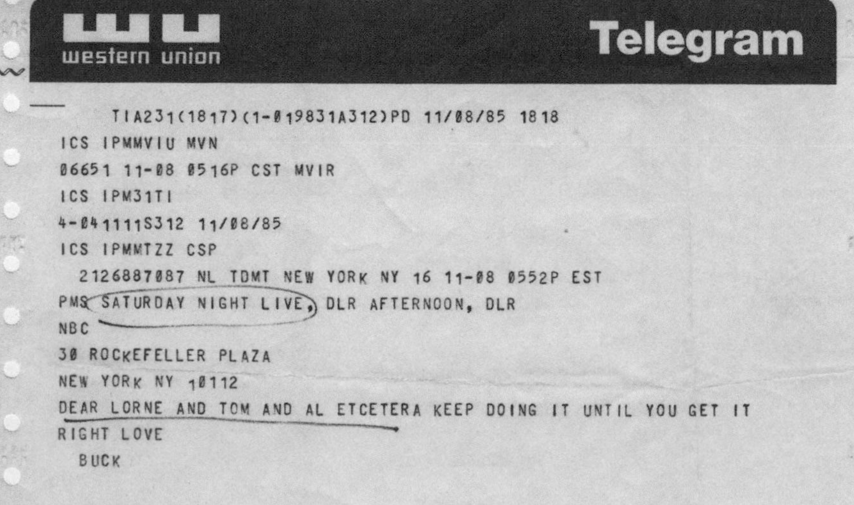

western union Telegram

TIA231(1817)(1-019831A312)PD 11/08/85 1818
ICS IPMMVIU MVN
06651 11-08 0516P CST MVIR
ICS IPM31TI
4-0411115312 11/08/85
ICS IPMMTZZ CSP
2126887087 NL TDMT NEW YORK NY 16 11-08 0552P EST
PMS SATURDAY NIGHT LIVE, DLR AFTERNOON, DLR
NBC
30 ROCKEFELLER PLAZA
NEW YORK NY 10112
DEAR LORNE AND TOM AND AL ETCETERA KEEP DOING IT UNTIL YOU GET IT
RIGHT LOVE
BUCK

1755 EST
SF-1201 (NY) (A-6/82)

To Lorne

Thank You

Thank you for all
of your help!
God Bless
Puff Daddy
98

A sampling of notes, telegrams, and letters sent to Lorne Michaels over the years.

The City of New York
Office of the Mayor
New York, N.Y. 10007

February 1, 1996

Mr. Lorne Michaels
The Brill Building
1619 Broadway, Ninth Floor
New York, New York 10019

Dear Lorne:

Thank you for your kind note of January 19. It was a pleasure to appear on Saturday Night Live, but until I get the call to return to the studio, I will keep my day job.

Best personal regards!

Sincerely,

Rudy

Rudolph W. Giuliani
Mayor

AMY POEHLER

Lorne—

Thank you for giving me my favorite job in my life so far.

Sincerely,
Amy Meredith Poehler

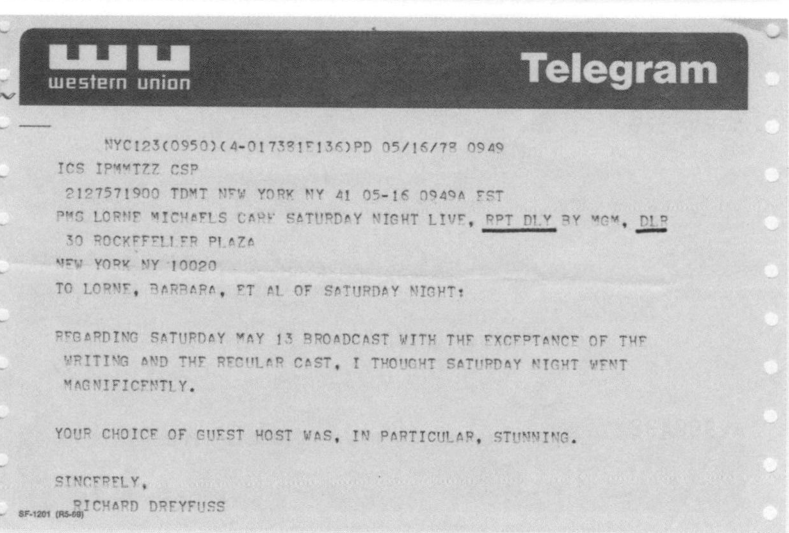

western union Telegram

NYC123(0950)(4-017381E136)PD 05/16/78 0949
ICS IPMMTZZ CSP
2127571900 TDMT NEW YORK NY 41 05-16 0949A EST
PMS LORNE MICHAELS CARE SATURDAY NIGHT LIVE, RPT DLY BY MGM, DLR
30 ROCKEFELLER PLAZA
NEW YORK NY 10020
TO LORNE, BARBARA, ET AL OF SATURDAY NIGHT:

REGARDING SATURDAY MAY 13 BROADCAST WITH THE EXCEPTANCE OF THE WRITING AND THE REGULAR CAST, I THOUGHT SATURDAY NIGHT WENT MAGNIFICENTLY.

YOUR CHOICE OF GUEST HOST WAS, IN PARTICULAR, STUNNING.

SINCERELY,
RICHARD DREYFUSS

SF-1201 (R5-69)

PHIL HARTMAN

Dear Lorne,

It was not without its blood, sweat and tears; but the thrills and the glory remain prominent in my mind.

Thanks for the opportunity to serve.

Forever yours,
Phil

October 30, 1978

Lorne -

This is a rough synopsis of the following fan mail. It is slightly imbalanced on the negative side as Kay has been protectively holding aside a lot of the general fan mail that's been negative.

Feedback on the Stones:

Obscene - 7 (about half were older parent types)

Positive - 1 letter plus 50 signitures

"I've been a fan since the show started, but I'm dissapointed in this season" - 13

Catholics upset about Pope & Cardinal jokes - 4

Too many commercials - 6

Don't like Bill in Update - 7

Love Greek Restaurant - 1

Loved Beatle sketch - 2

"Who are Devo?" - 3

Lucille Ball segment - cheap shot - 1

Music this year - terrible - 2

Danny's cheerleader commentary - great - 1

Scotch Tape Store - sensitively done - 1

Mr. Bill is wonderful - 1

Franken & Davis - always disgusting - 1

Oct. 21st show - terrific, best so far - 2
Loved Coneheads & Night on Freak Mountain

Sid Vicious - "unforgiveable" - 2 - from parent & relative of Nancy Spungen

Oct. 7th show - not funny - 5

Where is Chevy? - 3

Mongoloid joke - offensive - 1

Fan mail has always been reviewed and cataloged by the SNL staff.

Lorne Michaels

Q&A

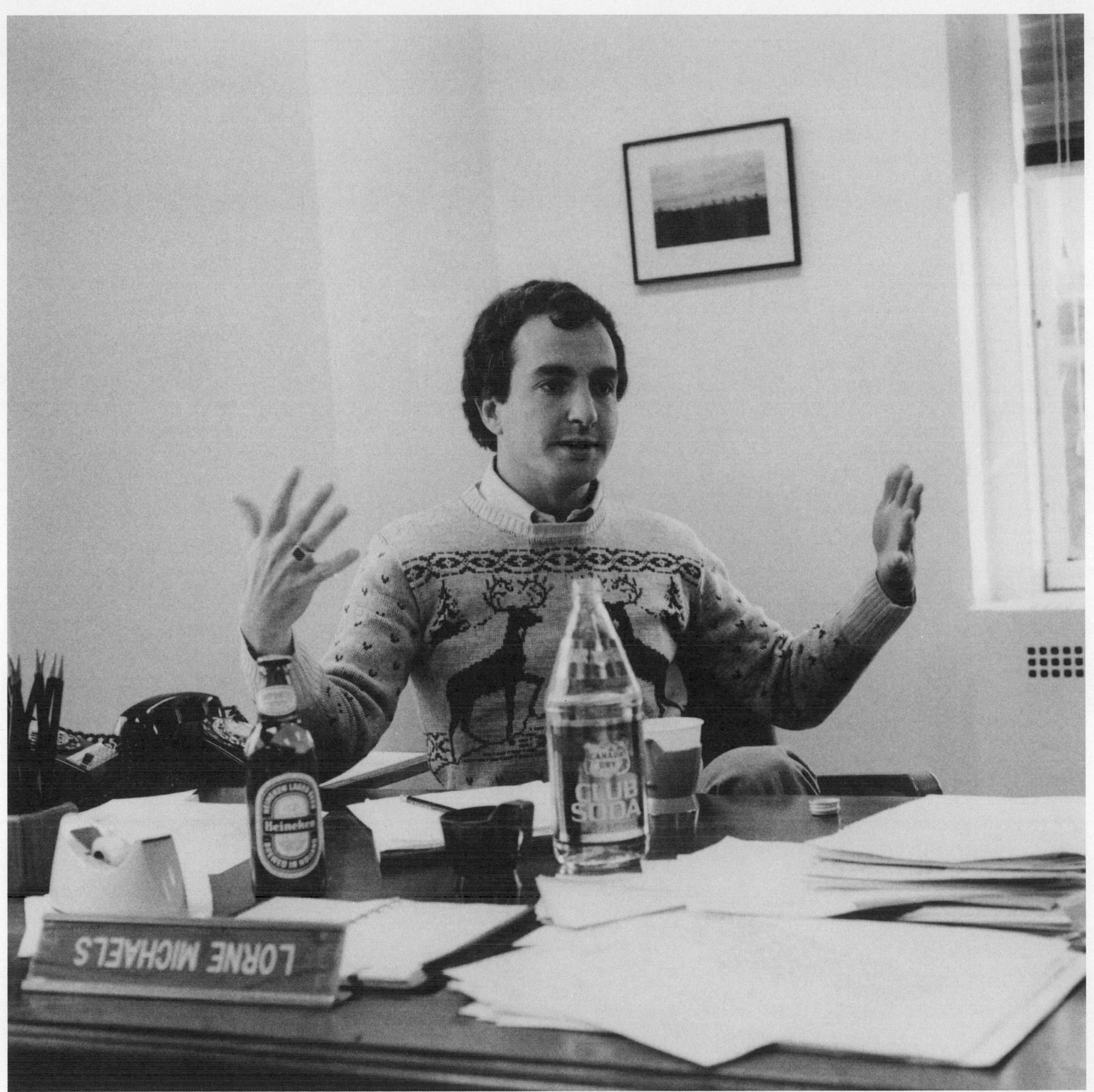

Michaels in his Rockefeller Plaza office. (1975)

RCA
NBC

Lorne Michaels in 2004.

Lorne Michaels in the SNL control room. (1978)

The Early Years

ALISON CASTLE: Are you planning anything special for April 1, 2015, to commemorate the 40 years since you signed the contract to do the show?
LORNE MICHAELS: No. If I get through the anniversary show on February 15, I think that'll be enough.

AC: Did you choose that day intentionally, the only "funny" day of the year?
LM: It just turned out that way. The day it happened, I just looked and realized it was April 1.

AC: The first season turned out, in many people's opinions, to be really the Chevy [Chase] season. The press and fans went wild over him. Looking at the pictures in the archives, and hearing people's recollections, it's clear you two were very close.
LM: Oh, we were very good friends. We were writing together, and with [Michael] O'Donoghue as well.

AC: Chevy had an amazing run the first season, got very successful, won an Emmy, and left. You didn't feel betrayed?
LM: No, I didn't at all, in no way. He did 40 shows, so in normal times that would be two years. He stayed until the beginning of '77, I think, when he exploded. He was on the covers of magazines…"New York" magazine had him on the cover in April of that year, calling him "the next Johnny Carson." Movies were being offered, and it was an incredibly exhilarating and confusing time. He was hired as a writer and at the time we only had a budget for six cast members, and I don't think anybody really was dealing with it because nobody thought the show would be on that much longer. I think that the network first approached him to do a primetime show, though the network was also tremendously supportive of his staying with "SNL." I think his agents were pressuring him to consider these offers for movies and other things, and he had a girlfriend in California and that was a lot of pressure…

AC: Were you closer with Chevy than you've ever been since with a cast member?
LM: I definitely had very close friendships, in many ways, with that original group. With Gilda [Radner], whom I had known before, and Laraine [Newman], and Danny [Aykroyd]. I'm trying to think… it just became different after that original period.

AC: I found a wonderful note from Gilda to you saying, "I love you."
LM: Aw…sweet. And Danny, I went up to Canada for his 60th birthday, not last summer but the summer before, with his family and Marty Short and some other friends. I said, "I've known you since you were 19." And he said, "Actually, I think you met me before…" Remember, everyone was so young. Chevy is a year older than I am, and I was 30. Ebersol was younger than me. So, you have a 30-year-old in charge of people who are 23, 24…with a level of fame and attention nobody was prepared for.

AC: Indeed. How many times did you quit over the years?
LM: Well, I quit after the fourth show, because they promised me a lighting director, and I was highly strung and dealing with pressure. I wasn't trying to extract anything. It was just, I felt betrayed and I had to fight for the show, and—

AC: Every time you quit, you came back. One time there was a long hiatus…
LM: Yeah. When I left in '80, it was more that I'd been offered a lot of stuff that I didn't know whether I wanted to do or not. The network was in a bad place, and I said in my meeting with [NBC president] Fred Silverman that I needed time, because I was just spent. And I said, "If I'm going to replace a whole cast and reinvent it, I'd rather come in, you know, mid-season. I just need time." I'd had six months with the first group. And he said, "Well, we've already sold the time through October." And I thought, "Can I do this and be compared to myself?" It was too daunting a task, and also we were in no way a priority at the network. We were still late-night, we didn't average into primetime ratings, we weren't really part of their core business. I sensed that. And also I didn't think I knew how to do it. So that was that.

Alan Zweibel, Chevy Chase, and Tom Davis watch from backstage at the 1976 Primetime Emmy Awards as Lorne Michaels accepts the award for Outstanding Comedy-Variety Series. (1976)

AC: What was your reaction when [director of comedy programming Brandon] Tartikoff chose [talent booker] Jean Doumanian to take over?

LM: I'd been talking to her when I was going back and forth about whether I thought I could do it; I certainly was talking to her—we were very close. So the fact that Brandon had approached her and talked to her... I remember because I was in Houston, oddly enough, for the premiere of "Urban Cowboy," and I got a call from Brandon, and he said, "I'm going to announce that Jean is going to take over," and I thought that was interesting because she wasn't connected to the core part, which was the writing/performing part. She was sophisticated and talented and all of that, she just wasn't from the 2-o'clock-in-the-morning part of it. And then Jean called me right after and said, "Brandon asked me not to talk to you about it." And it was just a grown-up moment for me because we were a very tight group, so I thought, "Oh, so it's different," that's all. But I was more surprised by it. Since I was leaving I didn't feel I had any right to comment. The one time Brandon talked to me, I said, "You have to keep the writing staff; that's the core thing." And by that point, Jim [Downey] had emerged as the strong voice, and he and Al [Franken] were good together, and he and Tom [Davis] were good together. I said, "Make sure that they are part of it." That was the only thing I really said.

AC: And everybody else left at that point. Then Dick [Ebersol] came back to the show in '81 after Jean was fired. From what I understand, you didn't have hard feelings. You even lent him your lucky pin for his first show as producer?

LM: A pin that I'd bought in LA that had a duck and three little ducks following. I wear it occasionally. Dick and I had dinner and I knew he was just there for me totally at the beginning of the show, and he said Brandon asked him to come in and do it and he wanted to do it and wanted my blessing, and I said that I would support it. I suggested he hire back a few people, and I think for the crew and for everyone else, his wearing that had some significance. I had assumed—naively, I think—that when I left—the entire writing staff, cast, designers... we all thought it would be taken off the air. Five years was a long time and we kind of limped to the finish line at the end of the fifth season.

AC: And the last shot of season 5 was of the ON AIR sign turning off. Clearly an intentional foreshadowing of what you saw happening.

LM: That's what we thought. For us, it was the end. I don't think we thought much about what would happen after that.

Writer James Downey, who was a featured player in season 5, as George H. W. Bush. (1980)

Writers and Writing

AC: Jim Downey said that the first five years of the show were so strong, it could survive anything. And it survived the first five years of the '80s. Ebersol's last season was really an all-star affair, but it was also really performer-oriented.
LM: It was a New York Yankees thing.

AC: Yes, whereas now it seems very much a writers' show.
LM: It goes back and forth. You happened to be here when that balance hit. But it tips back and forth. When the audience loves the cast, they say the writing is good. When the audience doesn't like the cast, they say that the writing is bad. But it's always the cast. And when it jells and when they've come into their own… A friend of mine who's a critic said to me the other day, "You know what, I always don't like them at the beginning, and there's no point in even reviewing it because you don't like them and you resist them, and then you find that you're crazy about them." I used to say that all babies are ugly, unless they're your baby. And then, when they're like two, three months old, you go, "Oh, cute baby." Newborns are, in their mothers' eyes, the greatest thing ever, but you don't look at them and go, "Wow, what a cute baby." It takes a while. And that's the same thing with the new cast. It's like someone saying, "Come to a dinner party; there will be 12 people you haven't met." Nobody's dying to run to that party.

AC: I may be biased, but I feel the writing has been very strong this season.
LM: But there's almost always great writing. And when people don't like the show, it's almost always the writing you can point to in any of the seasons. The '94–95 season was the end of a cycle, and the '95 season had a lot of new cast members—Will Ferrell, Cheri [Oteri], a lot of new people—and it wasn't treated well. And now it's, you know, beloved. Those transitions are difficult. And now people know that it's going to take some time.

AC: I'd like to talk about the creative side of comedy, and the balancing of the creative side with the network side. [Writer] Anne Beatts said that in the early years you created a protective atmosphere for the writers, sort of a buffer. Do you still feel like you perform that role?
LM: There's no real static for the network. There's budget issues, because the show has become more expensive—we're starting to do more film and studio things—because I'm going to go every week for what I think is the best show to put on—but they've been incredibly supportive, particularly since the Comcast transition. And I think that all of the people at the network, both in programming and in senior management, kind of grew up on the show. So it's been around long enough that nobody's going to suggest that it shouldn't be done the way it's done.

AC: So you don't feel like you ever have to defend your creative decisions?
LM: I do, when the numbers go down, of course. But as long as the ratings are high—and they are—then that's just that. I think we've earned the creative privilege. We've had more good years than bad years.

AC: From what I've gathered it wasn't the same thing in the early years; there was a lot more battling with the network.
LM: Oh yeah, because it was a different generation and you "couldn't do that on television." Cable has so overtaken that. And it's interesting today with Chelsea Handler going to Netflix—so she can say whatever language she wants, like Howard Stern—and we're still in 1975 mode of broadcast and commercials and the manners… and that's part of what we do.

AC: The familiarity of that is comforting, I think, to people of all generations.
LM: Jimmy Fallon is doing the same thing on "The Tonight Show" and that's working well.

AC: Some writers, such as Larry David or Bob Odenkirk, have gone on to greater success after briefly working for SNL. Does some writers' humor just not work for the show?
LM: Absolutely not. You've been to read-through; we're reading 40 pieces, and if the piece kills, nobody's looking to see who wrote it and then make a decision. It either worked or it didn't work. And people do get better. And whether they get better here… Bob had worked with Robert Smigel. I met him in Chicago, I liked him, and I brought him here, and I'm sure at some level, he was frustrated, because he wanted to be a performer more than he wanted to be a writer. It just is… life.

Michaels in his 9th-floor office, which overlooks Studio 8H.

Things People Say

AC: The press is, obviously, hugely polarized on the subject of the show. They either love it or hate it, and there's not much in between. And a lot of previous cast members have been very vocal in a similar way. This show elicits that kind of passion much more than any other show that I know of.
LM: It's a very intense experience, and generally for most people it's their first job. They're still being formed; they don't have the experience of "this isn't normal." A job where you work 14 hours a day 6 days in a row and then get time to do your laundry on Sunday is just a different level of intensity. And people are very committed and very passionate and care deeply.

AC: One of my favorite quotes of yours is that some people are just "collectors of injustices."
LM: Yeah, injustice collectors is a certain category of people—you can spend a lot of time trying to convince them that things are better than they feel...and anger is often at the root of comedy, frustration—all of those things are given a voice through comedy. But it isn't that, it's that, at a certain point, you go, "You either did it, or you didn't do it." And there are a million places now where people can display all their talent, and it's still the same. Some people catch fire and some people don't, and this is a place where the more time you're here, the more you work and you generally get better. Because in that Malcolm Gladwell 10,000 hours way they've been through fire—because there isn't a form of criticism that they haven't been through.

AC: Jay Mohr wrote in his book that there was a lot of vicious competition in the early '90s, and that at the read-throughs, people wouldn't laugh at other people's sketches. Which is absolutely not true now...
LM: I doubt that it was true then. But that's neither here nor there—that's what he felt. I like Jay, we get along, that isn't the issue. I think that year, [with] new management at the network, there was a more aggressive, hands-on approach to all programs, us included. That '86 cast—you know, Dana [Carvey], Phil [Hartman], Jan [Hooks], Nora [Dunn]—I'm leaving people out but I don't mean to—it was a very stable period that got better and better. And then, success happened for Mike [Myers] and Dana on a scale that was impossible to maintain. As big as, if not bigger than, what Chevy had gone through. And then with Farley and Sandler... the amount of things that were pulling them in another direction affected the cohesion of the show. And so, for the new people coming in, that was a hard thing to deal with. It wasn't a "normal" time.

AC: Do you feel the press has been out of sync with popular opinion?
LM: I think that in the beginning, in the '70s, the press was generational. We were dismissed by the "New York Times." John O'Connor, who was the first person to review it, reviewed the second show, which was Paul Simon. He says in the opening paragraphs of the review that he had got caught on the Long Island Rail Road and didn't get to see the show until 12:20. Reviewers were very annoyed that it was live because they were used to getting a cassette. So he saw Paul and Artie sing, he thought it was mostly a musical show, he didn't like some of the comedy, and that was that. And then in April of that season, I think, he reviewed it and was better about it. But I think the sensibility was just so aimed at people who were of a certain age. All of us had come from the audience and we were doing a show that we wanted to do—and we were the baby boom, by and large—and so there were a lot of us.

AC: I was really shocked by the "New York" article from 1995 that gave a negative portrayal of some of the cast and crew.
LM: The guy who wrote that was Chris Smith—you never forget *those* guys. It was just for a better story. Michael O'Donoghue had just died. Michael and Chevy and I had spent a lot of time together, and Cheryl [Hardwick], who was Michael's widow, was working here and had been with us since the beginning. Michael died on a Monday night or Tuesday, and my son, Eddie, was born in the same hospital that Wednesday. On the Friday there was this impromptu memorial at their apartment. We were in the studio until late, and Cheryl asked us to come down. Chevy called me and I asked him to come along. But Michael had been running successfully against Chevy for a few years by that point, and that had turned bitter. So my being there with Chevy was not a popular move, but for me it was an emotionally honest move, because I remembered them together—we shared a house together. So the writer was at that event, and he asked people about that. Everybody was emotional and devastated, and I got a couple letters of apology from people who said things. It didn't matter. What it was, it was an interesting period, because the baby boom was not prepared to accept the sensibility of the next generation. So people like Sandler and Farley were obvious targets. But they weren't playing to the older people,

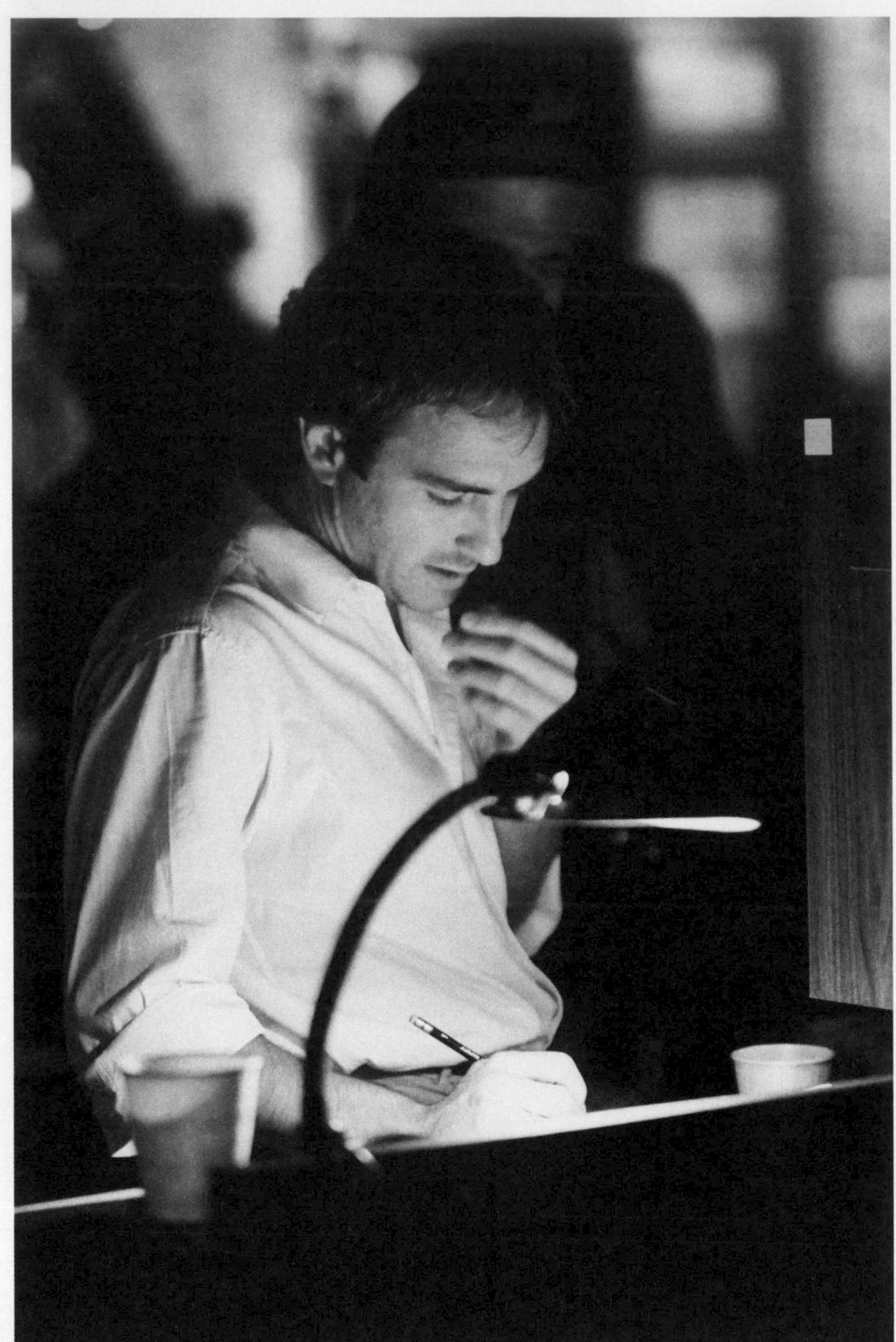

Michaels at his lectern during the live broadcast. (1979)

who were the baby boom; they were playing to a younger audience, to their own generation. So it was a different sensibility, and they weren't particularly political. And then [NBC president] Don Ohlmeyer thought none of them were funny. I said, "I understand why you love Bill Murray, and these guys grew up on Bill Murray, but it's a different thing [now], a different sensibility, and they're not playing to you." The year after, he called me to see if I could help him get a "Happy Gilmore" print for his kid's birthday party. And I said of course I would help. But it was just that thing, of the show being ahead of its time before it settled in.

AC: This year, it seems for the first time that the casting was affected by popular opinion, because you actively looked for a black female cast member.

LM: I was actually just talking to Sasheer [Zamata]; we were catching up before the summer officially begins. She came in during the middle of the season, in a very public way. We had used the same casting process that we'd always used: out in Chicago, LA, we looked at 80 or 90 people, narrowing it down to like 30 or 40, and then bringing them into the studio. And there were several black women we brought in, a couple of whom were very good and we were very hopeful. But the final test is how you do in the studio. And the one thing I don't like doing, because I have to admit I was wrong, is hiring people that I don't think have a real shot at succeeding. I never condescend, or never did, to like, "well, we just have to have this person because of..." But I think that over the years we became perceived as an institution, like a college or government institution, and people looked at us and went, "Hey, wait a minute."

AC: Like you had a social responsibility.

LM: Yes, and more importantly, four of the best men who had ever done the show had just left. With Kristen leaving the year before, I brought in three women, and that had gone really well, so the focus was on men, we weren't really looking for women. Then a journalist wrote a piece that went from a website to an editorial in the "New York Times" in about three weeks. And I thought about it, and realized I understood. Because it's such a large cast, it looked like a glaring omission. And I just dealt with it. And if I hadn't been so preoccupied with adjusting to those guys leaving, Seth [Meyers] leaving in the middle of the season, Jimmy's launch, then maybe I would have been more aware — it's not like me to not be aware of things — and it just happened. I didn't have any problem admitting that we'd made a mistake. So then we held a more intense round of auditions exclusively for black women, and there were four or five people we hadn't seen before, and out of that, Sasheer emerged.

Tradition

AC: You have some interesting habits and rituals, such as always having a basket of popcorn in your office.
LM: The popcorn came from, when I first started, I was smoking. And I was looking for something after I stopped smoking. The basket is just there and people come in for meetings and just reach in.

AC: There's a wonderful sense of tradition, in the same way that, say, Ivy League colleges have odd traditions that are kept alive out of a sense of pride. For example, the way the writers and cast members crowd in here for writers' meetings and sit on the floor—it's like family tradition despite being impractical. Is that a conscious thing?
LM: Oh, 100 percent conscious. I hold that writers' meeting for numerous reasons. In the early days, it was because I wanted to bring the hosts in early, in order for them not to bolt, to sort of say, "Here are some ideas that we're thinking of." And then later, as we became more successful, it became a way to say, "Yeah, I know last week was a huge success, but we're doing a new show now." It was a way to say the week was beginning. And nobody really has much on Monday. It's about saying, "We're back. I know you're not in a good mood, or you didn't get much sleep, and I know you are trying to get your dry cleaning in, or whatever."

AC: But sometimes those ideas get turned into sketches.
LM: No question. Now people save things.

AC: Also, there's an interesting relationship between dress [rehearsal] and air. Dress is a different audience and different feeling, so it's hard to gauge. Some things get a huge laugh at dress and not at air. Or they hold back at dress to save themselves for air, but if they hold back too much, the sketch might get cut because it doesn't work. You have 90 minutes between dress and air to make a ton of changes. I've witnessed this all from the various departments, and it's insane, it's one of the most amazing things I've ever seen. And yet, you're basing all of the decisions on a dress rehearsal with a completely different audience. How do you know how things will be different on air?

Martin Short, Paul McCartney, and Steve Martin with Lorne Michaels in the area under the bleachers where he watches the live show. (2006)

Michaels with Audrey Peart Dickman, the show's original supervising producer. (1976)

Dear Lorne -
I hope your
host pulls through
for you today -
Hope you have
a big success
your friend til
something changes
everything -
Steve

LM: You're giving notes as you're going; you know whether you can turn a piece around with a rewrite. The writers sit with me during the piece. If I say, "Lose that part" or "I think that's not playing," they'll go away, and I'll hear back from them generally before we go up for the meeting, and they'll show me what they rewrote, or show the head writer, who will tell me, and then you go upstairs and you're trying to cut it to time. Plus, the host usually has strong views. And you don't want to cut it so you have four pieces that are the same color, so you're balancing that, and music—a lot of balls in the air. And I ask a lot of people their opinion, and then I make my decision.

AC: Do you ever have to make decisions against your own personal opinion?
LM: Sometimes, if a host is really attached. I will make the case as to why I don't think it's going to work, but...you can't explain that we know the room better than they do. If they're emotionally attached, that's what it is, and you still need to get them through the whole show.

AC: I can't help but ask you this: who does the best Lorne impression?
LM: No idea.

AC: A lot of people, myself included, think [Robert] Smigel does it spot-on.
LM: Mark McKinney did it really well. You know, I'm the boss, and people make fun of the boss.

AC: They do it in a loving way.
LM: You can only hope.

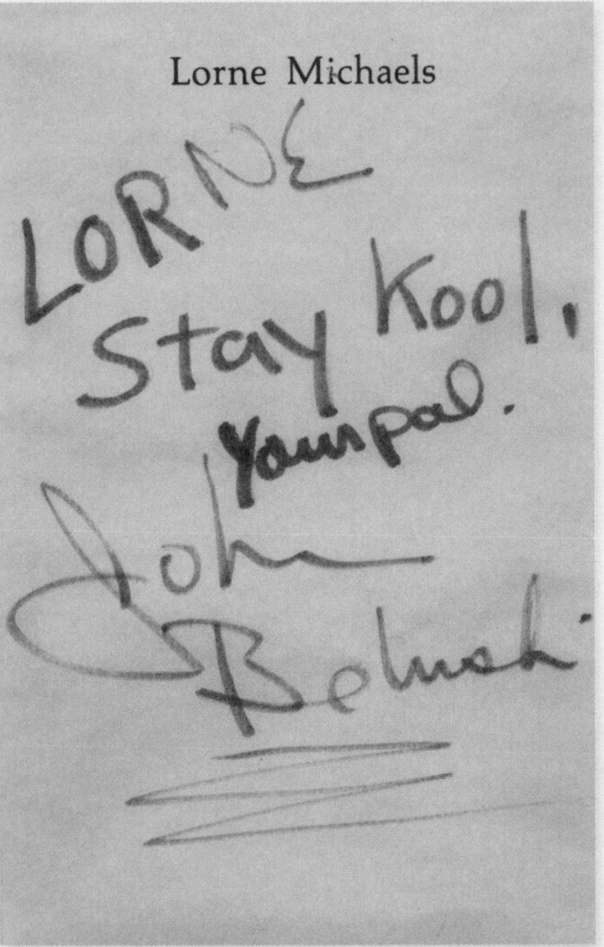

Lorne Michaels

LORNE
Stay kool,
Yourpal.
John
Belushi

Personal notes from Steve Martin (**TOP**) and John Belushi (**BOTTOM**).

As season 5 neared its end, with the cast and writers feeling burned out, Lorne Michaels felt the show needed to take a break and reinvent itself. When NBC insisted on rushing into season 6, Michaels announced he would not stay on and risk failure. He is seen here in Studio 8H on the night of the final episode of his original tenure. (1980)

Seasons

NB: Every episode is represented in the bumper galleries; however, for some episodes (particularly in the early seasons), the musical-guest bumper is missing because none was aired.

An illustrated encyclopedia of SNL. Cast head shots, bumper photography, episode lists, season highlights, and more.

The Players

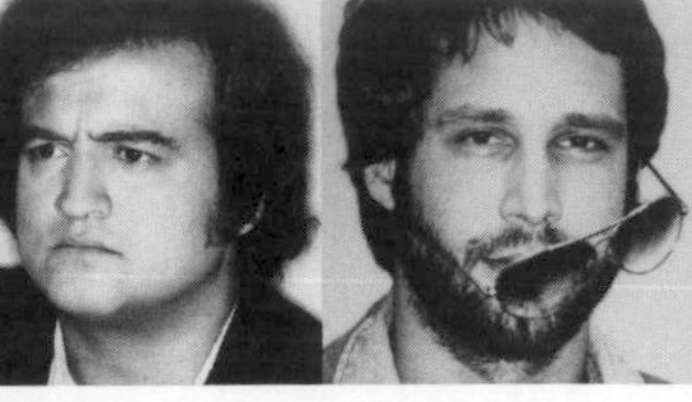

DAN AYKROYD
1-4 / 1975-79

JOHN BELUSHI
1-4 / 1975-79

CHEVY CHASE
1-2 / 1975-76

JANE CURTIN
1-5 / 1975-80

GARRETT MORRIS
1-5 / 1975-80

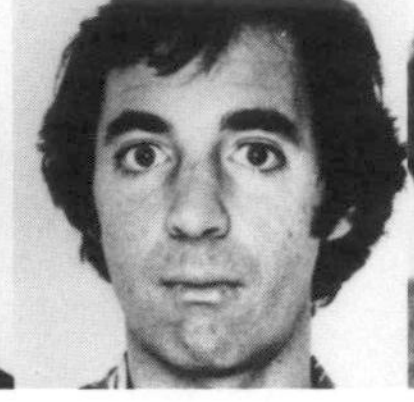

PAUL SHAFFER
5 / 1979-80

HARRY SHEARER
5,10 / 1979-80, 1984-85

ALAN ZWEIBEL
5 / 1979-80

DENNY DILLON
6 / 1980-81

ROBIN DUKE
6-9 / 1981-84

GILBERT GOTTFRIED
6 / 1980-81

TIM KAZURINSKY
6-9 / 1981-84

GAIL MATTHIUS
6 / 1980-81

EDDIE MURPHY
6-9 / 1980-84

JOE PISCOPO
6-9 / 1980-84

CHRISTOPHER GUEST
10 / 1984-85

RICH HALL
10 / 1984-85

MARTIN SHORT
10 / 1984-85

PAMELA STEPHENSON
10 / 1984-85

A. WHITNEY BROWN
11-16 / 1985-91

JOAN CUSACK
11 / 1985-86

ROBERT DOWNEY JR.
11 / 1985-86

NORA DUNN
11-15 / 1985-90

ANTHONY MICHAEL HALL
11 / 1985-86

JON LOVITZ
11 / 1985-90

MIKE MYERS
14-20 / 1989-95

BEN STILLER
14 / 1989

CHRIS FARLEY
16-20 / 1990-95

TIM MEADOWS
16-25 / 1991-2000

CHRIS ROCK
16-18 / 1990-93

ADAM SANDLER
16-20 / 1991-95

ROB SCHNEIDER
16-19 / 1990-94

DAVID SPADE
16-21 / 1990-96

JULIA SWEENEY
16-19 / 1990-94

BETH CAHILL
17 / 1991-92

JANEANE GAROFALO
20 / 1994-95

LAURA KIGHTLINGER
20 / 1994-95

MARK McKINNEY
20-22 / 1995-97

MOLLY SHANNON
20-26 / 1995-2001

JIM BREUER
21-23 / 1995-98

WILL FERRELL
21-27 / 1995-2002

DARRELL HAMMOND
21-34 / 1995-2001

CHRIS KATTAN
21-28 / 1996-2003

DAVID KOECHNER
21 / 1995-96

COLIN QUINN
21-25 / 1995-2000

MAYA RUDOLPH
25-33 / 2000-07

JERRY MINOR
26 / 2000-01

DEAN EDWARDS
27-28 / 2001-03

SETH MEYERS
27-39 / 2001-14

AMY POEHLER
27-34 / 2001-08

JEFF RICHARDS
27-29 / 2001-04

FRED ARMISEN
28-38 / 2002-13

WILL FORTE
28-35 / 2002-10

FINESSE MITCHELL
29-31 / 2003-06

KENAN THOMPSON
29- / 2003-

NASIM PEDRAD
35-39 / 2009-14

JENNY SLATE
35 / 2009-10

PAUL BRITTAIN
36-37 / 2010-12

TARAN KILLAM
36- / 2010-

JAY PHAROAH
36- / 2010-

KATE McKINNON
37- / 2012-

AIDY BRYANT
38- / 2012-

TIM ROBINSON
38 / 2012-13

CECILY STRONG
38- / 2012-

BECK BENNETT
39- / 2013-

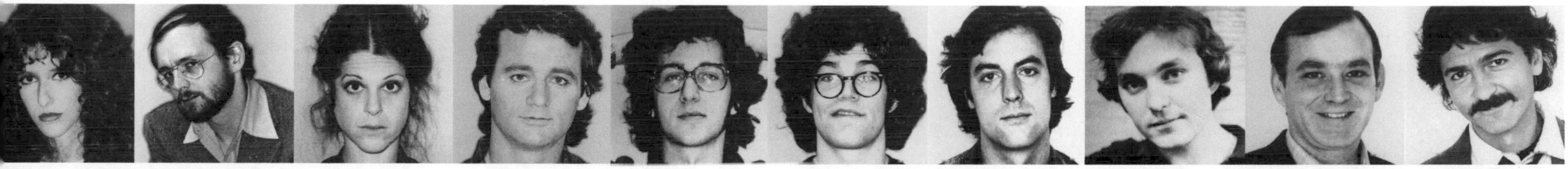

AINE NEWMAN
/ 1975-80

MICHAEL O'DONOGHUE
1 / 1975

GILDA RADNER
1-5 / 1975-80

BILL MURRAY
2-5 / 1977-80

TOM DAVIS
3-5 / 1977-80

AL FRANKEN
3-5, 11, 13-20 / 1977-80, 1985-86, 1988-95

PETER AYKROYD
5 / 1979-80

JAMES DOWNEY
5 / 1979-80

BRIAN E. DOYLE-MURRAY
5,7 / 1979-82

DON NOVELLO
5,11 / 1979-80, 1985-86

RISLEY
1980-81

CHARLES ROCKET
6 / 1980-81

CHRISTINE EBERSOLE
7 / 1981-82

MARY GROSS
7-10 / 1981-85

TONY ROSATO
7 / 1981-82

BRAD HALL
8-9 / 1982-84

GARY KROEGER
8-10 / 1982-85

JULIA LOUIS-DREYFUS
9-10 / 1982-85

JIM BELUSHI
9-10 / 1983-85

BILLY CRYSTAL
10 / 1984-85

NIS MILLER
16 / 1985-91

RANDY QUAID
11 / 1985-86

TERRY SWEENEY
11 / 1985-86

DANITRA VANCE
11 / 1985-86

DAMON WAYANS
11 / 1985-86

DANA CARVEY
12-18 / 1986-93

PHIL HARTMAN
12-19 / 1986-94

JAN HOOKS
12-16 / 1986-91

VICTORIA JACKSON
12-17 / 1986-92

KEVIN NEALON
12-20 / 1986-95

ANIE HUTSELL
19 / 1991-94

ELLEN CLEGHORNE
17-20 / 1992-95

SIOBHAN FALLON
17 / 1991-92

ROBERT SMIGEL
17-18 / 1991-93

NORM MACDONALD
19-23 / 1993-98

MICHAEL McKEAN
19-20 / 1994-95

JAY MOHR
19-20 / 1993-95

SARAH SILVERMAN
19 / 1993-94

MORWENNA BANKS
20 / 1995

CHRIS ELLIOTT
20 / 1994-95

CY WALLS
/ 1995-96

FRED WOLF
21 / 1995-96

TINA FEY
22-31 / 1997-2006

TRACY MORGAN
22-28 / 1996-2003

ANA GASTEYER
22-27 / 1996-2002

CHERI OTERI
22-25 / 1995-2000

JIMMY FALLON
24-29 / 1998-2004

CHRIS PARNELL
24-31 / 1998-2006

HORATIO SANZ
24-31 / 1998-2006

RACHEL DRATCH
25-31 / 1999-2006

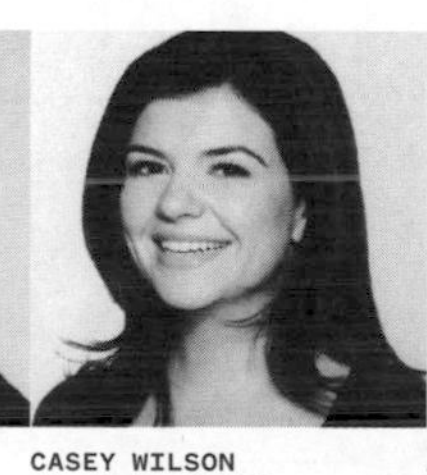

ON SUDEIKIS
38 / 2005-13

ROB RIGGLE
30 / 2004-05

BILL HADER
31-38 / 2005-13

ANDY SAMBERG
31-37 / 2005-12

KRISTEN WIIG
31-37 / 2005-12

CASEY WILSON
33-34 / 2008-09

ABBY ELLIOTT
34-37 / 2008-12

BOBBY MOYNIHAN
34- / 2008-

MICHAELA WATKINS
34 / 2008-09

VANESSA BAYER
35- / 2010-

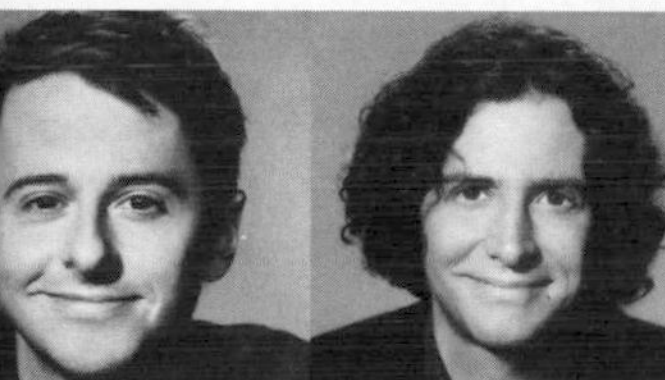

N MILHISER
/ 2013-14

KYLE MOONEY
39- / 2013-

MIKE O'BRIEN
39 / 2013-14

NOËL WELLS
39 / 2013-14

BROOKS WHEELAN
39 / 2013-14

SASHEER ZAMATA
39- / 2014-

COLIN JOST
39- / 2014-

Announcer

DON PARDO
1-6, 8-39 / 1975-2014

NBC's SATURDAY NIGHT

NBC's
SATURDAY
NIGHT

SATURDAY NIGHT
NBC's SATURDAY NIGHT
SATURDAY NIGHT
Cocktail LOUNGE
NBC's SATURDAY NIGHT
NBC's SATURDAY NIGHT
NBC's SATURDAY NIGHT
SATURDAY NIGHT
NBC's SATURDAY NIGHT

NBC's SATURDAY NIGHT
NBC's SATURDAY NIGHT
SATURDAY NIGHT

SATURDAY NIGHT

SEASON 01 / 1975-76

CAST

Dan Aykroyd
John Belushi
Chevy Chase
Jane Curtin
Garrett Morris
Laraine Newman
Gilda Radner

Featuring:
George Coe
Michael O'Donoghue

Weekend Update:
Chevy Chase

CREW

Executive Producer:
Lorne Michaels

Director: Dave Wilson

Writers: Anne Beatts, Chevy Chase, Tom Davis, Al Franken, Lorne Michaels, Rosie Shuster, Marilyn Suzanne Miller, Paul Mooney, Michael O'Donoghue, Herb Sargent, Tom Schiller, Alan Zweibel

Writing Supervisors:
Chevy Chase, Michael O'Donoghue, Rosie Shuster

Short Films:
Albert Brooks, Gary Weis

Supervising Producer:
Audrey Peart Dickman

Weekend Update Written and Produced by: Herb Sargent

Production Designer:
Eugene Lee

Lighting Designer:
Phil Hymes

Musical Director:
Howard Shore

Costume Designer: Franne Lee

Hair: Ted Long, Karen Specht

Makeup: Frances Kolar

Photographer: Edie Baskin

EPISODE LIST

EPISODE KEY:
H - Host
MG - Musical Guest
SG/C - Special Guests/Cameos

EPISODE 01: 10/11/75
H: George Carlin
MG: Janis Ian, Billy Preston
SG/C: Valri Bromfield, Wendell Craig, Clifford Einstein, Andy Kaufman, Jim Henson's Muppets, Paul Simon

EPISODE 02: 10/18/75
H: Paul Simon
MG: Paul Simon, Randy Newman, Phoebe Snow
SG/C: Marv Albert, Bill Bradley, Albert Brooks, Jessy Dixon, Clifford Einstein, Singers, Art Garfunkel, Connie Hawkins, Jim Henson's Muppets, Jerry Rubin, David Sanborn

EPISODE 03: 10/25/75
H: Rob Reiner
MG: John Belushi as Joe Cocker
SG/C: Denny Dillon, Mark Hampton, Jim Henson's Muppets, Andy Kaufman, The Lockers, Penny Marshall

EPISODE 04: 11/08/75
H: Candice Bergen
MG: Esther Phillips
SG/C: Rene Auberjonois, Albert Brooks, Andrew Duncan, Jim Henson's Muppets, Andy Kaufman, Kay Lenz

EPISODE 05: 11/15/75
H/MG: Robert Klein
MG: ABBA, Loudon Wainwright III
SG/C: Andrew Duncan, Jim Henson's Muppets

EPISODE 06: 11/22/75
H: Lily Tomlin
MG: Lily Tomlin, Howard Shore and his All Nurse Band
SG/C: Clifford Einstein, Jim Henson's Muppets

EPISODE 07: 12/13/75
H: Richard Pryor
MG: Gil Scott-Heron
SG/C: Albert Brooks, Annazette Chase, Kathrine McKee, Jim Henson's Muppets, Shelley Pryor, Thalmus Rasulala

EPISODE 08: 12/20/75
H: Candice Bergen
MG: Martha Reeves, The Stylistics
SG/C: Margaret Kuhn, Jim Henson's Muppets

EPISODE 09: 01/10/76
H: Elliott Gould
MG: Anne Murray
SG/C: Albert Brooks, James L. Brooks, Clifford Einstein, Jim Henson's Muppets, Paula Kahn, Julie Payne

EPISODE 10: 01/17/76
H: Buck Henry
MG: Bill Withers, Toni Basil
SG/C: Jim Henson's Muppets

EPISODE 11: 01/24/76
H: Peter Cook & Dudley Moore
MG: Neil Sedaka
SG/C: Jim Henson's Muppets, Abbie Hoffman

EPISODE 12: 01/31/76
H: Dick Cavett
MG: Jimmy Cliff
SG/C: Marshall Efron, Al Alen Petersen

EPISODE 13: 02/14/76
H: Peter Boyle
MG: Al Jarreau
SG/C: Andrew Duncan, The Shapiro Sisters

EPISODE 14: 02/21/76
H/MG: Desi Arnaz
SG/C: Desi Arnaz Jr., Taylor Mead

EPISODE 15: 02/28/76
H: Jill Clayburgh
MG: Leon Redbone
SG/C: Jonathan Dorn, Andy Kaufman, The Singing Idlers, Bill Wegman

EPISODE 16: 03/13/76
H: Anthony Perkins
MG: Betty Carter
SG/C: Taylor Mead, Jim Henson's Muppets, George Plimpton, Chuck Scarborough, Bill Wegman

EPISODE 17: 04/17/76
H: Ron Nessen
MG: Patti Smith Group
SG/C: Billy Crystal, President Gerald Ford, Jerry Rubin

EPISODE 18: 04/24/76
H: Raquel Welch
MG: Phoebe Snow, John Sebastian
SG/C: Jim Henson's Muppets

EPISODE 19: 05/08/76
H: Madeline Kahn
MG: Carly Simon
SG/C: Jim Henson's Muppets

EPISODE 20: 05/15/76
H: Dyan Cannon
MG: Leon & Mary Russell
SG/C: Buck Henry

EPISODE 21: 05/22/76
H: Buck Henry
MG: Gordon Lightfoot

EPISODE 22: 05/29/76
H: Elliott Gould
MG: Harlan Collins, Leon Redbone, Joyce Everson
SG/C: Wendell Craig, Jonathan Dorn, Charlie Lowe

EPISODE 23: 07/24/76
H: Louise Lasser
MG: The Preservation Hall Jazz Band
SG/C: Michael Sarrazin

EPISODE 24: 07/31/76
H: Kris Kristofferson
MG: Kris Kristofferson & Rita Coolidge

SEASON HIGHLIGHTS

Baba Wawa (Radner), Beatles Offer (Michaels), Bass-O-Matic (Aykroyd), Beethoven (Belushi), The Blues Brothers (Aykroyd/Belushi), The Courtroom (Chase/Curtin, et al.), Emily Litella (Radner), Gerald Ford (Chase), Homeward Bound (Weis), The Killer Bees (Aykroyd/Belushi, et al.), Land Shark (Chase), Mel's Char Palace (Aykroyd/Radner), Mighty Mouse (Kaufman), Mr. Bill (Dan Aykroyd), Nixon's Final Days (Aykroyd), Samurai Futaba (Belushi), Shimmer (Dan Aykroyd/Radner), Supreme Court Spot Check (Chase/Curtin, et al.), Word Association (Pryor/Chase)

BUMPER KEY (Pg. 324-325)

(Pg. 324-325)

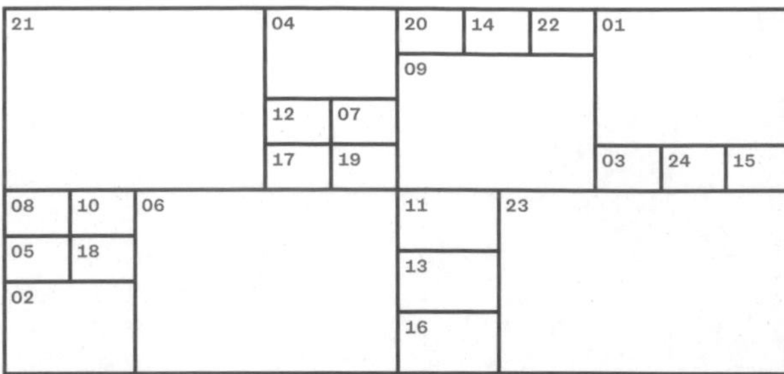

a.

b.

c.

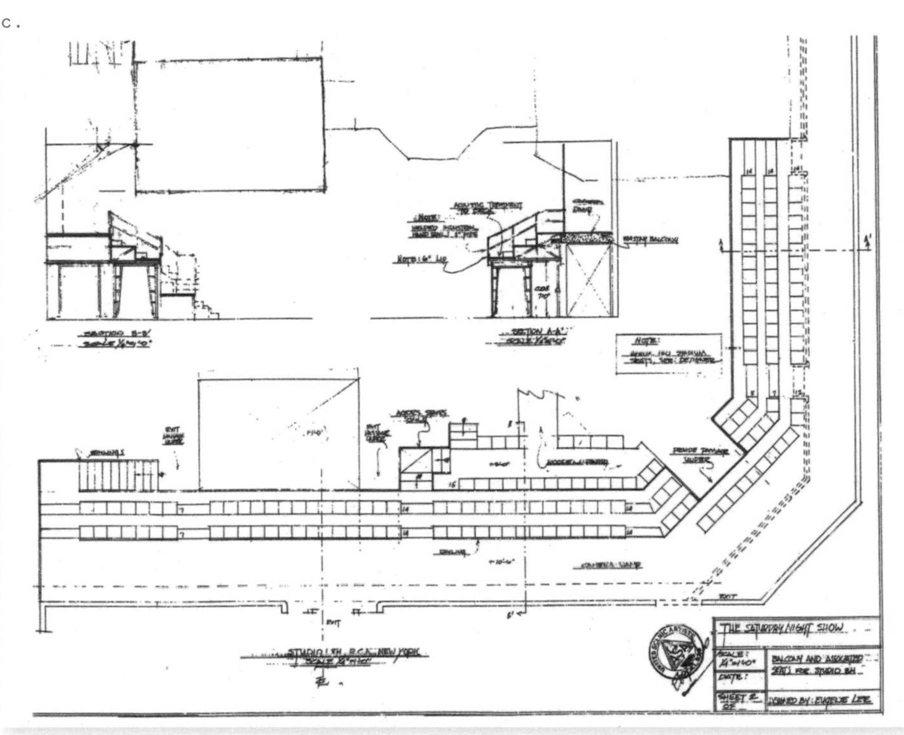

d.

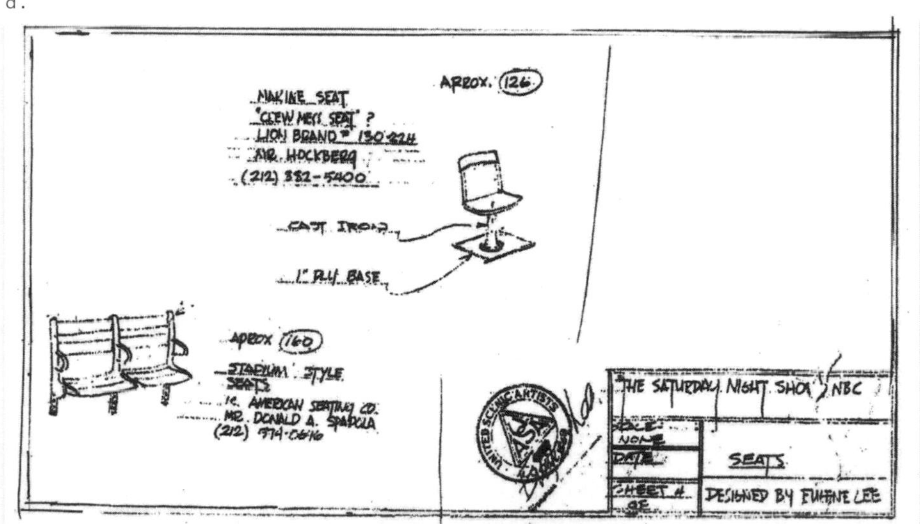

e.

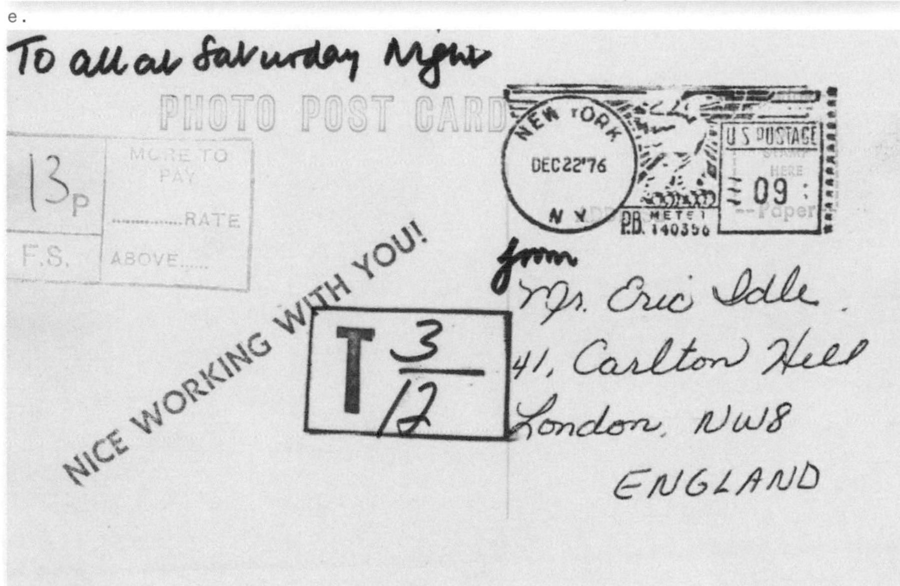

f.

a. The seven members of the season 1 cast.
b. Promotional flyer for the show's premiere.
c. Plan of the raised bleacher seating for Studio 8H.
d. Sketches of the bleachers and studio-floor seats.
e. Postcard from Eric Idle.
f. Writer Tom Schiller backstage with producer Dick Ebersol.

SEASON 02 /
1976–77

SATURDAY
NIGHT
SATURDAY
NIGHT
LIVE
SEASONS GREETINGS
FROM
SATURDAY NIGHT
SATURDAY
NIGHT
SATURDAY
NIGHT
SATURDAY
NIGHT
SATURDAY
NIGHT
SATURDAY
NIGHT
SATURDAY
NIGHT
SATURDAY
NIGHT
UCLA
SATURDAY
NIGHT

SATURDAY
NIGHT
LIVE
SATURDAY
NIGHT
LIVE
FORTY NINER
Yes! WE HAVE THE MOST BEAUTIFUL GIRLS IN TOWN
TOPLESS
DANCING NIGHTLY
Continuous Entertainment
SATURDAY
NIGHT
LIVE
SATURDAY
NIGHT
SATURDAY NIGHT
SATURDAY
NIGHT
SATURDAY
NIGHT
SATURDAY
NIGHT
LIVE
SATURDAY
NIGHT
SATURDAY
NIGHT
SATURDAY
NIGHT
LIVE
SATURDAY
NIGHT

SEASON 02 / 1976-77

CAST

Dan Aykroyd
John Belushi
Chevy Chase
Jane Curtin
Garrett Morris
Bill Murray
Laraine Newman
Gilda Radner

Weekend Update:
Chevy Chase
Jane Curtin

CREW

Executive Producer:
Lorne Michaels

Director: Dave Wilson

Writers: Dan Aykroyd, Anne Beatts, John Belushi, Chevy Chase, Tom Davis, James Downey, Al Franken, Bruce McCall, Lorne Michaels, Marilyn Suzanne Miller, Bill Murray, Michael O'Donoghue, Herb Sargent, Tom Schiller, Rosie Shuster, Alan Zweibel

Short Films: Gary Weis

Supervising Producer:
Audrey Peart Dickman

Weekend Update Written and Produced by: Herb Sargent

Production Designer:
Eugene Lee

Lighting Designers:
Phil Hymes, Howard Strawbridge

Musical Director:
Howard Shore

Costume Designer: Franne Lee

Hair: Alan Demkowicz, Karen Specht

Makeup: Frances Kolar

Photographer: Edie Baskin

EPISODE LIST

EPISODE KEY:
H - Host
MG - Musical Guest
SG/C - Special Guests/Cameos

EPISODE 01: 09/18/76
H: Lily Tomlin
MG: James Taylor
SG/C: Taylor Mead, Jim Henson's Muppets, David Sanborn, The Section

EPISODE 02: 09/25/76
H: Norman Lear
MG: Boz Scaggs
SG/C: Bea Arthur, Caroll O'Connor, Sherman Helmsley, Eric Idle, Kate Lear, Bernadette Peters, Isabel Sanford, Jean Stapleton, Nancy Walker

EPISODE 03: 10/02/76
H: Eric Idle
MG: Joe Cocker, Stuff
SG/C: Neil Innes, Gary Trudeau

EPISODE 04: 10/16/76
H: Karen Black
MG: John Prine
SG/C: George Schultz

EPISODE 05: 10/23/76
H: Steve Martin
MG: Kinky Friedman
SG/C: Bill Wegman

EPISODE 06: 10/30/76
H: Buck Henry
MG: The Band

EPISODE 07: 11/13/76
H: Dick Cavett
MG: Ry Cooder
SG/C: Chevy Chase, Flaco Jiménez

EPISODE 08: 11/20/76
H/MG: Paul Simon
SG/C: Chevy Chase, Shelley Duvall, George Harrison, Eric Idle, Neil Innes, Jim Keltner, Tom Scott, Ron Wood

EPISODE 09: 11/27/76
H: Jodie Foster
MG: Brian Wilson
SG/C: Chevy Chase

EPISODE 10: 12/11/76
H: Candice Bergen
MG: Frank Zappa
SG/C: Diana Nyad

EPISODE 11: 01/15/77
H: Ralph Nader
MG: George Benson
SG/C: Andrew Duncan, Andy Kaufman

EPISODE 12: 01/22/77
H: Ruth Gordon
MG: Chuck Berry
SG/C: Bob Dryden, Ricky Jay

EPISODE 13: 01/29/77
H: Fran Tarkenton
MG: Donny Harper & The Voice of Tomorrow, Leo Sayer

SNL LIVE FROM MARDI GRAS: 02/20/77
SG: Buck Henry, Eric Idle, Mayor Moon Landrieu, Penny Marshall, The New Leviathan Orchestra, Randy Newman, Cindy Williams, Henry Winkler

EPISODE 14: 02/26/77
H: Steve Martin
MG: The Kinks
SG/C: Buster Holmes, Lily Tomlin

EPISODE 15: 03/12/77
H: Sissy Spacek
MG: Richard Baskin

EPISODE 16: 03/19/77
H: Broderick Crawford
MG: Dr. John, Paul Butterfield, Levon Helm & The Meters
SG/C: Linda Ronstadt

EPISODE 17: 03/26/77
H: Jack Burns
MG: Santana

EPISODE 18: 04/09/77
H: Julian Bond
MG: Tom Waits, Brick
SG/C: Patti Smith

EPISODE 19: 04/16/77
H: Elliott Gould
MG: Roslyn Kind, The McGarrigle Sisters
SG/C: Chevy Chase

EPISODE 20: 04/23/77
H: Eric Idle
MG: Alan Price, Neil Innes
SG/C: Jeannette Charles

EPISODE 21: 05/14/77
H: Shelley Duvall
MG: Joan Armatrading
SG/C: Chevy Chase

EPISODE 22: 05/21/77
H: Buck Henry
MG: Jennifer Warnes, Kenny Vance
SG/C: Bella Abzug, Chevy Chase

SEASON HIGHLIGHTS

Ask President Carter (Aykroyd), Baba Wawa (Radner), Bill Murray's Apology (Murray), The Coneheads (Aykroyd/Curtin/Newman), Consumer Probe (Aykroyd), Emily Litella (Radner), The Killer Bees (Aykroyd/Belushi, et al.), Mr. Mike (O'Donoghue), Nick the Lounge Singer (Murray), Samurai Futaba (Belushi)

BUMPER KEY (Pg. 330-331)

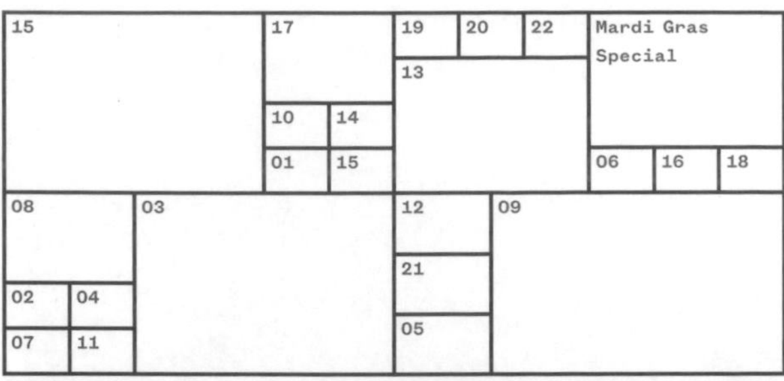

a.

b.

a. George Harrison and Paul Simon performing "Here Comes the Sun" and "Homeward Bound."
b. One of the show's early merchandising products was this coloring book.

c.

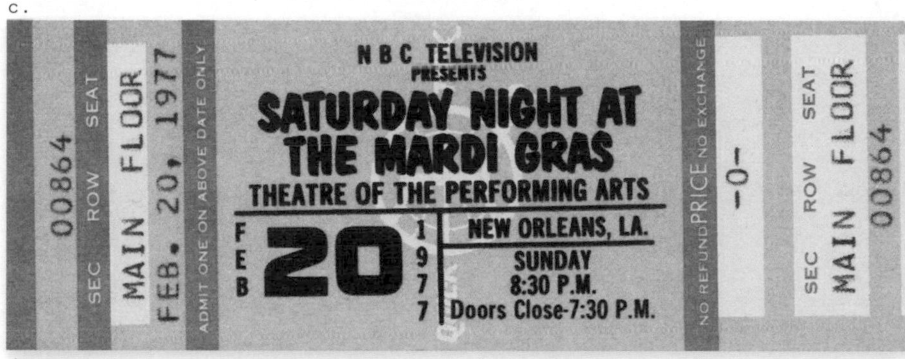

d.

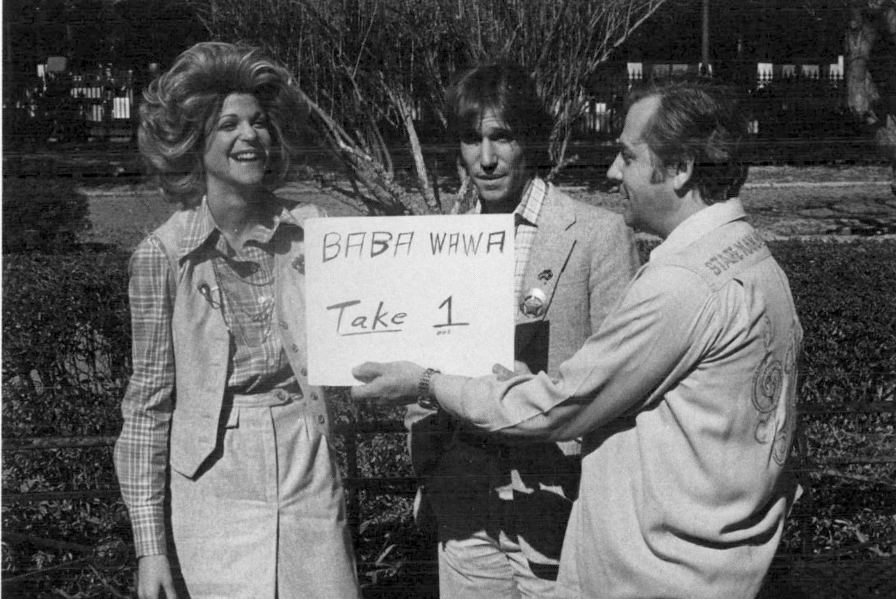

e.

f.

g.

h.

i.

The live-from-Mardi Gras primetime show didn't end up going quite as planned—not least of the problems was the fact that the parade got delayed and never made it to where Jane Curtin and Buck Henry were waiting for it (prompting Curtin to say, "Mardi Gras" is just the French word meaning 'no parade')."
c. A ticket for one of the show's venues. **d.** As Baba Wawa, Gilda Radner interviews "King of Bacchus" Henry Winkler. **e.** Production designer Eugene Lee (on phone) and costume designer Franne Lee on location. **f.** Lorne Michaels on location in New Orleans. **g.** Laraine Newman (rear) and Gilda Radner hitch rides with members of the Killer Bees Motorcycle Club. **h.** Franne Lee, writer Anne Beatts, and Eugene Lee. **i.** New Orleans native Garrett Morris as Fats Domino.

SATURDAY
NIGHT
LIVE

Saturday
Night
Live
Saturday
Night
Live
SATURDAY
NIGHT
LIVE
Saturday
Night
Live
Saturday
Night
Live

Saturday Night Live
Saturday Night Live
Saturday Night Live
SATURDAY NIGHT LIVE
Saturday Night Live
Saturday Night Live
Saturday Night Live
SATURDAY NIGHT LIVE
Saturday Night Live
Saturday Night Live
Saturday Night Live
SATURDAY NIGHT LIVE

SEASON 03 / 1977-78

CAST

Dan Aykroyd
John Belushi
Jane Curtin
Garrett Morris
Bill Murray
Laraine Newman
Gilda Radner

Weekend Update:
Dan Aykroyd
Jane Curtin

CREW

Executive Producer: Lorne Michaels

Director: Dave Wilson

Writers: Dan Aykroyd, Anne Beatts, John Belushi, Tom Davis, James Downey, Al Franken, Neil Levy, Lorne Michaels, Marilyn Suzanne Miller, Brian Doyle-Murray, Don Novello, Michael O'Donoghue, Herb Sargent, Tom Schiller, Rosie Shuster, Alan Zweibel

Production Designer: Eugene Lee

Lighting Designer: Phil Hymes

Musical Director: Howard Shore

Costume Designer: Franne Lee

Hair: Anthony Cortino, Alan Demkowicz

Makeup: Frances Kolar

Photographer: Edie Baskin

EPISODE LIST

EPISODE KEY:
H - Host
MG - Musical Guest
SG/C - Special Guests/Cameos

EPISODE 01: 09/24/77
H: Steve Martin
MG: Jackson Browne, The Section
SG/C: David Lindley

EPISODE 02: 10/08/77
H: Madeline Kahn
MG: Taj Mahal
SG/C: Barry Humphries

EPISODE 03: 10/15/77
H: Hugh Hefner
MG: Libby Titus
SG/C: Andy Kaufman

EPISODE 04: 10/29/77
H: Charles Grodin
MG: The Persuasions, Paul Simon
SG/C: Art Garfunkel, Toots Thielemans

EPISODE 05: 11/12/77
H/ MG: Ray Charles
SG/C: Franklyn Ajaye, Marcus Belgrave, Leroy Cooper, Hank Crawford, Phillip Guilbeau, Buck Henry, David "Fathead" Newman, The Raelettes

EPISODE 06: 11/19/77
H: Buck Henry
MG: Leon Redbone
SG/C: Deb Blair, Connie Crawford, Richard Kneip, David Lewis, The Original Sloth Band, Miskel Spillman

EPISODE 07: 12/10/77
H: Mary Kay Place
MG: Willie Nelson, Mary Kay Place
SG/C: Andy Kaufman

EPISODE 08: 12/17/77
H: Miskel Spillman
MG: Elvis Costello
SG/C: Joe Franken I, Phoebe Franken, Buck Henry

EPISODE 09: 01/21/78
H: Steve Martin
MG: Randy Newman & the Dirt Band
SG/C: Andrew Gold

EPISODE 10: 01/28/78
H: Robert Klein
MG: Bonnie Raitt

EPISODE 11: 02/18/78
H: Chevy Chase
MG: Billy Joel
SG/C: Valri Bromfield

EPISODE 12: 02/25/78
H: O.J. Simpson
MG: Ashford & Simpson

EPISODE 13: 03/11/78
H: Art Garfunkel
MG: Stephen Bishop, Art Garfunkel
SG/C: Andy Kaufman

EPISODE 14: 03/18/78
H: Jill Clayburgh
MG: Eddie Money

EPISODE 15: 03/25/78
H: Christopher Lee
MG: Meat Loaf
SG/C: Cheetah Chrome, Rick Overton, Stacy Keach

EPISODE 16: 04/08/78
H: Michael Palin
MG: Eugene Record

EPISODE 17: 04/15/78
H: Michael Sarrazin
MG: Gravity, Keith Jarrett

EPISODE 18: 04/22/78
H: Steve Martin
MG: The Blues Brothers

EPISODE 19: 05/13/78
H: Richard Dreyfuss
MG: Jimmy Buffett, Gary Tigerman

EPISODE 20: 05/20/78
H: Buck Henry
MG: Sun Ra

SEASON HIGHLIGHTS

Baba Wawa (Radner), The Blues Brothers (Aykroyd/Belushi), The Coneheads (Aykroyd/Curtin/Newman), Consumer Probe (Aykroyd/Curtin), Don't Look Back in Anger (Belushi), Father Guido Sarducci (Novello), The Festrunk Brothers (Aykroyd/Martin), The Franken and Davis Show (Davis/Franken), Hey You (Radner), Judy Miller (Radner), The Killer Bees (Aykroyd/Belushi, et al.), King Tut (Martin), La Dolce Gilda (Radner), Little Chocolate Donuts (Belushi), Mr. Mike (O'Donoghue), The Nerds (Radner), Olympia Cafe (Aykroyd/Belushi/Murray, et al.), Point/Counterpoint (Aykroyd/Curtin), Roseanne Roseannadanna (Radner), Royale Deluxe II (Aykroyd), Samurai Futaba (Belushi), Swan Lake (Weis/voice by Toni Basil)

BUMPER KEY (Pg. 336-337)

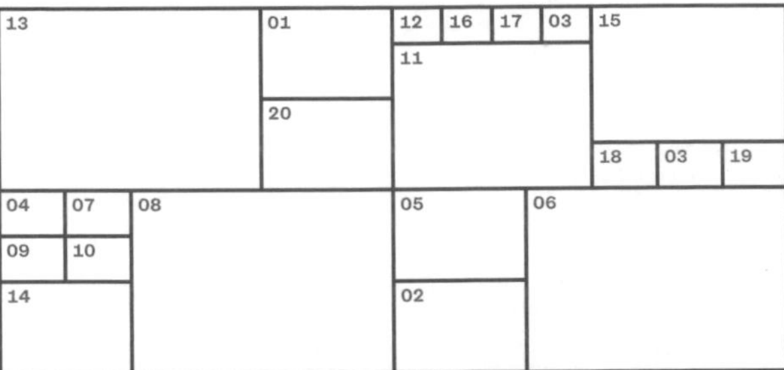

a.

b.

c.

d.

a. The Festrunk Brothers (Dan Aykroyd and Steve Martin) debuted in season 3. **b.** Michael Palin performed his monologue as Sid Biggs and entertained the audience by stuffing seafood salad and live cats down his pants. **c-d.** Sketch of John Belushi's Kuldroth costume for and photo of the "Return of the Coneheads" sketch.

SEASON 04 / 1978-79

CAST

Dan Aykroyd
John Belushi
Jane Curtin
Garrett Morris
Bill Murray
Laraine Newman
Gilda Radner

Featuring:
Tom Davis
Al Franken

Weekend Update:
Jane Curtin
Bill Murray

CREW

Executive Producer:
Lorne Michaels

Director: Dave Wilson

Writers: Dan Aykroyd, Anne Beatts, Tom Davis, James Downey, Brian Doyle-Murray, Al Franken, Brian McConnachie, Lorne Michaels, Don Novello, Herb Sargent, Tom Schiller, Rosie Shuster, Walter Williams, Alan Zweibel

Short Films: Tom Schiller

Production Designers:
Eugene Lee, Franne Lee

Lighting Designers:
Phil Hymes, Gene Martin

Musical Director:
Howard Shore

Costume Designer:
Karen Roston

Hair: Werner Sherer

Makeup: Frances Kolar

Photographer: Edie Baskin

EPISODE LIST

EPISODE KEY:
H - Host
MG - Musical Guest
SG/C - Special Guests/Cameos

EPISODE 01: 10/07/78
H/MG: The Rolling Stones
SG/C: Desi Arnaz Jr., Carrie Fisher, Steven Keats, Ed Koch

EPISODE 02: 10/14/78
H: Fred Willard
MG: Devo

EPISODE 03: 10/21/78
H/MG: Frank Zappa

EPISODE 04: 11/04/78
H: Steve Martin
MG: Van Morrison

EPISODE 05: 11/11/78
H: Buck Henry
MG: The Grateful Dead
CP: Rovco Chinch Ranch

EPISODE 06: 11/18/78
H: Carrie Fisher
MG: The Blues Brothers
SG/C: Tom Scott

EPISODE 07: 12/02/78
H: Walter Matthau
SG/C: Charlie Matthau

EPISODE 08: 12/09/78
H: Eric Idle
MG: Kate Bush

EPISODE 09: 12/16/78
H: Elliott Gould
MG: Peter Tosh
SG/C: Bob & Ray, Mick Jagger

EPISODE 10: 01/27/79
H: Michael Palin
MG: The Doobie Brothers

EPISODE 11: 02/10/79
H: Cicely Tyson
MG: Talking Heads

EPISODE 12: 02/17/79
H: Rick Nelson
MG: Rick Nelson, Judy Collins

EPISODE 13: 02/24/79
H: Kate Jackson
MG: Delbert McClinton
SG/C: Andy Kaufman

EPISODE 14: 03/10/79
H: Gary Busey
MG: Gary Busey, Eubie Blake, Gregory Hines

EPISODE 15: 03/17/79
H: Margot Kidder
MG: The Chieftains

EPISODE 16: 04/07/79
H: Richard Benjamin
MG: Rickie Lee Jones
SG/C: Nelson Briles, Rodney Dangerfield, Marvin Goldhar, Steve Henderson, Ed Kranepool

EPISODE 17: 04/14/79
H: Milton Berle
MG: Ornette Coleman, Prime Time
SG/C: Buddy Freed, Craig Nettles

EPISODE 18: 05/12/79
H: Michael Palin
MG: James Taylor
SG/C: Don Grolnick, The Section

EPISODE 19: 05/19/79
H: Maureen Stapleton
MG: Linda Ronstadt, Phoebe Snow
SG/C: Robert Fripp

EPISODE 20: 05/26/79
H: Buck Henry
MG: Bette Midler
SG/C: Luther Vandross

SEASON HIGHLIGHTS

Aviva Film: Bird Of All Seasons 4 (Murray), Baba Wawa (Radner), The Blues Brothers (Aykroyd/John Belushi), Candy Slice (Radner), The Coneheads (Aykroyd/Curtin/Newman), Consumer Probe (Aykroyd/Curtin), Emily Litella (Radner), Father Guido Sarducci (Novello), The Festrunk Brothers (Aykroyd/Steve Martin), The Killer Bees (Aykroyd/Belushi, et al.), The Nerds (Radner), Nick the Lounge Singer (Murray), Olympia Cafe (Aykroyd/Belushi/Murray, et al.), Roseanne Roseannadanna (Radner), Samurai Futaba (Belushi), Uncle Roy (Henry), The Widettes (Aykroyd/Belushi/Curtin/Radner)

BUMPER KEY (Pg. 340-341)

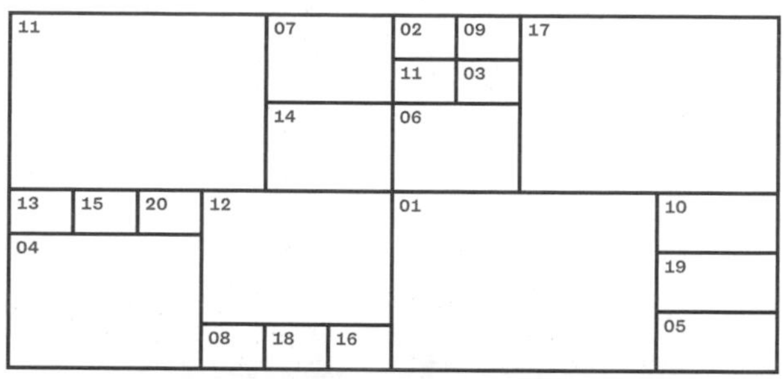

a.

b.

c.

d.

a. Dan Aykroyd as Ray from the sketch "Telepsychic."
b. Gilda Radner as poetic rocker Candy Slice, a character loosely inspired by Patti Smith.
c. Gilda Radner and Alan Zweibel as Lucille Ball and Gary Morton.
d. The Rolling Stones with Lorne Michaels (standing) and writer Alan Zweibel (seated, right) in Michaels's office.

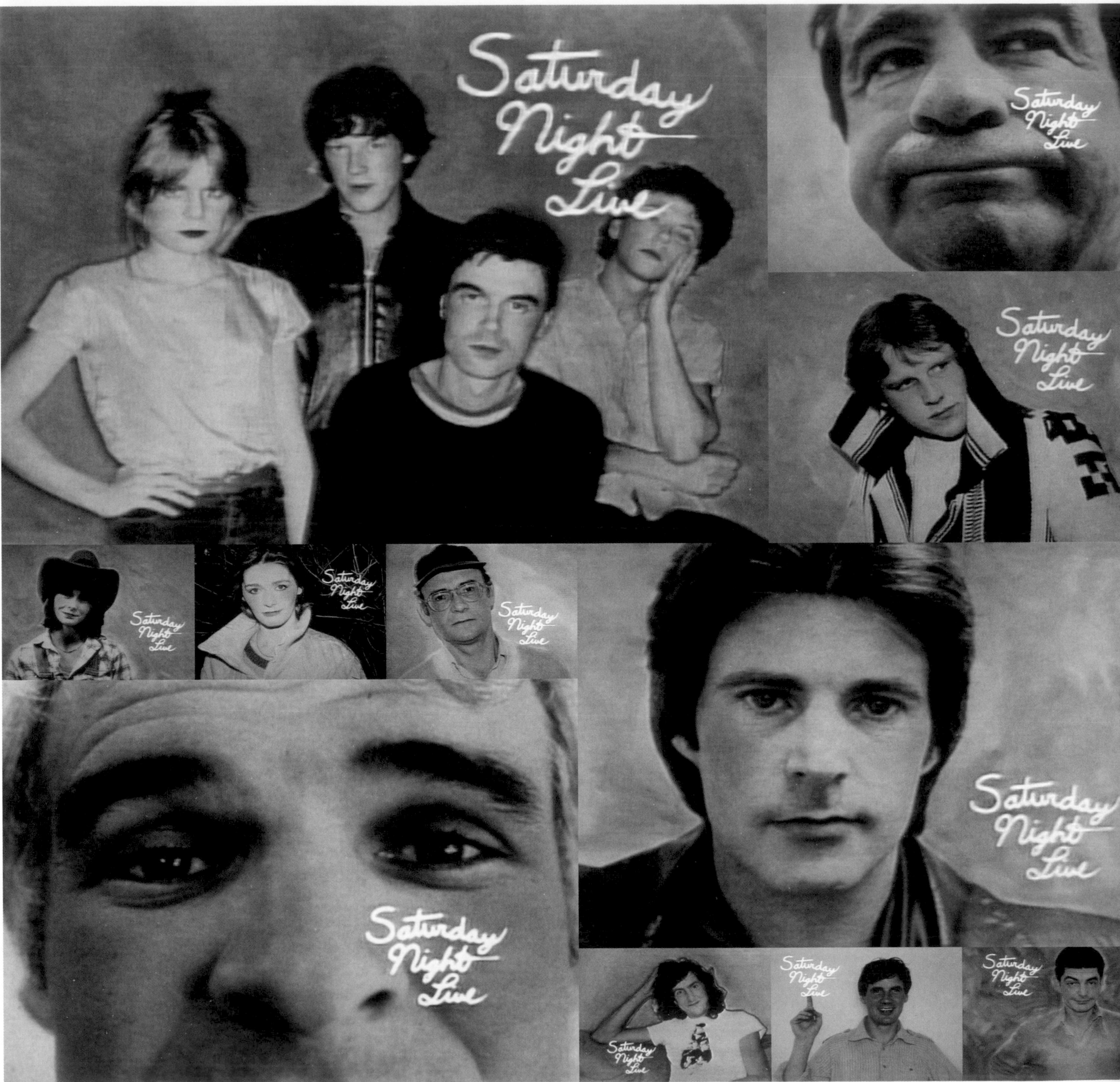
Saturday Night Live
Saturday Night Live
Saturday Night Live
Saturday Night Live
Saturday Night Live
Saturday Night Live
Saturday Night Live
Saturday Night Live
Saturday Night Live
Saturday Night Live
Saturday Night Live

Saturday Night Live
Saturday Night Live
Saturday Night Live
Saturday Night Live
Saturday Night Live
Saturday Night Live
Saturday Night Live
Saturday Night Live
Saturday Night Live
Saturday Night Live

Saturday
Night
Live

SEASON 05 / 1979-80

Saturday Night Live
Saturday Night Live
Saturday Night Live
Saturday Night Live
Saturday Night Live
Saturday Night Live
Saturday Night Live
Saturday Night Live
Saturday Night Live
Saturday Night Live
Saturday Night Live

SEASON 05 / 1979-80

CAST

Jane Curtin
Garrett Morris
Bill Murray
Laraine Newman
Gilda Radner
Harry Shearer

Featuring:
Peter Aykroyd
Tom Davis
James Downey
Brian Doyle-Murray
Al Franken
Don Novello
Tom Schiller
Paul Schaffer
Alan Zweibel

Weekend Update:
Jane Curtin
Bill Murray

CREW

Executive Producer: Lorne Michaels

Director: Dave Wilson

Writers: Peter Aykroyd, Anne Beatts, Tom Davis, James Downey, Brian Doyle-Murray, Al Franken, Tom Gammill, Lorne Michaels, Matt Neuman, Don Novello, Sarah Paley, Max Pross, Herb Sargent, Tom Schiller, Harry Shearer, Rosie Shuster, Alan Zweibel

Short Films: Tom Schiller

Production Designers: Eugene Lee, Franne Lee

Lighting Designers: Phil Hymes, Gene Martin

Musical Director: Howard Shore

Costume Designer: Karen Roston

Wardrobe: Margaret Karolyi

Hair: Lyn Quiyou

Makeup: Barbara Armstrong

Photographer: Edie Baskin

EPISODE LIST

EPISODE KEY:
H - Host
MG - Musical Guest
SG/C - Special Guests/Cameos

EPISODE 01: 10/13/79
H: Steve Martin
MG: Blondie
SG/C: Buck Henry

EPISODE 02: 10/20/79
H: Eric Idle
MG: Bob Dylan
SG/C: Buck Henry, Andy Kaufman, Fred Tackett, Bob Zmuda

EPISODE 03: 11/03/79
H: Bill Russell
MG: Chicago
SG/C: Ed Herlihy

EPISODE 04: 11/10/79
H: Buck Henry
MG: Tom Petty & The Heartbreakers

EPISODE 05: 11/17/79
H: Bea Arthur
MG: The Roches
SG/C: Andy Kaufman

EPISODE 06: 12/08/79
H: Howard Hesseman
MG: Randy Newman

EPISODE 07: 12/15/79
H: Martin Sheen
MG: David Bowie

EPISODE 08: 12/22/79
H: Ted Knight
MG: Desmond Child & Rouge
SG/C: Teri Garr, Andy Kaufman, Diana Peckham, Buddy Rogers, Bob Zmuda

EPISODE 09: 01/26/80
H: Teri Garr
MG: The B-52's
SG/C: John B. Anderson

EPISODE 10: 02/09/80
H: Chevy Chase
MG: Marianne Faithfull, Tom Scott
SG/C: Bert Convy

EPISODE 11: 02/16/80
H: Elliott Gould
MG: Gary Numan

EPISODE 12: 02/23/80
H: Kirk Douglas
MG: Sam & Dave
SG/C: Jack Garner, Joan Hackett, Lucie Lancaster

EPISODE 13: 03/08/80
H: Rodney Dangerfield
MG: The J. Geils Band

EPISODE 14 - 100TH ANNIVERSARY SHOW: 03/15/80
MG: David Sanborn, Paul Simon, James Taylor
SG/C: John Belushi, Carrie Fisher, Steve Jordan, Sen. Daniel P. Moynihan, Ralph Nader, Michael O'Donoghue, Michael Palin

EPISODE 15: 04/05/80
H: Paula Prentiss, Richard Benjamin
MG: The Grateful Dead

EPISODE 16: 04/12/80
H: Burt Reynolds
MG: Anne Murray

EPISODE 17: 04/19/80
H: Strother Martin
MG: The Specials

EPISODE 18: 05/10/80
H: Bob Newhart
MG: The Amazing Rhythm Aces, Bruce Cockburn

EPISODE 19: 05/17/80
H: Steve Martin
MG: 3-D, Paul McCartney, Linda McCartney

EPISODE 20: 05/24/80
H: Buck Henry
MG: Andrew Gold, Andrae Crouch, The Voices of Unity

SEASON HIGHLIGHTS

Baba Wawa (Radner), Father Guido Sarducci (Novello), The Franken and Davis Show (Davis/Franken), Nerds (Radner), Nick the Lounge Singer (Murray), Roseanne Roseannadanna (Radner), Uncle Roy (Henry)

BUMPER KEY (Pg. 344-345)

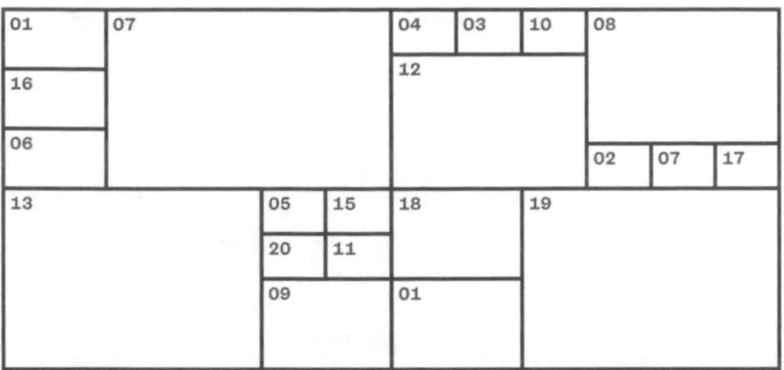

a.

b.

c.

d.

a. Peter Aykroyd, Bill Murray, and Garrett Morris in "New York State Wines." **b.** "I was just asking Lady Salisbury, 'Where the devil are those Douchebags?'" Lord Salisbury (Harry Shearer) with Lord and Lady Douchebag (Buck Henry and Gilda Radner) in "Royal Party." **c.** Plans for the Rockefeller Center subway home base set, which premiered for the 100th episode of the show (see photo a). **d.** Bob Dylan performing.

SEASON 06 / 1980-81

CAST

Denny Dillon
Robin Duke
Gilbert Gottfried
Tim Kazurinsky
Gail Matthius
Eddie Murphy
Joe Piscopo
Ann Risley
Charles Rocket
Tony Rosato

Featuring:
Yvonne Hudson
Matthew Laurance
Laurie Metcalf
Emily Prager
Patrick Weathers

Weekend Update:
Gail Matthius
Charles Rocket

CREW

Executive Producer:
Jean Doumanian

Director: Dave Wilson

Writers: Larry Arnstein, Barry W. Blaustein, Billy Brown, Ferris Butler, John DeBellis, Jean Doumanian, Nancy Dowd, Brian Doyle-Murray, Leslie Fuller, Mel Green, Mitchell Glazer, David Hurwitz, Judy Jacklin, Tim Kazurinsky, Sean Kelly, Mitchell Kriegman, Patricia Marx, Douglas McGrath, Tom Moore, Matt Neuman, Pamela Norris, Michael O'Donoghue, Mark Reisman, Tony Rosato, David Sheffield, Jeremy Stevens, Terrence Sweeney, Dick Wittenborn

Production Designer:
Akira Yoshimura

Lighting Designers:
Phil Hymes, Gene Martin

Musical Director:
Kenny Vance

Costume Designer:
Karen Roston

Wardrobe: Margaret Karolyi

Hair: Annette Bianco

Makeup: Barbara Armstrong

Photographer: Patti Perret

EPISODE LIST

EPISODE KEY:
H - Host
MG - Musical Guest
SG/C - Special Guests/Cameos

EPISODE 01: 11/15/80
H: Elliott Gould
MG: Kid Creole & The Coconuts

EPISODE 02: 11/22/80
H: Malcolm McDowell
MG: Captain Beefheart & The Magic Band

EPISODE 03: 12/06/80
H: Ellen Burstyn
MG: Aretha Franklin, Keith Sykes
SG/C: Bill Paxton

EPISODE 04: 12/13/80
H: Jamie Lee Curtis
MG: James Brown, Ellen Shipley
SG/C: Danny DeVito, William Duff-Griffin

EPISODE 05: 12/20/80
H: David Carradine
MG: The Cast of "Pirates of Penzance"
SG/C: Bill Irwin, Linda Ronstadt, George Rose, Rex Smith

EPISODE 06: 01/10/81
H: Ray Sharkey
MG: Jack Bruce & Friends

EPISODE 07: 01/17/81
H: Karen Black
MG: Cheap Trick, Stanley Clarke Trio

EPISODE 08: 01/24/81
H: Robert Hays
MG: Joe 'King' Carrasco & The Sounds/14 Karat Soul
SG/C: Harry Osborne, Michael Nesmith

EPISODE 09: 02/07/81
H: Sally Kellerman
MG: Jimmy Cliff
SG/C: Jim Fowler, Marc Weiner

EPISODE 10: 02/14/81
H: Deborah Harry
MG: Deborah Harry, Funky 4 + 1 More
SG/C: Clem Beck, Janice Pendarvis, Chris Stein, Marc Weiner

EPISODE 11: 02/21/81
H: Charlene Tilton
MG: Todd Rundgren, Prince
SG/C: Don King, Marc Weiner

EPISODE 12: 03/07/81
H: Bill Murray
MG: Delbert McClinton
SG/C: Bonnie Bramlett, Mark King

EPISODE 13: 4/11/81
MG: Junior Walker & The All Stars
SG/C: Chevy Chase, Al Franken, Christopher Reeve, Robin Williams

SEASON HIGHLIGHTS

Fish Heads (Bill Paxton), Mister Robinson's Neighborhood (Murphy), Nick the Lounge Singer (Murray)

BUMPER KEY (Pg. 348-349)

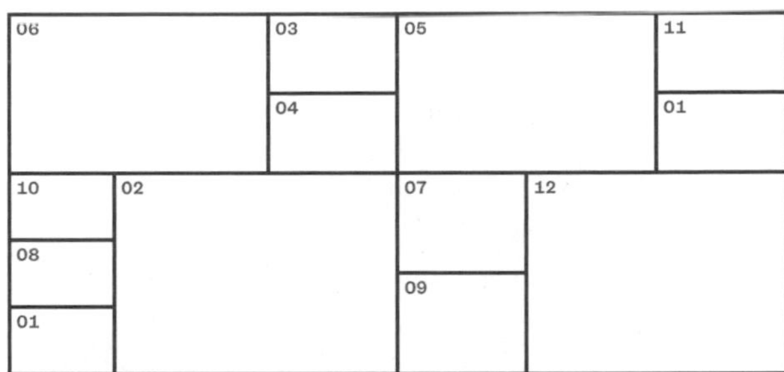

a.

b.

c.

a. The season 6 cast, selected by new executive producer Jean Doumanian.
b. Goodnights with host David Carradine.
c. Jean Doumanian with Charles Rocket.

Saturday Night Live
Saturday Night Live '80
Saturday Night Live '80
Saturday Night Live
Saturday Night Live
Saturday Night Live
NO PETS ALLOWED IN ZOO
Central Park ZOO AREA GATE CLOSING 6P.M. ALL VISITORS TO LEAVE
Saturday Night Live '80
Saturday Night Live '80

Saturday Night Live '80
Saturday Night Live
Saturday Night Live '80
Saturday Night Live
Saturday Night Live

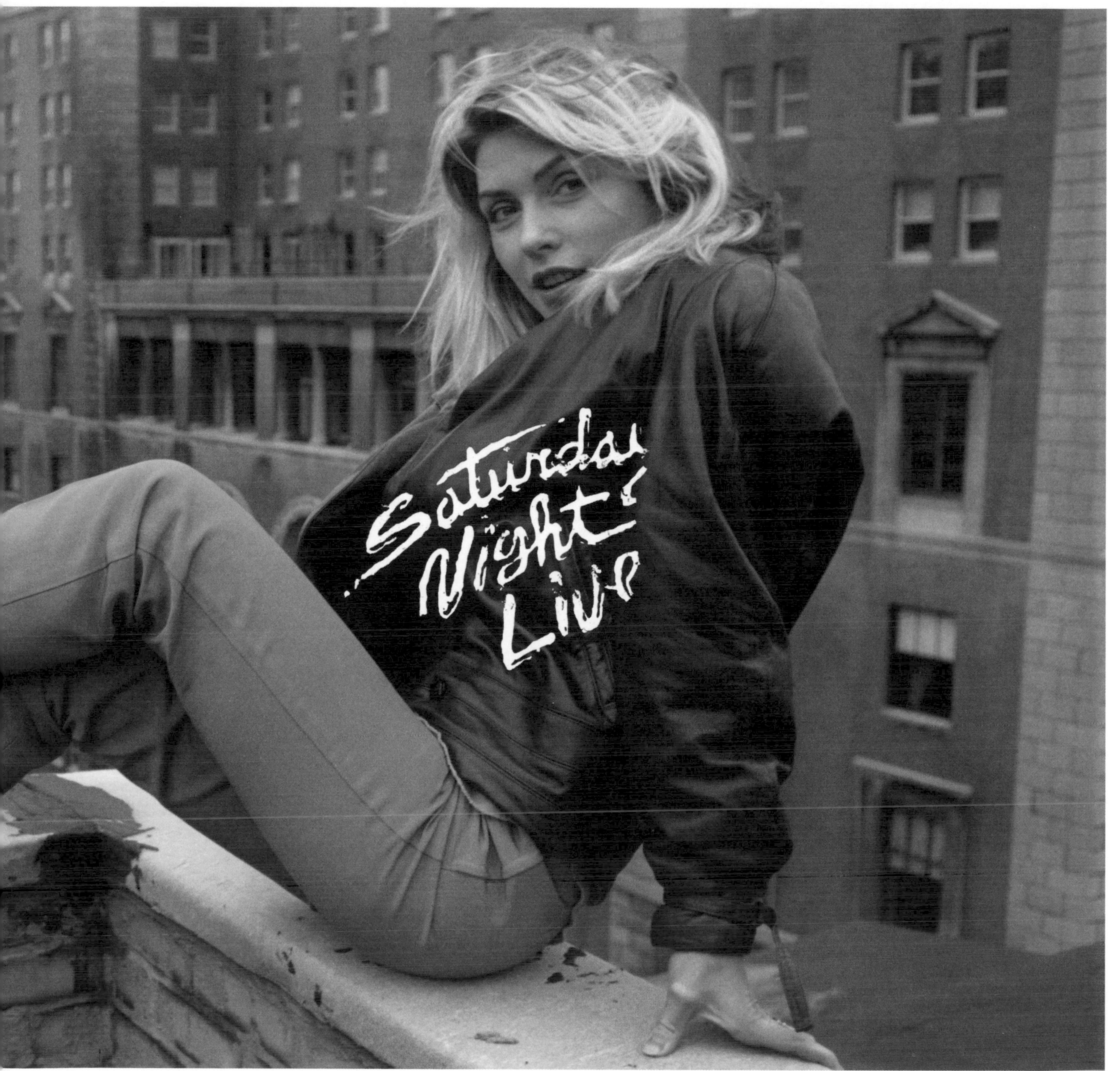

SEASON 07 / 1981-82

SATURDAY
NIGHT
LIVE

SATURDAY
NIGHT
LIVE

SATURDAY
NIGHT
LIVE

SATURDAY
NIGHT
LIVE

SATURDAY
NIGHT
LIVE

SATURDAY
NIGHT
LIVE

SATURDAY
NIGHT
LIVE

SATURDAY
NIGHT
LIVE

SATURDAY
NIGHT
LIVE

SATURDAY
NIGHT
LIVE

SATURDAY
NIGHT
LIVE

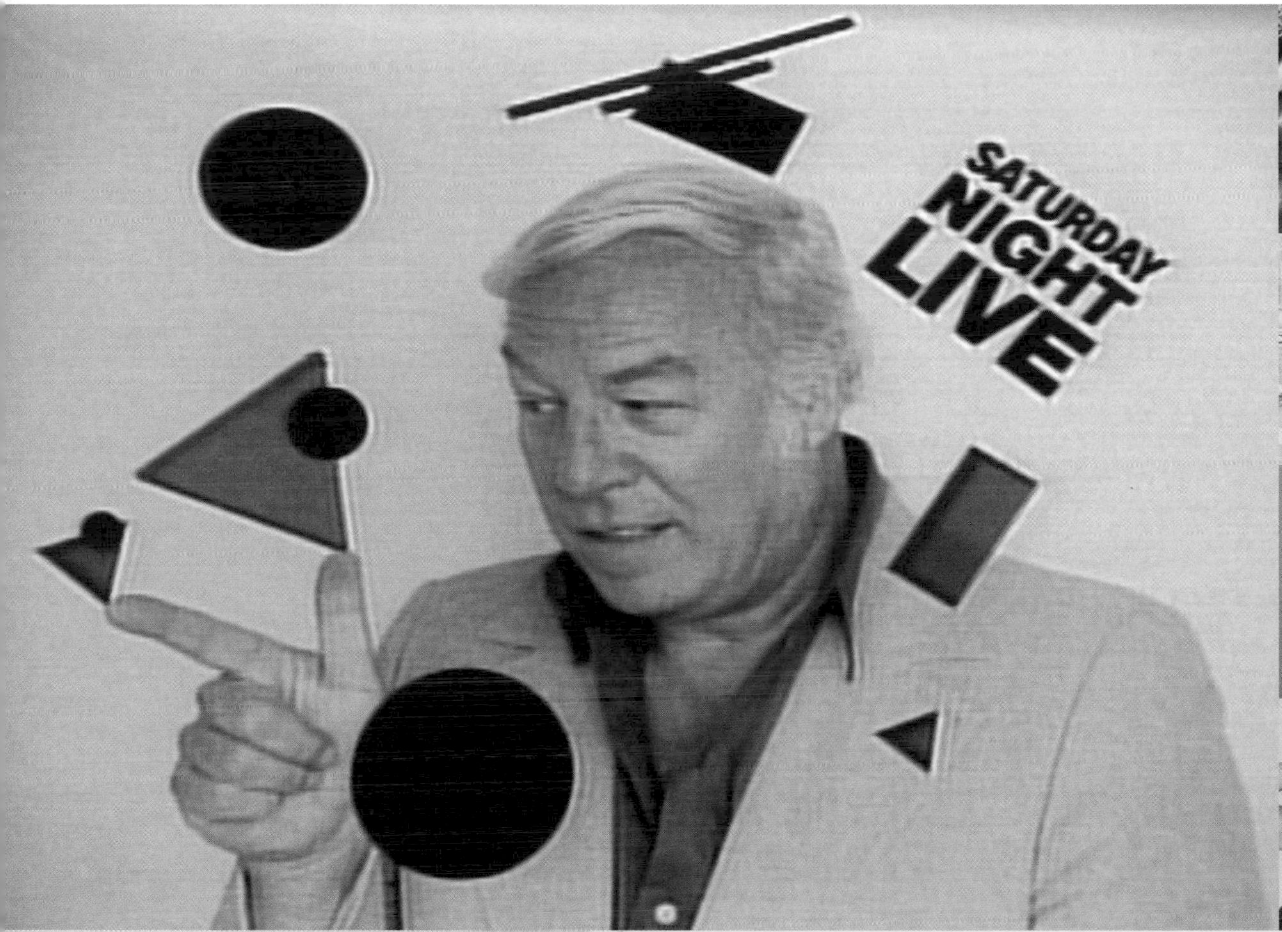

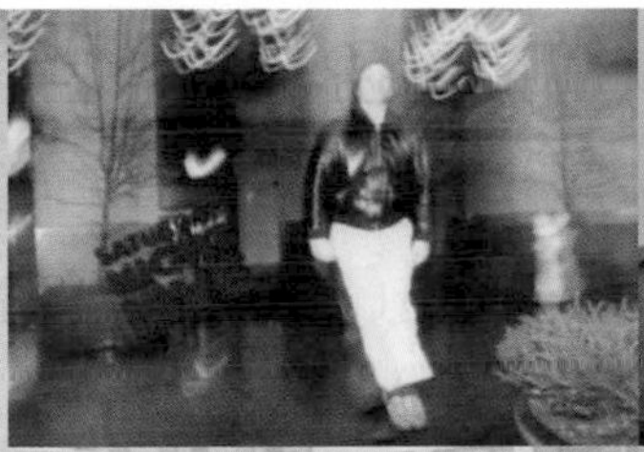

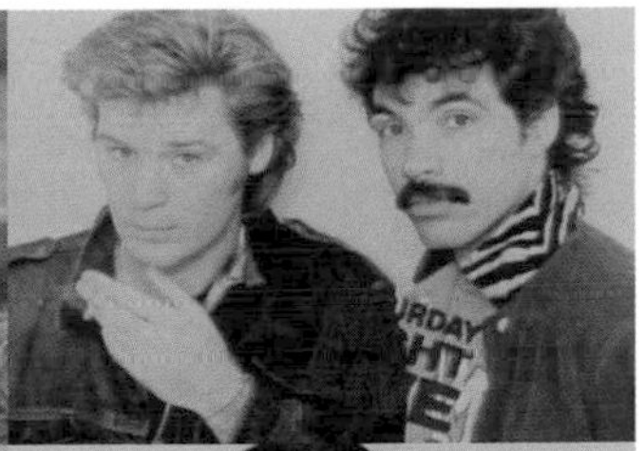

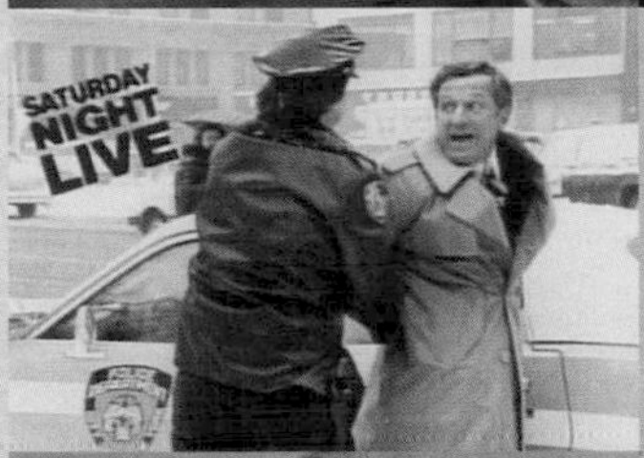

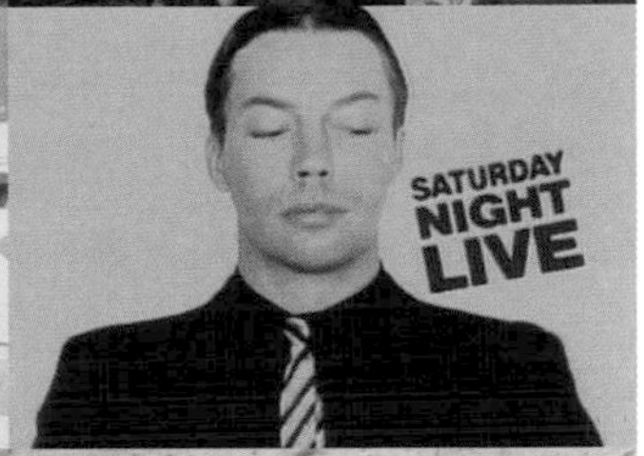

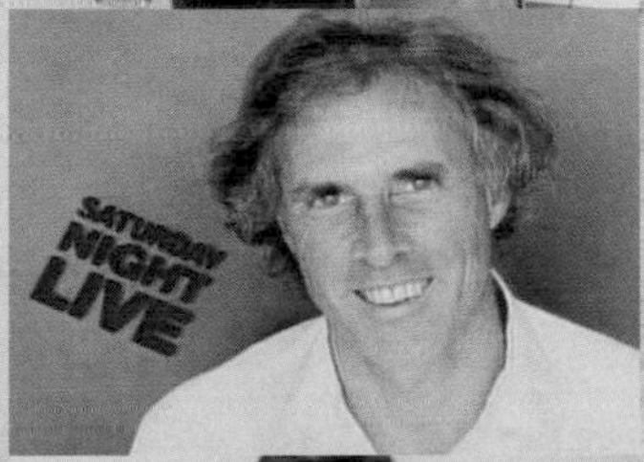

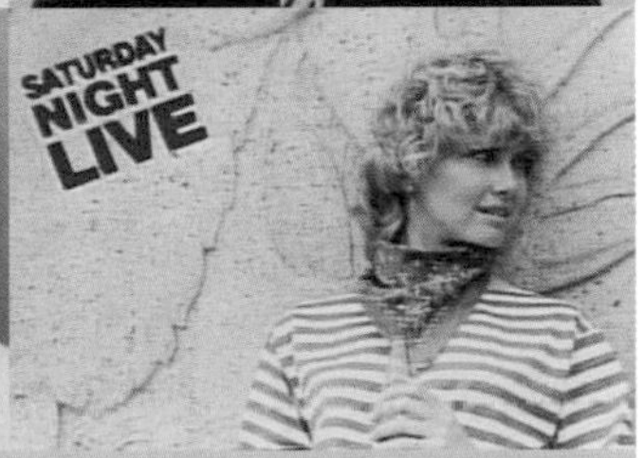

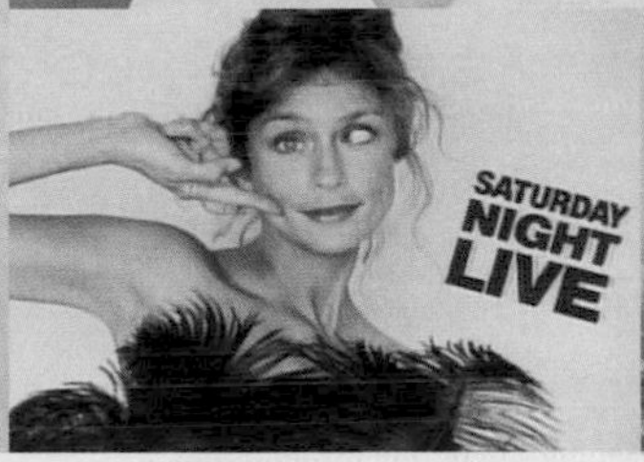

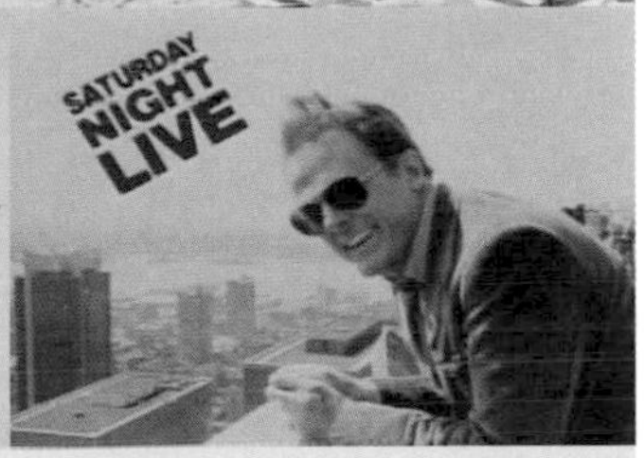

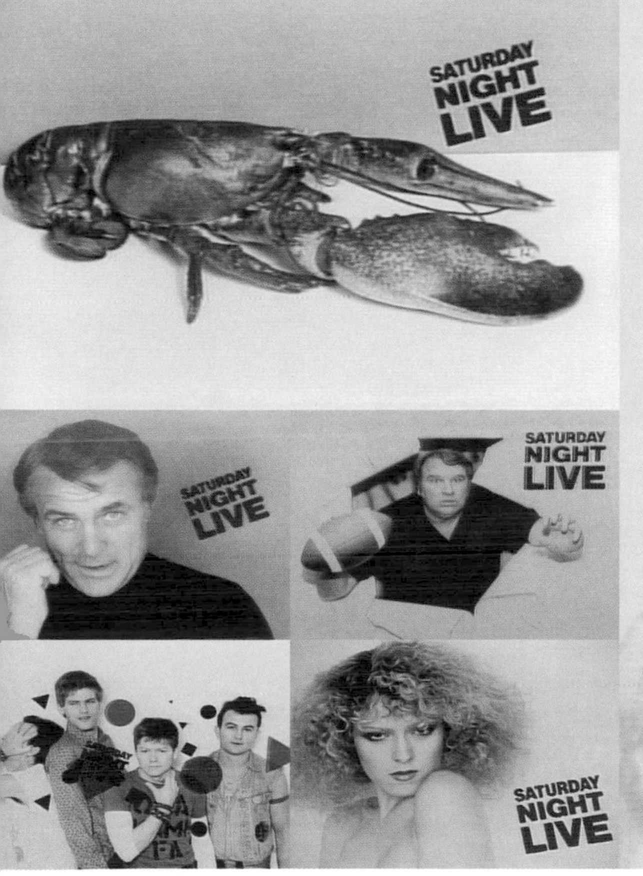

SATURDAY
NIGHT
LIVE

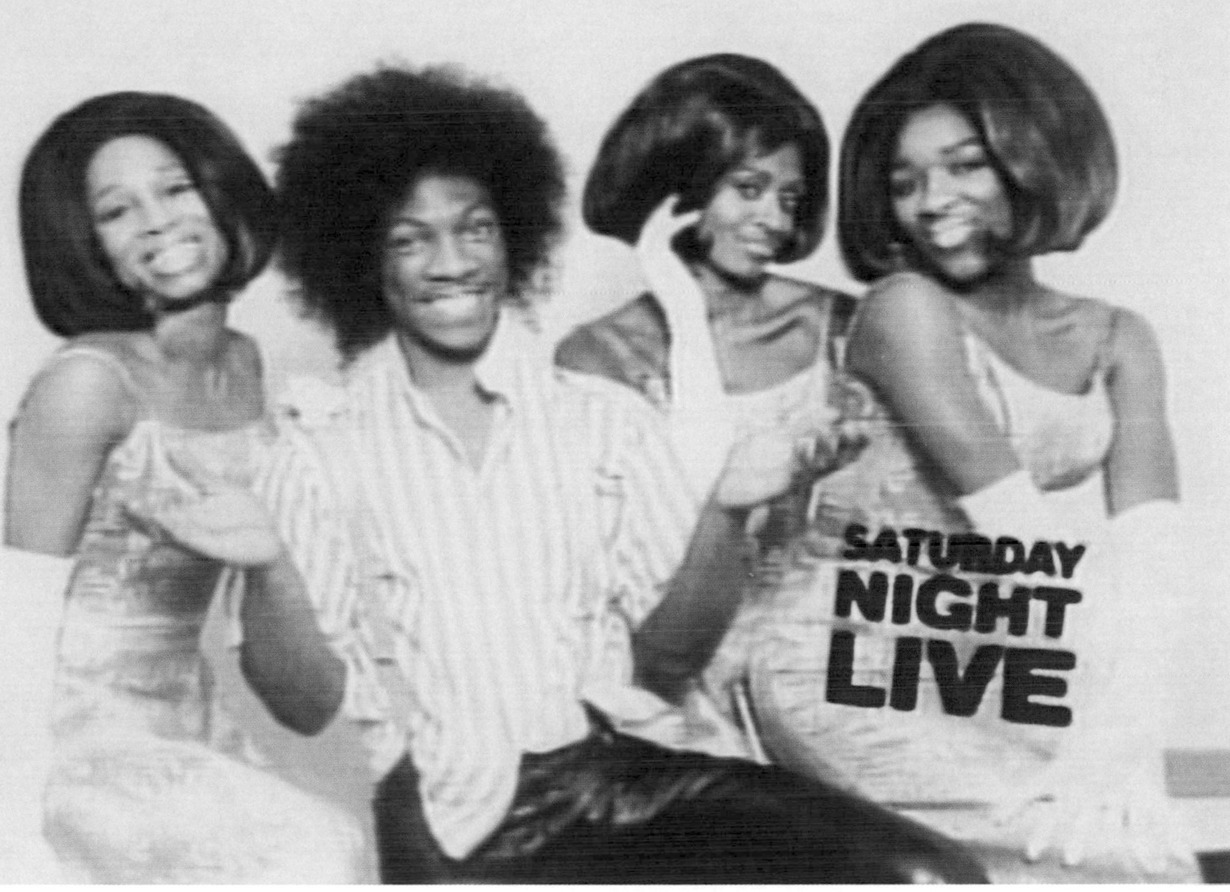

SATURDAY
NIGHT
LIVE

SEASON 07 / 1981-82

CAST

Denny Dillon
Robin Duke
Christine Ebersole
Mary Gross
Tim Kazurinsky
Eddie Murphy
Joe Piscopo
Tony Rosato

Featuring:
Brian Doyle-Murray

SNL Newsbreak:
Brian Doyle-Murray
Christine Ebersole
Mary Gross

CREW

Executive Producer:
Dick Ebersol

Director: Dave Wilson

Writers: Barry W. Blaustein, Joe Bodolai, Brian Doyle-Murray, Nate Herman, Tim Kazurinsky, Nelson Lyon, Marilyn Suzanne Miller, Pam Norris, Margaret Oberman, Mark O'Donnell, Michael O'Donoghue, Tony Rosato, David Sheffield, Rosie Shuster, Andrew Smith, Terry Southern, Bob Tischler, Eliot Wald

Supervising Producers:
Michael O'Donoghue,
Bob Tischler

Film Producer: Mary Salter

Production Designer:
Akira Yoshimura

Lighting Designers:
Phil Hymes, Gene Martin

Musical Director: Tom Malone

Costume Designer:
Karen Roston

Wadrobe: Margaret Karolyi

Hair: Annette Bianco

Makeup: Barbara Armstrong

Photographer: Edie Baskin

EPISODE LIST

EPISODE KEY:
H - Host
MG - Musical Guest
SG/C - Special Guests/Cameos

EPISODE 01: 10/03/81
MG: Rod Stewart
SG/C: Michael Davis, Tina Turner, Andy Warhol

EPISODE 02: 10/10/81
H: Susan Saint James
MG: The Kinks
SG/C: Andy Warhol

EPISODE 03: 10/17/81
H: George Kennedy
MG: Miles Davis
SG/C: Harry Anderson, John Candy, Ron Howard, Marcus Miller, Regis Philbin

EPISODE 04: 10/31/81
H: Donald Pleasence
MG: Fear
SG/C: John Belushi, Michael Davis, Andy Warhol

EPISODE 05: 11/07/81
H: Lauren Hutton
MG: Rick James
SG/C: William Burroughs, Stone City Band

EPISODE 06: 11/14/81
H: Bernadette Peters
MG: The Go-Go's/Billy Joel
SG/C: Bill Wegman

EPISODE 07: 12/05/81
H: Tim Curry
MG: Meat Loaf
SG/C: Bryant Gumbel, Frank Nelson

EPISODE 08: 12/12/81
H: Bill Murray
MG: The Spinners
SG/C: Michael Davis, Don Novello, The Yale Whiffenpoofs

EPISODE 09: 01/23/82
H: Robert Conrad
MG: The Allman Brothers Band

EPISODE 10: 01/30/82
H: John Madden
MG: Jennifer Holliday
SG/C: Andy Kaufman, Brent Musburger, Marv Throneberry, Bob Zmuda

EPISODE 11: 02/06/82
H: James Coburn
MG: Lindsey Buckingham, The Cholos
SG/C: Marc Weiner

EPISODE 12: 02/20/82
H: Bruce Dern
MG: Luther Vandross

EPISODE 13: 02/27/82
H: Elizabeth Ashley
MG: Daryl Hall & John Oates
SG/C: Harry Anderson, Joseph Papp

EPISODE 14: 03/20/82
H: Robert Urich
MG: Mink De Ville

EPISODE 15: 03/27/82
H: Blythe Danner
MG: Rickie Lee Jones
SG/C: Michael Davis

EPISODE 16: 04/10/82
H: Daniel J. Travanti
MG: John Cougar
SG/C: Susan Saint James, Barry Mitchell, Bruce Weitz

EPISODE 17: 04/17/82
H: Johnny Cash
MG: Johnny Cash, Elton John

EPISODE 18: 04/24/82
H: Robert Culp
MG: The Charlie Daniels Band

EPISODE 19: 05/15/82
H: Danny DeVito
MG: Sparks
SG/C: Tony Danza, Julia DeVito, Marilu Henner, Judd Hirsch, Andy Kaufman, Christopher Lloyd

EPISODE 20: 05/22/82
H/MG: Olivia Newton-John
SG/C: Graham Chapman, Michael Davis

SEASON HIGHLIGHTS

Aaron Film: Building Blowing Up (Davis/Prager), Buckwheat (Murphy), Dr. Jack Badofsky (Kazurinsky), Gumby (Murphy), Hidden Camera (Funt/Piscopo), James Brown Is Annie (Murphy), Mister Robinson's Neighborhood (Murphy), Our Gang Records (Murphy), Prose and Cons (Eddie's Part) (Murphy/Piscopo), Velvet Jones (Murphy), Warhol Film 1 (Andy Warhol), The Whiners (Duke/Piscopo)

BUMPER KEY (Pg. 354-355)

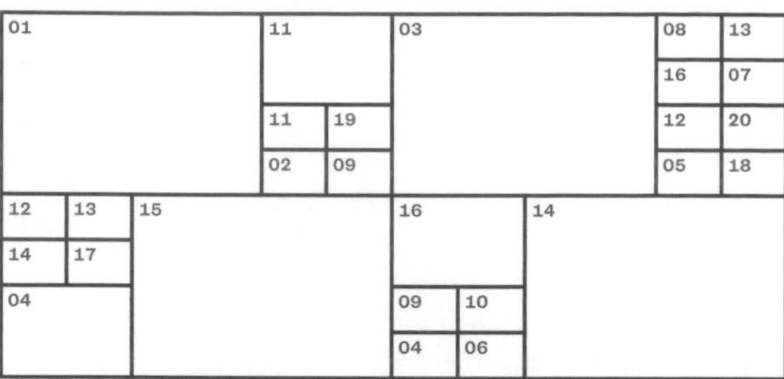

a.

b.

c.

a. For Danny DeVito's monologue, he was joined by fellow cast members of the recently cancelled series "Taxi" to say goodbye to the audience. **b.** Eddie Murphy as Velvet Jones of the Velvet Jones School of Technology. **c.** "Here's Cos" with Eddie Murphy as Bill Cosby.

CAST

Robin Duke
Mary Gross
Brad Hall
Tim Kazurinsky
Gary Kroeger
Julia Louis-Dreyfus
Eddie Murphy
Joe Piscopo

Saturday Night News:
Brad Hall

CREW

Executive Producer:
Dick Ebersol

Director: Dave Wilson

Producer: Bob Tischler

Writers: Paul Barrosse, Barry W. Blaustein, Robin Duke, Ellen L. Fogle, Nate Herman, Tim Kazurinsky, Andrew Kurtzman, Eddie Murphy, Pamela Norris, Margaret Oberman, Joe Piscopo, David Sheffield, Andrew Smith, Bob Tischler, Tracy Tormé, Eliot Wald

Writing Supervisors:
Barry W. Blaustein, David Sheffield

Film Producer: Mary Salter

Production Designer:
Akira Yoshimura

Lighting Designers:
Phil Hymes, Gene Martin

Musical Director: Tom Malone

Costume Designer:
Karen Roston

Wardrobe: Paul Buboltz, Margaret Karolyi

Hair: Annette Bianco

Makeup: Barbara Armstrong, Kevin Haney

Photographer: Mark Mullen

EPISODE LIST

EPISODE KEY:
H - Host
MG - Musical Guest
SG/C - Special Guests/Cameos

EPISODE 01: 09/25/82
H: Chevy Chase
MG: Queen
SG/C: Danny DeVito, Roger Ebert, Gene Siskel, John Zacherle

EPISODE 02: 10/02/82
H: Louis Gossett, Jr.
MG: George Thorogood & The Destroyers
SG/C: Mr. T

EPISODE 03: 10/09/82
H: Ron Howard
MG: The Clash
SG/C: Harry Anderson, Andy Griffith, Rex Reed

EPISODE 04: 10/23/82
H: Howard Hesseman
MG: Men at Work
SG/C: Bill Irwin, Susan Saint James, Milan Melvin

EPISODE 05: 10/30/82
H: Michael Keaton
MG: Joe Jackson
SG/C: Michael Palin

EPISODE 06: 11/13/82
H: Robert Blake
MG: Kenny Loggins
SG/C: Merv Griffin, Steve Jordan

EPISODE 07: 11/20/82
H: Drew Barrymore
MG: Squeeze
SG/C: Ed Asner

EPISODE 08: 12/04/82
H: Smothers Brothers
MG: Laura Branigan
SG/C: Lawrence K. Grossman

EPISODE 09: 12/11/82
H: Eddie Murphy
MG: Lionel Richie
SG/C: Harry Anderson, Seth Green, Steve Martin

EPISODE 10: 01/22/83
H/MG: Lily Tomlin
SG/C: Andy Kaufman, Barry Mitchell, Rick Moranis, Dave Thomas

EPISODE 11: 01/29/83
H: Rick Moranis/Dave Thomas
MG: The Bus Boys

EPISODE 12: 02/05/83
H: Sid Caesar
MG: Joe Cocker, Jennifer Warnes
SG/C: Harry Anderson

EPISODE 13: 02/19/83
H: Howard Hesseman
MG: Tom Petty & The Heartbreakers
SG/C: Milan Melvin

EPISODE 14: 02/26/83
H: Jeff & Beau Bridges
MG: Randy Newman
SG/C: Lloyd Bridges, Howard Hesseman, James Pickens Jr.

EPISODE 15: 03/12/83
H: Bruce Dern
MG: Leon Redbone

EPISODE 16: 03/19/83
H: Robert Guillaume
MG: Duran Duran
CP: Clysler-Prymouth, Adolf's Hits, Oil Guys

EPISODE 17: 04/09/83
H: Joan Rivers
MG: Musical Youth
SG/C: David Susskind

EPISODE 18: 04/16/83
H: Susan Saint James
MG: Michael McDonald
SG/C: Steven Wright, James Pickens Jr., Edgar Winter

EPISODE 19: 05/07/83
H/MG: Stevie Wonder
SG/C: Michael Davis, Greg Dean

EPISODE 20: 05/14/83
H: Ed Koch
MG: Kevin Rowland/Dexy's Midnight Runners
SG/C: Marv Albert, Harry Anderson, Don King, Leslie Pollack

SEASON HIGHLIGHTS

Alfalfa (Gross), Buckwheat (Murphy), Gumby (Murphy), Kannon AE-1 (Stevie Wonder), Land Shark (Chase), Mister Robinson's Neighborhood (Murphy), Velvet Jones (Murphy), The Whiners (Duke/Piscopo)

BUMPER KEY (Pg. 358-359)

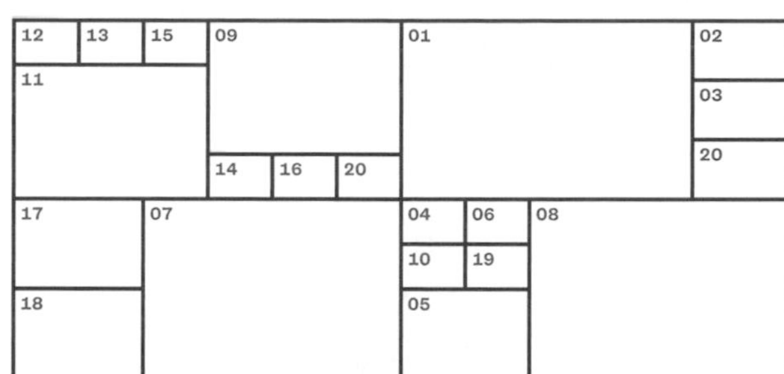

a.

b.

a. The Whiners (Robin Duke and Joe Piscopo) debuted in season 8.
b. Former "Little Rascal" Robert Blake with "Our Gang" members played by Julia Louis-Dreyfus, Eddie Murphy, Joe Piscopo, and Mary Gross.

SATURDAY NIGHT LIVE
SATURDAY NIGHT LIVE
SATURDAY NIGHT LIVE
SATURDAY NIGHT LIVE
UNITED STATES
SATURDAY NIGHT LIVE
SATURDAY NIGHT LIVE
Barrymore

SATURDAY
NIGHT
LIVE
SATURDAY
NIGHT
LIVE

.45
BY THE BOX
59
49¢
LOIN ENDS
29 LB
1.35 LB
OXTAILS
BEEF
FRESH
99¢
RABOS
BEEF
LIVER
FRESH
1.45
FONTINA
CARNE
1.59 lb.
COW
69
KIDNEYS
BEEF
FRESH
95¢ lb.
RIB
LAMB
79¢
LAMB
CHOPS
SHOULDER
SATURDAY
NIGHT
LIVE

SATURDAY
NIGHT
LIVE
WINGO
SATURDAY
NIGHT
LIVE
HAPPY
ST. PATRICK'S
DAY

SATURDAY NIGHT LIVE
15
SATURDAY NIGHT LIVE
SATURDAY NIGHT LIVE
St Station
CC
AA
SATURDAY NIGHT LIVE
SATURDAY NIGHT LIVE
POLICE LINE
OT CROSS
SATURDAY NIGHT LIVE
SATURDAY NIGHT LIVE
ST. TWIN
AMIE LEE CURTIS
E LETTER
SATURDAY NIGHT LIVE

SEASON 09 / 1983-84

CAST

Jim Belushi
Robin Duke
Mary Gross
Brad Hall
Tim Kazurinsky
Gary Kroeger
Julia Louis-Dreyfus
Eddie Murphy
Joe Piscopo

SNL Newsbreak:
Brad Hall

CREW

Executive Producer:
Dick Ebersol

Director: Dave Wilson

Head Writer: Andrew Smith

Producer: Bob Tischler

Writers: Jim Belushi, Andy Breckman, Robin Duke, Adam Green, Mary Gross, Nate Herman, Tino Insana, Tim Kazurinsky, Kevin Kelton, Andrew Kurtzman, Michael McCarthy, Eddie Murphy, Pamela Norris, Margaret Oberman, Joe Piscopo, Herb Sargent, Bob Tischler, Eliot Wald

Film Producer:
Barbara Lieberman

Production Designer:
Akira Yoshimura

Lighting Designers:
Leo Farrenkopf,
Howard Strawbridge

Musical Director: Tom Malone

Costume Designer:
Karen Roston

Wardrobe: Margaret Karolyi

Hair: Annette Bianco

Makeup: Barbara Armstrong, Kevin Haney

Photographer: Mark Mullen

EPISODE LIST

EPISODE KEY:
H - Host
MG - Musical Guest
SG/C - Special Guests/Cameos

EPISODE 01: 10/08/83
H: Brandon Tartikoff
MG: John Cougar
SG/C: Roger Ebert, Gene Siskel

EPISODE 02: 10/15/83
H: Danny DeVito, Rhea Perlman
MG: Eddy Grant
SG/C: Dick Cavett

EPISODE 03: 10/22/83
H: John Candy
MG: Men at Work

EPISODE 04: 11/05/83
H: Betty Thomas
MG: Stray Cats
SG/C: 14 Karat Soul

EPISODE 05: 11/12/83
H: Teri Garr
MG: Mick Fleetwood's Zoo
SG/C: Joel Hodgson

EPISODE 06: 11/19/83
H: Jerry Lewis
MG: Loverboy
SG/C: Florence Henderson

EPISODE 07: 12/03/83
H: Smothers Brothers
MG: Big Country
SG/C: Larry Holmes, Ron Luciano, Tom Seaver

EPISODE 08: 12/10/83
H: Flip Wilson
MG: Stevie Nicks
SG/C: Joel Hodgson

EPISODE 09: 01/14/84
H: Father Guido Sarducci
MG: Huey Lewis & The News
SG/C: Steven Wright

EPISODE 10: 01/21/84
H: Michael Palin & Mary Palin
MG: The Motels
SG/C: Eleanor McGovern, Frankie Pace, Clara Peller

EPISODE 11: 01/28/84
H: Don Rickles
MG: Billy Idol
SG/C: Dr. Joyce Brothers, John Madden, Brandon Tartikoff, Stevie Wonder

EPISODE 12: 02/11/84
H: Robin Williams
MG: Adam Ant
SG/C: Paula Poundstone

EPISODE 13: 02/18/84
H: Jamie Lee Curtis
MG: The Fixx
SG/C: Joel Hodgson, James Pickens Jr.

EPISODE 14: 02/25/84
H: Edwin Newman
MG: Kool & The Gang
SG/C: Harry Anderson, Robin Williams

EPISODE 15: 03/17/84
H: Billy Crystal
MG: Al Jarreau
SG/C: Ed Koch

EPISODE 16: 04/07/84
H: Michael Douglas
MG: Deniece Williams

EPISODE 17: 04/14/84
H: Sen. George McGovern
MG: Madness

EPISODE 18: 05/05/84
H: Barry Bostwick
MG: Spinal Tap
SG/C: A. Whitney Brown, Billy Crystal, Soupy Sales

EPISODE 19: 05/12/84
H: Billy Crystal, Ed Koch, Edwin Newman, Fr. Guido Sarducci, Betty Thomas
MG: The Cars
SG/C: Joel Hodgson, Timothy Hutton

SEASON HIGHLIGHTS

Buckwheat (Murphy), Father Guido Sarducci (Novello), Gumby (Murphy), James Brown's Celebrity Hot Tub Party (Murphy), Mister Robinson's Neighborhood (Murphy)

BUMPER KEY (Pg. 362-363)

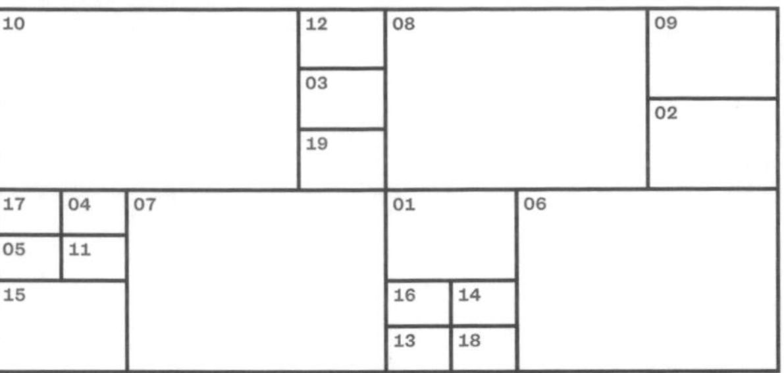

a. Gumby costume sketch.
b. "Gumby & Pokey" (Eddie Murphy and Joe Piscopo).
c. Eddie Murphy (as Jim Brown) with Joe Piscopo on "SNL Newsbreak."
d. "SNL Newsbreak" anchor Brad Hall with Julia Louis-Dreyfus.

a.

b.

c.

d.

SEASON 10 / 1984-85

CAST

Jim Belushi
Billy Crystal
Mary Gross
Christopher Guest
Rich Hall
Gary Kroeger
Julia Louis-Dreyfus
Harry Shearer
Martin Short
Pamela Stephenson

Saturday Night News:
Christopher Guest

CREW

Executive Producer: Dick Ebersol

Director: Dave Wilson

Producer: Bob Tischler

Writers: Jim Belushi, Andy Breckman, Billy Crystal, Larry David, James Downey, Christopher Guest, Rich Hall, Nate Herman, Kevin Kelton, Andy Kurtzman, Rob Riley, Herb Sargent, Harry Shearer, Martin Short, Bob Tischler, Eliot Wald

Film Producer: Barbara Lieberman

Production Designer: Akira Yoshimura

Musical Director: Tom Malone

Costume Designers: Vel Riberto, Lowell Detweiler

Wardrobe: Margaret Karolyi, Paul Buboltz

Hair: Annette Bianco

Makeup: Barbara Armstrong, Peter Montagna

Photographer: Mark Mullen

EPISODE LIST

EPISODE KEY:
H - Host
MG - Musical Guest
SG/C - Special Guests/Cameos

EPISODE 01: 10/06/84
MG: Thompson Twins
SG/C: Jamie Lee Curtis, Rob Reiner, Reginald VelJohnson

EPISODE 02: 10/13/84
H: Bob Uecker
MG: Peter Wolf
SG/C: Yogi Berra, Elliot Easton, Michael "Spaceman" Jonzun, Leon Mobley, Thommy Price, Maurice Starr, Dave Winfield, Gordon "Megabucks" Worthy

EPISODE 03: 10/20/84
H: Rev. Jesse Jackson
MG: Andrae Crouch/ Wintley Phipps

EPISODE 04: 11/03/84
H: Michael McKean
MG: Chaka Kahn
SG/C: Edwin Newman

EPISODE 05: 11/10/84
H: George Carlin
MG: Frankie Goes to Hollywood

EPISODE 06: 11/17/84
H: Ed Asner
MG: The Kinks

EPISODE 07: 12/01/84
H: Ed Begley, Jr.
MG: Billy Squier

EPISODE 08: 12/08/84
H: Ringo Starr
MG: Herbie Hancock
SG/C: Barbara Bach, James Pickens, Jr.

EPISODE 09: 12/15/84
H: Eddie Murphy
MG: Robert Plant & The Honeydrippers

EPISODE 10: 01/12/85
H: Kathleen Turner
MG: John Waite

EPISODE 11: 01/19/85
H: Roy Scheider
MG: Billy Ocean
SG/C: Steven Wright

EPISODE 12: 02/02/85
H: Alex Karras
MG: Tina Turner

EPISODE 13: 02/09/85
H: Harry Anderson
MG: Bryan Adams
SG/C: Carol Burnett, Johnny Cash, June Carter Cash, Christopher Reeve, Waylon Jennings

EPISODE 14: 02/16/85
H: Pamela Sue Martin
MG: Power Station
SG/C: Morgan Fairchild, Teri Garr, Susan Lucci, Ann-Margret, Lynn Swann

EPISODE 15: 03/30/85
H: Mr. T & Hulk Hogan
MG: The Commodores
SG/C: Steve Landesburg, Liberace, Bob Orton, Rowdy Roddy Piper

EPISODE 16: 04/06/85
H: Christopher Reeve
MG: Santana
SG/C: Steven Wright, Calvert DeForest

EPISODE 17: 04/13/85
H: Howard Cosell
MG: Greg Kihn

SEASON HIGHLIGHTS

Buckwheat (Murphy), Buddy Young, Jr. (Crystal), Ed Grimley (Short), Fernando's Hideaway (Crystal), Ricky & Phil (Crystal/Guest), Synchronized Swimming (Guest/Shearer/ Short), Syncronized Swimmers (Harry Shearer, Martin Short), That White Guy (Belushi), White Like Me (Murphy), Willie & Frankie (Crystal/Guest), White Like Me/White Like Eddie (Murphy), Wingtips/Walking After Midnight (Hall/Jim Belushi)

BUMPER KEY (Pg. 366-367)

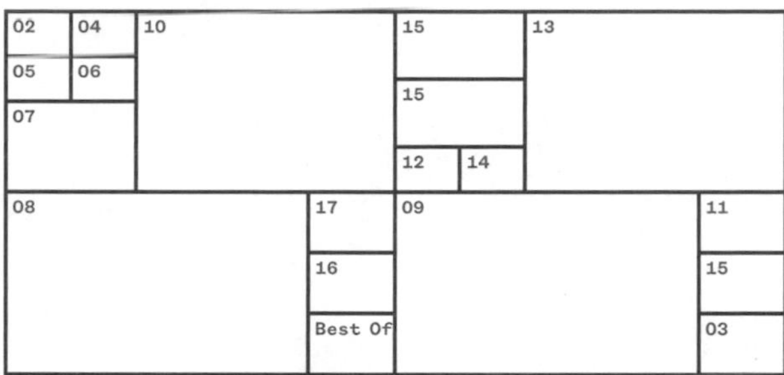

a.

b.

c.

d.

a. Martin Short as Jackie Rogers Jr. **b.** "I must say!" Ed Grimley was one of Short's most popular characters. **c.** Ringo Starr's monologue with Billy Crystal as Sammy Davis Jr. **d.** Jim Belushi as Bob Guccione on "Saturday Night News."

SATURDAY NIGHT LIVE
SATURDAY NIGHT LIVE
SATURDAY NIGHT LIVE
SATURDAY NIGHT LIVE
SATURDAY NIGHT LIVE
SATURDAY NIGHT LIVE
SATURDAY NIGHT LIVE
SATURDAY NIGHT LIVE
SNL Film Festival

SATURDAY
NIGHT
LIVE

SEASON 10 / 1984-85

SATURDAY
NIGHT
LIVE

SATURDAY NIGHT LIVE
VIDEO BOOTH
PUSSYCAT
phone

SATURDAY NIGHT LIVE
Subway
47-50 St Station
SATURDAY NIGHT LIVE

SEASON 11 / 1985-86

CAST

Joan Cusack
Robert Downey Jr.
Nora Dunn
Anthony Michael Hall
Jon Lovitz
Dennis Miller
Terry Sweeney
Randy Quaid
Danitra Vance

Featuring:
A. Whitney Brown
Al Franken
Don Novello
Dan Vitale
Damon Wayans

Weekend Update:
Dennis Miller

CREW

Executive Producer:
Lorne Michaels

Director: Dave Wilson

Head Writer: James Downey

Producers: Al Franken, Tom Davis

Writers: A. Whitney Brown, Tom Davis, James Downey, Al Franken, Jack Handey, Lanier Laney, Carol Leifer, George Meyer, Lorne Michaels, Don Novello, Michael O'Donoghue, R.D. Rosen, Herb Sargent, Suzy Schneider, Robert Smigel, John Swartzwelder, Terry Sweeney

Supervising Producer:
Audrey Peart Dickman

Film Producer: Mary Salter

Production Designers:
Eugene Lee, Akira Yoshimura

Music Produced by:
Howard Shore

Wardrobe: Margaret Karolyi, Paul Buboltz

Hair: Annette Bianco

Makeup: Barbara Armstrong, Peter Montagna

Costume Designer:
Carrie Robbins

Photographer: Isaiah Wyner

EPISODE LIST

EPISODE KEY:
H - Host
MG - Musical Guest
SG/C - Special Guests/Cameos

EPISODE 01: 11/09/85
H: Madonna
MG: Simple Minds
SG/C: Penn & Teller, Brandon Tartikoff

EPISODE 02: 11/16/85
H: Chevy Chase
MG: Sheila E.

EPISODE 03: 11/23/85
H: Pee-wee Herman
MG: Queen Ida

EPISODE 04: 12/07/85
H: John Lithgow
MG: Mr. Mister
SG/C: Sam Kinison

EPISODE 05: 12/14/85
H: Tom Hanks
MG: Sade
SG/C: Steven Wright

EPISODE 06: 12/21/85
H: Teri Garr
MG: Dream Academy/The Cult
SG/C: Penn & Teller

EPISODE 07: 01/18/86
H: Harry Dean Stanton
MG: The Replacements
SG/C: Sam Kinison

EPISODE 08: 01/25/86
H: Dudley Moore
MG: Al Green

EPISODE 09: 02/08/86
H: Ron Reagan
MG: The Nelsons
SG/C: Penn & Teller

EPISODE 10: 02/15/86
H: Jerry Hall
MG: Stevie Ray Vaughan, Double Tree
SG/C: Mick Jagger, Sam Kinison, Jimmie Vaughan

EPISODE 11: 02/22/86
H: Jay Leno
MG: The Neville Brothers
SG/C: Mike the Dog

EPISODE 12: 03/15/86
H: Griffin Dunne
MG: Rosanne Cash
SG/C: Penn & Teller

EPISODE 13: 03/22/86
H: George Wendt, Francis Ford Coppola
MG: Philip Glass
SG/C: Janice Pendarvis

EPISODE 14: 04/12/86
H: Oprah Winfrey
MG: Joe Jackson

EPISODE 15: 04/19/86
H: Tony Danza
MG: Laurie Anderson
SG/C: Penn & Teller

EPISODE 16: 05/10/86
H: Catherine Oxenberg, Paul Simon
MG: Ladysmith Black Mambazo
SG/C: Penn & Teller, Princess Elizabeth of Yugoslavia

EPISODE 17: 05/17/86
H: Jimmy Breslin
MG: Level 42, E.G. Daily
SG/C: Sam Kinison, Marvelous Marvin Hagler

EPISODE 18: 05/24/86
H: Anjelica Huston, Billy Martin
MG: George Clinton and the Parliament Funkadelic
SG/C: Thomas Dolby

SEASON HIGHLIGHTS

The Limits of the Imagination (various), Master Thespian (Lovitz), The Pat Stevens Show (Dunn), Tommy Flanagan the Pathological Liar (Lovitz)

BUMPER KEY (Pg. 370-371)

02 07 09 18 18 02 10
06 11 17
06 16 05 06 12 17
07 16 03 10 08 17 17
01 14 18 15 14
01 13 09 04
13 03 11
05 06 04 07
15 12

b.

SHOW #445
HOST: CHEVY CHASE

AIR: NOVEMBER 16, 1985
STUDIO 8H
NBC
30 Rockefeller Plaza
New York, NY

SATURDAY NIGHT LIVE

REHEARSAL AND STUDIO SCHEDULE

FRIDAY, NOVEMBER 15, 1985:

12:30P - 1:00P E.S.U.

CAMERA BLOCK: PG#

1:00P - 2:00P CRAIG SUNDBERG, IDIOT SAVANT
(Michael/Nora/Jon/Terry/Robert/Dan/Violinist/Pardo V.O.)

2:00P - 3:30P PARTY SCHOOL BOWL
(Chevy/Jon/Michael/Joan/Terry/Robert/Nora/Dan/Danitra/Pardo V.O.)

3:30P - 5:00P FORD/REAGAN
(Chevy/Randy/Terry/Jon/Dan)

5:00P - 6:00P MEAL BREAK

6:00P - 7:30P BLUE, GRAY, YELLOW
(Michael/Robert/Randy/Nora/Danitra/Joan/Jon V.O.)

7:30P - 8:30P QUIRKY
(Chevy/Joan)

8:30P - 9:30P THOSE UNLUCKY ANDERSONS
(Chevy/Nora/Michael/Joan/Jon/McKinney V.O./Damon/Dan)

9:30P - 11:00P DEATH OF A GUNFIGHTER
(Chevy/Robert/Randy/Jon/Extras)

INDIVIDUAL CALLS:

11A - 2P (CHEVY FILMS "DRUM AD")

(MORE)

a.

c.

d.

a. Robert Downey Jr. during dress rehearsal for "Models Against the Wilderness" (in the live sketch he wore a shirt). **b.** Rehearsal schedule for episode 2. **c.** Lorne Michaels, in his first season back on the show after a five-year hiatus, with new season 11 cast members. **d.** Paul Simon performing with Ladysmith Black Mambazo.

CAST

Dana Carvey
Nora Dunn
Phil Hartman
Jan Hooks
Victoria Jackson
Jon Lovitz
Dennis Miller

Featuring:
Kevin Nealon
A. Whitney Brown

Weekend Update:
Dennis Miller

CREW

Executive Producer:
Lorne Michaels

Director: Paul Miller

Writers: Andy Breckman, A. Whitney Brown, E. Jean Carroll, Tom Davis, James Downey, Al Franken, Eddie Gorodetsky, Phil Hartman, George Meyer, Lorne Michaels, Kevin Nealon, Herb Sargent, Marc Shaiman, Rosie Shuster, Robert Smigel, Bonnie Turner, Terry Turner, John Vitti, Christine Zander

Film Producer:
James Signorelli

Production Designers:
Eugene Lee, Akira Yoshimura

Musical Directors:
Cheryl Hardwick, G.E. Smith

Costume Designer:
Pam Peterson

Wardrobe: Margaret Karolyi, Paul Buboltz

Hair: Michael Kriston

Makeup: Peter Montagna

Photographer: Isaiah Wyner

EPISODE LIST

EPISODE KEY:
H - Host
MG - Musical Guest
SG/C - Special Guests/Cameos

EPISODE 01: 10/11/86
H: Sigourney Weaver
MG: Buster Poindexter
SG/C: Christopher Durang, Madonna, Buster Poindexter, Soozie Tyrell

EPISODE 02: 10/18/86
H: Malcolm-Jamal Warner
MG: Run-DMC
SG/C: Buster Poindexter, Sam Kinison, Spike Lee, Soozie Tyrell

EPISODE 03: 11/08/86
H: Rosanna Arquette
MG: Ric Ocasek
SG/C: Ron Darling, Bill Wegman

EPISODE 4: 11/15/86
H: Sam Kinison
MG: Lou Reed
SG/C: Seka

EPISODE 5: 11/22/86
H: Robin Williams
MG: Paul Simon
SG/C: Ladysmith Black Mambazo, Art Garfunkel, Whoopi Goldberg

EPISODE 6: 12/06/86
H: Chevy Chase, Steve Martin, Martin Short
MG: Randy Newman
SG/C: Eric Idle

EPISODE 7: 12/13/86
H: Steve Guttenberg
MG: The Pretenders
SG/C: Buster Poindexter, Penn & Teller, Tim Robbins, Eriq La Salle, Fisher Stevens

EPISODE 8: 12/20/86
H: William Shatner
MG: Lone Justice
SG/C: Griffin Dunne, Buster Poindexter, Kevin Meaney

EPISODE 9: 01/24/87
H: Joe Montana, Walter Payton
MG: Debbie Harry
SG/C: Chris Stein

EPISODE 10: 01/31/87
H: Paul Shaffer
MG: Bruce Hornsby & the Range

EPISODE 11: 02/14/87
H: Bronson Pinchot
MG: Paul Young
SG/C: Paulina Porizkova, Soozie Tyrell

EPISODE 12: 02/21/87
H/MG: Willie Nelson
SG/C: Danny DeVito

EPISODE 13: 02/28/87
H: Valerie Bertinelli
MG: The Robert Cray Band
SG/C: Edwin Newman, Eddie Van Halen

EPISODE 14: 03/21/87
H: Bill Murray
MG: Percy Sledge

EPISODE 15: 03/28/87
H: Charlton Heston
MG: Wynton Marsalis
SG/C: Danny Aiello, Don Braden, Bob Hurst, Julie Hagerty, John Mahoney, Anne Meara, Marcus Roberts, Ben Stiller, Jerry Stiller, Nina Tremblay, Jeff Watts

EPISODE 16: 04/11/87
H: John Lithgow
MG: Anita Baker

EPISODE 17: 04/18/87
H: John Larroquette
MG: Timbuk 3

EPISODE 18: 05/09/87
H: Mark Harmon
MG: Suzanne Vega

EPISODE 19: 05/16/87
H: Garry Shandling
MG: Los Lobos

EPISODE 20: 05/23/87
H: Dennis Hopper
MG: Roy Orbison

SEASON HIGHLIGHTS

Choppin' Broccoli (Carvey), Church Chat (Carvey), The Honest Man (Montana/Hartman/Hooks), Instant Coffee with Bill Smith (Nealon), Master Thespian (Lovitz), Mr. Subliminal (Nealon), Nick the Lounge Singer (Murray), The Pat Stevens Show (Dunn), The Sweeney Sisters (Hooks/Dunn/Shaiman)

BUMPER KEY (Pg. 374-375)

02 17 19 02 09 09 06
20 19 03 10
01 10 14
08 02 11 11 13 13
01 12 07 06
08 03 07 14
04 06
17 06 15 15 16
20 04 05 05 07 16 18 18

a.

b.

c.

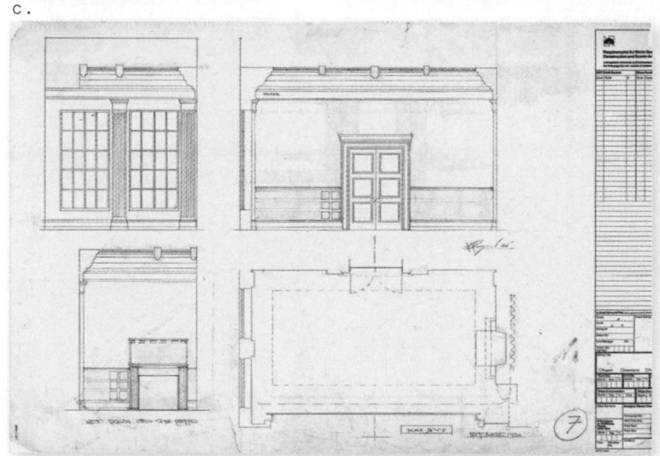

d.

a. Bill Murray and Nora Dunn in "Il Returno de Hercules." **b.** Production designer Keith Ian Raywood. **c.** Designs for the new season 12 home base. **b.** Cast and writers with Bronson Pinchot.

SATURDAY NIGHT LIVE

SEASON 12 / 1986-87

SATURDAY
NIGHT
LIVE

SATURDAY
NIGHT
LIVE
SATURDAY
NIGHT
LIVE
SATURDAY
NIGHT
LIVE
SATURDAY
NIGHT
LIVE
SATURDAY
NIGHT
LIVE
SATURDAY
NIGHT
LIVE
SATURDAY
NIGHT
LIVE
SATURDAY
NIGHT
LIVE
SATURDAY
NIGHT
LIVE
SATURDAY
NIGHT
LIVE
SATURDAY
NIGHT
LIVE

SEASON 13 / 1987-88

CAST

Dana Carvey
Nora Dunn
Phil Hartman
Jan Hooks
Victoria Jackson
Jon Lovitz
Dennis Miller
Kevin Nealon

Featuring:
A. Whitney Brown

Weekend Update:
Dennis Miller

CREW

Executive Producer:
Lorne Michaels

Director: Paul Miller

Producer: James Downey

Writers: A. Whitney Brown, Gregory Daniels, Tom Davis, James Downey, Al Franken, Jack Handey, Phil Hartman, George Meyer, Lorne Michaels, Conan O'Brien, Bob Odenkirk, Herb Sargent, Robert Smigel, Bonnie Turner, Terry Turner, Christine Zander

Film Producer:
James Signorelli

Production Designers:
Eugene Lee, Akira Yoshimura

Musical Directors:
Cheryl Hardwick, G.E. Smith

Costume Designer:
Pam Peterson

Wardrobe: Margaret Karolyi, Paul Buboltz

Hair: Gloria Rivera

Makeup: Peter Montagna

Photographer: Karen Kuehn

EPISODE LIST

EPISODE KEY:
H - Host
MG - Musical Guest
SG/C - Special Guests/Cameos

EPISODE 01: 10/17/87
H: Steve Martin
MG: Sting
SG/C: Bruce Babbitt, Branford Marsalis

EPISODE 02: 10/24/87
H: Sean Penn
MG: LL Cool J, The Pull

EPISODE 03: 10/31/87
H: Dabney Coleman
MG: The Cars
SG/C: Elvira

EPISODE 04: 11/14/87
H: Robert Mitchum
MG: Simply Red
SG/C: Jane Greer, Bentley Mitchum

EPISODE 05: 11/21/87
H: Candice Bergen
MG: Cher
SG/C: Sydney Biddle Barrows, Paul Shaffer

EPISODE 06: 12/05/87
H: Danny DeVito
MG: Bryan Ferry
SG/C: Rhea Perlman

EPISODE 07: 12/12/87
H: Angie Dickinson
MG: David Gilmour/Buster Poindexter
SG/C: The Banshees of Blue, Soozie Tyrell, The Uptown Horns

EPISODE 08: 12/19/87
H: Paul Simon
MG: Paul Simon, Linda Ronstadt
SG/C: Sen. Paul Simon, The Mariachi Vargas de Tecalitlán

EPISODE 09: 01/23/88
H: Robin Williams
MG: James Taylor
SG/C: Don Grolnick, Leland Sklar

EPISODE 10: 01/30/88
H: Carl Weathers
MG: Robbie Robertson
SG/C: BoDeans, Maria McKee

EPISODE 11: 02/13/88
H: Justine Bateman
MG: Terence Trent D'Arby
SG/C: Dan Aykroyd

EPISODE 12: 02/20/88
H: Tom Hanks
MG: Randy Travis

EPISODE 13: 02/27/88
H: Judge Reinhold
MG: 10,000 Maniacs

SEASON HIGHLIGHTS

Church Chat (Carvey), Girl Watchers (Hanks/Lovitz), Handi-Off (Victoria Jackson), Learning to Feel (Dunn), Master Thespian (Lovitz), The Pat Stevens Show (Dunn), Pumping Up with Hans & Franz (Carvey/Nealon), The Sweeney Sisters (Dunn/Hooks)

BUMPER KEY (Pg. 378-379)

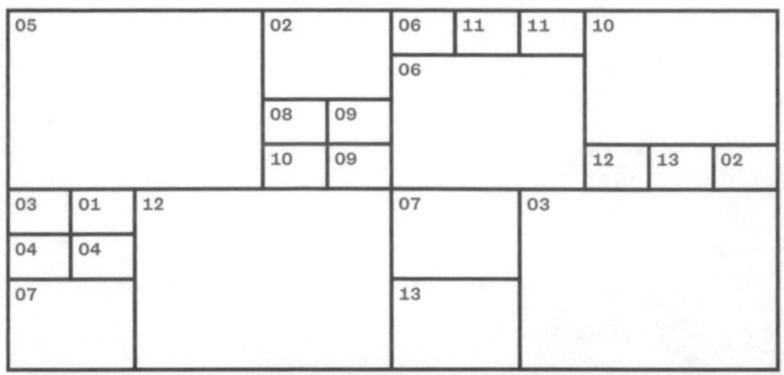

a.

b.

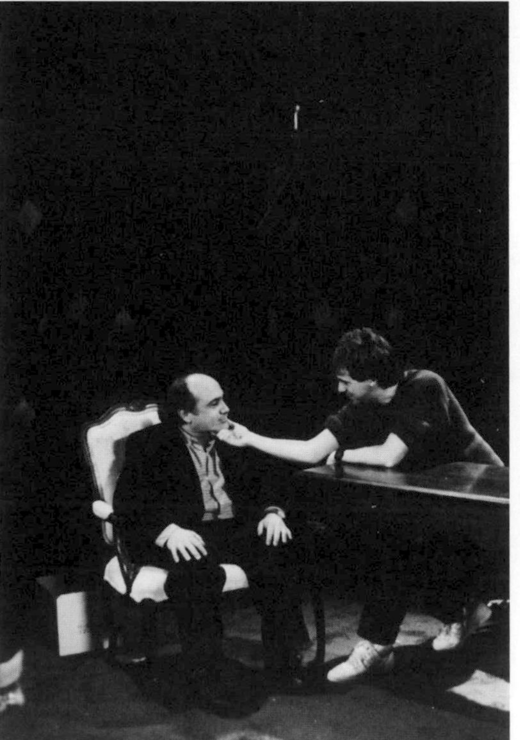

c.

a. "Church Chat" with Dana Carvey as the Church Lady and Sean Penn (prostrate).
b. Dana Carvey rehearsing "Church Chat" with Danny DeVito.
c. Steve Guttenberg rehearsing with Jon Lovitz, Al Franken, and Jan Hooks.

CAST

Dana Carvey
Nora Dunn
Phil Hartman
Jan Hooks
Victoria Jackson
Jon Lovitz
Dennis Miller
Kevin Nealon

Featuring:
A. Whitney Brown
Al Franken
Mike Myers
Ben Stiller

Weekend Update:
Dennis Miller

CREW

Executive Producer:
Lorne Michaels

Director: Paul Miller

Producer: James Downey

Writers: John Bowman, A. Whitney Brown, Gregory Daniels, Tom Davis, James Downey, Al Franken, Shannon Gaughan, Jack Handey, Phil Hartman, Lorne Michaels, Mike Myers, Conan O'Brien, Bob Odenkirk, Herb Sargent, Tom Schiller, Robert Smigel, Bonnie Turner, Terry Turner, Christine Zander

Film Producer:
James Signorelli

Production Designers:
Eugene Lee, Akira Yoshimura

Lighting Consultant:
Phil Hymes

Musical Directors:
Cheryl Hardwick, G.E. Smith

Costume Designer:
Pam Peterson

Wardrobe: Margaret Karolyi, Paul Buboltz

Hair: Gloria Rivera

Makeup: Peter Montagna

Photographers: Edie Baskin, Frank Ockenfels III

EPISODE LIST

EPISODE KEY:
H - Host
MG - Musical Guest
SG/C - Special Guests/Cameos

EPISODE 01: 10/08/88
H: Tom Hanks
MG: Keith Richards
SG/C: Steve Jordan, Ivan Neville

EPISODE 02: 10/15/88
H: Matthew Broderick
MG: The Sugarcubes
SG/C: Douglas McGrath, Laurie Metcalf, Fred Newman Catherine O'Hara

EPISODE 03: 10/22/88
H: John Larroquette
MG: Randy Newman

EPISODE 04: 11/05/88
H: Matthew Modine
MG: Edie Brickell & New Bohemians
SG/C: Morton Downey, Jr.

EPISODE 05: 11/12/88
H: Demi Moore
MG: Johnny Clegg & Savuka
SG/C: Kirsten Dunst, Bruce Willis

EPISODE 06: 11/19/88
H: John Lithgow
MG: Tracy Chapman

EPISODE 07: 12/03/88
H: Danny DeVito
MG: The Bangles
SG/C: Arnold Schwarzenegger

EPISODE 08: 12/10/88
H: Kevin Kline
MG: Bobby McFerrin

EPISODE 09: 12/17/88
H: Melanie Griffith
MG: Little Feat
SG/C: Don Johnson

EPISODE 10: 01/21/89
H: John Malkovich
MG: Anita Baker

EPISODE 11: 01/28/89
H: Tony Danza
MG: John Hiatt, The Goners

EPISODE 12: 02/11/89
H: Ted Danson
MG: Luther Vandross

EPISODE 13: 02/18/89
H: Leslie Nielsen
MG: Cowboy Junkies
SG/C: Kim Alexis, Beverly Johnson, Cheryl Tiegs

EPISODE 14: 02/25/89
H: Glenn Close
MG: Gipsy Kings
SG/C: William Hurt

EPISODE 15: 03/25/89
H: Mary Tyler Moore
MG: Elvis Costello

EPISODE 16: 04/01/89
H: Mel Gibson
MG: Living Colour
SG/C: Danny Glover

EPISODE 17: 04/15/89
H/MG: Dolly Parton

EPISODE 18: 04/22/89
H: Geena Davis
MG: John Mellencamp
SG/C: Lonnie Mack

EPISODE 19: 05/13/89
H: Wayne Gretzky
MG: Fine Young Cannibals

EPISODE 20: 05/20/89
H: Steve Martin
MG: Tom Petty & The Heartbreakers
SG/C: Timothy Busfield, Paulina Porizkova

SEASON HIGHLIGHTS

The New Coneheads (Dunn/Hartman/Jackson/Martin), A Grumpy Old Man (Carvey), Change Bank 2 (James Downey), Church Chat (Carvey), Cooking with the Anal Retentive Chef (Hartman), Girl Watchers (Hanks/Lovitz), Learning to Feel (Dunn), Love Is a Dream (Jan Hooks, Phil Hartman), Master Thespian (Lovitz), Mr. Short-Term Memory (Hanks), Mr. Subliminal (Nealon), The Pat Stevens Show (Dunn), Pumping Up with Hans & Franz (Carvey/Nealon), Sprockets (Myers), The Sweeney Sisters (Dunn/Hooks/Shaiman), Toonces the Cat Who Could Drive a Car (Carvey/Jackson), Wayne's World (Carvey/Myers)

BUMPER KEY (Pg. 382-383)

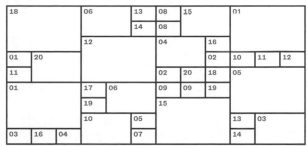

a.

b.

a. Jan Hooks and Glenn Close in "Jealous of Janelle."
b. Dana Carvey, Mel Gibson, and Danny Glover in "Lethal Weapon VI."

SATURDAY NIGHT LIVE
SATURDAY NIGHT LIVE
SATURDAY NIGHT LIVE
SATURDAY NIGHT LIVE
SATURDAY NIGHT LIVE
SATURDAY NIGHT LIVE

SATURDAY NIGHT LIVE

NIGHT
LIVE

NIGHT

SATURDAY * NIGHT * LIVE

SEASON 15 / 1989-90

CAST

Dana Carvey
Nora Dunn
Phil Hartman
Jan Hooks
Victoria Jackson
Jon Lovitz
Dennis Miller
Mike Myers
Kevin Nealon

Featuring:
A. Whitney Brown
Al Franken

Weekend Update:
Dennis Miller

CREW

Executive Producer:
Lorne Michaels

Director: Dave Wilson

Producer: James Downey

Writers: A. Whitney Brown, Gregory Daniels, Tom Davis, James Downey, Al Franken, Jack Handey, Tom Hymes, Lorne Michaels, Mike Myers, Conan O'Brien, Bob Odenkirk, Herb Sargent, Tom Schiller, Rob Schneider, Robert Smigel, David Spade, Bonnie Turner, Terry Turner, Christine Zander

Supervising Producer:
Ken Aymong

Film Producer:
James Signorelli

Production Designers:
Eugene Lee, Akira Yoshimura

Musical Directors:
Cheryl Hardwick, G.E. Smith

Costume Designer:
Ingrid Weber

Wardrobe: Dale Richards, Michael Wallace

Hair: Gloria Rivera

Makeup: Michael Laudati

Photographer: Edie Baskin

EPISODE LIST

EPISODE KEY:
H - Host
MG - Musical Guest
SG/C - Special Guests/Cameos

EPISODE 01: 09/30/89
H: Bruce Willis
MG: Neil Young
SG/C: Steve Jordan

EPISODE 02: 10/07/89
H: Rick Moranis
MG: Rickie Lee Jones

EPISODE 03: 10/21/89
H: Kathleen Turner
MG: Billy Joel

EPISODE 04: 10/28/89
H: James Woods
MG: Don Henley

EPISODE 05: 11/11/89
H: Chris Evert
MG: Eurythmics

EPISODE 06: 11/18/89
H: Woody Harrelson
MG: David Byrne

EPISODE 07: 12/02/89
H: John Goodman
MG: k.d. lang & The Reclines

EPISODE 08: 12/09/89
H: Robert Wagner
MG: Linda Ronstadt, Aaron Neville

EPISODE 09: 12/16/89
H: Andie MacDowell
MG: Tracy Chapman
SG/C: Joe Franken II

EPISODE 10: 01/13/90
H: Ed O'Neill
MG: Harry Connick, Jr.
SG/C: Maury Povich

EPISODE 11: 01/20/90
H: Christopher Walken
MG: Bonnie Raitt

EPISODE 12: 02/10/90
H: Quincy Jones
MG: Quincy Jones, Take 6, Tevin Campbell, Andrae Crouch, Sandra Crouch, Kool Moe Dee, Big Daddy Kane, Melle Mel, Quincy D III, Siedah Garrett, Al Jarreau

EPISODE 13: 02/17/90
H: Tom Hanks
MG: Aerosmith

EPISODE 14: 02/24/90
H: Fred Savage
MG: Technotronic
SG/C: Rosie Perez, Joanne Savage, Kala Savage

EPISODE 15: 03/17/90
H: Rob Lowe
MG: The Pogues
SG/C: Chevy Chase

EPISODE 16: 03/24/90
H: Debra Winger
MG: Eric Clapton

EPISODE 17: 04/14/90
H: Corbin Bernsen
MG: The Smithereens

EPISODE 18: 04/21/90
H: Alec Baldwin
MG: The B-52's

EPISODE 19: 5/12/90
H: Andrew Dice Clay
MG: The Spanic Boys, Julee Cruise

EPISODE 20: 05/19/90
H: Candice Bergen
MG: The Notting Hillbillies

SEASON HIGHLIGHTS

Church Chat (Carvey), Colon Blow (Phil Hartman), The Continental (Walken), Cooking with the Anal Retentive Chef (Hartman), Girl Watchers (Hanks/Lovitz), Mr. Short-Term Memory (Hanks), The Pat Stevens Show (Dunn), Pumping Up with Hans & Franz (Carvey/Nealon), Sprockets (Myers), Toonces the Cat Who Could Drive a Car (Carvey/Jackson), Wayne's World (Carvey/Myers)

BUMPER KEY (Pg. 386-387)

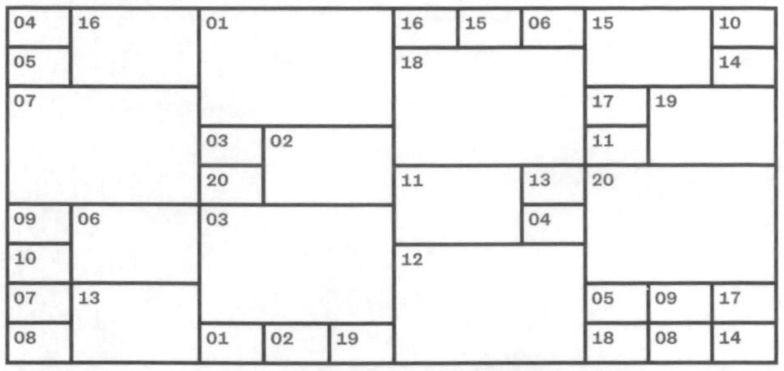

a.

b.

c.

a. Phil Hartman as Jack Nicholson in "Five Easy Pieces '89." **b.** Mike Myers and Dana Carvey in the wardrobe department. **c.** Alec Baldwin.

CAST

Dana Carvey
Phil Hartman
Jan Hooks
Victoria Jackson
Dennis Miller
Mike Myers
Kevin Nealon

Featuring:
A. Whitney Brown
Chris Farley
Al Franken
Tim Meadows
Chris Rock
Adam Sandler
Rob Schneider
David Spade
Julia Sweeney

Weekend Update:
Dennis Miller

CREW

Executive Producer:
Lorne Michaels

Director: Dave Wilson

Producers: James Downey, Al Franken, Jack Handey, Robert Smigel

Writers: A. Whitney Brown, Tom Davis, James Downey, Al Franken, Jack Handey, Lorne Michaels, Dennis Miller, Conan O'Brien, Bob Odenkirk, Andrew Robin, Adam Sandler, Herb Sargent, Rob Schneider, Robert Smigel, David Spade, Bonnie Turner, Terry Turner, Christine Zander

Supervising Producer:
Ken Aymong

Film Producer:
James Signorelli

Production Designers:
Eugene Lee, Akira Yoshimura

Lighting Consultant:
Phil Hymes

Musical Directors:
Cheryl Hardwick, G.E. Smith

Sketch Music Adaptation:
Hal Willner

Costume Designer:
Melina Root

Wardrobe: Dale Richards
Michael Wallace

Hair: Gloria Rivera

Makeup: Jennifer Aspinall

Photographer: Edie Baskin

EPISODE LIST

EPISODE KEY:
H - Host
MG - Musical Guest
SG/C - Special Guests/Cameos

EPISODE 01: 09/29/90
H: Kyle MacLachlan
MG: Sinead O'Connor

EPISODE 02: 10/06/90
H: Susan Lucci
MG: Hothouse Flowers
SG/C: Gene Rayburn

EPISODE 03: 10/20/90
H: George Steinbrenner
MG: The Time

EPISODE 04: 10/27/90
H: Patrick Swayze
MG: Mariah Carey
SG/C: Liza Niemi

EPISODE 05: 11/10/90
H: Jimmy Smits
MG: World Party
SG/C: Bob Costas

EPISODE 06: 11/17/90
H: Dennis Hopper
MG: Paul Simon
SG/C: Olodum, Bert Parks

EPISODE 07: 12/01/90
H: John Goodman
MG: Faith No More

EPISODE 08: 12/08/90
H: Tom Hanks
MG: Edie Brickell & New Bohemians
SG/C: Elliott Gould, Jon Lovitz, Steve Martin, Ralph Nader, Tony Randall, Paul Simon

EPISODE 09: 12/15/90
H: Dennis Quaid
MG: The Neville Brothers
SG/C: Jon Lovitz

EPISODE 10: 01/12/91
H: Joe Mantegna
MG: Vanilla Ice

EPISODE 11: 01/19/91
H/MG: Sting

EPISODE 12: 02/09/91
H: Kevin Bacon
MG: INXS

EPISODE 13: 02/16/91
H: Roseanne Barr
MG: Deee-Lite
SG/C: Tom Arnold, Bootsy Collins & The Rubber Band, Jon Lovitz

EPISODE 14: 02/23/91
H: Alec Baldwin
MG: Whitney Houston
SG/C: Evander Holyfield, Arthur Kent, Jon Lovitz

EPISODE 15: 03/16/91
H: Michael J. Fox
MG: The Black Crowes

EPISODE 16: 03/23/91
H: Jeremy Irons
MG: Fishbone
SG/C: Razor Ruddock

EPISODE 17: 04/13/91
H: Catherine O'Hara
MG: R.E.M.
SG/C: Evander Holyfield, Carole King, Kate Pierson, Randy Quaid

EPISODE 18: 04/20/91
H: Steven Seagal
MG: Michael Bolton

EPISODE 19: 05/11/91
H: Delta Burke
MG: Chris Isaak, Silvertone
SG/C: Madonna

EPISODE 20: 05/18/91
H: George Wendt
MG: Elvis Costello

SEASON HIGHLIGHTS

Bad Idea Jeans (Nealon), Bill Swerski's Superfans (Wendt/Smigel/Myers/Farley), Chia Head (Nealon/Hartman (Spade/Rock), Chippendales (Swayze/Farley), Church Chat (Carvey), Copy Machine (Schneider), Daily Affirmation with Stuart Smalley (Franken), The Dark Side (Rock), Deep Thoughts by Jack Handey (Hartman), Happy Fun Ball (Jan Hooks, Dana Carvey, Mike Myers), Nikey Turkey (Rock), Pat (Sweeney), Pumping Up with Hans & Franz (Carvey/Nealon), Simon (Myers), Sprockets (Myers), Toonces the Cat Who Could Drive a Car (Carvey/Jackson), Wayne's World (Carvey/Myers)

BUMPER KEY (Pg. 390-391)

01 10 03 03 13 18 16 12
01 09
02 11 02 10 15 14 14
16 05 08 05 13 12 15 04 17
06 08 09 17 18 19
04 06 07 07 19 20

a.

a. David Spade and Mike Myers backstage.
b. Chris Rock as Nat X.
c. "The Sinatra Group" with Phil Hartman as Frank Sinatra, Jan Hooks as Sinead O'Connor, and Sting as Billy Idol.

b.

c.

SATURDAY NIGHT LIVE
SATURDAY NIGHT LIVE
SATURDAY NIGHT LIVE
SATURDAY NIGHT LIVE
SATURDAY NIGHT LIVE
NIGHT LIVE

SATURDAY NIGHT LIVE

SEASON 16 / 1990-91

NIGHT

EARTH·HOPE·
HARMONY
COLOURS
UNITY·
ONE LOVE

SEASON 17 / 1991-92

SATURDAY
NIGHT
LIVE

JIMMY SWAG
SATURDAY ✦ NIGHT ✦ LIVE

SEASON 17 / 1991-92

CAST

Dana Carvey
Chris Farley
Phil Hartman
Victoria Jackson
Mike Myers
Kevin Nealon
Chris Rock
Julia Sweeney

Featuring:
Beth Cahill
Ellen Cleghorne
Siobhan Fallon
Al Franken
Melanie Hutsell
Tim Meadows
Adam Sandler
Rob Schneider
Robert Smigel
David Spade

Weekend Update:
Kevin Nealon

CREW

Executive Producer:
Lorne Michaels

Director: Dave Wilson

Producers: James Downey, Al Franken, Jack Handey, Robert Smigel

Writers: Tom Davis, James Downey, Al Franken, Jack Handey, Warren Hutcherson, Steven Koren, Daniel McGrath, Lorne Michaels, Adam Sandler, Herb Sargent, Rob Schneider, Robert Smigel, Bonnie Turner, Terry Turner, Christine Zander

Supervising Producer:
Ken Aymong

Film Producer:
James Signorelli

Production Designers:
Eugene Lee, Akira Yoshimura

Lighting Consultant:
Phil Hymes

Musical Directors:
Cheryl Hardwick, G.E. Smith

Sketch Music Adaptation:
Hal Willner

Costume Designer:
Melina Root

Wardrobe: Dale Richards

Hair: Gloria Rivera

Makeup: Jennifer Aspinall

Photographer: Edie Baskin

EPISODE LIST

EPISODE KEY:
H - Host
MG - Musical Guest
SG/C - Special Guests/Cameos

EPISODE 01: 09/28/91
H: Michael Jordan
MG: Public Enemy
SG/C: Jesse Jackson, Spike Lee, George Wendt

EPISODE 02: 10/05/91
H: Jeff Daniels
MG: Color Me Badd

EPISODE 03: 10/12/91
H: Kirstie Alley
MG: Tom Petty & the Heartbreakers
SG/C: Ted Danson, Kelsey Grammer, Woody Harrelson, George Wendt

EPISODE 04: 10/26/91
H: Christian Slater
MG: Bonnie Raitt
SG/C: John McLaughlin, Arnold Schwarzenegger

EPISODE 05: 11/02/91
H: Kiefer Sutherland
MG: Skid Row
SG/C: Ken Stabler

EPISODE 06: 11/16/91
H: Linda Hamilton
MG: Mariah Carey
SG/C: Edward Furlong, Martin Scorsese

EPISODE 07: 11/23/91
H: Macaulay Culkin
MG: Kieran Culkin, Tin Machine
SG/C: George Wendt

EPISODE 08: 12/07/91
H/MG: MC Hammer
SG/C: Christina Ricci, Jimmy Workman

EPISODE 09: 12/14/91
H: Steve Martin
MG: James Taylor
SG/C: Don Grolnick, Susan Lucci

EPISODE 10: 01/11/92
H: Rob Morrow
MG: Nirvana
SG/C: Charlie Musselwhite

EPISODE 11: 01/18/92
H: Chevy Chase
MG: Robbie Robertson
SG/C: Monk Boudreaux, Bruce Hornsby, Ivan Neville, George Wendt

EPISODE 12: 02/08/92
H: Susan Dey
MG: C+C Music Factory

EPISODE 13: 02/15/92
H: Jason Priestley
MG: Teenage Fanclub

EPISODE 14: 02/22/92
H: Roseanne & Tom Arnold
MG: The Red Hot Chili Peppers
SG/C: Madonna, Barbra Streisand

EPISODE 15: 03/14/92
H: John Goodman
MG: Garth Brooks

EPISODE 16: 03/21/92
H: Mary Stuart Masterson
MG: En Vogue

EPISODE 17: 04/11/92
H: Sharon Stone
MG: Pearl Jam
SG/C: Jon Lovitz, Ken Stabler

EPISODE 18: 04/18/92
H: Jerry Seinfeld
MG: Annie Lennox
SG/C: Johnny Winter

EPISODE 19: 05/09/92
H: Tom Hanks
MG: Bruce Springsteen
SG/C: Jay Leno

EPISODE 20: 05/16/92
H: Woody Harrelson
MG: Vanessa Williams
SG/C: Jon Lovitz

SEASON HIGHLIGHTS

Bill Swerski's Superfans (Farley/Myers/Smigel), The Chris Farley Show (Farley), Coffee Talk with Linda Richman (Myers), Coldcock (Meadows), Copy Machine (Schneider), Daily Affirmation with Stuart Smalley (Franken), The Dark Side (Rock), Deep Thoughts by Jack Handey (Hartman), Dick Clark's Receptionist (Spade), Love Toilet (Jackson/Nealon), Massive Headwound Harry (Carvey), Opera Man (Sandler), Pat (Sweeney), Pumping Up with Hans & Franz (Carvey/Nealon), Schmitts Gay (Sandler/Farley), Simon (Myers), Three Legged Jeans (Meadows/Rock), Toonces the Cat Who Could Drive a Car (various), Unfrozen Caveman Lawyer (Hartman), Wayne's World (Carvey/Myers)

d.

BUMPER KEY (Pg. 396-397)

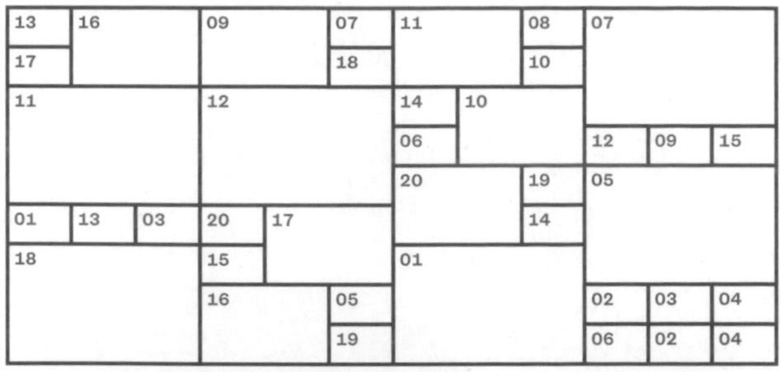

13 16 09 07 11 08 07
17 18 10
11 12 14 10
06 12 09 15
20 19 05
01 13 03 20 17 14
18 15 01
16 05 02 03 04
19 06 02 04

a.

b.

c.

e.

a. Bill Swerski's Superfans (Robert Smigel, Mike Myers, Chris Farley, and George Wendt) with host Michael Jordan. **b.** Ellen Cleghorne's Queen Shenequa character debuted in season 17. **c.** "Welcome to All Things Scottish. If it's not Scottish, it's craaaapp!!" Mike Myers as Stuart Rankin, with Phil Hartman. **d.** Adam Sandler as Opera Man. **e.** Phil Hartman (as Frank Sinatra) and David Spade in an unaired version of "Dick Clark's Receptionist."

CAST

Dana Carvey
Chris Farley
Phil Hartman
Mike Myers
Kevin Nealon
Chris Rock
Rob Schneider
Julia Sweeney

With:
Al Franken
Robert Smigel

Featuring:
Ellen Cleghorne
Melanie Hutsell
Tim Meadows
Adam Sandler
David Spade

Weekend Update:
Kevin Nealon

CREW

Executive Producer:
Lorne Michaels

Director: Dave Wilson

Producer: James Downey

Writers: Tom Davis, James Downey, Al Franken, Bruce Handey, Jack Handey, Warren Hutcherson, Dawna Kaufman, Steve Koren, David Mandel, Ian Maxtone-Graham, Tim Meadows, Lorne Michaels, Vanessa Middleton, Marilyn Suzanne Miller, Adam Sandler, Herb Sargent, Robert Smigel, David Spade, Bonnie Turner, Terry Turner, Christine Zander

Supervising Producer:
Ken Aymong

Film Producer:
James Signorelli

Production Designers:
Eugene Lee, Akira Yoshimura, Edie Baskin, Keith Ian Raywood

Lighting Consultant:
Phil Hymes

Musical Directors:
Cheryl Hardwick, G.E. Smith

Sketch Music Adaptation:
Hal Willner

Costume Designer:
Melina Root

Wardrobe: Dale Richards, Ellen Ellis Lee, Margaret Karolyi

Hair: Gloria Rivera

Makeup: Jennifer Aspinall

Photographer: Edie Baskin

EPISODE LIST

EPISODE KEY:
H - Host
MG - Musical Guest
SG/C - Special Guests/Cameos

EPISODE 01: 09/26/92
H: Nicolas Cage
MG: Bobby Brown
SG/C: Jan Hooks, Cher

EPISODE 02: 10/03/92
H: Tim Robbins
MG: Sinead O'Connor
SG/C: Susan Sarandon

EPISODE 03: 10/10/92
H: Joe Pesci
MG: Spin Doctors
SG/C: Robert De Niro, Martin Scorsese

EPISODE 04: 10/24/92
H: Christopher Walken
MG: Arrested Development
SG/C: Jan Hooks

EPISODE 05: 10/31/92
H: Catherine O'Hara
MG: 10,000 Maniacs

EPISODE 06: 11/14/92
H: Michael Keaton
MG: Morrissey

EPISODE 07: 11/21/92
H: Sinbad
MG: Sade

EPISODE 08: 12/05/92
H: Tom Arnold
MG: Neil Young
SG/C: Roseanne Arnold, George Wendt, Dick Butkus

EPISODE 09: 12/12/92
H: Glenn Close
MG: The Black Crowes
SG/C: Mary Beth Hurt, Jon Lovitz

EPISODE 10: 01/09/93
H: Danny DeVito
MG: Bon Jovi
SG/C: Mike Ditka, Jan Hooks, Joe Mantegna, George Wendt

EPISODE 11: 01/16/93
H: Harvey Keitel
MG: Madonna
SG/C: Jan Hooks

EPISODE 12: 02/06/93
H: Luke Perry
MG: Mick Jagger
SG/C: Giorgio Armani, Jan Hooks

EPISODE 13: 02/13/93
H: Alec Baldwin
MG: Paul McCartney

EPISODE 14: 02/20/93
H: Bill Murray
MG: Sting
SG/C: Steve Martin, Don Novello

EPISODE 15: 03/13/93
H: John Goodman
MG: Mary J. Blige
SG/C: Cora Blige, The Bravados

EPISODE 16: 03/20/93
H: Miranda Richardson
MG: Soul Asylum
SG/C: Marv Albert

EPISODE 17: 04/10/93
H: Jason Alexander
MG: Peter Gabriel

EPISODE 18: 04/17/93
H: Kirstie Alley
MG: Lenny Kravitz

EPISODE 19: 05/08/93
H: Christina Applegate
MG: Midnight Oil

EPISODE 20: 05/15/93
H: Kevin Kline
MG: Willie Nelson/Paul Simon
SG/C: Dan Ay

SEASON HIGHLIGHTS

The Chris Farley Show (Farley), Bill Swerski's Superfans (Farley/Myers/Smigel), Canis, Canteen Boy (Sandler), Cluckin' Chicken (Sandler/Hartman), Coffee Talk with Linda Richman (Myers), The Continental (Walken), Daily Affirmation with Stuart Smalley (Franken), The Dark Side (Rock), Deep Thoughts by Jack Handey (Hartman), Gap Girls (Farley/Sandler/Spade), Hibernol (Hartman), Hollywood Minute (Spade), Hub's Gyros (Farley/Sandler/Schneider/Smigel), Matt Foley Motivational Speaker (Farley), Pat (Sweeney), Pumping Up with Hanz & Franz (Carvey/Nealon), Simon (Myers), Unfrozen Caveman Lawyer (Hartman), Wayne's World (Carvey/Myers)

BUMPER KEY (Pg. 400-401)

a.

b.

c.

d.

e.

a. "Gap Girls" David Spade, Adam Sandler, and Chris Farley.
b. Harvey Keitel with Kevin Nealon in "Bathroom Attendant."
c. "You like-a da juice, huh?" Rob Schneider et al. in "Hub's Gyros."
d-e. "Deep Thoughts" was a recurring short segment featuring text by SNL writer Jack Handey and narrated by Phil Hartman.

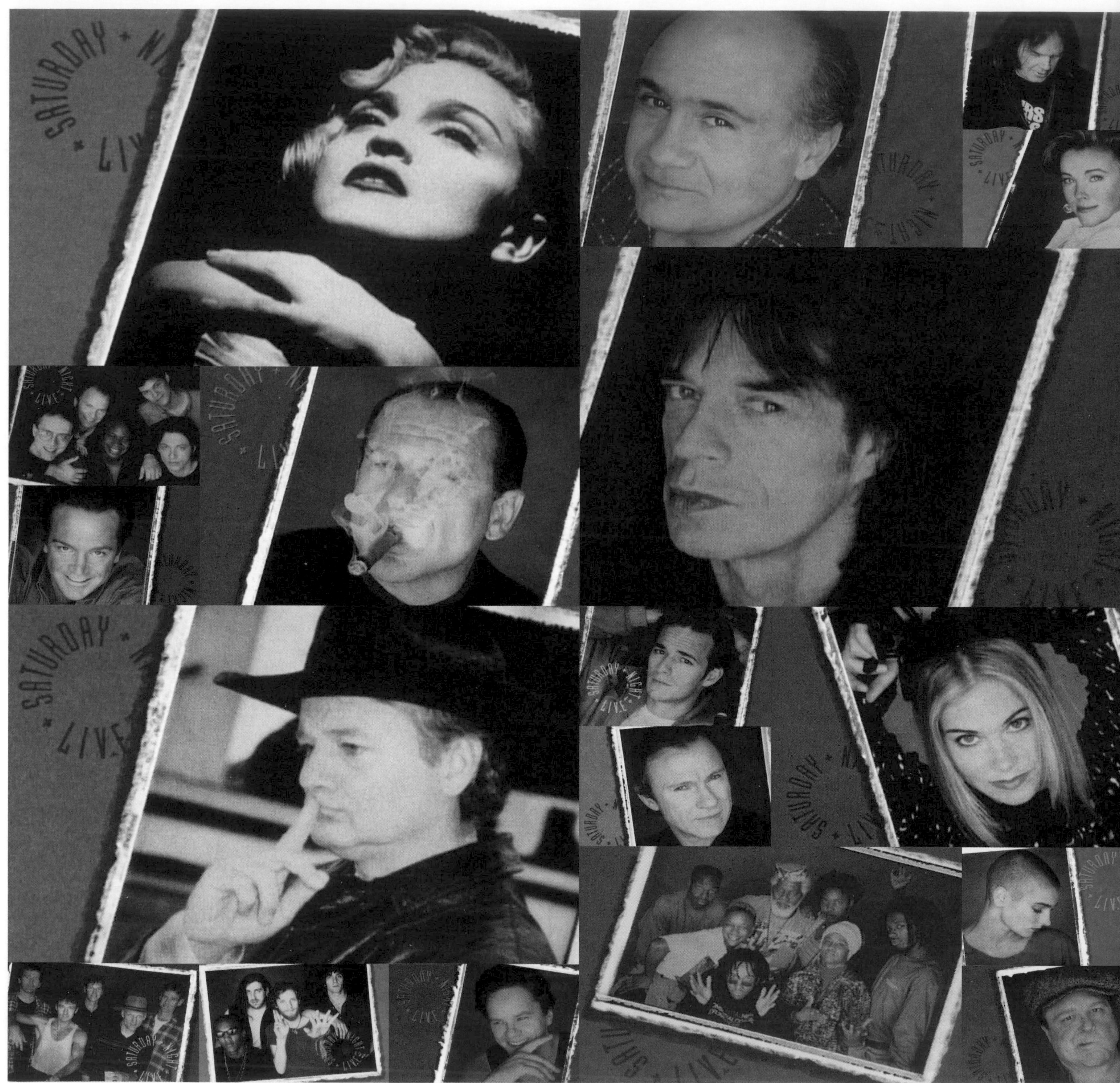
SATURDAY NIGHT LIVE

SATURDAY NIGHT LIVE
Molte Rumore
per Nulla

SEASON 18 / 1992-93

SATURDAY NIGHT LIVE

SATURDAY NIGHT LIVE
HILL

SATURDAY * NIGHT * LIVE

SEASON 19 / 1993-94

CAST

Ellen Cleghorne
Chris Farley
Phil Hartman
Melanie Hutsell
Michael McKean
Tim Meadows
Mike Myers
Kevin Nealon
Adam Sandler
Rob Schneider
David Spade
Julia Sweeney

Featuring:
Al Franken
Norm Macdonald
Jay Mohr
Sarah Silverman

Weekend Update:
Kevin Nealon

CREW

Executive Producer:
Lorne Michaels

Director: Dave Wilson

Producer: James Downey

Writers: Dave Attell, Tom Davis, Tony DeSena, James Downey, Al Franken, Tim Herlihy, Steve Koren, Steve Lookner, Norm Macdonald, David Mandel, Ian Maxtone-Graham, Lorne Michaels, Marilyn Suzanne Miller, Jay Mohr, Lewis Morton, Herb Sargent, Sarah Silverman, Fred Wolf

Supervising Producer:
Ken Aymong

Film Producer:
James Signorelli

Production Designers:
Eugene Lee, Akira Yoshimura, Edie Baskin, Keith Ian Raywood

Lighting Consultant:
Phil Hymes

Musical Directors:
Cheryl Hardwick, G.E. Smith

Sketch Music Adaptation:
Hal Willner

Costume Designer:
Melina Root

Wardrobe: Dale Richards, Ellen Ellis Lee, Margaret Karolyi

Hair: Gloria Rivera

Makeup: John Caglione Jr.

Photographer: Edie Baskin

EPISODE LIST

EPISODE KEY:
H - Host
MG - Musical Guest
SG/C - Special Guests/Cameos

EPISODE 01: 09/25/93
H: Charles Barkley
MG: Nirvana
SG/C: Muggsy Bouges, RuPaul, Skid Row

EPISODE 02: 10/02/93
H: Shannen Doherty
MG: Cypress Hill
SG/C: Ashley Hamilton

EPISODE 03: 10/09/93
H: Jeff Goldblum
MG: Aerosmith
SG/C: Laura Dern

EPISODE 04: 10/23/93
H: John Malkovich
MG: Billy Joel
SG/C: Jan Hooks

EPISODE 05: 10/30/93
H: Christian Slater
MG: Smashing Pumpkins
SG/C: Mark O'Connor

EPISODE 06: 11/13/93
H: Rosie O'Donnell
MG: James Taylor
SG/C: Don Grolnick, Casey Kasem

EPISODE 07: 11/20/93
H: Nicole Kidman
MG: Stone Temple Pilots
SG/C: Junior Brown, Dana Carvey, Christina Ricci, Jimmy Workman

EPISODE 08: 12/04/93
H: Charlton Heston
MG: Paul Westerberg

EPISODE 09: 12/11/93
H: Sally Field
MG: Tony! Toni! Toné!

EPISODE 10: 01/08/94
H: Jason Patric
MG: Blind Melon
SG/C: Richard Simmons

EPISODE 11: 01/15/94
H: Sara Gilbert
MG: Counting Crows

EPISODE 12: 02/05/94
H: Patrick Stewart
MG: Salt-N-Pepa
SG/C: Bernie Kopel

EPISODE 13: 02/12/94
H: Alec Baldwin, Kim Basinger
MG: UB40
SG/C: Billy Baldwin, Steven Baldwin

EPISODE 14: 02/19/94
H: Martin Lawrence
MG: Crash Test Dummies

EPISODE 15: 03/12/94
H: Nancy Kerrigan
MG: Aretha Franklin

EPISODE 16: 03/19/94
H: Helen Hunt
MG: Snoop Doggy Dogg
SG/C: Cindy Crawford

EPISODE 17: 04/09/94
H: Kelsey Grammer
MG: Dwight Yoakam
SG/C: Manute Bol, Jan Hooks, Sy Sperling

EPISODE 18: 04/16/94
H: Emilio Estevez
MG: Pearl Jam

EPISODE 19: 05/07/94
H: John Goodman
MG: The Pretenders
SG/C: Jan Hooks, Manute Bol

EPISODE 20: 05/14/94
H: Heather Locklear
MG: Janet Jackson
SG/C: Rafel Fuchs, Jay Leno

SEASON HIGHLIGHTS

Canteen Boy (Sandler), Coffee Talk with Linda Richman (Myers), Daily Affirmation with Stuart Smalley (Franken), Eych (Cleghorne), Matt Foley Motivational Speaker (Farley), Phillip the Hyper Hypo (Myers), Simon (Myers), Total Bastard Airlines (Spade), Wayne's World (Carvey/Myers)

BUMPER KEY (Pg. 404-405)

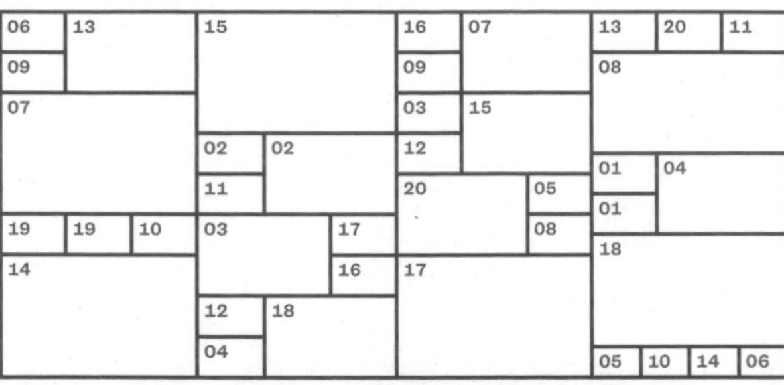

a.

b.

c.

d.

e.

a. Alec Baldwin with Adam Sandler as Canteen Boy. **b.** Chris Farley and Adam Sandler in "Lunchlady Land." **c.** Mike Myers as Simon, with host Sara Gilbert. **d.** "Buh-bye. Buh-bye. Buh-bye." David Spade, Tim Meadows, and Helen Hunt in "Total Bastard Airlines." **e.** Adam Sandler on "Weekend Update."

CAST

Morwenna Banks
Ellen Cleghorne
Chris Elliott
Chris Farley
Janeane Garofalo
Norm Macdonald
Michael McKean
Mark McKinney
Tim Meadows
Mike Myers
Kevin Nealon
Adam Sandler
David Spade

Featuring:
Al Franken
Laura Kightlinger
Jay Mohr
Molly Shannon

Weekend Update:
Norm Macdonald

CREW

Executive Producer:
Lorne Michaels

Director: Dave Wilson

Producer: James Downey

Writers: James Downey, Al Franken, Tim Herlihy, Norm Hiscock, Brian Kelley, Laura Kightlinger, Steve Koren, Steve Lookner, David Mandel, Ian Maxtone-Graham, Margo Meyer, Lorne Michaels, Marilyn Suzanne Miller, Lewis Morton, Adam Resnick, Herb Sargent, Drake Sather, Fred Wolf

Supervising Producer:
Ken Aymong

Film Producer:
James Signorelli

Production Designers:
Eugene Lee, Akira Yoshimura, Keith Ian Raywood

Lighting Consultant:
Phil Hymes

Musical Directors:
Cheryl Hardwick, G.E. Smith

Sketch Music Adaptation:
Hal Willner

Costume Designer:
Tom Broecker

Wardrobe: Dale Richards, Ellen Ellis Lee, Margaret Karolyi

Hair: Mary D'Angelo, Gloria Rivera

Makeup: John Caglione Jr., Jack Engel

Photographer: Edie Baskin

EPISODE LIST

EPISODE KEY:
H – Host
MG – Musical Guest
SG/C – Special Guests/Cameos

EPISODE 01: 09/24/94
H: Steve Martin
MG: Eric Clapton
SG/C: Bobby Bonilla, Roger Clemens, Lenny Dykstra, Brian Austin Green, Jac McDowell, Mo Vaughn

EPISODE 02: 10/01/94
H: Marisa Tomei
MG: Bonnie Raitt

EPISODE 03: 10/15/94
H: John Travolta
MG: Seal
SG/C: Steve Buscemi, Dave Edmunds, David Lander

EPISODE 04: 10/22/94
H: Dana Carvey
MG: Edie Brickell
SG/C: President George Bush, Paul Simon

EPISODE 05: 11/12/94
H: Sarah Jessica Parker
MG: R.E.M.
SG/C: Bill Murray

EPISODE 06: 11/19/94
H: John Turturro
MG: Tom Petty & The Heartbreakers
SG/C: Joey Buttafuoco, Davo Grohl, David Hasselhoff

EPISODE 07: 12/03/94
H: Roseanne
MG: Green Day
SG/C: Rip Taylor

EPISODE 08: 12/10/94
H: Alec Baldwin
MG: Beastie Boys
SG/C: Buddy Guy, Christian Slater

EPISODE 09: 12/17/94
H: George Foreman
MG: Hole
SG/C: Michael Buffer

EPISODE 10: 01/14/95
H: Jeff Daniels
MG: Luscious Jackson

EPISODE 11: 01/21/95
H: David Hyde Pierce
MG: Live

EPISODE 12: 02/11/95
H: Bob Newhart
MG: Des'ree, Suzanne Pheshette

EPISODE 13: 02/18/95
H: Deion Sanders
MG: Manute Bol, Bon Jovi

EPISODE 14: 02/25/95
H: George Clooney
MG: The Cranberries

EPISODE 15: 03/18/95
H: Paul Reiser
MG: Billy Grundfest, Annie Lennox

EPISODE 16: 03/25/95
H: John Goodman
MG: The Tragically Hip
SG/C: Dan Aykroyd, Brian Dennehy, George Wendt

EPISODE 17: 04/08/95
H: Damon Wayans
MG: Dionne Farris
SG/C: David Alan Grier

EPISODE 18: 04/15/95
H: Courteney Cox
MG: Dave Matthews Band
SG/C: Bela Fleck

EPISODE 19: 05/06/95
H: Bob Saget
MG: TLC

EPISODE 20: 05/13/95
H: David Duchovny
MG: Rod Stewart
SG/C: Michael Argarno, Naomi Campbell

SEASON HIGHLIGHTS

Bill Swerski's Super Fans (Aykroyd/Farley/Goodman/Smigel), The Blues Brothers (Aykroyd/Goodman), Canteen Boy (Sandler), Coffee Talk with Linda Richman (Myers), Daily Affirmations with Stuart Smalley (Franken), ETERNA REST (Michael Mckean), Film Beat (Daniels), Gap Girls (Farley/Sandler/Spade), Matt Foley, Motivational Speaker (Farley), Opera Man (Sandler), Total Bastard Airlines (Spade), Zagat's (Farley/Sandler)

BUMPER KEY (Pg. 408-409)

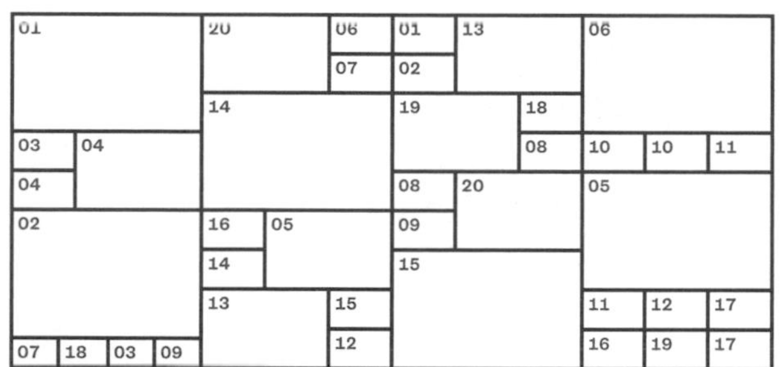

a.

b.

c.

a. Janeane Garofalo and Sarah Jessica Parker in "Munchkinland." **b.** "Coffee Talk" with Mike Myers as Linda Richman and John Travolta as Barbra Streisand. **c.** Damon Wayans, David Alan Grier, and Chris Farley (as Roger Ebert) in "Men on Film."

SATU
1975

S

SEASON 21 /
1995-96

SNL
SNL
SNL
SNL
SATURDAYNIGHTLIVE
SATURDAYNIGHTLIVE
SNL
SNL
SNL
SNL
SATURDAYNIGHTLIVE
SNL
SNL
SNL
SATURDAYNIGHTLIVE
SATURDAYNIGHTLIV
SATURDAYNIGHTLIV

SNL
SATURDAYNIGHTLIVE
SATURDAYNIGHTLIVE
SNL
SNL
SNL
SNL
SNL
SNL
SNL
SNL
SATURDAYNIGHTLIVE
SATURDAYNIGHTLIVE
SNL
SNL
SATURDAYNIGHTLIVE
SNL
SATURDAYNIGHTLIVE
SATURDAYNIGHTLIVE
SNL
USA

SEASON 21 / 1995-96

CAST

Jim Breuer
Will Ferrell
Darrell Hammond
David Koechner
Norm Macdonald
Mark McKinney
Tim Meadows
Cheri Oteri
Molly Shannon
David Spade
Nancy Walls

Featuring:
Chris Kattan
Colin Quinn
Fred Wolf

Weekend Update:
Norm Macdonald

CREW

Executive Producer:
Lorne Michaels

Director: Beth McCarthy

Writers: Ross Abrash, Cindy Caponera, James Downey, Hugh Fink, Peter Gaulke, Tom Gianas, Jack Handey, Tim Herlihy, Steve Higgins, Norm Hiscock, Steve Koren, Erin Maroney, Adam McKay, Dennis McNicholas, Lorne Michaels, Lori Nasso, Paula Pell, Colin Quinn, Frank Sebastiano, Andrew Steele, Fred Wolf

Writing Supervisors:
Steve Higgins, Fred Wolf

Supervising Producer:
Ken Aymong

Film Producer:
James Signorelli

Weekend Update Produced by:
James Downey

Production Designers:
Eugene Lee, Akira Yoshimura, Keith Ian Raywood

Lighting Consultant:
Phil Hymes

Musical Directors: Cheryl Hardwick, Lenny Pickett

Sketch Music Adaptation:
Hal Willner

Costume Designer:
Tom Broecker

Wardrobe: Dale Richards, Ellen Ellis Lee, Margaret Karolyi

Hair: Lawrence-Gregory Gladstone III, David Lawrence

Makeup: Mike Maddi

Photographer: Edie Baskin

EPISODE LIST

EPISODE KEY:
H - Host
MG - Musical Guest
SG/C - Special Guests/Cameos

EPISODE 01: 09/30/95
H: Mariel Hemingway
MG: Blues Traveler

EPISODE 02: 10/07/95
H: Chevy Chase
MG: Lisa Loeb
SG/C: Mariel Hemingway, Don Novello

EPISODE 03: 10/21/95
H: David Schwimmer
MG: Natalie Merchant
SG/C: Jennifer Aniston, Gary Coleman, Katell Keineg, Lisa Kudrow, Jennifer Turner, Jimmy Walker, Barry Williams

EPISODE 04: 10/28/95
H: Gabriel Byrne
MG: Alanis Morissette
SG/C: Lamar Alexander, Bill Bradley, Tom Glavine, Chrissie Hynde, Chipper Jones, Mark Wohlers

EPISODE 05: 11/11/95
H: Quentin Tarantino
MG: The Smashing Pumpkins
SG/C: Robert Hegyes

EPISODE 06: 11/18/95
H: Laura Leighton
MG: Rancid
SG/C: Sean Penn, Grant Show, Sam Waterston

EPISODE 07: 12/02/95
H: Anthony Edwards
MG: Foo Fighters

EPISODE 08: 12/09/95
H: David Alan Grier
MG: Silverchair

EPISODE 09: 12/16/95
H: Madeline Kahn
MG: Bush
SG/C: Sam Waterston

EPISODE 10: 01/13/96
H: Christopher Walken
MG: Joan Osborne
SG/C: Rudy Giuliani, George Pataki

EPISODE 11: 01/20/96
H: Alec Baldwin
MG: Tori Amos

EPISODE 12: 02/10/96
H: Danny Aiello
MG: Coolio
SG/C: Larry Brown, L.V., Chris Farley

EPISODE 13: 02/17/96
H: Tom Arnold
MG: Tupac Shakur
SG/C: Danny Boy, Adam Sandler, Roger Troutman

EPISODE 14: 02/24/96
H: Elle Macpherson
MG: Sting

EPISODE 15: 03/16/96
H: John Goodman
MG: Everclear
SG/C: Kurt Loder, Elle Macpherson

EPISODE 16: 03/23/96
H: Phil Hartman
MG: Gin Blossoms

EPISODE 17: 04/13/96
H: Steve Forbes
MG: Rage Against the Machine
SG/C: Sabina Beekman, Catherine Forbes, Elizabeth Forbes, Moira Forbes, Roberta Forbes, Sabina Forbes

EPISODE 18: 04/20/96
H: Teri Hatcher
MG: Dave Matthews Band
SG/C: Sam Waterston

EPISODE 19: 05/11/96
H: Christine Baranski
MG: The Cure
SG/C: Jim Gaffigan, Dennis Rodman

EPISODE 20: 05/18/96
H: Jim Carrey
MG: Soundgarden

SEASON HIGHLIGHTS

A.M. Ale (Koechner), Bill Brasky (Ferrell/Koechner/McKinney/Meadows), Bug-Off (Ferrell), The Continental (Walken), Father Guido Sarducci (Novello), Fuzzy Memories: Dog Head, Grayson Moorehead (Downey), Jimmy Tango's Fat Busters (Carrey), The Joe Pesci Show (Breuer), Leg Up (Oteri/Shannon), Mary Katherine Gallagher "Superstar" (Shannon), Old Glory (Waterson), Petchow Rat Poison (Ferrell), The Roxbury Guys (Ferrell/Kattan), Spartan Cheerleaders (Ferrell/Oteri), Unfrozen Caveman Lawyer (Hartman)

BUMPER KEY (Pg. 414-415)

a.

b.

c.

WEDNESDAY

a/o June 28, 1995 12:56 PM

SNL AUDITIONS

DATE: JUNE 28, 1995

SATURDAY NIGHT LIVE

AUDITIONS SCHEDULE

WEDNESDAY, JUNE 28, 1995

4:00P - 9:00P	VTR: SNL AUDITIONS	STUDIO 8H
	Jenna Jolovitz	-E. Dole wig
	Adam McKay	-stool
	Jon Glaser	-chair, tape player
	Chris Kattan	-tape player, stool -chalkboard/chalk -2 chairs, table
	Will Ferrell	-tape player, chair -stand mic
	Jennifer Coolidge	
	Luke Torres	
	James Stephens III	-cassette player
	Elon Gold	-stool
	Jay Lacopo	-dual cassette player -stand mic, chair
	Darrell Hammond	-stool, stand mic
	D.C. Benny	-stool
	Cheri Oteri	
	Ricky Harris	-stand mic, stool
	Dina Pearlman	-stool
	Paula Jai Parker	
	Gordie Brown	-2 stand mics
	Matt Dwyer	-stool -mic stand
	Greer Barnes	-stool, stand mic
	Pat Finn	

a. "British Fops" Lucien Callow and Fagan (Mark McKinney and David Koechner) shooting a promo with Alec Baldwin. **b.** Molly Shannon and Cheri Oteri as Ann Miller and Debbie Reynolds in "Leg Up." **c.** Season 21 audition schedule.

SEASON 22 / 1996-97

CAST

Jim Breuer
Will Ferrell
Ana Gasteyer
Darrell Hammond
Chris Kattan
Norm Macdonald
Mark McKinney
Tim Meadows
Tracy Morgan
Cheri Oteri
Molly Shannon

Featuring:
Colin Quinn
Fred Wolf

Weekend Update:
Norm Macdonald

CREW

Executive Producer:
Lorne Michaels

Director: Beth McCarthy

Producers: Steve Higgins, James Downey, Fred Wolf

Writers: Ross Abrash, David Breckman, Cindy Caponera, Robert Carlock, James Downey, Hugh Fink, Tom Gianas, Tim Herlihy, Steve Higgins, Norm Hiscock, Adam McKay, Dennis McNicholas, Lorne Michaels, Lori Nasso, Paula Pell, Matt Piedmont, Colin Quinn, Frank Sebastiano, Robert Smigel, Andrew Steele, Scott Wainio, Fred Wolf

Writing Supervisors:
Tim Herlihy, Adam McKay

Supervising Producer:
Ken Aymong

Film Producer:
James Signorelli

Weekend Update Produced by:
James Downey

Production Designers:
Eugene Lee, Akira Yoshimura, Keith Ian Raywood

Lighting Consultant:
Phil Hymes

Musical Directors:
Cheryl Hardwick, Lenny Pickett

Sketch Music Adaptation:
Hal Willner

Costume Designer:
Tom Broecker

Wardrobe: Dale Richards, Margaret Karolyi, J. Douglas James, Bruce Brumage

Hair: Lawrence-Gregory Gladstone III

Makeup: Mike Maddi

Photographer: Edie Baskin

EPISODE LIST

EPISODE KEY:
H - Host
MG - Musical Guest
SG/C - Special Guests/Cameos

EPISODE 01: 09/28/96
H: Tom Hanks
MG: Tom Petty & The Heartbreakers
SG/C: Kerri Strug

EPISODE 02: 10/05/96
H: Lisa Kudrow
MG: Sheryl Crow
SG/C: David Lander

EPISODE 03: 10/19/96
H: Bill Pullman
MG: New Edition

EPISODE 04: 10/26/96
H: Dana Carvey
MG: Dr. Dre

EPISODE 05: 11/02/96
H: Chris Rock
MG: The Wallflowers
SG/C: Dana Carvey, Abe Vigoda

EPISODE 06: 11/16/96
H: Robert Downey Jr.
MG: Fiona Apple
SG/C: Bob Dole, Elizabeth Dole, Evander Holyfield

EPISODE 07: 11/23/96
H: Phil Hartman
MG: Bush
SG/C: Rodney Dangerfield, Cliff Robertson

EPISODE 08: 12/07/96
H: Martin Short
MG: No Doubt
SG/C: Chevy Chase

EPISODE 09: 12/14/96
H: Rosie O'Donnell
MG: Whitney Houston
SG/C: Penny Marshall, Georgia Mass Choir

EPISODE 10: 01/11/97
H: Kevin Spacey
MG: Beck
SG/C: John Cleese, Michael Palin

EPISODE 11: 01/18/97
H: David Alan Grier
MG: Snoop Doggy Dogg
SG/C: Daz Dillinger, Charlie Wilson

EPISODE 12: 02/08/97
H: Neve Campbell
MG: David Bowie
SG/C: David Spade

EPISODE 13: 02/15/97
H: Chevy Chase
MG: Live

EPISODE 14: 02/22/97
H: Alec Baldwin
MG: Tina Turner
SG/C: Howard Stern

EPISODE 15: 03/15/97
H: Sting
MG: Veruca Salt
SG/C: Mark Hamill

EPISODE 16: 03/22/97
H: Mike Myers
MG: Aerosmith

EPISODE 17: 04/12/97
H: Rob Lowe
MG: Spice Girls
SG/C: Robert De Niro, Joe Pesci

EPISODE 18: 04/19/97
H: Pamela Lee
MG: Rollins Band
SG/C: Tommy Lee

EPISODE 19: 05/10/97
H: John Goodman
MG: Jewel
SG/C: Mike Myers

EPISODE 20: 05/17/97
H: Jeff Goldblum
MG: En Vogue

SEASON HIGHLIGHTS

The Ambiguously Gay Duo (Smigel), Barbara Walters (Oteri), Big Brawn (Ferrell), Bill Brasky (Ferrell, et al.), Caribbean Essence (Morgan), Celebrity Jeopardy! (Ferrell/Hammond/Macdonald, et al.), Church Chat (Carvey), Coffee Talk with Linda Richman (Myers), The Culps (Ferrell/Gasteyer), The Dark Side (Rock), Death Row Bloopers (Grier/Kattan), Delicious Dish (Gasteyer/Shannon), Goth Talk (Breuer/Kattan/Shannon), The Joe Pesci Show (Breuer), Mr. Peepers (Kattan), The Roxbury Guys (Ferrell/Kattan), Spartan Cheerleaders (Ferrell/Oteri), Sprockets (Myers), Star Wars Screen Test (Spacey/Hammond), Star Wars Screen Test 2 (Spacey/Hammond), The X-Presidents (Smigel)

BUMPER KEY (Pg. 418-419)

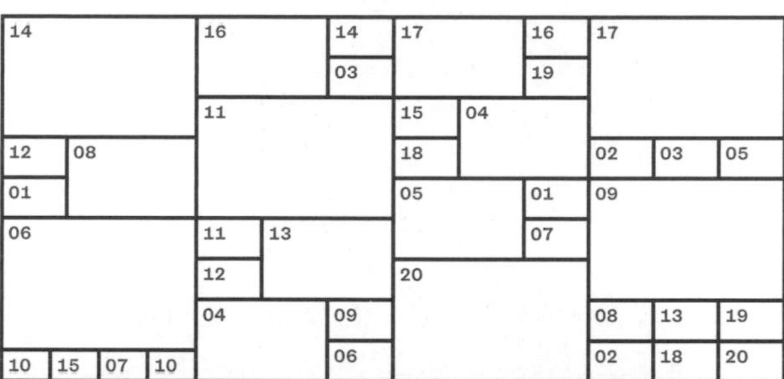

a.

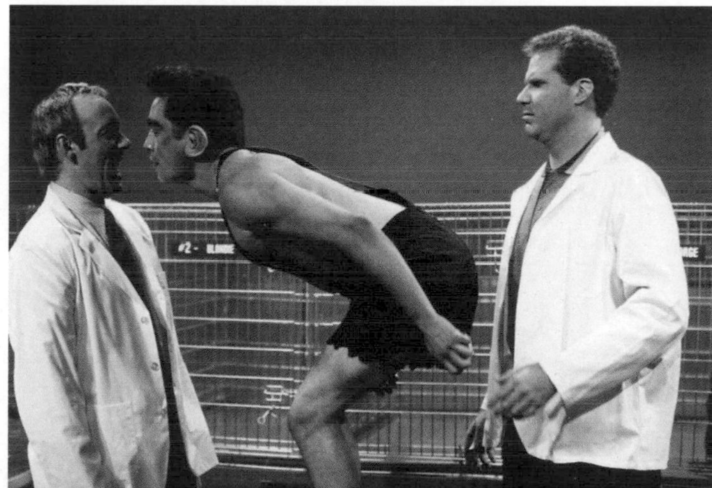

b.

c.

d.

a. Chris Kattan as Mr. Peepers in "Monkey Lab," with Kevin Spacey and Will Ferrell.
b. Chris Kattan, Molly Shannon, and Jeff Goldblum in "Goth Talk."
c. Performance by the Spice Girls.
d. "This may be the Benzedrine talking, but you're a slice of man meat, and this prescription says take with food, huh?" Cheri Oteri as Collette Reardon, with John Goodman.

SNL
SNL
SATURDAYNIGHTLIVE
SATURDAYNIGHTLIVE
SNL
SNL
SNL
SNL
SNL
SNL
SNL
SNL
SNL
SNL
SATURDAYNIGHTLIVE
SNL
SNL
SNL

SNL
SATURDAYNIGHTLIVE
SNL
SATURDAYNIGHTLIVE
SNL
SNL
SNL
SNL
SNL
SNL
SNL
SATURDAYNIGHTLIVE
SNL
SNL
SATURDAYNIGHTLIVE
SNL
SATURDAYNIGHTLIVE
SNL
SNL
SNL
SATURDAYNIGHTLIVE

SEASON 22 /
1996-97

SNL

SATURDAYNIGHTLIVE
SATURDAYNIGHTLIVE
SATURDAYNIGHTLIVE
SNL
SNL
SNL
SATURDAYNIGHTLIVE
SNL
SNL
SATURDAYNIGHTLIVE
SATURDAYNIGHTLIVE
SNL
SNL
SNL
SATURDAYNIGHTLIVE
SNL
SNL
SATURDAYNIGHTLIVE
SNL

SNL
SATURDAYNIGHTLIVE
SNL
SNL
SNL
SNL
SNL
SNL
SNL
SNL
SNL
SNL
SATURDAYNIGHTLIVE
SNL
SATURDAYNIGHTLIVE
SNL
SATURDAYNIGHTLIVE
SNL
SATURDAYNIGHTLIVE

SEASON 23 / 1997-98

CAST

Jim Breuer
Will Ferrell
Ana Gasteyer
Darrell Hammond
Chris Kattan
Norm Macdonald
Tim Meadows
Tracy Morgan
Cheri Oteri
Colin Quinn
Molly Shannon

Weekend Update:
Norm Macdonald
Colin Quinn

CREW

Executive Producer:
Lorne Michaels

Director: Beth McCarthy

Producers: Tim Herlihy, Steve Higgins

Writers: Ross Abrash, Cindy Caponera, Robert Carlock, James Downey, Tina Fey, Hugh Fink, Tom Gianas, Tim Herlihy, Steve Higgins, Michael McCullers, Adam McKay Dennis McNicholas, Lorne Michaels, Lori Nasso, Paula Pell, Matt Piedmont, Michael Schur, Frank Sebastiano, Andrew Steele, Scott Wainio

Writing Supervisor:
Adam McKay

Supervising Producer:
Ken Aymong

Film Producer:
James Signorelli

Weekend Update Produced by:
James Downey

Production Designers:
Eugene Lee, Akira Yoshimura, Keith Ian Raywood

Lighting Consultant:
Phil Hymes

Musical Directors:
Cheryl Hardwick, Lenny Pickett

Sketch Music Adaptation:
Hal Willner

Costume Designer:
Tom Broecker

Wardrobe: Dale Richards, Margaret Karolyi, J. Douglas James, Bruce Brumage

Hair: Bobby H. Grayson

Makeup: Louie Zakarian

Photographer: Edie Baskin

EPISODE LIST

EPISODE KEY:
H - Host
MG - Musical Guest
SG/C - Special Guests/Cameos

EPISODE 01: 09/27/97
H: Sylvester Stallone
MG: Jamiroquai
SG/C: Richard Jewell

EPISODE 02: 10/04/97
H: Matthew Perry
MG: Oasis

EPISODE 03: 10/18/97
H: Brendan Fraser
MG: Björk
SG/C: Eric Dickerson

EPISODE 04: 10/25/97
H: Chris Farley
MG: The Mighty Mighty Bosstones
SG/C: Chevy Chase, Mike Ditka, Bill Kurtis, Chris Rock, George Wendt

EPISODE 05: 11/08/97
H: Jon Lovitz
MG: Jane's Addiction
SG/C: Dana Carvey, Flea

EPISODE 06: 11/15/97
H: Claire Danes
MG: Mariah Carey

EPISODE 07: 11/22/97
H: Mayor Rudy Giuliani
MG: Sarah McLachlan

EPISODE 08: 12/06/97
H: Nathan Lane
MG: Metallica
SG/C: The Dallas Cowboys Cheerleaders, Marianne Faithfull, Ernie Sabella

EPISODE 09: 12/13/97
H: Helen Hunt
MG: Hanson
SG/C: Pedro Borbón Jr, Marty Cordova, Russ Davis, Jeff Fasssero, Cliff Floyd, Mark Grudzielanek, David Howard, Todd Hundly, Gregg Jefferies, Jack Nicholson, Scott Rolen, Mike Sweeny, Rondell White, Gerald Williams, Mark Wohlers, Todd Zeile

EPISODE 10: 01/10/98
H: Samuel L. Jackson
MG: Ben Folds Five

EPISODE 11: 01/17/98
H: Sarah Michelle Gellar
MG: Portishead

EPISODE 12: 02/07/98
H: John Goodman
MG: Paula Cole
SG/C: Dan Aykroyd

EPISODE 13: 02/14/98
H: Roma Downey
MG: Missy 'Misdemeanor' Elliott
SG/C: Magoo, Timbaland

EPISODE 14: 02/28/98
H/MG: Garth Brooks
SG/C: Robert Duvall

EPISODE 15: 03/07/98
H: Scott Wolf
MG: Natalie Imbruglia

EPISODE 16: 03/14/98
H: Julianne Moore
MG: Backstreet Boys

EPISODE 17: 04/04/98
H: Steve Buscemi
MG: Third Eye Blind
SG/C: Didi Conn, Natasha Henstridge, John Hurt, Lewis Lapham

EPISODE 18: 04/11/98
H: Greg Kinnear
MG: All Saints
SG/C: Bob Hoskins

EPISODE 19: 05/02/98
H: Matthew Broderick
MG: Natalie Merchant
SG/C: Regis Philbin, Tenacious D

EPISODE 20: 05/09/98
H: David Duchovny
MG: Puff Daddy, Jimmy Page
SG/C: Paula Abdul, John Goodman, Matt Lauer, Nicholas Lea, Jimmy Page, Al Roker

SEASON HIGHLIGHTS

The Ambiguously Gay Duo (Smigel), Barbara Walters (Oteri), Bill Swerski's Superfans (Farley/Smigel et al.), The Blues Brothers (Aykroyd), Celebrity Jeopardy! (Ferrell/Hammond/ MacDonald, et al.), Chess for Girls (Shannon/Ferrell), Cookie Dough (Will Ferrell), The Culps (Ferrell/Gasteyer), Delicious Dish (Gasteyer/ Shannon), Goth Talk (Breuer/ Kattan/Shannon), The Joe Pesci Show (Breuer), The Ladies' Man (Meadows), Mango (Kattan), Matt Foley Motivational Speaker (Farley), Mr. Peepers (Kattan), The Roxbury Guys (Ferrell/Kattan), Spartan Cheerleaders (Ferrell/ Oteri), Star Wars Screen Test (Spacey/Hammond), Star Wars Screen Test 2 (Spacey/ Hammond), The X-Presidents (Smigel)

BUMPER KEY (Pg. 422-423)

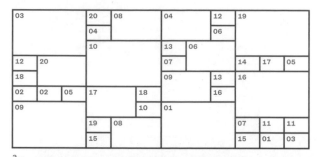

03 20 08 04 12 19
04 06
10 13 06
12 20 07 14 17 05
18 09 13 16
02 02 05 17 18 16
09 10 01
19 08 07 11 11
15 15 01 03

a.

b.

a. "I'm Leon Phelps, and how y'all doin' tonight?" Tim Meadows as the Ladies' Man.
b. Title card of TV Funhouse's "X-Presidents."

CAST

Will Ferrell
Ana Gasteyer
Darrell Hammond
Chris Kattan
Tim Meadows
Tracy Morgan
Cheri Oteri
Colin Quinn
Molly Shannon

Featuring:
Jimmy Fallon
Chris Parnell
Horatio Sanz

Weekend Update:
Colin Quinn

CREW

Executive Producer:
Lorne Michaels

Director: Beth McCarthy

Producers: Steve Higgins, Tim Herlihy

Writers: Robert Carlock, Jerry Collins, Steven Cragg, Tony Daro, Tina Fey, Hugh Fink, Rich Francese, Matt Graham, Tim Herlihy, Steve Higgins, Ray James, Adam McKay, Dennis McNicholas, Lorne Michaels, Lori Nasso, Paula Pell, Matt Piedmont, Michael Schur, T. Sean Shannon, Andrew Steele, Scott Wainio

Writing Supervisor:
Adam McKay

Supervising Producer:
Ken Aymong

Film Producer:
James Signorelli

Production Designers:
Eugene Lee, Akira Yoshimura, Keith Ian Raywood

Lighting Consultant:
Phil Hymes

Musical Directors:
Cheryl Hardwick, Lenny Pickett

Sketch Music Adaptation:
Hal Willner

Costume Designer:
Tom Broecker

Wardrobe: Dale Richards, Margaret Karolyi, J. Douglas James, Bruce Brumage

Hair: Bobby H. Grayson

Makeup: Louie Zakarian

Photographer: Edie Baskin

EPISODE LIST

EPISODE KEY:
H - Host
MG - Musical Guest
SG/C - Special Guests/Cameos

EPISODE 01: 09/26/98
H: Cameron Diaz
MG: The Smashing Pumpkins
SG/C: Dan Aykroyd, John Goodman, Tommy Larkins, Steve Martin, Jonathan Richman

EPISODE 02: 10/03/98
H: Kelsey Grammer
MG: Sheryl Crow
SG/C: Christine Baranski, Hal Linden, Patti LuPone, Wendy Melvoin, Shaquille O'Neal

EPISODE 03: 10/17/98
H: Lucy Lawless
MG: Elliott Smith
SG/C: Chucky, Judge Judy Sheindlin

EPISODE 04: 10/24/98
H: Ben Stiller
MG: Alanis Morissette
SG/C: David Cone, Chili Davis, Graeme Lloyd, Tino Martinez, David Wells

EPISODE 05: 11/07/98
H: David Spade
MG: Eagle-Eye Cherry
SG/C: Brad Pitt, Chris Rock

EPISODE 06: 11/14/98
H: Joan Allen
MG: Jewel
SG/C: John Goodman

EPISODE 07: 11/21/98
H: Jennifer Love Hewitt
MG: Beastie Boys
SG/C: John Goodman, Muse Watson

EPISODE 08: 12/05/98
H: Vince Vaughn
MG: Lauryn Hill

EPISODE 09: 12/12/98
H: Alec Baldwin
MG: Luciano Pavarotti, Vanessa Williams
SG/C: John Goodman, Janice Pendarvis

EPISODE 10: 01/09/99
H: Bill Paxton
MG: Beck
SG/C: James Cameron, Debbie Matenopoulos

EPISODE 11: 01/16/99
H: James Van Der Beek
MG: Everlast

EPISODE 12: 02/06/99
H: Gwyneth Paltrow
MG: Barenaked Ladies
SG/C: Ben Affleck

EPISODE 13: 02/13/99
H: Brendan Fraser
MG: Busta Rhymes, The Roots
SG/C: The Roots, Tom Davis, John Goodman, Fiaco Jiménez, George Plimpton

EPISODE 14: 02/20/99
H: Bill Murray
MG: Lucinda Williams
SG/C: Chevy Chase, Stephanie Seymour

EPISODE 15: 03/13/99
H: Ray Romano
MG. The Corrs
SG/C: Peter Boyle, Doris Roberts

EPISODE 16: 03/20/99
H: Drew Barrymore
MG: Garbage
SG/C: Edward Norton

EPISODE 17: 04/10/99
H: John Goodman
MG: Tom Petty & the Heartbreakers

EPISODE 18: 05/08/99
H: Cuba Gooding Jr.
MG: Ricky Martin
SG/C: John Goodman, Monica Lewinsky

EPISODE 19: 05/15/99
H: Sarah Michelle Gellar
MG: Backstreet Boys
SG/C: David Boreanaz, Seth Green, Lee Ranaldo

SEASON HIGHLIGHTS

The Ambiguously Gay Duo (Smigel), Barbara Walters (Oteri), Bill Brasky (Ferrell), Brian Fellow's Safari Planet (Morgan), Celebrity Jeopardy! (Ferrell/Hammond et al.), The Culps (Ferrell/Gasteyer), Delicious Dish (Gasteyer/Shannon), The Festrunk Brothers (Aykroyd/Martin), Goth Talk (Kattan/Shannon), The Ladies' Man (Meadows), Mango (Kattan), Mr. Peepers (Kattan), Oops I Crapped My Pants (Ana Gasteyer), The Roxbury Guys (Ferrell/Kattan), Spartan Cheerleaders (Ferrell/Oteri), SportsCenter (Meadows), The X-Presidents (Smigel)

BUMPER KEY (Pg. 426-427)

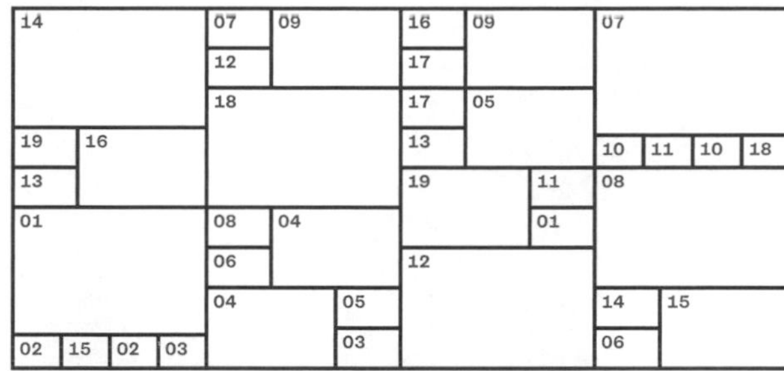

a.

b.

Lorne,
I just wanted to thank you for the opportunity to test for SNL. It was very exciting for me. I hope you have a great season.
Sincerely,
Jimmy Fallon
P.S. Happy Halloween!

c.

d.

a. Charlie Brown gets a massive head injury when Lucy pulls the football away in "You're a Champion, Charlie Brown."
b. Note from Jimmy Fallon to Lorne Michaels.
c. "Does your name ever make you hungry?" Harry Carey (Will Ferrell) interviewing Linda Ham (Joan Allen) in "Space: The Infinite Frontier."
d. John Goodman, Will Ferrell, and Alec Baldwin in "Bill Brasky on Wall Street."

30 ROCKEFELLER PLAZA
SNL
SATURDAYNIGHTLIVE
SATURDAYNIGHTLIVE
SATURDAYNIGHTLIVE
SNL
SNL
SNL
SNL
SNL
SNL
SNL
SNL
SATURDAYNIGHTLIVE
SNL
SNL
SATURDAYNIGHTLIVE
SATURDAYNIGHTLIVE
SATURDAYNIGHTLIVE
SN

SNL
SNL
SATURDAYNIGHTLIVE
SATURDAYNIGHTLIVE
SATURDAYNIGHTLIVE
SCORPIO !!!
SATURDAYNIGHTLIVE
SNL
SATURDAYNIGHTLIVE
SNL
SATURDAYNIGHTLIVE
SATURDAYNIGHTLIVE
SATURDAYNIGHTLIVE
SATURDAYNIGHTLIVE
SNL
SATURDAYNIGHTLIVE
SATURDAYNIGHTLIVE

SEASON 24 / 1998-99

SEASON 25 / 1999-2000

SNL
SATURDAYNIGHTLIVE25
SNL25
SNL25
SNL
SATURDAYNIGHTLIVE25
SNL25
SNL25
SNL25
SATURDAYNIGHTLIVE25
SATURDAYNIGHTLIVE25
SNL25
SNL25
SNL25
SATURDAYNIGHTLIVE25

SNL25
SATURDAYNIGHTLIVE25
SNL25
SNL25
456
SNL25
SNL25
SNL25
SNL25
SATURDAYNIGHTLIVE25
SNL25
LOS ANGELES LAKERS
SNL25
SNL25
SATURDAYNIGHTLIVE25
SATURDAYNIGHTLIVE25
SATURDAYNIGHTLIVE25
SATURDAYNIGHTLIVE25
SATURDAYNIGHTLIVE25
SNL25

SEASON 25 / 1999-2000

CAST

Jimmy Fallon
Will Ferrell
Ana Gasteyer
Darrell Hammond
Chris Kattan
Tim Meadows
Tracy Morgan
Cheri Oteri
Chris Parnell
Colin Quinn
Horatio Sanz
Molly Shannon

Featuring:
Rachel Dratch
Maya Rudolph

Weekend Update:
Colin Quinn

CREW

Executive Producer:
Lorne Michaels

Director:
Beth McCarthy-Miller

Producers: Steve Higgins, Tim Herlihy

Writers: Kevin Brennan, Robert Carlock, Jerry Collins, Steven Cragg, Tony Daro, Ali Farahnakian, Tina Fey, Hugh Fink, Rich Francese, Tim Herlihy, Steve Higgins, Adam McKay, Dennis McNicholas, Lorne Michaels, Paula Pell, J.J. Philbin, Matt Piedmont, Michael Schur, T. Sean Shannon, Andrew Steele, Scott Wainio

Writing Supervisor: Tina Fey

Short Films: Adam McKay

Supervising Producer:
Ken Aymong

Film Producer:
James Signorelli

Production Designers:
Eugene Lee, Akira Yoshimura, Keith Ian Raywood

Lighting Consultant:
Phil Hymes

Musical Directors:
Cheryl Hardwick, Lenny Pickett

Sketch Music Adaptation:
Hal Willner

Costume Designer:
Tom Broecker

Wardrobe: Dale Richards, Margaret Karolyi, J. Douglas James, Bruce Brumage

Hair: Bobby H. Grayson

Makeup: Louie Zakarian

Photographers: Edie Baskin, Mary Ellen Matthews

EPISODE LIST

EPISODE KEY:
H - Host
MG - Musical Guest
SG/C - Special Guests/Cameos

EPISODE 01: 10/02/99
H: Jerry Seinfeld
MG: David Bowie
SG/C: A.J. Benza, Rick Ludwin, Harold Perineau, J.K. Simmons, Lee Tergesen, Dean Winters

EPISODE 02: 10/16/99
H: Heather Graham
MG: Marc Anthony
SG/C: Dana Carvey, Kevin Nealon

EPISODE 03: 10/23/99
H: Norm Macdonald
MG: Dr. Dre, Snoop Dogg, Eminem
SG/C: Savion Glover

EPISODE 04: 11/06/99
H: Dylan McDermott
MG: Foo Fighters

EPISODE 05: 11/13/99
H: Garth Brooks
MG: Chris Gaines

EPISODE 06: 11/20/99
H: Jennifer Aniston
MG: Sting
SG/C: John Carpenter, Cheb Mami

EPISODE 07: 12/04/99
H: Christina Ricci
MG: Beck

EPISODE 08: 12/11/99
H: Danny DeVito
MG: R.E.M.
SG/C: Al Franken, Joe Franken II, The Rockettes

EPISODE 09: 01/08/00
H: Jamie Foxx
MG: Blink-182
SG/C: Jared "Choclatt" Crawford, John Goodman, Larry Wright

EPISODE 10: 01/15/00
H: Freddie Prinze Jr.
MG: Macy Gray
SG/C: Angie Everhart

EPISODE 11: 02/05/00
H: Alan Cumming
MG: Jennifer Lopez
SG/C: Fat Joe, Ben Stiller

EPISODE 12: 02/12/00
H: Julianna Margulies
MG: DMX
SG/C: Noah Wyle

EPISODE 13: 02/19/00
H: Ben Affleck
MG: Fiona Apple
SG/C: Gwyneth Paltrow, G.E. Smith

EPISODE 14: 03/11/00
H: Joshua Jackson
MG: *NSYNC
SG/C: Cameos: Badal Roy, The Stratler Brothers

EPISODE 15: 03/18/00
H: The Rock
MG: AC/DC
SG/C: Big Show, Mick Foley, Vince McMahon, Triple H

EPISODE 16: 04/08/00
H: Christopher Walken
MG: Christina Aguilera
SG/C: Dana Carvey, J. Mascis

EPISODE 17: 04/15/00
H: Tobey Maguire
MG: Sisqó
SG/C: Clarence "Gatemouth" Brown, Steve Buscemi

EPISODE 18: 05/06/00
H: John Goodman
MG: Neil Young
SG/C: Roc Raida

EPISODE 19: 05/13/00
H/MG: Britney Spears
SG/C: Sarah Michelle Gellar, Gaetano Thomas Oteri

EPISODE 20: 05/20/00
H: Jackie Chan
MG: Kid Rock
SG/C: Trey Anastasio, Sarah Michelle Gellar, Gina Gershon, Florence Henderson, G.E. Smith

SEASON HIGHLIGHTS

The Ambiguously Gay Duo (Smigel), Barbara Walters (Oteri), Behind the Music: Blue Oyster Cult (Walken/ Ferrell, et al.), Boston Teens (Dratch/Fallon), Celebrity Jeopardy! (Ferrell/ Hammond, et al.), Colonel Belmont's Old Fashioned Horse Glue (Will Ferrell), The Continental (Walken), The Culps (Ferrell/Gasteyer), Delicious Dish (Gasteyer/ Shannon), Desire, Gap Fat (Horatio Sanz), Goth Talk (Kattan/Shannon), The Ladies' Man (Meadows), Litter Critters (Oteri/ Parnell), Mango (Kattan), Mr. Peepers (Kattan/The Rock), Oz (Seinfeld), Spartan Cheerleaders (Ferrell/Oteri), Uncle Jemimah's Pure Mash Liquor (Tracy Morgan), Where Are They Now? Hans & Franz (Carvey/Nealon)

BUMPER KEY (Pg. 432-433)

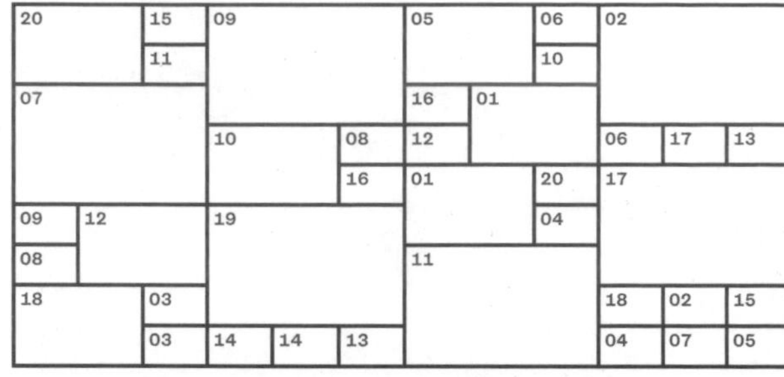

a.

b.

c.

a. Jimmy Fallon and Rachel Dratch as Sully and Denise in "Boston Teens," with Garth Brooks. **b.** Britney Spears with Cheri Oteri and Will Ferrell in "Morning Latte." **c.** Mary Katherine Gallagher (Molly Shannon) flirts with Lenny Schwartzman (Jerry Seinfeld), "the Jewish Michael Jordan."

SEASON 26 / 2000-01

CAST

Jimmy Fallon
Will Ferrell
Ana Gasteyer
Darrell Hammond
Chris Kattan
Tracy Morgan
Chris Parnell
Horatio Sanz
Molly Shannon

Featuring:
Rachel Dratch
Tina Fey
Jerry Minor
Maya Rudolph

Weekend Update:
Jimmy Fallon
Tina Fey

CREW

Executive Producer:
Lorne Michaels

Director:
Beth McCarthy Miller

Producer: Steve Higgins

Writers: James Anderson, Robert Carlock, Tony Daro James Downey, Tina Fey, Hugh Fink, Melanie Graham, Steve Higgins, Erik Kenward, Adam McKay, Dennis McNicholas, Lorne Michaels, Jerry Minor, Matt Murray, Paula Pell, Matt Piedmont, Jon Rosenfeld, Michael Schur, Frank Sebastiano, T. Sean Shannon, Robert Smigel, Barry Sobel, Andrew Steele, Scott Wainio

Writing Supervisor: Tina Fey

Short Films: Adam McKay

Supervising Producer:
Ken Aymong

Film Producer:
James Signorelli

Weekend Update Produced by:
Robert Carlock

Production Designers:
Eugene Lee, Akira Yoshimura, Keith Ian Raywood

Lighting Consultant:
Phil Hymes

Musical Director:
Lenny Pickett

Sketch Music Adaptation:
Hal Willner

Costume Designer:
Tom Broecker

Hair: Kym Coats, Clariss Morgan, Linda Rice

Makeup: Louie Zakarian

Photographer:
Mary Ellen Matthews

EPISODE LIST

EPISODE KEY:
H - Host
MG - Musical Guest
SG/C - Special Guests/Cameos

EPISODE 01: 10/07/00
H: Rob Lowe
MG: Eminem
SG/C: Dido, Brendan Fraser, Tim Meadows, Ralph Nader

EPISODE 02: 10/14/00
H: Kate Hudson
MG: Radiohead
SG/C: Nomar Garciaparra

EPISODE 03: 10/21/00
H: Dana Carvey
MG: Wallflowers
SG/C: Robert De Niro, Baha Men

EPISODE 04: 11/04/00
H: Charlize Theron
MG: Paul Simon

EPISODE 05: 11/11/00
H: Calista Flockhart
MG: Ricky Martin
SG/C: Giovanni Hidalgo

EPISODE 06: 11/18/00
H: Tom Green
MG: David Gray
SG/C: Drew Barrymore, Mary Jane Green, Richard Green, Shawn Greenson, Derek Harvie, Glenn Humplik, Gwyneth Paltrow

EPISODE 07: 12/09/00
H: Val Kilmer
MG: U2
SG/C: Maceo Parker

EPISODE 08: 12/16/00
H: Lucy Liu
MG: Jay-Z
SG/C: Beanie Sigel, Memphis Bleek

EPISODE 09: 01/13/01
H: Charlie Sheen
MG: Nelly Furtado
SG/C: Pamelia Kurstin

EPISODE 10: 01/20/01
H: Mena Suvari
MG: Lenny Kravitz
SG/C: Janet Reno, Fred Wesley

EPISODE 11: 02/10/01
H/MG: Jennifer Lopez
SG/C: Tom Hanks

EPISODE 12: 02/17/01
H: Sean Hayes
MG: Shaggy
SG/C: Rayvon, Rikrok, G.E. Smith, T-Bone Wolk

EPISODE 13: 02/24/01
H: Katie Holmes
MG: Dave Matthews Band
SG/C: Junior Brown

EPISODE 14: 03/10/01
H: Conan O'Brien
MG: Don Henley
SG/C: Ben Affleck, Max Weinberg, Becky Weinberg

EPISODE 15: 03/17/01
H: Julia Stiles
MG: Aerosmith
SG/C: David Copperfield

EPISODE 16: 04/07/01
H: Alec Baldwin
MG: Coldplay
SG/C: Kid Rock, David Spade

EPISODE 17: 04/14/01
H: Renée Zellweger
MG: Eve
SG/C: Molly Shannon, Gwen Stefani

EPISODE 18: 05/05/01
H: Pierce Brosnan
MG: Destiny's Child
SG/C: Molly Shannon, Julia Stiles

EPISODE 19: 05/12/01
H: Lara Flynn Boyle
MG: Bon Jovi
SG/C: Delbert McClinton, Lou Reed

EPISODE 20: 05/19/01
H: Christopher Walken
MG: Weezer
SG/C: Kevin Nealon, Winona Ryder

SEASON HIGHLIGHTS

Brian Fellow's Safari Planet (Morgan), Celebrity Jeopardy! (Ferrell/Hammond), Centaur (Walken/Parnell/Kattan), Church Chat (Carvey), The Continental (Walken), Cracklin' Oat Flakes (Ferrell/Gasteyer), The Delicious Dish (Gasteyer/Shannon), Gemini's Twin (Rudolph/Gasteyer), Homocil (Ferrell, Gasteyer), Janet Reno's Dance Party (Ferrell/Reno), Jarret's Room (Fallon/Sanz), Jeffrey's (Ferrell/Fallon/Hayes), The Lovers (Ferrell/Dratch), Magic Mouth (Ferrell), Mango (Kattan), Mr. Tarkanian Angry Boss (Ferrell/Brosnan), Reliable Investments (Baldwin/Gasteyer), Subshack (Fallon), The X-Presidents (Smigel), Wade Blasingame (Ferrell)

BUMPER KEY (Pg. 436-437)

02 01 01 03 15 10 18 17
16 06 13 13
05 10 17 08 08 14
11 14 20 20 19
04 09 04 07
19 02 03 07 05 16 06 09 15 12 12 18

a.

b.

c.

d.

a. Dana Carvey and Will Ferrell as George Bush Sr. and Jr. in "Dad & Son Go Hunting." **b.** Conan O'Brien as early-20th-century heavyweight champion James "The Gentleman Masher" Corcoran. **c.** Radiohead performing "Idioteque." **d.** Jimmy Fallon cracked up at Will Ferrell's performance as supervisor of a designer boutique in this "Jeffrey's" sketch (with host Sean Hayes).

SNL
NEW
YORK
SNL
SNL
SNL
SNL
SNL
SATURDAYNIGHTLIVE
SATURDAYNIGHTLIVE
SATURDAYNIGHTLIVE
SATURDAYNIGHTLIVE
SATURDAYNIGHTLIVE
SATURDAYNIGHTLIVE
SATURDAYNIGHTLIVE
SATURDAYNIGHTLIVE

SATURDAYNIGHTLIVE
SNL
SATURDAYNIGHTLIVE
SNL
SNL
SNL
SNL
SATURDAYNIGHTLIVE
SATURDAYNIGHTLIVE
SATURDAYNIGHTLIVE
SATURDAYNIGHTLIVE
SNL
SATURDAYNIGHTLIVE
SNL

SEASON 26 / 2000-01

SNL

SNL
SATURDAYNIGHTLIVE

SNL
SATURDAYNIGHTLIVE
SNL
SNL
SATURDAYNIGHTLIVE
SNL
SNL
SATURDAYNIGHTLIVE
SNL
SATURDAYNIGHTLIVE
SATURDAYNIGHTLIVE
SNL

SEASON 27 / 2001-02

CAST

Rachel Dratch
Jimmy Fallon
Will Ferrell
Tina Fey
Ana Gasteyer
Darrell Hammond
Chris Kattan
Tracy Morgan
Chris Parnell
Amy Poehler
Maya Rudolph
Horatio Sanz

Featuring:
Dean Edwards
Seth Meyers
Jeff Richards

Weekend Update:
Jimmy Fallon
Tina Fey

CREW

Executive Producer:
Lorne Michaels

Director:
Beth McCarthy-Miller

Head Writers: Tina Fey, Dennis McNicholas

Producer: Steve Higgins

Writers: Doug Abeles, James Anderson, Max Brooks, James Downey Tina Fey, Hugh Fink, Charlie Grandy, Jack Handey, Steve Higgins, Erik Kenward, Dennis McNicholas, Lorne Michaels, Matt Murray, Paula Pell, Matt Piedmont, Ken Scarborough, Michael Schur, Frank Sebastiano, T. Sean Shannon, Robert Smigel, Emily Spivey, Andrew Steele, Scott Wainio

Writing Supervisors:
Paula Pell, Andrew Steele

Supervising Producer:
Ken Aymong

Film Producer:
James Signorelli

Weekend Update Produced by:
Robert Carlock

Production Designers:
Eugene Lee, Akira Yoshimura, Keith Ian Raywood

Lighting Consultant:
Phil Hymes

Musical Director:
Lenny Pickett

Sketch Music Adaptation:
Hal Willner

Costume Designer:
Tom Broecker

Wardrobe: Dale Richards, Margaret Karolyi, J. Douglas James, Bruce Brumage

Hair: Michael Anthony, Mitch Ely, Clariss Morgan, Linda Rice

Makeup: Louie Zakarian

Photographer:
Mary Ellen Matthews

EPISODE LIST

EPISODE KEY:
H - Host
MG - Musical Guest
SG/C - Special Guests/Cameos

EPISODE 01: 9/29/01
H: Reese Witherspoon
MG: Alicia Keys
SG/C: Rudy Giuliani, Paul Simon

EPISODE 02: 10/06/01
H: Seann William Scott
MG: Sum 41
SG/C: Chevy Chase

EPISODE 03: 10/13/01
H: Drew Barrymore
MG: Macy Gray
SG/C: Tom Green, John Popper, Colin Quinn

EPISODE 04: 11/03/01
H: John Goodman
MG: Ja Rule
SG/C: Ashanti, Dan Aykroyd, Case

EPISODE 05: 11/10/01
H: Gwyneth Paltrow
MG: Ryan Adams, Dr. John
SG/C: Matt Damon

EPISODE 06: 11/17/01
H: Billy Bob Thornton
MG: Creed
SG/C: Ashton Kutcher

EPISODE 07: 12/01/01
H: Derek Jeter
MG: Bubba Sparxxx/Shakira
SG/C: David Cone, David Wells

EPISODE 08: 12/08/01
H: Hugh Jackman
MG: Mick Jagger

EPISODE 09: 12/15/01
H: Ellen DeGeneres
MG: No Doubt
SG/C: Rudy Giuliani

EPISODE 10: 1/12/02
H: Josh Hartnett
MG: Pink

EPISODE 11: 1/19/02
H: Jack Black
MG: The Strokes
SG/C: Kyle Gass

EPISODE 12: 2/02/02
H/MG: Britney Spears
SG/C: Dan Aykroyd, Justin Timberlake

EPISODE 13: 3/2/02
H: Jonny Moseley
MG: Outkast
SG/C: Rip Taylor

EPISODE 14: 3/9/02
H: Jon Stewart
MG: India.Arie
SG/C: George Plimpton

EPISODE 15: 3/16/02
H: Ian McKellan
MG: Kylie Minogue

EPISODE 16: 4/6/02
H: Cameron Diaz
MG: Jimmy Eat World

EPISODE 17: 4/13/02
H: The Rock
MG: Andrew W.K.

EPISODE 18: 4/20/02
H: Alec Baldwin
MG: P.O.D.

EPISODE 19: 5/11/02
H: Kirsten Dunst
MG: Eminem
SG/C: Proof

EPISODE 20: 5/18/02
H: Winona Ryder
MG: Moby
SG/C: Neil Diamond, Alex Trebek

SEASON HIGHLIGHTS

Amber the One-Legged Hypoglycemic (Poehler), Astronaut Jones (Morgan), Blues Brothers (Aykroyd), Boston Teens (Dratch/Fallon), Brian Fellow's Safari Planet (Morgan), Celebrity Jeopardy! (Ferrell/Hammond, et al.), Clear Results (Gasteyer/Parnell), Delicious Dish (Gasteyer/Shannon), Dissing Your Dog (Ferrell), Donatella Versace (Rudolph), E.P.T. (Meyers/Poehler), Herbal Essences (Ferrell/Poehler), Jarret's Room (Fallon/Sanz), Kotex Classics (Dratch/Fey/Poehler/Rudolph), Land Shark (Chase), The Lovers (Dratch/Ferrell), Mango (Kattan), Mr. Peepers (Kattan), Preparation H (Fallon), The X-Presidents (Smigel)

BUMPER KEY (Pg. 440-441)

11 16 01 17 09 16
02 15
08 13 09
03 01 06 11 17 13
03 12 10 14
19 04 04 10
05 20
05 14 18 06 02
07 07 08 19 18 15 20

a.

b.

c.

a. The Land Shark (Chevy Chase) makes a cameo on "Weekend Update" (with Jimmy Fallon). **b.** In her monologue, Drew Barrymore alludes to the panic that had ensued at 30 Rock after that week's anthrax attacks. **c.** Winona Ryder and cast in "Girl Next Door," featuring Amy Poehler as Amber the One-Legged Hypoglycemic, with Rachel Dratch, Maya Rudolph, and Ana Gasteyer.

SEASON 28 / 2002-03

CAST

Rachel Dratch
Jimmy Fallon
Tina Fey
Darrell Hammond
Chris Kattan
Tracy Morgan
Chris Parnell
Amy Poehler
Maya Rudolph
Horatio Sanz

Featuring:
Fred Armisen
Dean Edwards
Will Forte
Seth Meyers
Jeff Richards

Weekend Update:
Jimmy Fallon
Tina Fey

CREW

Executive Producer:
Lorne Michaels

Director:
Beth McCarthy-Miller

Head Writers:
Tina Fey, Dennis McNicholas

Produced by:
Steve Higgins, Marci Klein, Mike Shoemaker

Writers: Doug Abeles, Leo Allen, James Anderson, Max Brooks, James Downey, James Eagan, Tina Fey, Charlie Grandy, Steve Higgins, Erik Kenward, Dennis McNicholas, Lorne Michaels, Corwin Moore, Matt Murray, Paula Pell, Ken Scarborough, Michael Schur, Frank Sebastiano, T. Sean Shannon, Eric Slovin, Robert Smigel, Emily Spivey, Andrew Steele, Scott Wainio

Writing Supervisors:
Paula Pell, Andrew Steele

Supervising Producer:
Ken Aymong

Film Producer:
James Signorelli

Weekend Update Produced by:
Michael Schur

Production Designers:
Eugene Lee, Akira Yoshimura, Keith Ian Raywood

Lighting Consultant:
Phil Hymes

Musical Directors:
Lenny Pickett, Leon Pendarvis

Sketch Music Adaptation:
Hal Willner

Costume Designer:
Tom Broecker

Wardrobe: Dale Richards, Margaret Karolyi, J. Douglas James, Bruce Brumage

Hair: Michael Anthony, Clariss Morgan, Linda Rico

Makeup: Andrea Miller, Louie Zakarian

Photographer:
Mary Ellen Matthews

EPISODE LIST

EPISODE KEY:
H - Host
MG - Musical Guest
SG/C - Special Guests/Cameos

EPISODE 01: 10/5/02
H: Matt Damon
MG: Bruce Springsteen & The E Street Band
SG/C: Soozie Tyrell

EPISODE 02: 10/12/02
H: Sarah Michelle Gellar
MG: Faith Hill

EPISODE 03: 10/19/02
H: Senator John McCain
MG: The White Stripes

EPISODE 04: 11/2/02
H: Eric McCormack
MG: Jay-Z
SG/C: Lenny Kravitz, Beyoncé

EPISODE 05: 11/9/02
H: Nia Vardalos
MG: Eve
SG/C: Jean Fey

EPISODE 06: 11/16/02
H: Brittany Murphy
MG: Nelly
SG/C: Garrett Morris, Kelly Rowland, Adam Sandler, Rob Schneider

EPISODE 07: 12/7/02
H: Robert De Niro
MG: Norah Jones
SG/C: Harvey Keitel

EPISODE 08: 12/13/02
H: Al Gore
MG: Phish
SG/C: Al Franken, Tipper Gore, Allison Janney, Richard Schiff, Martin Sheen, John Spencer, Bradley Whitford

EPISODE 09: 1/11/03
H: Jeff Gordon
MG: Avril Lavigne

EPISODE 10: 1/18/03
H: Ray Liotta
MG: The Donnas

EPISODE 11: 2/8/03
H: Matthew McConaughey
MG: The Dixie Chicks

EPISODE 12: 2/15/03
H: Jennifer Garner
MG: Beck

EPISODE 13: 2/22/03
H: Christopher Walken
MG: Foo Fighters
SG/C: Jim Carrey, Will Ferrell, Steve Martin, Britney Spears

EPISODE 14: 3/8/03
H: Queen Latifah
MG: Ms. Dynamite
SG/C: Dan Aykroyd

EPISODE 15: 3/15/03
H: Salma Hayek
MG: Christina Aguilera
SG/C: Edward Norton

EPISODE 16: 4/5/03
H: Bernie Mac
MG: Good Charlotte

EPISODE 17: 4/12/03
H: Ray Romano
MG: Zwan

EPISODE 18: 5/3/03
H: Ashton Kutcher
MG: 50 Cent
SG/C: G-Unit, Nate Dogg

EPISODE 19: 5/10/03
H: Adrien Brody
MG: Sean Paul & Wayne Wonder
SG/C: Elliot Brody, Sylvia Plachy

EPISODE 20: 5/17/03
H: Dan Aykroyd
MG: Beyoncé
SG/C: Jay-Z, Jim Belushi, John Goodman, Kip King

SEASON HIGHLIGHTS

Amber the One-Legged Hypoglycemic (Poehler), The Ambiguously Gay Duo (Smigel), Astronaut Jones (Morgan), Boston Teens (Dratch/Fallon), Brian Fellow's Safari Planet (Morgan), The Continental (Walken), Corona Ads (Fallon/Poehler), Daily Affirmation with Stuart Smalley (Franken), Donatella Versace (Rudolph), The Falconer (Forte), Jarret's Room (Fallon/Sanz), The Lovers (Dratch/Ferrell), McCain Sings Streisand (McCain), Mom Jeans (Dratch/Fey/Poehler/Rudolph), NRA Ads (Fallon/Meyers/Sanz), Swiffer Sleepers (Poehler), Tim Calhoun (Forte), The X-Presidents (Smigel)

BUMPER KEY (Pg. 444-445)

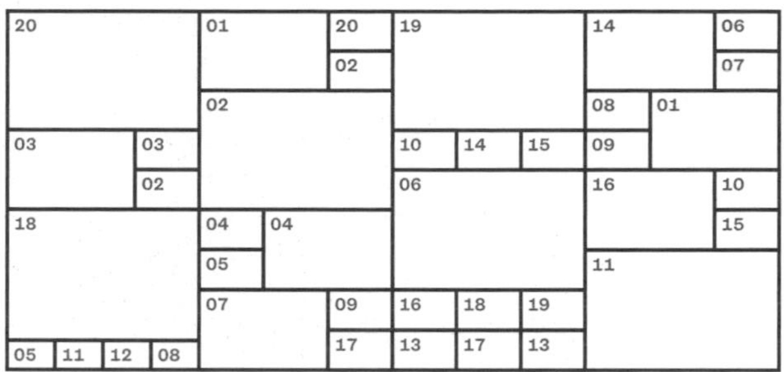

a.

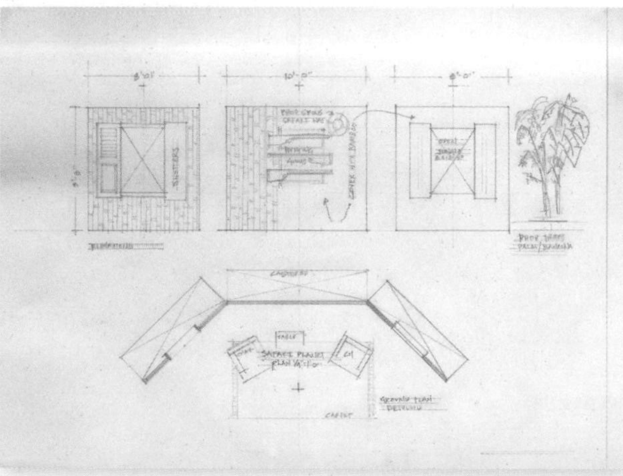

b.

c.

a. "Safari Planet" set design. **b.** Matt Damon and Tracy Morgan in "Brian Fellow's Safari Planet." **c.** Al Gore as Dr. Ralph Wormly Curtis in "Jarret's Room," with Jimmy Fallon and Horatio Sanz.

50 ROCKEFELLER PLAZA
Saturday Night Live
SNL
SNL
SATURDAYNIGHTLIVE
SNL
SATURDAYNIGHTLIVE
SATURDAYNIGHTLIVE
SATURDAYNIGHTLIVE
SNL
SATURDAYNIGHTLIVE
SATURDAYNIGHTLIVE
SNL
SNL
SNL
SNL
SNL
SATURDAYNIGHTLIVE

SNL
SATURDAYNIGHTLIVE

SEASON 28 / 2002-03

SNL
SD

SNL
SNL
SATURDAYNIGHTLIVE
SNL
SATURDAYNIGHTLIVE
SNL
SNL
SNL
SNL
SNL
SATURDAYNIGHTLIVE
SNL
SNL
SATURDAYNIGHTLIVE

SATURDAYNIGHTLIVE
SATURDAYNIGHTLIVE
PENNSYLVANIA
55
SNL
SNL
SNL
SNL
SNL
SNL
SNL
SNL
SNL
SNL
SNL
SNL
SNL
SNL

SEASON 29 / 2003-04

CAST

Rachel Dratch
Jimmy Fallon
Tina Fey
Will Forte
Darrell Hammond
Seth Meyers
Chris Parnell
Amy Poehler
Jeff Richards
Maya Rudolph
Horatio Sanz

Featuring:
Fred Armisen
Finesse Mitchell
Kenan Thompson

Weekend Update:
Jimmy Fallon
Tina Fey

CREW:

Executive Producer:
Lorne Michaels

Produced by: Steve Higgins

Director:
Beth McCarthy-Miller

Head Writers: Tina Fey, Dennis McNicholas

Producers: Marci Klein, Michael Shoemaker

Writers: Doug Abeles, Leo Allen, James Anderson, Jordan Black, Liz Cackowski, James Downey, James Eagan, Tina Fey, Charlie Grandy, Steve Higgins, David Iserson, Joe Kelly, Erik Kenward, John Lutz, Dennis McNicholas, Lorne Michaels, Matt Murray, Paula Pell, Ken Scarborough, Michael Schur, Frank Sebastiano, T. Sean Shannon, Eric Slovin, Robert Smigel, JB Smoove, Emily Spivey, Andrew Steele, Jason Sudeikis, Rich Talarico

Writing Supervisors:
Paula Pell, T. Sean Shannon, Andrew Steele

Supervising Producer:
Ken Aymong

Film Producer:
James Signorelli

Weekend Update Produced by:
Michael Schur

Production Designers:
Eugene Lee, Akira Yoshimura, Keith Ian Raywood

Lighting Consultant:
Phil Hymes

Musical Directors:
Lenny Pickett, Leon Pendarvis

Sketch Music Adaptation:
Hal Willner

Costume Designer:
Tom Broecker

Wardrobe: Dale Richards
Margaret Karolyi,
J. Douglas James, Bruce Brumage

Hair: Michael Anthony, Clariss Morgan, Linda Rice

Makeup: Andrea Miller, Louie Zakarian

Photographer:
Mary Ellen Matthews

EPISODE LIST

EPISODE KEY:
H - Host
MG - Musical Guest
SG/C - Special Guests/Cameos

EPISODE 01: 10/4/03
H: Jack Black
MG: John Mayer
SG/C: Will Ferrell, Kyle Gass

EPISODE 02: 10/11/03
H/MG: Justin Timberlake
SG/C: Carl Weathers

EPISODE 03: 10/18/03
H: Halle Berry
MG: Britney Spears
SG/C: George Wendt

EPISODE 04: 11/1/03
H: Kelly Ripa
MG: Outkast
SG/C: Chris Kattan

EPISODE 05: 11/8/03
H: Andy Roddick
MG: Dave Matthews
SG/C: Trey Anastasio, John McEnroe

EPISODE 06: 11/15/03
H: Alec Baldwin
MG: Missy Elliott
SG/C: Mike Myers

EPISODE 07: 12/6/03
H: Reverend Al Sharpton
MG: Pink
SG/C: Paris Hilton, Tracy Morgan

EPISODE 08: 12/13/03
H: Elijah Wood
MG: Jet
SG/C: Chris Kattan

EPISODE 09: 1/10/04
H: Jennifer Aniston
MG: The Black Eyed Peas
SG/C: Al Franken

EPISODE 10: 1/17/04
H: Jessica Simpson & Nick Lachey
MG: G-Unit
SG/C: Joe

EPISODE 11: 2/7/04
H: Megan Mullally
MG: Clay Aiken
SG/C: Nick Offerman

EPISODE 12: 2/14/04
H: Drew Barrymore
MG: Kelis

EPISODE 13: 2/21/04
H: Christina Aguilera
MG: Maroon 5

EPISODE 14: 3/6/04
H: Colin Firth
MG: Norah Jones
SG/C: Ana Gasteyer

EPISODE 15: 3/13/04
H: Ben Affleck
MG: N.E.R.D.
SG/C: Kelly Ripa

EPISODE 16: 4/3/04
H: Donald Trump
MG: Toots & The Maytals
SG/C: Bootsy Collins, Ben Harper, Jack Johnson, Carolyn Kepcher, The Roots, George Ross

EPISODE 17: 4/10/04
H/MG: Janet Jackson
SG/C: Simon Cowell, Chris Kattan, Tracy Morgan

EPISODE 18: 5/1/04
H: Lindsay Lohan
MG: Usher
SG/C: Ludacris

EPISODE 19: 5/8/04
H: Snoop Dogg
MG: Avril Lavigne

EPISODE 20: 5/15/04
H: Mary-Kate & Ashley Olsen
MG: J-Kwon

SEASON HIGHLIGHTS

The Barry Gibb Talk Show (Fallon/Timberlake), Boston Teens (Dratch/Fallon), Brian Fellow's Safari Planet (Morgan), Debbie Downer (Dratch), Donatella Versace (Rudolph), Dynacorp: Starkist (Simpson), The Falconer (Forte), Fear Factor Junior (Armisen), Gaystrogen (Parnell/Armisen), Huggies Thong (Dratch/ Rudolph), Jarret's Room (Fallon/Sanz), Mary Kate & Ashley (Olsen/ Olsen), Mascots (Timberlake), Only Bangkok (Affleck/Meyers/ Poehler), The Prince Show (Armisen/Rudolph), Tressant Supreme (Ripa), Trump's House of Wings (Trump), Turlington's Tattoo Remover (Parnell)

BUMPER KEY (Pg. 448-449)

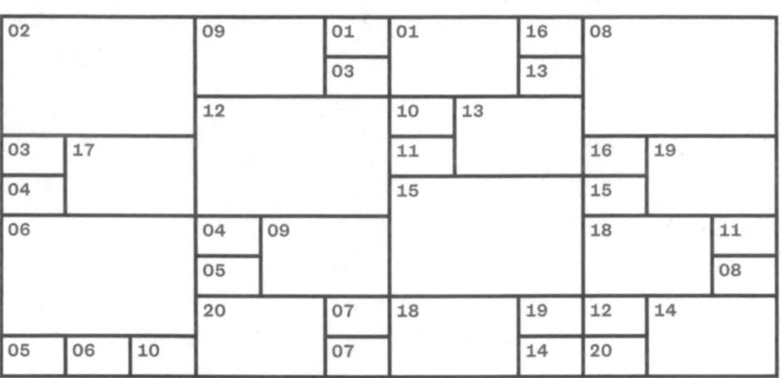

a-b. Plans and completed set for the Grand Central home base that debuted in 2003. **c-d.** Drawing for Chris Parnell's "Benny's vs. Omeletteville" costume and photo of the performance, with Justin Timberlake as the Omelette. **e.** Seth Meyers and Ben Affleck in "Appalachian Emergency Room."

a.

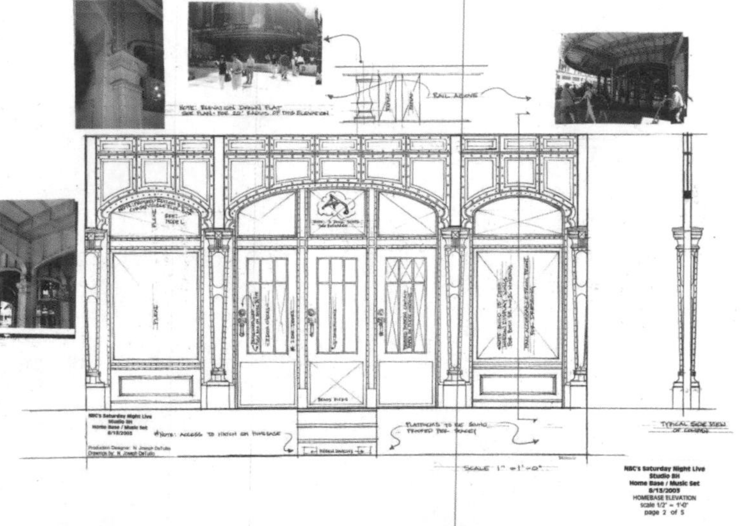

b.

c.

e.

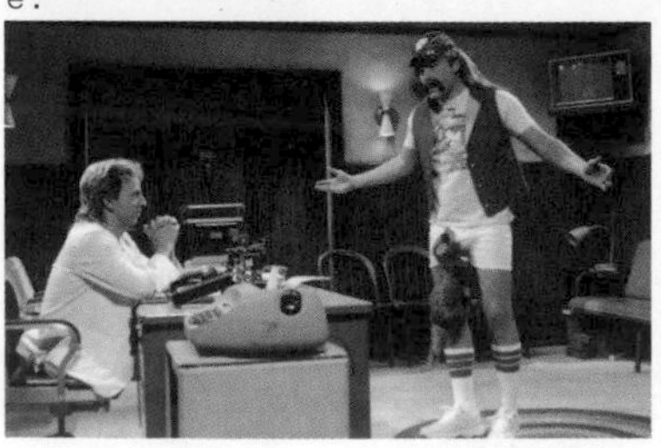

d.

SEASON 30 / 2004-05

CAST

Fred Armisen
Rachel Dratch
Tina Fey
Will Forte
Darrell Hammond
Seth Meyers
Chris Parnell
Amy Poehler
Maya Rudolph
Horatio Sanz

Featuring:
Finesse Mitchell
Rob Riggle
Jason Sudeikis
Kenan Thompson

Weekend Update:
Tina Fey
Amy Poehler

CREW

Executive Producer:
Lorne Michaels

Produced by: Steve Higgins

Director:
Beth McCarthy-Miller

Head Writers:
Tina Fey, Andrew Steele

Producers: Marci Klein, Michael Schoemaker

Writers: Doug Abeles, Leo Allen, James Anderson, Alex Baze, Liz Cackowski, James Downey, Tina Fey, Charlie Grandy, Steve Higgins, Joe Kelly, Erik Kenward, John Lutz, Lorne Michaels, Matt Murray, Paula Pell, Lauren Pomerantz, Frank Sebastiano, T. Sean Shannon, Eric Slovin, Robert Smigel, JB Smoove, Emily Spivey, Andrew Steele, Jason Sudeikis, Rich Talarico

Writing Supervisors:
Paula Pell, T. Sean Shannon

Supervising Producer:
Ken Aymong

Film Producer:
James Signorelli

Weekend Update Produced by:
Charlie Grandy

Weekend Update Head Writer:
Doug Abeles

Production Designers:
Eugene Lee, Akira Yoshimura, Keith Ian Raywood

Lighting Consultant:
Phil Hymes

Musical Directors:
Lenny Pickett, Leon Pendarvis

Sketch Music Adaptation:
Hal Willner

Costume Designer:
Tom Broecker

Wardrobe: Dale Richards, Margaret Karolyi, J. Douglas James, Bruce Brumage

Hair: Michael Anthony, Clariss Morgan, Linda Rice

Makeup: Andrea Miller, Louie Zakarian

Photographer:
Mary Ellen Matthews

EPISODE LIST

EPISODE KEY:
H - Host
MG - Musical Guest
SG/C - Special Guests/Cameos

EPISODE 01: 10/2/04
H: Ben Affleck
MG: Nelly
SG/C: Alec Baldwin, James Gandolfini, Jaheim

EPISODE 02: 10/9/04
H/MG: Queen Latifah
SG/C: Chris Kattan

EPISODE 03: 10/23/04
H: Jude Law
MG: Ashlee Simpson

EPISODE 04: 10/30/04
H: Kate Winslet
MG: Eminem
SG/C: Johnny Damon, Proof

EPISODE 05: 11/13/04
H: Liam Neeson
MG: Modest Mouse

EPISODE 06: 11/20/04
H: Luke Wilson
MG: U2

EPISODE 07: 12/11/04
H: Colin Farrell
MG: Scissor Sisters
SG/C: Brett Hull, Lindsay Lohan

EPISODE 08: 12/18/04
H: Robert De Niro
MG: Destiny's Child
SG/C: Jim Henson's Muppets, Lil Wayne

EPISODE 09: 1/15/05
H: Topher Grace
MG: The Killers

EPISODE 10: 1/22/05
H: Paul Giamatti
MG: Ludacris, Sum 41

EPISODE 11: 2/5/05
H: Paris Hilton
MG: Keane

EPISODE 12: 2/12/05
H: Jason Bateman
MG: Kelly Clarkson

EPISODE 13: 2/19/05
H: Hilary Swank
MG: 50 Cent
SG/C: Olivia

EPISODE 14: 3/12/05
H: David Spade
MG: Jack Johnson
SG/C: G. Love

EPISODE 15: 3/19/05
H: Ashton Kutcher
MG: Gwen Stefani
SG/C: Eve, Demi Moore

EPISODE 16: 4/9/05
H: Cameron Diaz
MG: Green Day
SG/C: Drew Barrymore, Jimmy Fallon, Justin Timberlake

EPISODE 17: 4/16/05
H: Tom Brady
MG: Beck
SG/C: Martin Short

EPISODE 18: 5/7/05
H: Johnny Knoxville
MG: System of a Down
SG/C: Paula Abdul, Patti Forte

EPISODE 19: 5/14/05
H: Will Ferrell
MG: Queens of the Stone Age

EPISODE 20: 5/21/05
H: Lindsay Lohan
MG: Coldplay

SEASON HIGHLIGHTS

The Barry Gibb Talk Show (Fallon/Timberlake), Bear City: Smokes (Willard), Celebrity Jeopardy! (Ferrell/Hammond, et al.), CheapKids.Net (Meyers/Parnell), Debbie Downer (Dratch), Donatella Versace (Rudolph), Dr. Porkenheimers Bone Juice (Poehler), Dyson (Armisen), Excedrin: Racial Tension (Latifah), The Falconer (Forte), Federlines (Kutcher), Me-Harmony (Forte), Nuni and Nuni Schoener, Art Dealers (Armisen/Rudolph), The Prince Show (Armisen/Parnell/Rudolph), Short & Curly (Seth Meyers), Woomba (Dratch/Fey/Poehler/Rudolph), The X-Presidents (Smigel)

BUMPER KEY (Pg. 452-453)

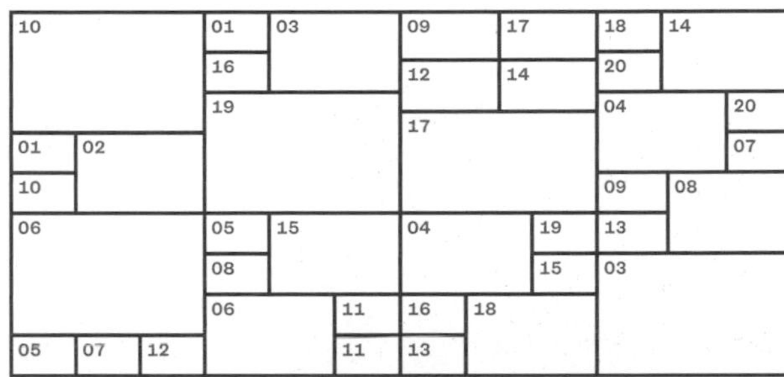

a.

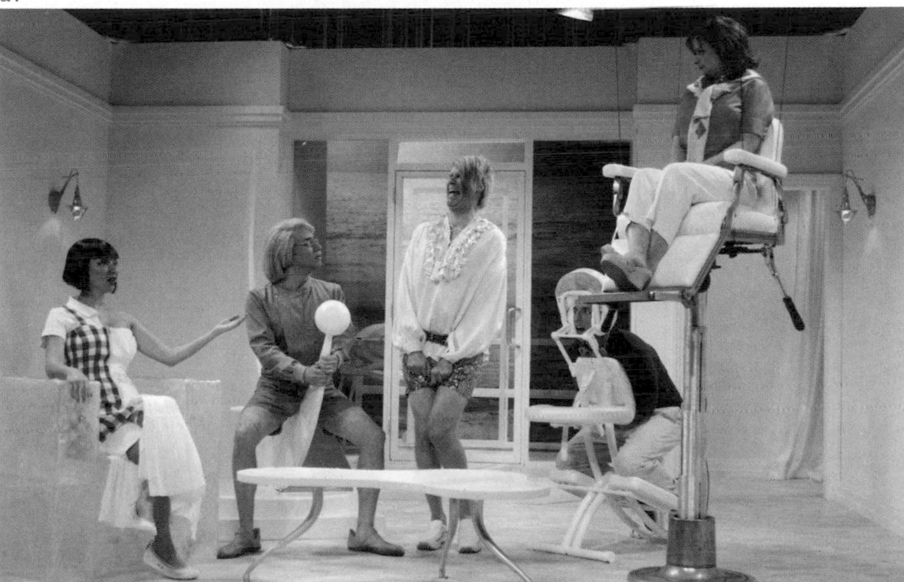

b.

c.

a. Maya Rudolph and Fred Armisen as "Nuni and Nuni Schoener, Art Dealers," with Will Ferrell, Seth Meyers, and Rachel Dratch.
b-c. Costume design for and performance of "Gays in Space" (with host Ashton Kutcher).

SNL
SNL
SNL
SATURDAY NIGHT LIVE
SNL
SNL
SNL
SATURDAY NIGHT LIVE
SNL
SATURDAY NIGHT LIVE
362553 206
11 20 04
SNL
SATURDAY NIGHT LIVE
SNL
SNL
SNL
SNL
SNL

SATURDAY NIGHT LIVE
SNL
SATURDAYNIGHTLIVE
SATURDAYNIGHTLIVE
SNL
SATURDAY NIGHT LIVE
SATURDAY NIGHT LIVE
SATURDAY NIGHT LIVE
SNL
SNL
SNL
SNL
SNL
SNL
SNL
SNL
SNL
SNL
SNL

SEASON 30 / 2004-05

SAT

SEASON 31 / 2005-06

SATURDAYNIGHTLIVE
SATURDAYNIGHTLIVE
SNL
SNL
SNL
SATURDAY NIGHT LIVE
SATURDAY NIGHT LIVE
SATURDAYNIGHTLIVE
SNL
SNL
SNL
SNL
SNL
SATURDAY
NIGHT LIVE
SATURDAYNIGHTLIVE
SNL
SATURDAY NIGHT LIVE

SNL
SNL
SATURDAY NIGHT LIVE
SNL
SNL
SATURDAY NIGHT LIVE
STOP WARS
SNL
SATURDAYNIGHTLIVE
SATURDAY NIGHT LIVE
SATURDAY NIGHT LIVE
SATURDAYNIGHTLIVE
SNL
SATURDAY NIGHT LIVE
SNL
SATURDAY NIGHT LIVE
SNL
SATURDAYNIGHTLIVE
SATURDAY NIGHT LIVE
SNL

SEASON 31 / 2005-06

CAST

Fred Armisen
Rachel Dratch
Tina Fey
Will Forte
Darrell Hammond
Seth Meyers
Finesse Mitchell
Chris Parnell
Amy Poehler
Maya Rudolph
Horatio Sanz
Kenan Thompson

Featuring:
Bill Hader
Andy Samberg
Jason Sudeikis
Kristen Wiig

Weekend Update:
Tina Fey
Amy Poehler
Horatio Sanz

CREW:

Executive Producer:
Lorne Michaels

Produced by: Steve Higgins

Director:
Beth McCarthy-Miller

Head Writers: Tina Fey, Seth Meyers, Andrew Steele

Producers: Marci Klein, Michael Shoemaker

Writers: Doug Abeles, James Anderson, Alex Baze, Liz Cackowski, Tina Fey, Charlie Grandy, Steve Higgins, Colin Jost, Erik Kenward, John Lutz, Seth Meyers, Lorne Michaels, Matt Murray, Paula Pell, Akiva Schaffer, Frank Sebastiano, T. Sean Shannon, Robert Smigel, J.B. Smoove, Emily Spivey, Andrew Steele, Jorma Taccone, Bryan Tucker

Supervising Producer:
Ken Aymong

Film Producer:
James Signorelli

Weekend Update Produced by:
Charlie Grandy

Weekend Update Head Writer:
Doug Abeles

Production Designers:
Eugene Lee, Akira Yoshimura, Keith Ian Raywood

Lighting Consultant:
Phil Hymes

Musical Directors:
Lenny Pickett, Leon Pendarvis

Sketch Music Adaptation:
Hal Willner

Costume Designers:
Tom Broecker, Eric Justian

Wardrobe: Dale Richards, Margaret Karolyi, J. Douglas James, Tim Alberts, Bruce Brumage

Hair: Michael Anthony, Clariss Morgan, Linda Rice

Makeup: Andrea Miller Louie Zakarian

Photographer:
Mary Ellen Matthews

EPISODE LIST

EPISODE KEY:
H - Host
MG - Musical Guest
SG/C - Special Guests/Cameos

EPISODE 01: 10/1/05
H: Steve Carell
MG: Kanye West
SG/C: Adam Levine, Mike Myers

EPISODE 02: 10/8/05
H: Jon Heder
MG: Ashlee Simpson

EPISODE 03: 10/22/05
H: Catherine Zeta-Jones
MG: Franz Ferdinand

EPISODE 04: 10/29/05
H: Lance Armstrong
MG: Sheryl Crow
SG/C: Scott Podsednik

EPISODE 05: 11/12/05
H: Jason Lee
MG: Foo Fighters

EPISODE 06: 11/19/05
H: Eva Longoria
MG: Korn

EPISODE 07: 12/3/05
H: Dane Cook
MG: James Blunt

EPISODE 08: 12/10/05
H: Alec Baldwin
MG: Shakira
SG/C: Tim Meadows, Alejandro Sanz

EPISODE 09: 12/17/05
H: Jack Black
MG: Neil Young
SG/C: Kyle Gass, Johnny Knoxville, Darlene Love, Tracy Morgan

EPISODE 10: 1/14/06
H: Scarlett Johansson
MG: Death Cab for Cutie

EPISODE 11: 1/21/06
H: Peter Sarsgaard
MG: The Strokes
SG/C: Drew Barrymore

EPISODE 12: 2/4/06
H: Steve Martin
MG: Prince
SG/C: Alec Baldwin, Jimmy Fallon, Scarlett Johansson, Conan O'Brien, Kelly Ripa, Tamar, Brian Williams, Gideon Yago

EPISODE 13: 3/4/06
H: Natalie Portman
MG: Fall Out Boy
SG/C: Dennis Haysbert

EPISODE 14: 3/11/06
H: Matt Dillon
MG: Arctic Monkeys

EPISODE 15: 4/8/06
H: Antonio Banderas
MG: Mary J. Blige
SG/C: Chris Kattan

EPISODE 16: 4/15/06
H: Lindsay Lohan
MG: Pearl Jam
SG/C: Michael Lohan

EPISODE 17: 5/6/06
H: Tom Hanks
MG: Red Hot Chili Peppers

EPISODE 18: 5/13/06
H: Julia Louis-Dreyfus
MG: Paul Simon
SG/C: Jason Alexander, Al Gore, Jerry Seinfeld

EPISODE 19: 5/20/06
H: Kevin Spacey
MG: Nelly Furtado
SG/C: Timbaland

SEASON HIGHLIGHTS

Black Eyed Peas Ad (Hader/Heder/Poehler/Thompson), Dad (Forte/Poehler), Debbie Downer and Bob Bummer (Carell/Dratch), Deep House Dish (Dratch/Samberg/Thompson), The Falconer (Forte), Lazy Sunday (Parnell/Samberg), Nelson's Baby Toupees (Hader), Nuni and Nuni Schoener, Art Dealers (Armisen/Parnell/Rudolph), The Prince Show (Armisen/Rudolph), Taco Town (Hader/Samberg/Sudeikis), The Target Lady (Wiig), Two A-Holes (Sudeikis/Wiig), Tylenol BM (Baldwin/Dratch), Vincent Price's Holiday Special (Hader)

BUMPER KEY (Pg. 458-459)

01 04 03 06 17 16 18
04 13 18
13 02 12 02
01 05 19
11 06
09 07 11 07 19 09 16 15
17 12 15
08 08 05
14 14 03 10 10

a.

b.

c.

d.

a-b. Costume design for and performance of "Elf Motivation," with Alec Baldwin. **c.** Jason Sudeikis and Kristen Wiig as "Two A-Holes Buying a Christmas Tree," with Jack Black. **d.** "Deep House Dish" hosts DJ Dynasty Handbag (Kenan Thompson) and Tiara Zee (Rachel Dratch) interview Donna Smalls English (Scarlett Johansson).

SEASON 32 / 2006-07

CAST

Fred Armisen
Will Forte
Bill Hader
Darrell Hammond
Seth Meyers
Amy Poehler
Maya Rudolph
Andy Samberg
Jason Sudeikis
Kenan Thompson
Kristen Wiig

Weekend Update:
Seth Meyers
Amy Poehler

CREW

Executive Producer:
Lorne Michaels

Produced by: Steve Higgins

Director: Don Roy King

Head Writers: Seth Meyers, Andrew Steele, Paula Pell

Producers: Marci Klein, Michael Shoemaker

Writers: Doug Abeles, James Anderson, Alex Baze, James Downey, Charlie Grandy, Steve Higgins, Colin Jost, Erik Kenward, John Lutz, Seth Meyers, Lorne Michaels, Matt Murray, Paula Pell, Marika Sawyer, Akiva Schaffer, Robert Smigel, John Solomon, Emily Spivey, Andrew Steele, Jorma Taccone, Bryan Tucker

Supervising Producer:
Ken Aymong

Film Producer:
James Signorelli

Weekend Update Produced by:
Charlie Grandy

Weekend Update Head Writer:
Doug Abeles

Production Designers:
Eugene Lee, Akira Yoshimura, Keith Ian Raywood

Lighting Consultant:
Phil Hymes

Musical Directors:
Lenny Pickett, Leon Pendarvis

Sketch Music Adaptation:
Hal Willner

Costume Designers:
Tom Broecker, Eric Justian

Wardrobe: Dale Richards, Margaret Karolyi, J. Douglas James, Tim Alberts, Bruce Brumage

Hair: Jodi Mancuso, Anne Michelle Radcliffe, Linda Rice, Bettie O. Rogers, Inga Thrasher

Makeup: Louie Zakarian

Photographer:
Mary Ellen Matthews

EPISODE LIST

EPISODE KEY:
H - Host
MG - Musical Guest
SG/C - Special Guests/Cameos

EPISODE 01: 9/30/06
H: Dane Cook
MG: The Killers
SG/C: Brian Williams

EPISODE 02: 10/7/06
H: Jaime Pressly
MG: Corinne Bailey Rae

EPISODE 03: 10/21/06
H: John C. Reilly
MG: My Chemical Romance
SG/C: Will Ferrell

EPISODE 04: 10/28/06
H: Hugh Laurie
MG: Beck
SG/C: Sacha Baron Cohen, Ken Davitan

EPISODE 05: 11/11/06
H: Alec Baldwin
MG: Christina Aguilera
SG/C: Tony Bennett, Tina Fey, Takeru Kobayashi, Steve Martin, Paul McCartney, Tracy Morgan, Martin Short

EPISODE 06: 11/18/06
H/MG: Ludacris
SG/C: Mary J. Blige

EPISODE 07: 12/2/06
H: Matthew Fox
MG: Tenacious D

EPISODE 08: 12/9/06
H: Annette Bening
MG: Gwen Stefani and Akon
SG/C: Alec Baldwin, Matthew Fox

EPISODE 09: 12/16/06
H/MG: Justin Timberlake
SG/C: Cameron Diaz, Jimmy Fallon

EPISODE 10: 1/13/07
H: Jake Gyllenhaal
MG: The Shins

EPISODE 11: 1/20/07
H: Jeremy Piven
MG: AFI
SG/C: Common

EPISODE 12: 2/3/07
H: Drew Barrymore
MG: Lily Allen
SG/C: Horatio Sanz

EPISODE 13: 2/10/07
H: Forest Whitaker
MG: Keith Urban

EPISODE 14: 2/24/07
H: Rainn Wilson
MG: Arcade Fire
SG/C: Rashida Jones

EPISODE 15: 3/17/07
H: Julia Louis-Dreyfus
MG: Snow Patrol
SG/C: Chris Rock

EPISODE 16: 3/24/07
H: Peyton Manning
MG: Carrie Underwood
SG/C: Dan Aykroyd, Archie Manning, Eli Manning, Olivia Manning

EPISODE 17: 4/14/07
H: Shia LaBeouf
MG: Avril Lavigne
SG/C: Alec Baldwin

EPISODE 18: 4/21/07
H: Scarlett Johansson
MG: Björk
SG/C: Sen. Charles Schumer

EPISODE 19: 5/12/07
H: Molly Shannon
MG: Linkin Park

EPISODE 20: 5/19/07
H: Zach Braff
MG: Maroon 5

SEASON HIGHLIGHTS

Aunt Linda (Wiig), The Barry Gibb Talk Show (Fallon/Timberlake), Bronx Beat (Poehler/Rudolph), Deep Dish House (Samberg/Thompson), Dick in a Box (Samberg/Timberlake), Donatella Versace (Rudolph), La Rivista Della Televisione (Hader), Locker Room Motivation (Forte/Manning), MacGruber (Forte), Mary Katherine Gallagher "Superstar" (Shannon), Mascots (Timberlake), Nuni and Nuni Schoener, Art Dealers (Armisen/Parnell/Rudolph), Penelope (Wiig), The Prince Show (Armisen/Rudolph), The Target Lady (Wiig), TV Funhouse: Maraka (Smigel), Two A-Holes (Sudeikis/Wiig), United Way (Manning)

BUMPER KEY (Pg. 462-463)

01 | 01 02 02 | 20 | 08 | 18
09 | 08
03 04 | 14 | 19 16
03 20 | 12
05 06 07
15
07 10 14 | 10 | 19 05
11 | 17 18
11 12
04
13 13 | 15 17 16

a.

b.

c.

a. Amy Poehler and Maya Rudolph as "Bronx Beat" hosts Betty Caruso and Jodi Dietz. **b.** "New Jersey Gay Couple" (Fred Armisen and Bill Hader) bring their own mistletoe to "Weekend Update." **c.** "And the Oscar does NOT go to: the war epic 'Letters from Iwo Jima'! Excuse me? Everyone's Asian and subtitled? I have two letters for you, Clark Eastwood: F. U.! Yeah, I give this toilet log a big, fat 'Oh, Criiippes!'" Kristen Wiig as Aunt Linda.

SATURDAY NIGHT LIVE
SATURDAY NIGHT LIVE
SATURDAY NIGHT LIVE
SATURDAY NIGHT LIVE
SNL
SATURDAY NIGHT LIVE
SNL
SNL
SNL
SNL
SATURDAY NIGHT LIVE
SATURDAY NIGHT LIVE
SNL
SATURDAY NIGHT LIVE
SATURDAY NIGHT LIVE
SNL
SATURDAY NIGHT LIVE
SNL
SNL
SATURDAY NIGHT LIVE
SNL

SATURDAY NIGHT LIVE
SATURDAY NIGHT LIVE
SATURDAY NIGHT LIVE
SATURDAY NIGHT LIVE
SNL
SNL
SNL
SNL
SNL
SATURDAY NIGHT LIVE
SNL
SNL
SNL
SNL
SATURDAY NIGHT LIVE
SATURDAY NIGHT LIVE
SATURDAY NIGHT LIVE

SNL

SEASON 33 /
2007-08

SNL

SATURDAY NIGHT LIVE

SNL

SNL

SATURDAY NIGHT LIVE

SNL

SATURDAY NIGHT LIVE

SNL

SATURDAY NIGHT LIVE

SNL

SNL

PRESS

UNDERWOOD

SATURDAY NIGHT LIVE
SATURDAY NIGHT LIVE
SATURDAY NIGHT LIVE
SATURDAY NIGHT LIVE
SATURDAY NIGHT LIVE
SNL
SATURDAY NIGHT LIVE
SATURDAY NIGHT LIVE
SATURDAY NIGHT LIVE
SNL
SNL

SEASON 33 / 2007-08

CAST

Fred Armisen
Will Forte
Bill Hader
Darrell Hammond
Seth Meyers
Amy Poehler
Maya Rudolph
Andy Samberg
Jason Sudeikis
Kenan Thompson
Kristen Wiig

Featuring:
Casey Wilson

Weekend Update:
Seth Meyers
Amy Poehler

CREW

Executive Producer:
Lorne Michaels

Produced by: Steve Higgins

Director: Don Roy King

Head Writers: Seth Meyers, Andrew Steele, Paula Pell

Producers: Marci Klein, Michael Shoemaker

Writers: Doug Abeles, James Anderson, Alex Baze, James Downey, Charlie Grandy, Steve Higgins, Colin Jost, Erik Kenward, Rob Klein, John Lutz, Seth Meyers, Lorne Michaels, Paula Pell, Simon Rich, Marika Sawyer, Akiva Schaffer, Robert Smigel, John Solomon, Emily Spivey, Andrew Steele, Kent Sublette, Jorma Taccone, Bryan Tucker

Supervising Producer:
Ken Aymong

Film Producer:
James Signorelli

Weekend Update Produced by:
Charlie Grandy

Weekend Update Head Writer:
Doug Abeles

Production Designers:
Eugene Lee, Akira Yoshimura, Keith Ian Raywood

Lighting Consultant:
Phil Hymes

Musical Directors:
Lenny Pickett, Leon Pendarvis, Katreese Barnes

Sketch Music Adaptation:
Hal Willner

Costume Designers:
Tom Broecker, Eric Justian

Wardrobe: Dale Richards, Margaret Karolyi, J. Douglas James, Tim Alberts, Bruce Brumage

Hair: Jodi Mancuso, Linda Rice, Bettie O. Rogers, Inga Thrasher

Makeup: Louie Zakarian

Photographer:
Mary Ellen Matthews

EPISODE LIST

EPISODE KEY:
H - Host
MG - Musical Guest
SG/C - Special Guests/Cameos

EPISODE 01: 9/29/07
H: LeBron James
MG: Kanye West
SG/C: Jake Gyllenhaal, Adam Levine

EPISODE 02: 10/6/07
H: Seth Rogen
MG: Spoon
SG/C: Chevy Chase

EPISODE 03: 10/13/07
H: Jon Bon Jovi
MG: Foo Fighters
SG/C: Bon Jovi, Jack Nicholson

EPISODE 04: 11/3/07
H: Brian Williams
MG: Feist
SG/C: Bono, Matt Lauer, Barack Obama, Al Roker, Horatio Sanz

WGA (WRITERS GUILD OF AMERICA) WRITER'S STRIKE
11/5/07-2/12/08

EPISODE 05: 2/23/08
H: Tina Fey
MG: Carrie Underwood
SG/C: Amber Lee Ettinger, Mike Huckabee, Steve Martin

EPISODE 06: 3/1/08
H: Ellen Page
MG: Wilco
SG/C: Hillary Clinton, Vincent D'Onofrio, Rudy Giuliani

EPISODE 07: 3/8/08
H: Amy Adams
MG: Vampire Weekend

EPISODE 08: 3/15/08
H: Jonah Hill
MG: Mariah Carey
SG/C: Tracy Morgan, T-Pain

EPISODE 09: 4/5/08
H: Christopher Walken
MG: Panic! at the Disco
SG/C: Christopher Dodd, Tina Fey

EPISODE 10: 4/12/08
H: Ashton Kutcher
MG: Gnarls Barkley
SG/C: Cameron Diaz, Demi Moore

EPISODE 11: 5/10/08
H: Shia LaBeouf
MG: My Morning Jacket

EPISODE 12: 5/17/08
H: Steve Carell
MG: Usher feat. Young Jeezy
SG/C: Sen. John McCain, Ricky Gervais, Young Jeezy, Nancy Walls

SEASON HIGHLIGHTS

The Ambiguously Gay Duo (Smigel), Annuale (Fey), Bronx Beat (Poehler/Rudolph), Dating Downey (Downey/Hill/Samberg), Japanese Office (Carell/Gervais), La Rivista Della Televisione (Hader), MacGruber (Forte), Sue (Wiig), The Target Lady (Wiig), Two A-Holes (Sudeikis/Wiig), Walker Family Reunion (Poehler/Walken, et al.)

BUMPER KEY (Pg. 466-467)

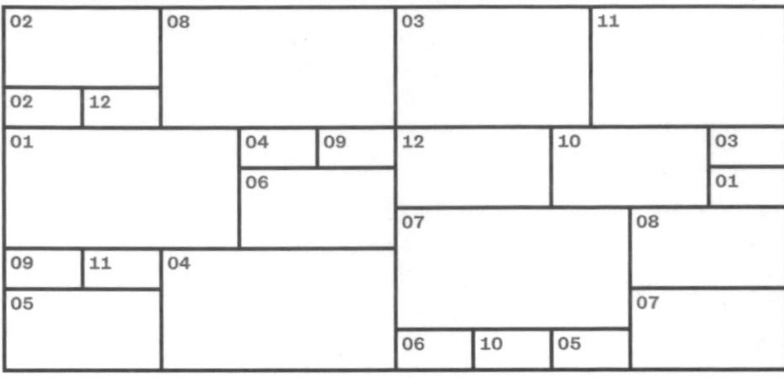

a.

c.

d.

b.

a-b. Costume designs for the aliens in and performance of "Where's My Purse." (With Maya Rudolph, Andy Samberg, Fred Armisen, and Jason Sudeikis.)
c. Fred Armisen as Barack Obama, with hair stylist Jodi Mancuso.
d. "My hands are paralyzed!" Kristen Wiig as Sue, losing control of herself in anticipation of a surprise party.

CAST

Fred Armisen
Will Forte
Bill Hader
Darrell Hammond
Seth Meyers
Amy Poehler
Andy Samberg
Jason Sudeikis
Kenan Thompson
Kristen Wiig

Featuring:
Abby Elliott
Bobby Moynihan
Michaela Watkins
Casey Wilson

Weekend Update:
Seth Meyers
Amy Poehler

CREW

Executive Producer: Lorne Michaels

Produced by: Steve Higgins

Director: Don Roy King

Head Writer: Seth Meyers

Producers: Marci Klein, Michael Shoemaker

Writers: Doug Abeles, James Anderson, Alex Baze, Jessica Conrad, James Downey, Steve Higgins, Colin Jost, Erik Kenward, Rob Klein, John Lutz, Seth Meyers, Lorne Michaels, John Mulaney, Paula Pell, Simon Rich, Marika Sawyer, Akiva Schaffer, John Solomon, Emily Spivey, Kent Sublette, Jorma Taccone, Bryan Tucker

Writing Supervisor: Paula Pell

Supervising Producer: Ken Aymong

Film Producer: James Signorelli

Weekend Update Produced by: Doug Abeles

Weekend Update Head Writer: Alex Baze

Production Designers: Eugene Lee, Akira Yoshimura, Keith Ian Raywood

Lighting Consultant: Phil Hymes

Musical Directors: Lenny Pickett, Leon Pendarvis, Katreese Barnes

Sketch Music Adaptation: Hal Willner

Costume Designers: Tom Broecker, Eric Justian

Wardrobe: Dale Richards, Margaret Karolyi, J Douglas James, Tim Alberts, Bruce Brumage

Hair: Jodi Mancuso, Linda Rice, Bettie O. Rogers, Inga Thrasher

Makeup: Louie Zakarian

Photographer: Mary Ellen Matthews

EPISODE LIST

EPISODE KEY:
H - Host
MG - Musical Guest
SG/C - Special Guests/Cameos

EPISODE 01: 9/13/08
H: Michael Phelps
MG: Lil Wayne
SG/C: Tina Fey, Jared Fogel, Debbie Phelps, William Shatner

EPISODE 02: 9/20/08
H: James Franco
MG: Kings of Leon
SG/C: Cameron Diaz, Blake Lively, Kumail Nanjiani

EPISODE 03: 9/27/08
H: Anna Faris
MG: Duffy
SG/C: Tina Fey, Chris Parnell

EPISODE 04: 10/4/08
H: Anne Hathaway
MG: The Killers
SG/C: Tina Fey, Queen Latifah

EPISODE 05: 10/18/08
H: Josh Brolin
MG: Adele
SG/C: Alec Baldwin, Tina Fey, Sarah Palin, Oliver Stone, Mark Wahlberg

EPISODE 06: 10/25/08
H: Jon Hamm
MG: Coldplay
SG/C: Elisabeth Moss, Maya Rudolph, John Slattery

EPISODE 07: 11/1/08
H: Ben Affleck
MG: David Cook
SG/C: Tina Fey, Cindy McCain, Sen. John McCain

EPISODE 08: 11/15/08
H: Paul Rudd
MG: Beyoncé
SG/C: Justin Timberlake

EPISODE 09: 11/22/08
H: Tim McGraw
MG: Ludacris/T-Pain

EPISODE 10: 12/6/08
H: John Malkovich
MG: T.I.
SG/C: Swizz Beats, Jamie-Lynn Sigler, Molly Sims, Justin Timberlake

EPISODE 11: 12/13/08
H: Hugh Laurie
MG: Kanye West
SG/C: Maya Rudolph

EPISODE 12: 1/10/09
H: Neil Patrick Harris
MG: Taylor Swift
SG/C: Liza Minnelli

EPISODE 13: 1/17/09
H: Rosario Dawson
MG: Fleet Foxes

EPISODE 14: 1/31/09
H: Steve Martin
MG: Jason Mraz
SG/C: Colbie Caillat, Michael Daves, Craig Eastman, Britney Haas, Skip Ward

EPISODE 15: 2/7/09
H: Bradley Cooper
MG: TV on the Radio
SG/C: Drew Barrymore, James Lipton, T-Pain

EPISODE 16: 2/14/09
H: Alec Baldwin
MG: Jonas Brothers
SG/C: Dan Aykroyd, Alia Baldwin, Hailey Baldwin Cameron Diaz, Jack McBrayer

EPISODE 17: 3/7/09
H: Dwayne Johnson
MG: Ray LaMontagne
SG/C: Richard Dean Anderson, Jessica Biel, Justin Timberlake

EPISODE 18: 3/14/09
H: Tracy Morgan
MG: Kelly Clarkson
SG/C: John Cena, Tina Fey

EPISODE 19: 4/4/09
H: Seth Rogen
MG: Phoenix

EPISODE 20: 4/11/09
H: Zac Efron
MG: Yeah Yeah Yeahs

EPISODE 21: 5/9/09
H: Justin Timberlake
MG: Ciara
SG/C: Jessica Biel, Patricia Clarkson, Jimmy Fallon, Leonard Nimoy, Chris Pine, Zachary Quinto, Susan Sarandon

EPISODE 22: 5/16/09
H: Will Ferrell
MG: Green Day
SG/C: Tom Hanks, Anne Hathaway, Artie Lange, Norm Macdonald, Elisabeth Moss, Amy Poehler, Paul Rudd, Maya Rudolph

SEASON HIGHLIGHTS

Astronaut Jones (Morgan), The Barry Gibb Talk Show (Fallon/Timberlake), Beyoncé Video Shoot (Moynihan/Rudd/Samberg/Timberlake), Brian Fellow's Safari Planet (Morgan), Bronx Beat (Poehler/Rudolph), Celebrity Jeopardy! (Ferrell/Hammond), Deep House Dish (Samberg/Thompson), Don Draper's Guide to Picking Up Women (Hamm), Gilly (Wiig), Kissing Family (Armisen/Hader/Wiig), La Rivista Della Televisione (Hader), The Lawrence Welk Show (Armisen/Wiig), MacGruber (Forte), Mascots (Timberlake), Stefon (Hader), Sue (Wiig), The Target Lady (Wiig), Two A-Holos (Sudeikis/Wiig), Vincent Price's Holiday Special (Hader)

a. In "J'accuzzi," John Malkovich reprises his "Dangerous Liaisons" role, "Except this time, all the seduction, lust, and deception take place in a hot tub." (With Andy Samberg.) **b.** "Gonna need your vote in the next election! / Can I get a what-what from the senior section?" Amy Poehler does Sarah Palin's rap when the latter (far right) gets cold feet. (With Jason Sudeikis as Todd Palin and Fred Armisen and Andy Samberg as Eskimos.) **c.** To mask where Dooneese's tiny prosthetic hands are attached to her costume, her dress was designed with long sleeves and wrist cuffs, and the dresses for the other singers were designed to match. **d.** Kristen Wiig (as Dooneese) with Anne Hathaway on "The Lawrence Welk Show."

BUMPER KEY (Pg. 470-471)

14 | 03 | 09 | 02 | 04 | 21 | 06
10 | 09 | 10 | 08
19 | 05 | 15
22 | 01 | 12 | 19 | 20 | 13
01 | 02 | 18 | 08
18 | 06 | 16 | 21 | 11 | 17
20 | 13 | 17
04 | 11 | 07 | 03 | 22
14 | 12 | 05 | 15 | 07 | 16

a.

b.

c.

d.

SATURDAY NIGHT LIVE
SATURDAY NIGHT LIVE
SNL
SATURDAY NIGHT LIVE
SATURDAY NIGHT LIVE
SNL
SATURDAY NIGHT LIVE
SNL
SATURDAY NIGHT LIVE
SATURDAY NIGHT LIVE
SNL
SNL
SATURDAY NIGHT LIVE
SATURDAY NIGHT LIVE
SNL
SNL
Saturday Night Live
SNL
SNL
SATURDAY NIGHT LIVE
SATURDAY NIGHT LIVE
SATURDAY NIGHT LIVE
SNL
SNL
SNL

SNL
SNL
SNL
SNL
SNL
SNL
SATURDAY NIGHT LIVE
SNL
SATURDAY NIGHT LIVE
SNL
SNL
SATURDAY NIGHT LIVE
SNL
SNL
SNL
SATURDAY NIGHT LIVE
SATURDAY NIGHT LIVE

SEASON 34 /
2008-09

SEASON 35 /
2009-10

SNL
SNL
SATURDAY NIGHT LIVE
SNL
SNL
SNL
SNL
SATURDAY NIGHT LIVE
SNL
SNL
SNL
SNL
SATURDAY NIGHT LIVE
SATURDAY NIGHT LIVE
SATURDAY NIGHT LIVE
SNL
SNL
SATURDAY NIGHT LIVE

SNL
SNL
SNL
SNL
SNL
SNL
SNL
SATURDAY NIGHT LIVE
SNL
SNL 35
SNL
SATURDAY NIGHT LIVE
SNL
SNL
SNL
SATURDAY NIGHT LIVE
SNL
SATURDAY NIGHT LIVE
SNL

SEASON 35 / 2009-10

CAST

Fred Armisen
Will Forte
Bill Hader
Seth Meyers
Andy Samberg
Jason Sudeikis
Kenan Thompson
Kristen Wiig

Featuring:
Abby Elliott
Bobby Moynihan
Nasim Pedrad
Jenny Slate

Weekend Update:
Seth Meyers

CREW

Executive Producer:
Lorne Michaels

Produced by: Steve Higgins

Director: Don Roy King

Head Writer: Seth Meyers

Producer: Marci Klein

Writers: Doug Abeles, James Anderson, Alex Baze, Jillian Bell, Hannibal Buress, Jessica Conrad, James Downey, Steve Higgins, Colin Jost, Erik Kenward, Jessi Klein, Rob Klein, John Lutz, Seth Meyers, Lorne Michaels, John Mulaney, Christine Nangle, Michael Patrick O'Brien, Paula Pell, Ryan Perez, Simon Rich, Marika Sawyer, Akiva Schaffer, John Solomon, Emily Spivey, Kent Sublette, Jorma Taccone, Bryan Tucker

Writing Supervisors:
Emily Spivey, Colin Jost, John Mulaney, Bryan Tucker

Supervising Producer:
Ken Aymong

Film Producer:
James Signorelli

Weekend Update Produced by:
Doug Abeles

Weekend Update Head Writer:
Alex Baze

Production Designers:
Eugene Lee, Akira Yoshimura, Keith Ian Raywood, N. Joseph DeTullio

Lighting Designer:
Phil Hymes

Musical Directors:
Lenny Pickett, Leon Pendarvis, Katreese Barnes

Sketch Music Adaptation:
Hal Willner

Costume Designers:
Tom Broecker, Eric Justian

Wardrobe: Dale Richards, Margaret Karolyi, J Douglas James, Brian Hemesath, Tim Alberts

Hair: Jodi Mancuso, Bettie O. Rogers, Inga Thrasher

Makeup: Louie Zakarian

Photographer:
Mary Ellen Matthews

EPISODE LIST

EPISODE KEY:
H - Host
MG - Musical Guest
SG/C - Special Guests/Cameos

EPISODE 01: 9/26/09
H: Megan Fox
MG: U2
SG/C: Brian Austin Green

EPISODE 02: 10/3/10
H: Ryan Reynolds
MG: Lady Gaga
SG/C: Darrell Hammond, Scarlett Johansson, Madonna, Elijah Wood

EPISODE 03: 10/10/09
H: Drew Barrymore
MG: Regina Spektor
SG/C: Justin Long

EPISODE 04: 10/17/09
H: Gerard Butler
MG: Shakira
SG/C: James Franco, Dwayne Johnson

EPISODE 05: 11/7/09
H/MG: Taylor Swift
SG/C: Amy Poehler

EPISODE 06: 11/14/09
H: January Jones
MG: Black Eyed Peas
SG/C: Darrell Hammond

EPISODE 07: 11/21/09
H: Joseph Gordon-Levitt
MG: Dave Matthews Band
SG/C: Al Gore, Mindy Kaling

EPISODE 08: 12/5/09
H: Blake Lively
MG: Rihanna
SG/C: Young Jeezy

EPISODE 09: 12/12/09
H: Taylor Lautner
MG: Bon Jovi

EPISODE 10: 12/19/09
H: James Franco
MG: Muse
SG/C: Jack McBrayer, Mike Tyson

EPISODE 11: 1/9/10
H: Charles Barkley
MG: Alicia Keys

EPISODE 12: 1/16/10
H: Sigourney Weaver
MG: The Ting Tings
SG/C: James Cameron, Darrell Hammond

EPISODE 13: 1/30/10
H: Jon Hamm
MG: Michael Bublé
SG/C: Sharon Jones

EPISODE 14: 2/6/10
H: Ashton Kutcher
MG: Them Crooked Vultures

EPISODE 15: 2/27/10
H/MG: Jennifer Lopez

EPISODE 16: 3/6/10
H: Zach Galifianakis
MG: Vampire Weekend
SG/C: Anthony Anderson, Jack McBrayer, Jane Krakowski, Dr. Mehmet Oz, Frank Rich, Paul Rudd, Jeremy Sisto, Brian Williams

EPISODE 17: 3/13/10
H: Jude Law
MG: Pearl Jam
SG/C: Julian Casablancas, Jerry Seinfeld

EPISODE 18: 4/10/10
H: Tina Fey
MG: Justin Bieber
SG/C: Steve Martin, Mark Sanchez

EPISODE 19: 4/17/10
H: Ryan Phillippe
MG: Ke$ha

EPISODE 20: 4/24/10
H: Gabourey Sidibe
MG: MGMT

EPISODE 21: 5/8/10
H: Betty White
MG: Jay-Z
SG/C: Rachel Dratch, Tina Fey, Ana Gasteyer, Mr. Hudson, Bridget Kelly, Amy Poehler, Maya Rudolph, Molly Shannon

EPISODE 22: 5/15/10
H: Alec Baldwin
MG: Tom Petty & The Heartbreakers
SG/C: Steve Martin

SEASON HIGHLIGHTS

Deep House Dish (Samberg/Thompson), Delicious Dish (Gasteyer/Shannon), Garth and Kat (Armisen/Wiig), Gilly (Wiig), Kissing Family (Armisen/Hader/Wiig), La Rivista Della Televisione (Hader), The Lawrence Welk Show (Armisen/Wiig), MacGruber (Forte), The Manuel Ortiz Show (Armisen), Secret Word (Hader/Wiig), Stefon (Hader), Sue (Wiig), The Target Lady (Wiig), Vincent Price's Holiday Special (Hader), What Up with That? (Armisen/Hader/Sudeikis/Thompson)

b.

a. Jason Sudeikis and Will Forte as ladies'-sport commentators Pete Twinkle and Greg Stink. **b.** Bill Hader as Stefon. **c.** Taylor Swift, Bobby Moynihan, and Kenan Thompson in "Scared Straight." **d.** The F-bomb Jenny Slate accidentally dropped on air during "Biker Chick Chat" (seen here with Kristen Wiig) was actually not the first on SNL: Paul Shaffer and Charles Rocket, e.g., made the same mistake.

BUMPER KEY (Pg. 474-475)

04 12 16 22 17 22 06 06
14 07 07
01 01 05
18 14 13
17 18 02 21 08 08
12 20 20 19 21 09 09
16 10 10
02 03 15
03 11 19 13 04 11

a.

c.

d.

476

SEASON 36 / 2010-11

CAST

Fred Armisen
Abby Elliott
Bill Hader
Seth Meyers
Bobby Moynihan
Andy Samberg
Jason Sudeikis
Kenan Thompson
Kristen Wiig

Featuring:
Vanessa Bayer
Paul Brittain
Taran Killam
Nasim Pedrad
Jay Pharoah

Weekend Update:
Seth Meyers

CREW:

Executive Producer: Lorne Michaels

Produced by: Steve Higgins

Director: Don Roy King

Head Writer: Seth Meyers

Writers: Doug Abeles, James Anderson, Alex Baze, Heather Anne Campbell, Jessica Conrad, Matt Craig, James Downey, Tom Flanigan, Shelly Gossman, Steve Higgins, Colin Jost, Erik Kenward, Rob Klein, Jonathan Krisel, Seth Meyers, Lorne Michaels, John Mulaney, Christine Nangle, Michael Patrick O'Brien, Paula Pell, Simon Rich, Marika Sawyer, Akiva Schaffer, Sarah Schneider, John Solomon, Kent Sublette, Bryan Tucker

Writing Supervisors: Colin Jost, John Mulaney, Bryan Tucker

Supervising Producer: Ken Aymong

Film Producer: James Signorelli

Weekend Update Produced by: Doug Abeles

Weekend Update Head Writer: Alex Baze

Production Designers: Eugene Lee, Akira Yoshimura, Keith Ian Raywood, N. Joseph DeTullio

Lighting Designer: Phil Hymes

Musical Directors: Lenny Pickett, Leon Pendarvis, Katreese Barnes

Sketch Music Adaptation: Hal Willner

Costume Designers: Tom Broecker, Eric Justian

Hair: Jodi Mancuso, Bettie O. Rogers, Inga Thrasher

Makeup: Louie Zakarian

Photographer: Mary Ellen Matthews

EPISODE LIST

EPISODE KEY:
H - Host
MG - Musical Guest
SG/C - Special Guests/Cameos

EPISODE 01: 9/25/10
H: Amy Poehler
MG: Katy Perry
SG/C: Rachel Dratch, Jimmy Fallon, Tina Fey, Maya Rudolph, Peter Sarsgaard, Justin Timberlake

EPISODE 02: 10/2/10
H: Bryan Cranston
MG: Kanye West
SG/C: Ernest Borgnine, Morgan Freeman, Helen Mirren, Pusha T

EPISODE 03: 10/9/10
H: Jane Lynch
MG: Bruno Mars

EPISODE 04: 10/23/10
H: Emma Stone
MG: Kings of Leon

EPISODE 05: 10/30/10
H: Jon Hamm
MG: Rihanna

EPISODE 06: 11/13/10
H: Scarlett Johansson
MG: Arcade Fire

EPISODE 07: 11/20/10
H: Anne Hathaway
MG: Florence + the Machine

EPISODE 08: 12/4/10
H: Robert De Niro
MG: Diddy-Dirty Money
SG/C: Swizz Beatz, Ben Stiller, Robin Williams

EPISODE 09: 12/11/10
H: Paul Rudd
MG: Paul McCartney
SG/C: Mario Batali

EPISODE 10: 12/18/10
H: Jeff Bridges
MG: Eminem, Lil Wayne
SG/C: Akon, Jessica Alba, Blake Lively, John McEnroe, Jim Henson's Muppets

EPISODE 11: 1/8/11
H: Jim Carrey
MG: The Black Keys

EPISODE 12: 1/15/11
H: Gwyneth Paltrow
MG: Cee Lo Green
SG/C: Anderson Cooper, Pee-wee Herman

EPISODE 13: 1/29/11
H: Jesse Eisenberg
MG: Nicki Minaj
SG/C: Mark Zuckerberg, John Waters

EPISODE 14: 2/5/11
H: Dana Carvey
MG: Linkin Park
SG/C: Justin Bieber, Dex Carvey, Tom Carvey, Jesse Eisenberg, Jon Lovitz, Mike Myers

EPISODE 15: 2/12/11
H: Russell Brand
MG: Chris Brown

EPISODE 16: 3/5/11
H: Miley Cyrus
MG: The Strokes

EPISODE 17: 3/12/11
H: Zach Galifianakis
MG: Jessie J feat. B.o.B.

EPISODE 18: 4/2/11
H/MG: Elton John
SG/C: Carmelo Anthony, Will Forte, Jake Gyllenhaal, Tom Hanks, Leon Russell

EPISODE 19: 4/9/11
H: Helen Mirren
MG: Foo Fighters

EPISODE 20: 5/7/11
H: Tina Fey
MG: Ellie Goulding
SG/C: Michael Bolton, Darrell Hammond, Maya Rudolph, Robin Wright

EPISODE 21: 5/14/11
H: Ed Helms
MG: Paul Simon
SG/C: Steve Carell, Stephen Colbert, Chris Colfer, Jimmy Fallon, Jon Hamm

EPISODE 22: 5/21/11
H: Justin Timberlake
MG: Lady Gaga
SG/C: Patricia Clarkson, Bradley Cooper, Lindsey Buckingham, Jimmy Fallon, Jon Hamm, Susan Sarandon

SEASON HIGHLIGHTS

A Message from the TSA (Hader/Moynihan/Thompson), The Ambiguously Gay Duo (Smigel), Anthony Crispino (Moynihan), The Barry Gibb Talk Show (Fallon/Timberlake), Bronx Beat (Poehler/Rudolph), Church Chat (Carvey), Dictator's Two Best Friends from Growing Up (Armisen/Bayer), Don' You Go Rounin' Roun To Re Ro (British Movie) (Brand/Hader), Jacob the Bar Mitzvah Boy (Bayer), Kissing Family (Armisen/Hader/Rudd/Wiig), The Lawrence Welk Show (Wiig), Les Jeunes de Paris (Killam), The Manuel Ortiz Show (Armisen), Mascots (Timberlake), The Miley Cyrus Show (Bayer), Mom on Facebook (Samberg/Lynch), Principal Daniel Frye (Pharoah), Sarah Palin (Fey), Secret Word (Hader/Wiig), Stefon (Hader), Vincent Price's Holiday Special (Hader), Wayne's World (Carvey/Myers), What Up with That? (Armisen/Hader/Sudeikis/Thompson)

BUMPER KEY (Pg. 478-479)

17 06 10 15 20 03 19
11 02 08 13
14 21 09 01 22
05 06 08 13
12 07 12 04
05 03 10 01 20
07 14 17 21
18 22 16 16 19
15 09 02 04 11

a.

b.

a. Host Paul Rudd locks lips with Bill Hader in "Kissing Family." **b.** Fred Armisen as Queen Elizabeth II, with Bill Hader (as Prince Philip) and Anne Hathaway (as Kate Middleton). **c.** Bill Hader as curmudgeonly TV reporter Herb Welch. **d.** "Happy Thanksgiving! I'm not thankful four anything—I'm thankful five, so, more than you!" Kristen Wiig as Penelope (with Kenan Thompson). **e.** "Attention teachers and stoo-dins..." Jay Pharoah as Principal Frye in "Holiday Jam." (With Paul Rudd.)

c.

d.

e.

SATURDAY NIGHT LIVE
SNL
SATURDAY NIGHT LIVE
SNL
SATURDAY NIGHT LIVE
SATURDAY NIGHT LIVE
SNL
SATURDAY NIGHT LIVE
SATURDAY NIGHT LIVE
SNL
SNL
SNL
SNL
SNL
SNL
SATURDAY NIGHT LIVE

SNL
SATURDAY NIGHT LIVE
SNL
SNL
SNL
SNL
SNL
SNL
SNL
SNL
SNL
SNL
SNL
SATURDAY NIGHT LIVE
SNL
SNL
SNL
SATURDAY NIGHT LIVE
SNL
SNL
SATURDAY NIGHT LIVE
SATURDAY NIGHT LIVE

SEASON 36 / 2010-11

SATURDAY
NIGHT
LIVE

SEASON 37 / 2011-12

SATURDAY NIGHT LIVE
SATURDAY NIGHT LIVE
SNL
SNL
SATURDAY NIGHT LIVE
SATURDAY NIGHT LIVE
SATURDAY NIGHT LIVE
SNL
SNL
SNL
SNL
SNL
SNL
SNL
SNL
SNL
SATURDAY NIGHT LIVE
SNL
SNL
SNL
Saturday Night Live

SNL
SNL
SNL
SNL
SATURDAY NIGHT LIVE
SNL
SNL
SNL
SNL
SNL
SATURDAY NIGHT LIVE
SNL
SNL
NEW YORK POST
BROLIN HOSTS SNL
SNL
SNL
SNL
SATURDAY NIGHT LIVE
SNL
SNL
SNL
SATURDAY NIGHT LIVE
SNL

SEASON 37 / 2011-12

CAST

Fred Armisen
Abby Elliott
Bill Hader
Seth Meyers
Bobby Moynihan
Nasim Pedrad
Andy Samberg
Jason Sudeikis
Kenan Thompson
Kristen Wiig

Featuring:
Vanessa Bayer
Paul Brittain
Taran Killam
Kate McKinnon
Jay Pharoah

Weekend Update:
Seth Meyers

CREW

Executive Producer: Lorne Michaels

Produced by: Steve Higgins

Director: Don Roy King

Head Writer: Seth Meyers

Producers: Erik Kenward, John Mulaney

Writers: James Anderson, Alex Baze, Jessica Conrad, James Downey, Shelly Gossman, Steve Higgins, Colin Jost, Zach Kanin, Chris Kelly, Erik Kenward, Rob Klein, Seth Meyers, Lorne Michaels, John Mulaney, Christine Nangle, Michael Patrick O'Brien, Paula Pell, Marika Sawyer, Sarah Schneider, Pete Schultz, John Solomon, Kent Sublette, Bryan Tucker

Writing Supervisors: Bryan Tucker, Colin Jost

Supervising Producer: Ken Aymong

Film Producer: Rhys Thomas

Weekend Update Produced and Written by: Alex Baze

Production Designers: Eugene Lee, Akira Yoshimura, Keith Ian Raywood, N. Joseph DeTullio

Lighting Designer: Phil Hymes

Musical Directors: Lenny Pickett, Leon Pendarvis, Eli Brueggemann

Sketch Music Adaptation: Hal Willner

Costume Designers: Tom Broecker, Eric Justian

Wardrobe: Dale Richards, Margaret Karolyi, J Douglas James, Tim Alberts

Hair: Jodi Mancuso, Bettie O. Rogers, Inga Thrasher

Makeup: Louie Zakarian

Photographer: Mary Ellen Matthews

EPISODE LIST

EPISODE KEY:
H - Host
MG - Musical Guest
SG/C - Special Guests/Cameos

EPISODE 01: 9/24/11
H: Alec Baldwin
MG: Radiohead
SG/C: Steve Martin, Seth Rogen

EPISODE 02: 10/1/11
H: Melissa McCarthy
MG: Lady Antebellum

EPISODE 03: 10/8/11
H: Ben Stiller
MG: Foster the People
SG/C: Hugh Jackman, Kenny G

EPISODE 04: 10/15/11
H: Anna Faris
MG: Drake
SG/C: Nicki Minaj

EPISODE 05: 11/05/11
H: Charlie Day
MG: Maroon 5
SG/C: Danny DeVito, Travie McCoy

EPISODE 06: 11/12/11
H: Emma Stone
MG: Coldplay
SG/C: Andrew Garfield

EPISODE 07: 11/19/11
H: Jason Segel
MG: Florence + the Machine
SG/C: Jim Henson's Muppets, Paul Rudd, Olivia Wilde

EPISODE 08: 12/3/11
H: Steve Buscemi
MG: The Black Keys
SG/C: Maya Rudolph

EPISODE 09: 12/10/11
H: Katy Perry
MG: Robyn
SG/C: Alec Baldwin, Matt Damon, Darrell Hammond, Val Kilmer

EPISODE 10: 12/17/11
H: Jimmy Fallon
MG: Michael Bublé
SG/C: Rachel Dratch, Tina Fey, Chris Kattan, Jude Law, Tracy Morgan, Amy Poehler, Horatio Sanz

EPISODE 11: 1/7/12
H: Charles Barkley
MG: Kelly Clarkson

EPISODE 12: 1/14/12
H: Daniel Radcliffe
MG: Lana Del Rey

EPISODE 13: 2/4/12
H: Channing Tatum
MG: Bon Iver

EPISODE 14: 2/11/12
H: Zooey Deschanel
MG: Karmin
SG/C: Nicolas Cage, Jean Dujardin

EPISODE 15: 2/18/12
H: Maya Rudolph
MG: Sleigh Bells
SG/C: Bill O'Reilly, Amy Poehler, Paul Simon, Justin Timberlake, Kate Upton

EPISODE 16: 3/3/12
H: Lindsay Lohan
MG: Jack White
SG/C: Ruby Amanfu, Jimmy Fallon, Jon Hamm

EPISODE 17: 3/10/12
H: Jonah Hill
MG: The Shins
SG/C: Tom Hanks, John McEnroe

EPISODE 18: 4/7/12
H: Sofia Vergara
MG: One Direction
SG/C: Manolo Gonzalez

EPISODE 19: 4/14/12
H: Josh Brolin
MG: Gotye
SG/C: Kimbra, Steven Spielberg

EPISODE 20: 5/5/12
H: Eli Manning
MG: Rihanna
SG/C: David Baas, Sacha Baron Cohen, David Diehl, Abby McGrew, Shaun O'Hara, Martin Scorsese, Chris Snee

EPISODE 21: 5/12/12
H: Will Ferrell
MG: Usher
SG/C: Kay Ferrell, Will Forte, Ana Gasteyer, Liam Neeson, Justin Bieber, Michael Bolton, Julian Casablancas, Jon Hamm, Natalie Portman, Justin Timberlake

EPISODE 22: 5/19/12
H: Mick Jagger
MG: Mick Jagger feat. Arcade Fire, Foo Fighters, Jeff Beck
SG/C: Rachel Dratch, Will Forte, Nikolai Fraiture, Jon Hamm, Chris Kattan, Steve Martin, Chris Parnell, Amy Poehler

SEASON HIGHLIGHTS

Bronx Beat (Poehler/Rudolph), The Californians (Armisen/Bayer/Hader/Thompson/Wiig), The Culps (Ferrell/Gasteyer), Drunk Uncle (Moynihan), Gilly (Wiig), J-Pop America Fun Time Now (Bayer/Killam), Janet Peckinpaugh (Moynihan), Kissing Family (Armisen/Hader/Wiig), The Lawrence Welk Show (Armisen/Wiig), Lil' Poundcake (Bayer), The Manuel Ortiz Show (Armisen), The Real Housewives of Disney (Lohan/Elliott), Red Flag Parfum (Wiig), Secret Word (Hader/Wiig), Stefon (Hader), Sue (Wiig), The Target Lady (Wiig), What Up with That? (Armisen/Hader/Sudeikis/Thompson)

BUMPER KEY (Pg. 484-485)

01 01 02 16 07 10 13 14
21 22 15 15
02 14 20 03 08
18 12 13
05 11 06 08
05 03 10 19 04 19
16 17 06 17 07
09 09 12
21 22 20 11 18 04

a.

b.

c.

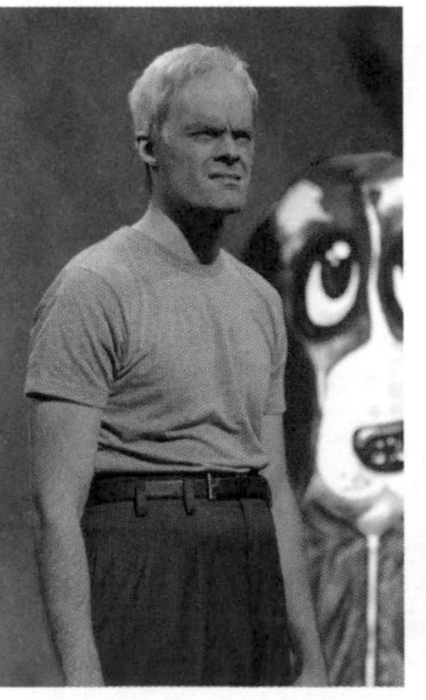

d.

a. Jason Segel's jealous "Muppet Movie" co-stars crash his monologue. **b.** Josh Brolin and cast in "The Californians." **c.** Bill Hader as Clint Eastwood in "Doggie Duty." **d.** As Tom Brady, Channing Tatum falls for Janet Peckinpaugh (Bobby Moynihan).

SEASON 38 / 2012-13

CAST

Fred Armisen
Vanessa Bayer
Bill Hader
Taran Killam
Seth Meyers
Bobby Moynihan
Nasim Pedrad
Jay Pharoah
Jason Sudeikis
Kenan Thompson

Featuring:
Aidy Bryant
Kate McKinnon
Tim Robinson
Cecily Strong

Weekend Update:
Seth Meyers

CREW

Executive Producer:
Lorne Michaels

Produced by: Steve Higgins, Erik Kenward

Director: Don Roy King

Head Writers: Seth Meyers, Colin Jost

Producers: Lindsay Shookus, Erin Doyle

Writers: James Anderson, Alex Baze, Neil Casey, Michael Che, James Downey, Steve Higgins, Colin Jost, Zach Kanin, Chris Kelly, Joe Kelly, Erik Kenward, Rob Klein, Seth Meyers, Lorne Michaels, John Mulaney, Mike O'Brien, Josh Patten, Paula Pell, Marika Sawyer, Sarah Schneider, Pete Schultz, John Solomon, Kent Sublette, Bryan Tucker

Writing Supervisors:
Bryan Tucker, Marika Sawyer

Supervising Producer:
Ken Aymong

Film Producer: Rhys Thomas

Weekend Update Written and Produced by: Alex Baze

Production Designers:
Eugene Lee, Akira Yoshimura, Keith Ian Raywood, N. Joseph DeTullio

Lighting Designer:
Phil Hymes

Musical Directors:
Lenny Pickett, Leon Pendarvis, Eli Brueggemann

Sketch Music Adaptation:
Hal Willner

Costume Designers:
Tom Broecker, Eric Justian

Wardrobe: Dale Richards, Margaret Karolyi, J. Douglas James, Tim Alberts

Hair: Jodi Mancuso, Bettie O. Rogers, Inga Thrasher

Makeup: Louie Zakarian

Photographer:
Mary Ellen Matthews

EPISODE LIST

EPISODE KEY:
H - Host
MG - Musical Guest
SG/C - Special Guests/Cameos

EPISODE 01: 9/15/12
H: Seth MacFarlane
MG: Frank Ocean
SG/C: John Mayer, Psy

EPISODE 02: 9/22/12
H: Joseph Gordon-Levitt
MG: Mumford & Sons

EPISODE 03: 10/6/12
H: Daniel Craig
MG: Muse
SG/C: Jim Henson's Muppets, Chris Parnell

EPISODE 04: 10/13/12
H: Christina Applegate
MG: Passion Pit
SG/C: Usain Bolt

EPISODE 05: 10/20/12
H/MG: Bruno Mars
SG/C: Tom Hanks

EPISODE 06: 11/3/12
H: Louis C.K.
MG: FUN.

EPISODE 07: 11/10/12
H: Anne Hathaway
MG: Rihanna

EPISODE 08: 11/17/12
H: Jeremy Renner
MG: Maroon 5
SG/C: Chris Christie

EPISODE 09: 12/8/12
H: Jamie Foxx
MG: Ne-Yo
SG/C: 2 Chainz, Charlie Day, Dermot Mulroney

EPISODE 10: 12/15/12
H: Martin Short
MG: Paul McCartney
SG/C: Alec Baldwin, Carrie Brownstein, The New York City Children's Chorus, Jimmy Fallon, Tina Fey, Dave Grohl, Tom Hanks, Samuel L. Jackson, Krist Novoselic, Paul Shaffer, Pat Smear, Kristen Wiig, Joe Walsh

EPISODE 11: 1/19/13
H: Jennifer Lawrence
MG: The Lumineers

EPISODE 12: 1/26/13
H: Adam Levine
MG: Kendrick Lamar
SG/C: Cameron Diaz, Mickey Madden, Danny McBride, Andy Samberg, Jerry Seinfeld

EPISODE 13: 2/9/13
H/MG: Justin Bieber
SG/C: Whoopi Goldberg

EPISODE 14: 2/16/13
H: Christoph Waltz
MG: Alabama Shakes

EPISODE 15: 3/2/13
H: Kevin Hart
MG: Macklemore & Ryan Lewis
SG/C: Ray Dalton, Wanz

EPISODE 16: 3/9/13
H/MG: Justin Timberlake
SG/C: Dan Aykroyd, Alec Baldwin, Candice Bergen, Chevy Chase, Tom Hanks, Jay-Z, Steve Martin, Andy Samberg, Martin Short, Paul Simon

EPISODE 17: 4/6/13
H: Melissa McCarthy
MG: Phoenix
SG/C: Peter Dinklage, Dennis Rodman

EPISODE 18: 4/13/13
H: Vince Vaughn
MG: Miguel
SG/C: Steve Jones

EPISODE 19: 5/4/13
H: Zach Galifianakis
MG: Of Monsters and Men
SG/C: Bradley Cooper, Nikolaj Coster-Waldau, Jon Hamm, Ed Helms

EPISODE 20: 5/11/13
H: Kristen Wiig
MG: Vampire Weekend
SG/C: Jonah Hill, Maya Rudolph

EPISODE 21: 5/18/13
H: Ben Affleck
MG: Kanye West
SG/C: Carrie Brownstein, Anderson Cooper, Jennifer Garner, Kim Gordon, Steve Jones, Aimee Mann, J. Mascis, Michael Penn, Amy Poehler

SEASON HIGHLIGHTS

The Californians (Armisen/Bayer/Hader, et al.), Djesus Uncrossed (Waltz), Drunk Uncle (Moynihan), The Ex Porn Stars (Bayer/Strong), Five Timer's Club (Timberlake et al.), History of Punk (Armisen), It's a Date—Festrunk Brothers (Aykroyd/Chase/Samberg/Timberlake), J-Pop America Fun Time Now (Bayer/Killam) Last Call (McKinnon/Thompson), The Lawrence Welk Show (Armisen/Wiig), Lincoln (Louis C.K.), Loving Couple (Armisen), Maine Justice (Sudeikis/Foxx, et al.), The Miley Cyrus Show (Bayer), Puppetry Class (Bayer/Hader/MacFarlane), Rosetta Stone (Hader/Killam/Moynihan), Sopranos High (Armisen/Moynihan), Stefon (Hader), Stefon's Wedding (Hader), The Target Lady (Wiig), Tres Equis (Gordon-Levitt), Verismo (Bayer), What Up with That? (Armisen/Hader/Sudeikis/Thompson), Xanax for Gay Summer Weddings (Killam/Sudeikis)

BUMPER KEY (Pg. 488-489)

12 18 17 04 03 11 09 12
21 14 18 07 04
13 01 11 10 03
14
02 08
02 8 06 15 15 01 20 05
10 21 09 17
16
06 07 19 20 19

a.

b.

c.

d.

a. Paul McCartney and the New York City Children's Chorus perform "Wonderful Christmas Time." **b.** Louis C.K. and Kate McKinnon as Dan Pants and Sheila Sovage in "Last Call." **c.** "Five-Timers' Club" members Dan Aykroyd, Candice Bergen, Tom Hanks, Alec Baldwin, Steve Martin, Chevy Chase, and Martin Short welcome Justin Timberlake. **d.** "I lost part of my foot. It broke off in a butt. And I've regretted it ever since. But I don't regret wearing…crystals." Vanessa Bayer and Cecily Strong in "Swarovski Crystals."

SNL
SNL
SNL
SATURDAY NIGHT LIVE
SNL
SNL
SNL
SNL
SNL
SATURDAY NIGHT LIVE
SNL
SNL
SNL
VOTE FOR FUN
VOTE FOR FUN.
VOTE FOR FUN.
polaroid
SNL
SATURDAY NIGHT LIVE
SNL
SNL

SATURDAY NIGHT LIVE
SNL
SNL
SNL
SNL
SNL
SNL
SNL
SNL
SNL
SNL
SNL
SNL
SNL
SNL
SATURDAY NIGHT LIVE
SNL
SNL
SATURDAY NIGHT LIVE

SEASON 38 / 2012-13

SEASON 39 /
2013-14

IGHT LIVE

SNL
SNL
SNL
SNL
SNL
SNL
SNL
SNL
SNL
SATURDAY NIGHT LIVE
SNL
SNL
SATURDAY NIGHT LIVE
SNL
SNL
SNL
SNL

SNL
SNL
SATURDAY NIGHT LIVE
SNL
SNL
SNL
SNL
SNL
SNL
SATURDAY NIGHT LIVE
SNL
SNL
SATURDAY NIGHT LIVE
SNL
SNL
SATURDAY NIGHT LIVE
SNL
SNL
SNL

SEASON 39 / 2013-14

CAST

Vanessa Bayer
Aidy Bryant
Taran Killam
Kate McKinnon
Seth Meyers
Bobby Moynihan
Nasim Pedrad
Jay Pharoah
Cecily Strong
Kenan Thompson

Featuring:
Beck Bennett
Colin Jost
John Milhiser
Kyle Mooney
Mike O'Brien
Noël Wells
Brooks Wheelan
Sasheer Zamata

Weekend Update:
Seth Meyers
Cecily Strong
Colin Jost

CREW

Executive Producer:
Lorne Michaels

Produced by: Steve Higgins, Erik Kenward

Director: Don Roy King

Head Writers:
Seth Meyers, Colin Jost, Rob Klein, Bryan Tucker

Producers: Lindsay Shookus, Erin Doyle

Writers: James Anderson, Alex Baze, Michael Che, Mikey Day, Steve Higgins, Leslie Jones, Colin Jost, Zach Kanin, Chris Kelly, Erik Kenward, Lorne Michaels, Claire Mulaney, Josh Patten, Paula Pell, Katie Rich, Tim Robinson, Marika Sawyer, Sarah Schneider, Pete Schultz, John Solomon, Kent Sublette, LaKendra Tookes, Bryan Tucker

Writing Supervisors:
Bryan Tucker, Marika Sawyer, John Solomon

Supervising Producer:
Ken Aymong

Film Producer:
Rhys Thomas

Weekend Update Written and Produced by: Alex Baze, Pete Schultz

Production Designers:
Eugene Lee, Akira Yoshimura, Keith Ian Raywood, N. Joseph DeTullio

Lighting Designer:
Phil Hymes

Musical Directors:
Lenny Pickett, Leon Pendarvis, Eli Brueggemann

Sketch Music Adaptation:
Hal Willner

Costume Designers:
Tom Broecker, Eric Justian

Wardrobe: Dale Richards, J. Douglas James, Tim Alberts

Hair: Bettie O. Rogers, Jodi Mancuso, Inga Thrasher

Makeup: Louie Zakarian

Photographer:
Mary Ellen Matthews

EPISODE LIST

EPISODE KEY:
H - Host
MG - Musical Guest
SG/C - Special Guests/Cameos

EPISODE 01: 9/28/13
H: Tina Fey
MG: Arcade Fire
SG/C: Aaron Paul

EPISODE 02: 10/5/13
H/MG: Miley Cyrus

EPISODE 03: 10/12/13
H: Bruce Willis
MG: Katy Perry
SG/C: Aaron Paul

EPISODE 04: 10/26/13
H: Edward Norton
MG: Janelle Monáe
SG/C: Alec Baldwin, Miley Cyrus

EPISODE 05: 11/2/13
H: Kerry Washington
MG: Eminem
SG/C: Skylar Grey, Rick Rubin, Al Sharpton

EPISODE 06: 11/16/13
H/MG: Lady Gaga
SG/C: R. Kelly

EPISODE 07: 11/23/13
H: Josh Hutcherson
MG: HAIM

EPISODE 08: 12/7/13
H: Paul Rudd
MG: One Direction
SG/C: Fred Armisen, Steve Carell, Will Ferrell, David Koechner, Kristen Wiig

EPISODE 09: 12/14/13
H: John Goodman
MG: Kings of Leon
SG/C: Robert De Niro, Sylvester Stallone, Wale

EPISODE 10: 12/21/13
H: Jimmy Fallon
MG: Justin Timberlake
SG/C: Michael Bloomberg, Barry Gibb, Madonna, Paul McCartney, Chris Rock

EPISODE 11: 1/18/14
H/MG: Drake
SG/C: Jhené Aiko

EPISODE 12: 1/25/14
H: Jonah Hill
MG: Bastille
SG/C: Michael Cera, Leonardo DiCaprio

EPISODE 13: 2/1/14
H: Melissa McCarthy
MG: Imagine Dragons
SG/C: Fred Armisen, Bill Hader, Kendrick Lamar, Amy Poehler, Andy Samberg

EPISODE 14: 3/1/14
H: Jim Parsons
MG: Beck

EPISODE 15: 3/8/14
H: Lena Dunham
MG: The National
SG/C: Fred Armisen, Jon Hamm, Liam Neeson

EPISODE 16: 3/29/14
H: Louis C.K.
MG: Sam Smith

EPISODE 17: 4/5/14
H: Anna Kendrick
MG: Pharrell
SG/C: Hans Zimmer, Icona Pop

EPISODE 18: 4/12/14
H: Seth Rogen
MG: Ed Sheeran
SG/C: Zooey Deschanel, James Franco, Taylor Swift

EPISODE 19: 5/3/14
H: Andrew Garfield
MG: Coldplay
SG/C: Mary Lynn Rajskub, Emma Stone, Kiefer Sutherland

EPISODE 20: 5/10/14
H: Charlize Theron
MG: The Black Keys
SG/C: Barbara Walters

EPISODE 21: 5/17/14
H: Andy Samberg
MG: St. Vincent
SG/C: 2 Chainz, Fred Armisen, Bill Hader, Seth Meyers, Paul Rudd, Maya Rudolph, Martin Short, Jorma Taccone, Kristen Wiig, Pharrell Williams

SEASON HIGHLIGHTS

24 Hour Energy Drink (Thompson/Bayer), 80s song (Bayer/Hutcherson), The Barry Gibb Talk Show (Fallon/Timberlake), The Beygency (Killam), Bill Brasky (Ferrell/Koechner/Rudd), Boy Dance Party (Willis/Killam), (Do It On My) Twin Bed (McKinnon/Bryant), Drunk Uncle (Moynihan), Dyke & Fats (McKinnon/Bryant), E-Meth (Killam/Wheelan/McKinnon), The Ex Porn Stars (Bayer/Strong), Kissing Family (Armisen/Hader/Samberg/Wiig), Girls Promo (Fey/Strong), Jebediah Atkinson (Killam), Jos A Bank Cleaning (Bayer), Mascots (Timberlake), Me (Hill/Cera), The Midnight Coterie of Sinister Intruders (Norton), Mornin' Miami! (Bayer/McKinnon/Moynihan), Mr. Patterson (Bennett), Waking Up with Kimye (Pedrad/Pharoah), We Did Stop (The Government) (Killam/Cyrus)

BUMPER KEY (Pg. 494-495)

12 05 03 07 04 16 11 03
07 04 19 15
16 09 21 20
01
06 09 18 21
01 13 15 02 10
08 13 05
17 14 14
12 18 19 17 20

a.

b.

a. Miley Cyrus, Bobby Moynihan, and Kate McKinnon in "Mornin' Miami."
b. Lady Gaga as an Apple Store employee on "Waking Up with Kimye," with Nasim Pedrad as Kim Kardashian and Jay Pharoah as Kanye West.

c.

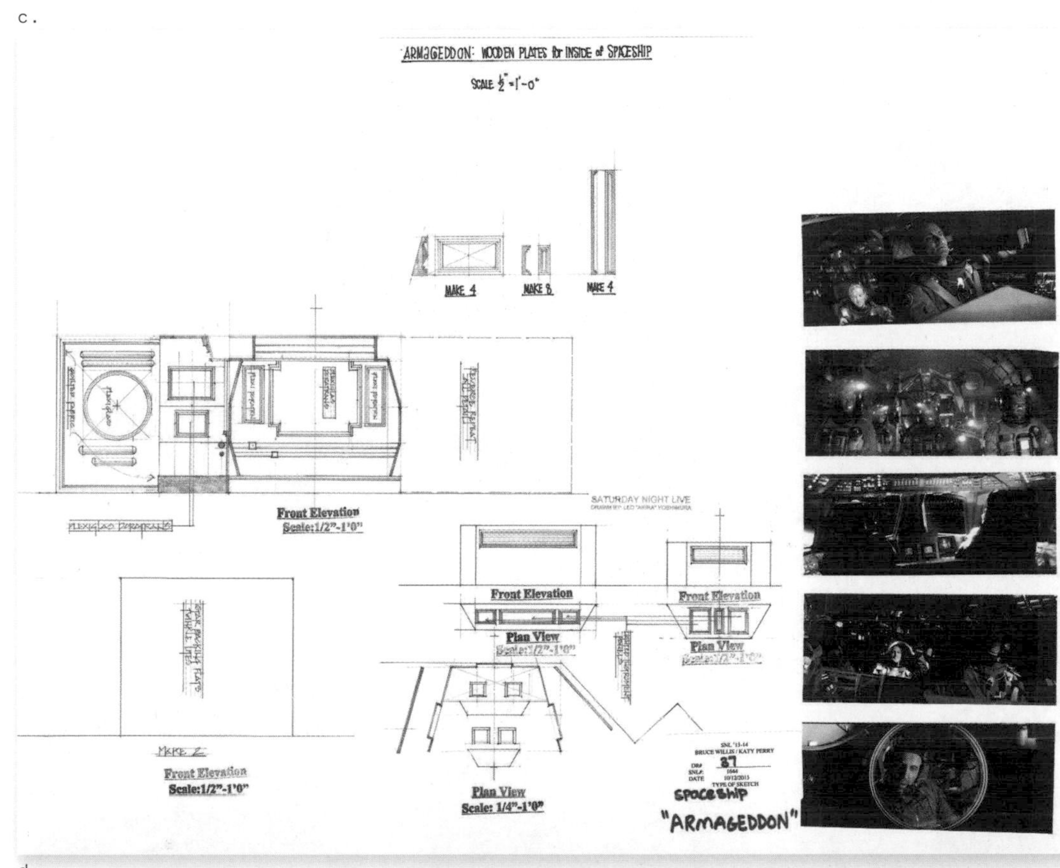

d.

e.

f.

g.

c. Plans and reference photos for "Armageddon." **d.** Bobby Moynihan as a kitty-cat-obsessed astronaut (right), with Taran Killam, Beck Bennett, Kenan Thompson, and host Bruce Willis, in "Armageddon." **e.** "Little Buff Boys," a sketch about a child bodybuilding competition, was cut after dress rehearsal. (With host Lena Dunham, second from left.) **f.** Producer Lindsay Shookus (right) supervises Charlize Theron's promo shoot in the control room. **g.** Bandleader Lenny Pickett.

The Manuel Ortiz Show
THE HOW DO YOU SAY? AH YES, SHOW WITH ANTONIO BANDERAS
$ You Can't Win! $
SPROCKETS
WAKE UP WAKEFIELD!
Mr. Short-Term Memory
WAYNE'S WORLD
THE Pat Stevens SHOW
Fiesta Politica
Church Chat
THE Franken & Davis SHOW
PUMPING UP WITH HANS & FRANZ
THE CALIFORNIANS
THE BARRY GIBB TALK SHOW
SAMURAI BAKERY
THE LADIES' MAN
Daily Affirmation with STUART SMALLEY
ASTRONAUT JONES
The Tony Bennett show
GREAT MOMENTS IN HERSTORY
MACGRUBER
The Night Hanukkah Harry Saved Christmas
GIRLFRIENDS TALK SHOW
THE DATING ZONE
Goth Talk
DEBBIE DOWNER
Fernando's HIDEAWAY
SECRET WORD
BABA WAWA AT LARGE
THE ROCK OBAMA
The Ferey Mühtar Talk Show
THE CONEHEADS
THEODORIC of YORK MEDIEVAL JUDGE
AN SNL DIGITAL SHORT
Prince Show
THE JOE PESCI SHOW
La Rivista Della Televisione con VINNY VEDECCI
FRED GARVIN: MALE PROSTITUTE
what up with that
DEEP HOUSE DISH
TALK OR DIE
gilly!
Spy Glass
Bronx Beat with Betty & Jodi
Master Thespian
Brian Fellow's SAFARI PLANET
LOTHAR OF THE HILL PEOPLE
Low Class Italian Theater
The Killer Bees
BLACK PERSPECTIVE
FALCONER
MERV THE PERV
Bee Centennial Minute
APPALACHIAN EMERGENCY ROOM
Derek Jeter's Taco Hole
the COUGAR den
TOP O' THE MORNING
BAD NEWS Bees
CAROL!
MISTER ROBINSON'S NEIGHBORHOOD

Acknowledgements

A vital element of my research for this book consisted of spending time backstage during the 39th season of "Saturday Night Live." I would like to thank the entire cast and crew for their hospitality, and in particular the following individuals who allowed me to watch them work, took time to explain and answer questions, and enabled me to gain an insider's perspective on the making of the show:

Ken Aymong
Laurie Berdan
Tom Broecker
Mikey Day
N. Joseph DeTullio
Erin Doyle
Dana Edelson
Steve Higgins
Emily Hoffman
Eric Justian
Chris Kelly
Erik Kenward
Don Roy King
Rob Klein
Eugene Lee
Jodi Mancuso
Mary Ellen Matthews
Seth Meyers
Lorne Michaels
Adam Nicely
Nasim Pedrad
Keith Ian Raywood
Dale Richards
Bettie O. Rogers
Gena Rositano
Lindsay Shookus
Inga Thrasher
Akira Yoshimura
Louie Zakarian

A very special thanks to Nina Wiener and Lawrence Schiller, who were instrumental in making this book happen, and to my publisher, Benedikt Taschen, for believing in me time and time again.

I am also indebted to the following people for their assistance, advice, patience, dedication, and/or encouragement during the making of this book:

Andrea Angiolillio
Fred Armisen
Edie Baskin
Vee Benard
Ryan Bocskay
Candace Bothwell
Austin Breslow
Bella Bronson
Megan Callahan
Mattison Carter
Jonathan Correira
Tara Donnelly
James Downey
Suzy M. Drasnin
Dick Ebersol
Lucas Engel
Jimmy Fallon
Tatiana Farfan-Narcisse
Samantha Garrett
Howard Groudan
Bill Hader
Jessica Hoffmann
Marc Jacoby
Mark Lach
Erica Lancaster
Nasya Lee
Blossom Lefcourt
Michael Lesko
Learah Lockhart
Gillian Lusins
Rachele Lynn
Caroline Maroney
Cristina McGinniss
Justus McLarty
Kate Miller
Mark Mullen
Najen Naylor
Laraine Newman
Robert Noble
Amber Noland
Emily Oberman
Kelly Powers
Blake Rosenberg
Tonia Sawyer
Herb Schlosser
Jacob Septimus
Mike Shoemaker
Robert Smigel
Kevin Spencer
Alex Stikeleather
Juliana Stone
Jason Sudeikis
Jack Sullivan
Britta von Schoeler
Chris Voss
Anna Weinstein
Kristen Wiig
Matt Yonks
Doug Zeider
Lucas Zelnick

—Alison Castle,
New York, 2014

Comments or questions? Please feel free to contact me via Twitter (@alisoncastle) or email (a.castle@taschen.com).

Credits

PRINCIPAL PHOTOGRAPHY BY:
Edie Baskin
Mary Ellen Matthews

BUMPER PHOTOGRAPHY BY:
Edie Baskin
Karen Kuehn
Mary Ellen Matthews
Mark Mullen
Frank Ockenfels III
Patti Perret
Isaiah Wyner

EPISODIC AND BACKSTAGE PHOTOGRAPHY BY:
Edie Baskin
Suzy M. Drasnin
Dana Edelson
Karen Kuehn
Mary Ellen Matthews
Mark Mullen
Norman Ng
Patti Perret
Isaiah Wyner

ADDITIONAL PHOTOGRAPHS BY:
AP Photo/Reed Saxon
Herb Ball
Fred Bronson
Alison Castle
F.T. Fyre
Sharon Haskell
Fred Hermansky
Al Levine
R.M. Lewis Jr.
Cristina McGinniss
Jean Pigozzi
Alan Singer
Brooks Wheelan

ORIGINAL DRAWINGS PROVIDED BY:
Tom Broecker
N. Joseph DeTullio
Eugene Lee
Keith Ian Raywood
Karen Roston
J.J. Sedelmaier Productions, Inc.
Akira Yoshimura

RECOMMENDED READING:

Beatts, Anne and John Head, eds.; "Saturday Night Live." New York: Avon Books, 1977.

Cader, Michael, ed.; "Saturday Night Live: The First Twenty Years." New York: Houghton Mifflin, 1994.

Hill, Doug and Jeff Weingrad; "Saturday Night: A Backstage History of Saturday Night Live." New York: Beech Tree Books, 1986.

Marx, Nick, Matt Sienkiewicz, and Ron Becker, eds.; "Saturday Night Live & American TV." Bloomington: Indiana University Press, 2013.

Shales, Tom, and James Andrew Miller; "Live from New York: An Uncensored History of Saturday Night Live, as Told by Its Stars, Writers, and Guests." New York: Little, Brown and Company, 2002.

Tropiano, Stephen; "Saturday Night Live FAQ." Milwaukee: Applause Theatre & Cinema Books, 2013.

CITATIONS:

16: "[T]hat the network had gone home…"
—Lorne Michaels quoted in Hill/Weingrad

16: "[A] lava lamp with sound"
—Hill/Weingrad

16: "[A] motley crew"
—Dave Tebet quoted in Hill/Weingrad

23: "[D]ecent Viking Funeral"
—Michael O'Donoghue quoted in Hill/Weingrad

23: "[B]asically pulled a Steinbrenner…"
—Jim Belushi in "SNL in the '80s: Lost and Found" (dir. Kenneth Bowser, 2005)

213: "[H]e was sitting there thinking…"
—Jon Lovitz quoted in Shales

The following quotations were received directly from their sources:

129: "[P]retty much an eyelash distance…"
—Laraine Newman

222: "Will decided between the dress and air…"
—Eric Justian

a.

b.

c.

d.

a. Music producer Hal Willner and writer T. Sean Shannon backstage during season 27. **b.** Cristina McGinniss (assistant to Lorne Michaels) and Jennifer Pinkham (assistant to Laraine Newman) in 1980. **c.** Stagehand Speedy Rosenthal. (2011) **d.** John Head, the talent producer during the show's early years.

EACH AND EVERY TASCHEN BOOK PLANTS A SEED!

TASCHEN is a carbon neutral publisher.
Each year, we offset our annual carbon emissions with carbon credits at the Instituto Terra, a reforestation program in Minas Gerais, Brazil, founded by Lélia and Sebastião Salgado. To find out more about this ecological partnership, please check: www.taschen.com/zerocarbon
Inspiration: unlimited. Carbon footprint: zero.

To stay informed about upcoming TASCHEN titles, please subscribe to our free Magazine at www.taschen.com/magazine, find our Magazine app for iPad on iTunes, follow us on Twitter and Facebook, or e-mail us at contact@taschen.com for any questions about our program.

Hohenzollernring 53, D-50672 Köln
www.taschen.com

Editor: Alison Castle, New York
Design: Pentagram, New York
Production: Jennifer Patrick, Los Angeles

Typeset in “Founders Grotesk”
designed by Kris Sowersby

Printed in Slovakia
ISBN 978-3-8365-5241-7

FISH
AND A VEST
30
NYPD